O'KEEFE'S COMMENTARY ON THE 1970 UNESCO CONVENTION

Volume 4 in the Art Law Library series

This new edition of Patrick O'Keefe's classic book presents up-to-date analysis of the 1970 UNESCO Convention on the Means of Prohibiting and Preventing the Illicit Import, Export and Transfer of Ownership of Cultural Property, contributing to a detailed article-by-article commentary on the Convention's provisions, while providing historical context to the Convention's adoption and a contemporary understanding of its stature today.

The traffic in cultural artefacts has been a major challenge for the international community, especially when it involves cross-border smuggling and the potentially conflicting application of different national laws. The UNESCO Convention was adopted in 1970 to confront this challenge, setting out important mechanisms for the protection and the return of cultural objects. While the direct legal effect of the Convention is debatable, it has without doubt become the quintessential marker in the fight against the illicit antiquities trade, coming to influence standards across the entire cultural sector. With almost 150 States Parties, the Convention has had an indelible impact on the ethical landscape affecting acquisitions and due diligence amongst museums and the art market.

The book highlights the background which led to the creation of the Convention and offers a critical look at how it has been interpreted over the years by commentators and international bodies. It also examines in detail specific implementation of the Convention across a number of important States.

The 1970 Convention is a watershed, an aspiration, an icon – and an eternal compromise. This book shows how the Convention has come to be all these things at once, and what its future may hold.

THE ART LAW LIBRARY

The Art Law Library includes books on all aspects of the law relating to art in its widest sense, including antiquities, museums, intangible cultural heritage, archives, intellectual property and human remains. Titles in the series are invaluable to those working and studying in the fields of law, museums, galleries, libraries, planning, archaeology and law enforcement. The series continues the imprint of the Institute of Art and Law.

Series Editor: Ruth Redmond-Cooper, Editor of Art Antiquity and Law, and founder of the Institute of Art and Law

RECENT TITLES IN THE SERIES

Volume 1: *The Parthenon Marbles Dispute: Heritage, Law, Politics*
Alexander Herman

Volume 2: *Digitising Cultural Heritage: Clashes with Copyright Law*
Pinar Oruç

Volume 3: *Beyond Restitution: Exploring the Stories of Cultural Objects After their Return*
Kristin Hausler and Elke Selter

Volume 4: *O'Keefe's Commentary on the 1970 UNESCO Convention*
Alexander Herman

O'Keefe's Commentary on the 1970 UNESCO Convention

Third Edition

Alexander Herman

•HART•

OXFORD • LONDON • NEW YORK • NEW DELHI • SYDNEY

HART PUBLISHING
Bloomsbury Publishing Plc
Kemp House, Chawley Park, Cumnor Hill, Oxford, OX2 9PH, UK
1385 Broadway, New York, NY 10018, USA
Bloomsbury Publishing Ireland Limited, 29 Earlsfort Terrace, Dublin 2, D02 AY28, Ireland

HART PUBLISHING, the Hart/Stag logo, BLOOMSBURY and the Diana logo are trademarks of Bloomsbury Publishing Plc
First published in Great Britain 2026

1

A catalogue record for this book is available from the British Library.

Library of Congress Cataloging-in-Publication Data

Names: O'Keefe, Patrick J. writer of added commentary | Herman, Alexander (Writer on art and heritage law) author

Title: O'keefe's commentary on the 1970 unesco convention / Alexander Herman.

Other titles: Commentary on the 1970 UNESCO Convention

Description: Third edition. | Gordonsville : Hart Publishing, 2026. | Series: The art law library ; vol 4 | Includes bibliographical references and index. | Summary: "This new edition of Patrick O'Keefe's classic book provides up-to-date analysis of the 1970 UNESCO Convention on the Means of Prohibiting and Preventing the Illicit Import, Export and Transfer of Ownership of Cultural Property. The new edition also includes a detailed article-by-article commentary on the provisions of the Convention, a comprehensive telling of the historical background that led to the adoption of the Convention and an examination of its impact today. The illicit traffic in objects of great cultural importance continues to be a massive challenge for the international community, especially when it involves cross-border smuggling and the conflicting application of differing national laws. The UNESCO Convention has become an iconic marker in the fight against the illicit trade, providing important mechanisms for the protection and the return of cultural objects, while influencing standards across the cultural sector. Adopted by some 150 States, it has had an indelible impact on the ethical landscape affecting museums, especially in relation to acquisitions, and the art market. The book highlights the background which led to the creation of the Convention, and takes a critical look at how it has been interpreted and implemented around the world, including by UNESCO bodies and States Parties to the Convention. The Convention has unmistakably contributed to the discourse around the restitution of cultural objects to countries of origin. It has also inspired a range of other instruments for the protection and acquisition of cultural objects, such as codes of ethics and museum acquisition policies. These instruments are analysed in the book, while suggestions are made for improving the overall framework for the protection of cultural objects"– Provided by publisher.

Identifiers: LCCN 2026030550 (print) | LCCN 2026030551 (ebook) | ISBN 9781509986927 hardback | ISBN 9781509986880 paperback | ISBN 9781509986910 epub | ISBN 9781509986903 pdf

Subjects: LCSH: Convention on the Means of Prohibiting and Preventing the Illicit Import, Export, and Transfer of Ownership of Cultural Property (1970 November 14) | Cultural property–Protection (International law) | Cultural property–Protection–Law and legislation

Classification: LCC K3791.A4197 O44 2026 (print) | LCC K3791.A4197 (ebook)

LC record available at https://lccn.loc.gov/2026030550

LC ebook record available at https://lccn.loc.gov/2026030551

ISBN: HB: 978-1-50998-692-7
ePDF: 978-1-50998-690-3
ePub: 978-1-50998-691-0

Typeset by Lumina Datamatics Ltd

For product safety related questions contact productsafety@bloomsbury.com

To find out more about our authors and books visit www.hartpublishing.co.uk. Here you will find extracts, author information, details of forthcoming events and the option to sign up for our newsletters.

ACKNOWLEDGMENTS

Updating a renowned commentary on an international convention is no easy feat. It could not have been done without a wonderfully supportive team at the Institute, starting with Ruth Redmond-Cooper and Emily Gould. Thanks are due to researchers Ilaria Bortot, Lilian Palmer and Ephraim Tan, as well as those who assisted with insights from particular jurisdictions, including Makoto Shimada (Japan), Ronan Bergin (Ireland), Ian McDonald (Australia), Jihon Kim (South Korea), Hao Liu (China), representatives at the Swiss Office for Culture specialising in the international transfer of cultural property, and especially Patty Gerstenblith (USA). Thank you also to Andrzej Jakubowski for his wisdom on the history of international law, and to staff at UNESCO for their support. All errors are of course my own.

TABLE OF CONTENTS

II: ARTICLE-BY-ARTICLE ANALYSIS

III: INTERPRETING THE CONVENTION

IV: THE WIDER CONTEXT

V: STATE IMPLEMENTATION

TABLE OF CASES

International

Australia

Canada

France

Germany

Italy

Netherlands

Switzerland

United Kingdom

United States of America

TABLE OF STATUTES

Nigeria

Norway

Qatar

South Korea

Switzerland

United Arab Emirates

United Kingdom

United States of America

TABLE OF INTERNATIONAL INSTRUMENTS

CONVENTION ON THE MEANS OF PROHIBITING AND PREVENTING THE ILLICIT IMPORT, EXPORT AND TRANSFER OF OWNERSHIP OF CULTURAL PROPERTY

The General Conference of the United Nations Educational, Scientific and Cultural Organization, meeting in Paris from 12 October to 14 November 1970, at its sixteenth session,

Recalling the importance of the provisions contained in the Declaration of the Principles of International Cultural Co-operation, adopted by the General Conference at its fourteenth session,

Considering that the interchange of cultural property among nations for scientific, cultural and educational purposes increases the knowledge of the civilization of Man, enriches the cultural life of all peoples and inspires mutual respect and appreciation among nations,

Considering that cultural property constitutes one of the basic elements of civilization and national culture, and that its true value can be appreciated only in relation to the fullest possible information regarding is origin, history and traditional setting,

Considering that it is incumbent upon every State to protect the cultural property existing within its territory against the dangers of theft, clandestine excavation, and illicit export,

Considering that, to avert these dangers, it is essential for every State to become increasingly alive to the moral obligations to respect its own cultural heritage and that of all nations,

Considering that, as cultural institutions, museums, libraries and archives should ensure that their collections are built up in accordance with universally recognized moral principles,

Considering that the illicit import, export and transfer of ownership of cultural property is an obstacle to that understanding between nations which it is part of UNESCO's mission to promote by recommending to interested States, international conventions to this end,

Considering that the protection of cultural heritage can be effective only if organized both nationally and internationally among States working in close co-operation,

Considering that the UNESCO General Conference adopted a Recommendation to this effect in 1964,

Having before it further proposals on the means of prohibiting and preventing the illicit import, export and transfer of ownership of cultural property, a question which is on the agenda for the session as item 19,

Having decided, at its fifteenth session, that this question should be made the subject of an international convention,

Adopts this Convention on the fourteenth day of November 1970.

Article 1
For the purposes of this Convention, the term "cultural property" means property which, on religious or secular grounds, is specifically designated by each State as being of importance for archaeology, prehistory, history, literature, art or science and which belongs to the following categories:

a. Rare collections and specimens of fauna, flora, minerals and anatomy, and objects of palaeontlogical interest;
b. property relating to history, including the history of science and technology and military and social history, to the life of national leaders, thinkers, scientists and artists and to events of national importance;
c. products of archaeological excavations (including regular and clandestine) or of archaeological discoveries;
d. elements of artistic or historical monuments or archaeological sites which have been dismembered;
e. antiquities more than one hundred years old, such as inscriptions, coins and engraved seals;
f. objects of ethnological interest;
g. property of artistic interest, such as:
    i. pictures, paintings and drawings produced entirely by hand on any support and in any material (excluding industrial designs and manufactured articles decorated by hand);
    ii. original works of statuary art and sculpture in any material;
    iii. original engravings, prints and lithographs;
    iv. original artistic assemblages and montages in any material;
h. rare manuscripts and incunabula, old books, documents and publications of special interest (historical, artistic, scientific, literary, etc.) singly or in collections;

i. postage, revenue and similar stamps, singly or in collections;
j. archives, including sound, photographic and cinematographic archives;
k. articles of furniture more than one hundred years old and old musical instruments.

Article 2

1. The States Parties to this Convention recognise that the illicit import, export and transfer of ownership of cultural property is one of the main causes of the impoverishment of the cultural heritage of the countries of origin of such property and that international co-operation constitutes one of the most efficient means of protecting each country's cultural property against all the dangers resulting therefrom.
2. To this end, the States Parties undertake to oppose such practices with the means at their disposal, and particularly by removing their causes, putting a stop to current practices, and by helping to make the necessary reparations.

Article 3

The import, export or transfer of ownership of cultural property effected contrary to the provisions adopted under this Convention by the States Parties thereto, shall be illicit.

Article 4

The States Parties to this Convention recognise that for the purpose of the Convention property which belongs to the following categories forms part of the cultural heritage of each State:

a. cultural property created by the individual or collective genius of nationals of the State concerned, and cultural property of importance to the State concerned created within the territory of that State by foreign nationals or stateless persons resident within such territory;
b. cultural property found within the national territory;
c. cultural property acquired by archaeological, ethnological or natural science missions, with the consent of the competent authorities of the country of origin of such property;
d. cultural property which has been the subject of a freely agreed exchange;
e. cultural property received as a gift or purchased legally with the consent of the competent authorities of the country of origin of such property.

Article 5

To ensure the protection of their cultural property against illicit import, export and transfer of ownership, the States Parties to this Convention undertake, as appropriate for each country, to set up within their territories one or more national services, where such services do not already exist, for the protection of the cultural heritage, with a qualified staff sufficient in number for the effective carrying out of the following functions:

a. contributing to the formation of draft laws and regulations designed to secure the protection of the cultural heritage and particularly prevention of the illicit import, export and transfer of ownership of important cultural property;
b. establishing and keeping up to date, on the basis of a national inventory of protected property, a list of important public and private cultural property whose export would constitute an appreciable impoverishment of the national cultural heritage;
c. promoting the development or the establishment of scientific and technical institutions (museums, libraries, archives, laboratories, workshops...) required to ensure the preservation and presentation of cultural property;
d. organising the supervision of archaeological excavations, ensuring the preservation "in situ" of certain cultural property, and protecting certain areas reserved for future archaeological research;
e. establishing, for the benefit of those concerned (curators, collectors, antique dealers, etc.) rules in conformity with the ethical principles set forth in this Convention; and taking steps to ensure the observance of those rules;
f. taking educational measures to stimulate and develop respect for the cultural heritage of all States, and spreading knowledge of the provisions of this Convention;
g. seeing that appropriate publicity is given to the disappearance of any items of cultural property.

Article 6
The States Parties to this Convention undertake:

a. to introduce an appropriate certificate in which the exporting State would specify that the export of the cultural property in question is authorised. The certificate should accompany all items of cultural property exported in accordance with the regulations;
b. to prohibit the exportation of cultural property from their territory unless accompanied by the abovementioned export certificate;
c. to publicise this prohibition by appropriate means, particularly among persons likely to export or import cultural property.

Article 7
The States Parties to this Convention undertake:

a. To take the necessary measures, consistent with national legislation, to prevent museums and similar institutions within their territories from acquiring cultural property originating in another State Party which has been illegally exported after entry into force of this Convention, in the States concerned. Whenever possible, to inform a State of origin Party to this Convention of an offer of such cultural property illegally removed from that State after the entry into force of this Convention in both States;
b. i. to prohibit the import of cultural property stolen from a museum or a religious or secular public monument or similar institution in another State

Party to this Convention after the entry into force of this Convention for the States concerned, provided that such property is documented as appertaining to the inventory of that institution;

ii. at the request of the State Party of origin, to take appropriate steps to recover and return any such cultural property imported after the entry into force of this Convention in both States concerned, provided, however, that the requesting State shall pay just compensation to an innocent purchaser or to a person who has valid title to that property. Requests for recovery and return shall be made through diplomatic offices. The requesting Party shall furnish, at its expense, the documentation and other evidence necessary to establish its claim for recovery and return. The Parties shall impose no customs duties or other charges upon cultural property returned pursuant to this Article. All expenses incident to the return and delivery of the cultural property shall be borne by the requesting Party.

Article 8

The States Parties to this Convention undertake to impose penalties or administrative sanctions on any person responsible for infringing the prohibitions referred to under Articles 6(b) and 7(b) above.

Article 9

Any State Party to this Convention whose cultural patrimony is in jeopardy from pillage of archaeological or ethnological materials may call upon other States Parties who are affected. The States Parties to this Convention undertake, in these circumstances, to participate in a concerted international effort to determine and to carry out the necessary concrete measures, including the control of exports and imports and international commerce in the specific materials concerned. Pending agreement each State concerned shall take provisional measures to the extent feasible to prevent irremediable injury to the cultural heritage of the requesting State.

Article 10

The States Parties to this Convention undertake:

a. to restrict by education, information and vigilance, movement of cultural property illegally removed from any State Party to this Convention and, as appropriate for each country, oblige antique dealers, subject to penal or administrative sanctions, to maintain a register recording the origin of each item of cultural property, names and addresses of the supplier, description and price of each item sold and to inform the purchaser of the cultural property of the export prohibition to which such property may be subject;

b. to endeavour by educational means to create and develop in the public mind a realization of the value of cultural property and the threat to the cultural heritage created by theft, clandestine excavations and illicit exports.

Article 11
The export and transfer of ownership of cultural property under compulsion arising directly or indirectly from the occupation of a country by a foreign power shall be regarded as illicit.

Article 12
The States Parties to this Convention shall respect the cultural heritage within the territories for the international relations of which they are responsible, and shall take all appropriate measures to prohibit and prevent the illicit import, export and transfer of ownership of cultural property in such territories.

Article 13
The States Parties to this Convention also undertake, consistent with the laws of each State:

a. To prevent by all appropriate means transfers of ownership of cultural property likely to promote the illicit import or export of such property;
b. to ensure that their competent services co-operate in facilitating the earliest possible restitution of illicitly exported cultural property to its rightful owner;
c. to admit actions for recovery of lost or stolen items of cultural property brought by or on behalf of the rightful owners;
d. to recognise the indefeasible right of each State Party to this Convention to classify and declare certain cultural property as inalienable which should therefore ipso facto not be exported, and to facilitate recovery of such property by the State concerned in cases where it has been exported.

Article 14
In order to prevent illicit export and to meet the obligations arising from the implementation of this Convention, each State Party to the Convention should, as far as it is able, provide the national services responsible for the protection of its cultural heritage with an adequate budget and, if necessary, should set up a fund for this purpose.

Article 15
Nothing in this Convention shall prevent States Parties thereto from concluding special agreements among themselves or from continuing to implement agreements already concluded regarding the restitution of cultural property removed, whatever the reason, from its territory of origin, before the entry into force of this Convention for the States concerned.

Article 16

The States Parties to this Convention shall in their periodic reports submitted to the General Conference of the United Nations Educational, Scientific and Cultural Organization on dates and in a manner to be determined by it, give information on the legislative and administrative provisions which they have adopted and other action which they have taken for the application of this Convention, together with details of the experience acquired in this field.

Article 17

1. The States Parties to this Convention may call on the technical assistance of the United Nations Educational, Scientific and Cultural Organization, particularly as regards:
   a) Information and education;
   b) consultation and expert advice;
   c) co-ordination and good offices.
2. The United Nations Educational, Scientific and Cultural Organization may, on its own initiative conduct research and publish studies on matters relevant to the illicit movement of cultural property.
3. To this end, the United Nations Educational, Scientific and Cultural Organization may also call on the co-operation of any competent non-governmental organization.
4. The United Nations Educational, Scientific and Cultural Organization may, on its own initiative, make proposals to States Parties to this Convention for its implementation.
5. At the request of at least two States Parties to this Convention which are engaged in a dispute over its implementation, UNESCO may extend its good offices to reach a settlement between them.

Article 18

This Convention is drawn up in English, French, Russian and Spanish, the four texts being equally authoritative.

Article 19

1. This Convention shall be subject to ratification or acceptance by States Members of the United Nations Educational, Scientific and Cultural Organization in accordance with their respective constitutional procedures.
2. The instruments of ratification or acceptance shall be deposited with the Director-General of the United Nations Educational, Scientific and Cultural Organization.

Article 20

1. This Convention shall be open to accession by all States not members of the United Nations Educational, Scientific and Cultural Organization which are invited to accede to it by the Executive Board of the Organization.
2. Accession shall be effected by the deposit of an instrument of accession with the Director-General of the United Nations Educational, Scientific and Cultural Organization.

Article 21

This Convention shall enter into force three months after the date of the deposit of the third instrument of ratification, acceptance or accession, but only with respect to those States which have deposited their respective instruments on or before that date. It shall enter into force with respect to any other State three months after the deposit of its instrument of ratification, acceptance or accession.

Article 22

The States Parties to this Convention recognise that the Convention is applicable not only to their metropolitan territories but also to all territories for the international relations of which they are responsible; they undertake to consult, if necessary, the governments or other competent authorities of these territories on or before ratification, acceptance or accession with a view to securing the application of the Convention to those territories, and to notify the Director-General of the United Nations Educational, Scientific and Cultural Organization of the territories to which it is applied, the notification to take effect three months after the date of its receipt.

Article 23

1. Each State Party to this Convention may denounce the Convention on its own behalf or on behalf of any territory for whose international relations it is responsible.
2. The denunciation shall be notified by an instrument in writing, deposited with the Director-General of the United Nations Educational, Scientific and Cultural Organization.
3. The denunciation shall take effect twelve months after the receipt of the instrument of denunciation.

Article 24

The Director-General of the United Nations Educational, Scientific and Cultural Organization shall inform the States members of the Organization, the States not members of the Organization which are referred to in Article 20, as well as the United Nations, of the deposit of all the instruments of ratification, acceptance and accession provided for in Articles 19 and 20, and of the notifications and denunciations provided for in Articles 22 and 23 respectively.

Article 25

1. This Convention may be revised by the General Conference of the United Nations Educational, Scientific and Cultural Organization. Any such revision shall, however, bind only the States which shall become Parties to the revising convention.
2. If the General Conference should adopt a new convention revising this Convention in whole or in part, then, unless the new convention otherwise provides, this Convention shall cease to be open to ratification, acceptance or accession, as from the date on which the new revising convention enters into force.

Article 26

In conformity with Article 102 of the Charter of the United Nations, this Convention shall be registered with the Secretariat of the United Nations at the request of the Director-General of the United Nations Educational, Scientific and Cultural Organization.

Done in Paris this seventeenth day of November 1970, in two authentic copies bearing the signature of the President of the sixteenth session of the General Conference and of the Director-General of the United Nations Educational, Scientific and Cultural Organization, which shall be deposited in the archives of the United Nations Educational, Scientific and Cultural Organization, and certified true copies of which shall be delivered to all the States referred to in Articles 19 and 20 as well as to the United Nations.

INTRODUCTION TO THE NEW EDITION

On 14 November 1970, a Convention was adopted by UNESCO's General Conference at the Organization's headquarters in Paris. The vote was by show of hands: 77 in favour, one against with eight abstentions. Three days later, the Convention on the Means of Prohibiting and Preventing the Illicit Import, Export and Transfer of Ownership of Cultural Property (the 1970 Convention) was signed by both the President of the General Conference and the UNESCO Director-General. The Director-General was a Frenchman named René Maheu who had done so much in steering the Convention through the Organization and obtaining the final approval.

The 1970 Convention is a watershed, an aspiration, an icon – and an eternal compromise. Today, it serves as a guiding light to governments, museums, the art trade and law enforcement around the world, but is also seen as a limp legal instrument that prompts more questions than answers. It has been said to have 'changed forever the ethical landscape of the museum world'[1] but was also declared, as long as 30 years ago, 'outdated in its spirit and its terms'.[2] So what is the Convention, *really*?

This book will take us through it all: from the history that predated the adoption in Paris to the roll-out and implementation across multiple States; and, regarding the Convention's often inscrutable provisions, from the hopeful preamble to the very last Article. Along the way, we will be guided by Patrick O'Keefe's great wisdom and supported by the insights that came from his experiences with UNESCO over the years, and indeed with the Convention itself. A lawyer, international adviser and scholar of cultural heritage law, O'Keefe took on many important UNESCO commissions from the 1980s to the 2000s, often working alongside his wife Professor Lyndel Prott, while they co-authored numerous contributions to the field.[3] In the first two editions of this book, as well as his 2017 work *Protecting*

[1] N Brodie, J Doole and P Watson, *Stealing History: The Illicit Trade in Cultural Material* (Cambridge, McDonald Institute for Archaeological Research, 2000) 9. Similarly, the 2005 Guidance from the UK's Department for Culture, Media and Sport stated that the Convention 'transformed the ethical landscape of the museum world': *Combating Illicit Trade* (October 2005) 4.

[2] 'Dépassé dans son esprit et sa teneur': Q Byrne-Sutton and MA Renold, 'Rôle et contenu d'une nouvelle réglementation Suisse en matière de circulation des biens culturels' in Q Byrne-Sutton, F Marièthoz and MA Renold (eds), *La réglementation Suisse de l'importation et de l'exportation des biens culturels* (Schulthess Polygraphischer Verlag, 1994) 15, 36.

[3] For example, see their monumental three-volume work, *Law and the Cultural Heri*tage (London, Butterworths, 1984–1989); also the *Handbook of National Regulations Concerning the Export of Cultural Property* (Paris, UNESCO, 1988); *Cultural Heritage Conventions and Other Instruments* (eds) (Builth Wells, Institute of Art and Law, 2011); L Prott, R Redmond-Cooper and S Urice (eds), *Realising Cultural Heritage Law: Festschrift for Patrick O'Keefe* (Builth Wells, Institute of Art and Law, 2013); 'Cultural Heritage or Cultural Property?' (1992) 1 *International Journal of Cultural Property* 307.

Cultural Objects, O'Keefe set the bar high. We now hope to honour his contributions, while also highlighting the significant developments that have taken place around the Convention since those earlier works.[4]

The Story of the Ife Head – the Convention's Shortcomings

The image on the cover of the present edition evokes both the promise and the frustration of the 1970 Convention. It shows a copper alloy head, often referred to as a 'bronze', cast around 1200 CE, originating from the West African Ife kingdom. In 1938, it was discovered along with 17 others in what was called the 'Wunmonije' compound in the town of Ife, Nigeria. At the time, Nigeria was a colony and protectorate of the United Kingdom. Of the impressive discoveries, one head ended up at the British Museum in London, while the others remained in Nigeria.[5] The latter heads were eventually housed at the Jos Museum, West Africa's first public art museum, founded in 1952 and located north-east of the Nigerian capital of Abuja. The head we are looking at was noted for an abrasion on the left side of its face, like a gunshot wound that tore through the upper part of the cheek, very close to the corner of the eye.[6]

Many years later, in 1987, tragedy struck the Jos Museum. A brazen theft took place on the night of 14 January, in which nine key artefacts, including this one, were taken.[7] Independent from Britain since 1960, Nigeria had been the third State to ratify the 1970 Convention, which it did on 24 January 1972, prompting the Convention's international entry into force three months later on 24 April 1972 (in accordance with the requirements of Article 21 of the Convention). It was clear that within Nigeria much hope was placed on the Convention as a way to help protect objects of Nigerian heritage looted from the country – especially those of the ancient Nok, Nri and Ife civilisations – should they end up overseas. For instance, Article 7(b) of the Convention requires States Parties to prohibit the import of 'cultural property' stolen from a museum in another State Party if it has been properly documented on the inventory of that institution. Museum objects

[4] His latest work *Protecting Cultural Objects: Before and After 1970* (Builth Wells, Institute of Art and Law, 2017) was a notable expansion on the original commentary text with additional material on the history behind the Convention and further examples of restitution. For present purposes, I am not treating this 2017 version as a formal edition of the Commentary.

[5] T Llywelyn Evans, 'Collecting Copper Alloy Portrait Heads: A History of the Acquisition and Export of the Wúnmọníjẹ̀ Heads in Late Colonial Nigeria' (2024) 36 *Journal of the History of Collections* 101–16. The one at the British Museum seems to have been smuggled out of Nigeria in 1939 by Bates and then sold to Kenneth Clark, who donated it to the Museum.

[6] It was loaned to the British Museum for an exhibition on Ife Bronzes in 1947, and was photographed during this time.

[7] B Phillips, 'Nigerian Ife Head: Why UK Police are Holding a Priceless Sculpture' *BBC News* (26 June 2022).

such as the Ife heads were of significant importance to the State and the export of antiquities from Nigeria had been controlled, in any event, since the 1950s.[8] The thefts were promptly reported by Nigeria's National Commission for Museums and Monuments (NCMM) to UNESCO and published, along with photographs of the missing pieces, in one of UNESCO's museum journals later that year.[9] Two of the photographs clearly depict the Ife Head with its noticeable abrasion on the cheek.

Twenty years later, in 2007, the head turned up in Belgium at a sale by the Belgian State. Law enforcement authorities were selling confiscated property in circumstances that to this day remain unclear. It was purchased by a Belgian dealer for €200 plus tax, reportedly alongside an acoustic guitar.[10] Ten years later, in 2017, the work was sent via an intermediary to London for a potential sale through the auctioneers Woolley & Wallis. After checking with experts and reviewing international databases, the auction house's Deputy Chair realised it had been stolen from the Jos Museum and refused to sell it, handing it over to UK law enforcement, specifically to the Art and Antiques Unit at London's Metropolitan Police, through an intermediary law firm.[11] Nigeria's NCMM was informed, as was the dealer, who refused to agree to the return of the head to Nigeria, even though there was no doubt this was the same piece that had been stolen (the hole in the face was the obvious indicator).

Quite apart from the question of whether or not English law might serve to assist the Nigerian State in recovering its stolen property, one might have assumed that an international treaty such as the 1970 Convention could provide for a prompt and seamless restitution. Nigeria and the UK were party to the Convention, Nigeria since 1972 and the UK since 2002, both ratifications easily predating the Head's appearance on British territory in 2017. But here the intricacies – and gaps – of the Convention become evident. Article 3 sets out that exports contrary to the Convention 'shall be illicit', but does not provide a direct recourse for victim States like Nigeria. Meanwhile, Article 7(b) prohibits the import of cultural property stolen from a museum, but only for thefts occurring *after* the Convention entered into force in both States concerned. In any event, Article 7(b) subjects any return to a payment of 'just compensation' to the innocent purchaser or valid title holder – as the Belgian dealer might here describe himself. Article 13 might seem relevant, as it requires cooperation amongst national services to facilitate 'the earliest possible restitution of illicitly exported cultural property' and

[8] See C Bos, '"How Our Heritage is Looted": Legal Meaning-Making, Cultural Property, and Customs Enforcement in Nigeria, 1938–79' (2024) *Journal of African History* 1, 9: The 1953 Antiquities Ordinance and the 1957 Antiquities Regulations were incorporated into the 1979 law creating the National Commission for Museums and Monuments: decree no. 77, *Federal Gazette* 47 (September 1979): A506-522.

[9] *Museum* (Quarterly Review) No 156, Vol XXXIX, no 4 (Paris, UNESCO, 1987) 302.

[10] Phillips (n 7).

[11] Certain details were provided to the author by the then Deputy Chair, now Chair, of Woolley & Wallis, John Axford.

the admission of actions for recovery brought by 'rightful owners'. However, these State obligations are less precise than others in the Convention, and are made subject to existing domestic law. While the presence of the Head on UK territory may contravene the spirit of the Convention, did it actually breach the strict letter of the law?

The dealer made clear that he would return the head to Nigeria only if he was duly compensated. This was reported to be for an initial sum in the millions, though he subsequently appears to have come down to €40,000, certainly less than the normal value of an artefact of this vintage, but around 200 times more than he had paid.[12] Nigeria refused. In 2020, the State instead brought the matter to UNESCO's Intergovernmental Committee for Promoting the Return of Cultural Property to its Countries of Origin or its Restitution in Case of Illicit Appropriation (ICPRCP), the prolixly titled body that seeks to assist States in reaching consensual resolutions in cultural property disputes.

The ICPRCP liaised with authorities in Belgium, the UK and Nigeria in order to seek a settlement. But after more than five years, there was no sign of the dispute being resolved.[13] In some respects it should be applauded that an international forum exists for the resolution of cultural property disputes, even where disputes fall outside the strictures of the Convention. The ICPRCP was founded in 1978 at the behest of UNESCO Director-General Amadou-Mahtar M'Bow to serve as an 'intergovernmental committee', but was incapable of issuing binding resolutions on States Parties to the Convention because (as O'Keefe reminds us in his commentary) no provision had been made for such a body in the Convention itself.[14] After nearly 50 years of existence, the successes of the body in 'promoting return or restitution' (as its title suggests) have been modest. The ICPRCP website lists only six resolutions during this period, and in some of these cases the body's involvement in the result might have been indirect to say the least.[15] The most famous cultural heritage claim of all, that of Greece for the return of the Parthenon Marbles in the UK, has sat on the ICPRCP docket since 1984 – 40 years and counting – with still no resolution in sight.[16]

The failure to reach any resolution in the case of the Ife Head – a piece so obviously stolen from a museum in a State Party to the 1970 Convention – must give us pause for thought. Is the 1970 Convention entirely supine? Is it legally dysfunctional? Or was this case simply a question of personalities, institutional inertia and, as ever, inter-state politics? In some respects, the intent in 1970 was for the

[12] Phillips (n 7).

[13] The author would like to thank Ilaria Bortot and Lilian Palmer for their research on this matter.

[14] See below, I, ch 4.

[15] See below, I, ch 4.

[16] Report of the 4th Session of the ICPRCP, CLT-85/Conf.202/2 (Paris, UNESCO, 1985). For more on the ICPRCP case involving the Parthenon Marbles, see LM Haertel, 'The Past, Present: The Parthenon Sculptures dispute as an Example of the ICPRCP's Role on Claims Barred by the Non-Retroactivity of the 1970 UNESCO Convention' (2021) 28 *International Journal of Cultural Property* 479–504; and A Herman, *The Parthenon Marbles Dispute: Heritage, Law, Politics* (Oxford, Hart Publishing, 2023) 71-2, 82-3, 152-3.

Convention to overcome such hurdles, to create a clear and practical framework for the return of illegally removed objects of cultural property, especially those that had been stolen from museums. The benefit of a treaty is to provide legal rights which can cut through the morass, allowing an effective remedy when the law of one country has so clearly been violated. But here, one unfortunate aspect of the 1970 Convention has been revealed: on purely legal grounds, it might be unhelpful to countries of origin seeking to recover stolen cultural property. The compromise at the heart of 1970 undercut what could have been an effective mechanism for recovery and return. And yet…

Despite the apparent legal lacunae in the case of the Ife head, the Convention has had a marked impact on global practice. The 1970 date has remarkably developed a recognisable stature in the cultural world, especially for museums making acquisitions or considering donations. The date provides a bright-line rule for examining provenance and deciding on acquisitions of objects for collections. As O'Keefe explains, the year has 'come to occupy a special place in the consciousness of those engaging in, or affected by, the trade in cultural heritage',[17] creating a clear demarcation between 'before' and 'after', between 'pre' and 'post', between – in many respects – legitimacy and illegitimacy. It has come to represent a particular approach to provenance, whereby evidence must demonstrate that an object left its country of origin before 1970, or that it otherwise left lawfully.

So how can the 1970 Convention be two things at once? The answer lies in this book – and in O'Keefe's commentary. It has to do with the drafting of the Convention, a history that stretches back well before the sessions at UNESCO in the 1960s. It also comes from the text of the Convention itself. It has to do with the manner in which the Convention has been implemented, both in States Parties and at an institutional level (at museums, for instance). And finally, it has to do with outside factors, including those emanating from law enforcement, international agencies, governments, museum associations and the antiquities trade. All of this has created the Schrodinger's Cat of international cultural heritage, a creature that is both dead and at the same time very much alive.

The Spirit of 1970

The irony of the 1970 Convention is that even the text itself never established '1970' as a cut-off date. Internationally, the Convention had no force of law until 24 April 1972 and, even so, the direct legal application for States depends on the date on which each one of them brought the Convention into force. For example – as seen with the Ife Head – the obligation on States Parties to recover and return designated cultural property stolen from a museum (Article 7(b)(ii)) applies only

[17] P O'Keefe, *Protecting Cultural Objects: Before and After 1970* (Builth Wells, Institute of Art and Law, 2017) 37. See also below, I, ch 3.

to material stolen *after* the Convention has entered into force for both the States in question: in the case of the Ife Head, the threshold would have been 1 November 2002, three months after the UK accepted the Convention;[18] in any event, a long time after 14 November 1970.

And yet sector practice around '1970' has had a mind of its own. Museums, government bodies and sector associations will often use 1970 as a provenance threshold, meaning that objects will not be acquired unless they have 'clean' provenance dating back to that year.[19] The British Museum first used the date for its acquisitions procedures as far back as 1998.[20] The UK government adopted it as part of its policy for museum acquisitions in 2005.[21] The American Association of Art Museum Directors did the same in 2008, referring to the date of the Convention's formal *enactment* (17 November 1970) – not of its adoption, nor its entry into force, interestingly – as 'the most pertinent threshold for the application of more rigorous standards to the acquisition of archaeological materials and ancient art'.[22]

And yet the Convention's salience is not only as an ethical yardstick. Its incorporation into the domestic law of States Parties has gone a long way towards affirming its impact. While the case of the Ife Head has revealed the gaps of the Convention in a strict sense, certain States have been wide-reaching in their methods of implementation. Canada, for instance, became a State Party quite early, in 1978, after passing a federal law that provided a broad scope for intervention involving cultural property illegally exported from another State Party to the 1970 Convention.[23] Australia introduced an even more comprehensive law in 1986,[24] leading up to its acceptance of the Convention in 1989. This law provided the basis in 2014 for the seizure by the Commonwealth Government of artefacts that had been illegally removed from India and brought into Australia[25] and, more recently, a Bolivian artefact from a commercial gallery seeking its import into Australia.[26] The United States, which accepted the Convention in 1983, provides under its

[18] As per Art 21 of the Convention.

[19] P Gerstenblith, 'The Meaning of 1970 for the Acquisition of Archaeological Objects' (2013) 38 *Journal of Field Archaeology* 364; K Hausler and E Selter, *Beyond Restitution: Exploring the Stories of Cultural Objects after their Return* (Oxford, Hart Publishing, 2025) 7–9.

[20] British Museum, 'Statement by the Trustees of the British Museum on the Acquisition of Antiquities (1998)' as reproduced in C Renfrew, *Loot, Legitimacy and Ownership: The Ethical Crisis in Archaeology* (London, Duckworth, 2000) Appendix 5. Reference to the 1970 date continues to the 2018 iteration, though it appears that by 2024 the policy had been shortened and now only refers to the 1970 Convention in broad terms. See below I, ch 3.

[21] Department for Culture, Media and Sport, *Combating Illicit Trade: Due Diligence Guidelines for Museums, Libraries, Archives on Collecting and Borrowing Cultural Material* (2005) 2.

[22] Association of Art Museum Directors, *The Acquisition of Archaeological Material and Ancient Art*, as updated in 2013 (relevant text of provisions quoted has remained the same).

[23] The Cultural Property Export and Import Act, which first came into force in 1977, s 37. The implementing provision provided the basis for the prosecution of a high-profile dealer who had been importing Bolivian artefacts into Canada in the 1980s: R v Yorke [1998] NSCA 58.

[24] Protection of Movable Cultural Heritage Act 1986.

[25] The National Gallery of Australia and the Art Gallery of New South Wales had bought these Indian artefacts from the (now convicted) dealer Subash Kapoor at his New York gallery, Art of the Past.

[26] Seized in 2020: *Commonwealth v Palmanova* [2025] HCA 35.

implementing law for both import restrictions and seizure provisions relating to cultural property exported illegally from any State with which it has a bilateral agreement in place. The United States has now entered into bilateral agreements with over 30 States.[27] In fact, most States implementing the 1970 Convention have done so using specific legislation, occasionally also in combination with civil or criminal law.[28]

The European Union has also paid tribute to the Convention. Although the EU has not formally adopted the Convention (there is no mechanism for a regional body to do so), all but one of its 27 Member States are individually party to it.[29] The EU has often expressed support for the 1970 Convention in its official documents[30] and it has sought to combat the illicit trade in cultural property in line with the principles of the Convention. For instance, the EU brought into its customs legislation important restrictions on cultural goods coming into the EU. Regulation 2019/880 on the Introduction and the Import of Cultural Goods requires authorities in Member States to check the provenance of such goods going back, in many cases, to the recognisable date of 24 April 1972, the Convention's international entry into force. Documentation is therefore required from the importer to demonstrate that an object's export from its country of origin after that date was lawful, unless that country cannot be reliably determined.[31] If there is evidence that the goods were unlawfully exported from an overseas country, their introduction into the EU territory will be prohibited.[32] While the Regulation does not directly implement the provisions of the 1970 Convention into EU law, it achieves a goal quite similar by turning ethical due diligence into a legal requirement. In doing so, it can be said to go beyond even what the Convention itself sought to do.

The 1970 Convention has therefore left an indelible mark on the ethics of the museum sector, and increasingly on those of the art market. Meanwhile, through the various implementing laws in different States Parties, it has had an impact on the legal rules across many jurisdictions – even if that impact might be unrelated to specific provisions in the Convention. Since the beginning of the present century, the Convention has really gained momentum. Indeed, as we will see, it has been pushed along by champions in different parts of the world.

[27] Convention on Cultural Property Implementation Act. Bilateral Agreements are listed by the Department of State on its website: 'Current Agreements and Import Restrictions'.

[28] For the 2019–2022 reporting cycle, UNESCO has noted that, of the 91 States reporting on implementation of the Convention, over 70% did so by a special law either alone or in combination with civil and/or criminal law, while 66% reported a change in legal framework as a result of ratification: Subsidiary Committee of the Meeting of States Parties, 11th Session, C70/23/11.SC/7 (Paris, UNESCO, 1–2 June 2023) pp 6–7.

[29] The last, Ireland, is at the time of writing working towards depositing its instruments of ratification. It has already passed legislation to this effect, with the relevant provisions awaiting entry into force: the Historic and Archaeological Heritage and Miscellaneous Provisions Act 2023, ss 125–130. The author thanks Dublin barrister Ronan Bergin for this information.

[30] See Regulation 2019/880 on the Introduction and the Import of Cultural Goods, Preamble.

[31] See Regulation 2019/880, Arts 3–5. Note there are threshold requirements in certain cases: see Annex.

[32] Art 3(1).

The Convention in the Twenty-first Century

When the first edition of this book came out in 2000, the Convention was less than 30 years old and was not in a particularly enviable position. Ninety States had ratified it, yet none of those States Parties had major art markets, apart from France (which had only ratified recently, in 1997) and the United States. The United States had implemented the Convention only partially[33] and, at the time, had cultural property agreements in place with only five other States.[34] The overall impact of the Convention on the market and museum practice was therefore muted. O'Keefe nevertheless wrote defiantly at the time that the Convention was 'acquiring greater significance than at any other point in its history'.[35]

Much has changed since that first edition. In fact, the landscape is almost unrecognisable. Since 2000, 60 more States have ratified or accepted the Convention, including principal art market States: the UK and Japan in 2002, Switzerland in 2003, Germany in 2007, the Netherlands and Belgium in 2009, Austria and Luxembourg in 2015, and Monaco and the United Arab Emirates in 2017. The US has 25 more bilateral agreements than it had in 2000, and is home to assertive public prosecutors looking to seize and confiscate cultural objects on the basis that they have been looted from their countries of origin. Actions by the US Attorney and the Manhattan District Attorney often take place outside the strict scope of the 1970 Convention or the federal law implementing it (the Convention on Cultural Property Implementation Act), yet they have promoted an environment that honours the interests of countries of origin in recovering lost cultural property. This then helps to emphasise the critical nature of provenance research and due diligence in the acquisition and possession of works of art, whether by collectors, dealers or museums. The Manhattan DA's office proudly declares that it has seized over 6,000 antiquities, valued at $480 million, since the founding of the Antiquities Trafficking Unit in 2012, and has repatriated the vast majority to countries of origin, totalling 32 in number, including to Pakistan, India, Turkey, Greece, Italy and Mexico.[36] The US art market has been put on notice. While this goes beyond the strict scope of the 1970 Convention, these actions chime with the Convention's broader principles.

O'Keefe's first edition came out in the wake of another important attempt to curb the illicit trade in cultural material, the 1995 UNIDROIT Convention on Stolen or Illegally Exported Cultural Objects, which entered into force with five ratifications in July 1998.[37] It was hoped (including by O'Keefe and by Professor

[33] Choosing to implement into domestic law only Arts 7(b) and 9.

[34] The US bilateral agreements at the time were with four Latin American States (El Salvador, Guatemala, Nicaragua and Peru) and Mali. It did then have emergency restrictions for material coming from Cambodia, Cyprus and Iraq, though without bilateral agreements for those States.

[35] PJ O'Keefe, *Commentary on the 1970 Convention*, 1st edn (Leicester, Institute of Art and Law, 2000) 9.

[36] New York County DA's Office press release, 'DA Bragg Announces Return of 43 Antiquities to the People of Türkiye' (10 December 2025).

[37] As per Art 12.

Prott[38]) that this instrument would fill some of the legal gaps left by the earlier Convention, coming as it did out of international discussions at UNESCO dating back to the 1980s.[39] The 1970 Convention applies only to State-designated 'cultural property' and its most forceful provision for importing States, Article 7(b), is very limited. The UNIDROIT Convention, by contrast, uses the more encompassing term 'cultural object' and gives rights of recovery to private owners, as well as to States, in relation to a broader category of material: both stolen and illegally exported cultural objects. Unlike the 1970 Convention which provides recourse only through diplomatic offices,[40] the UNIDROIT Convention offers rights of action through the courts of the State Party where the objects are located.[41]

And yet, over the past 25 years, the 1970 Convention has in some ways overtaken the more ambitious UNIDROIT Convention. The former has 150 States Parties, the latter only 56: and, while this figure includes States such as Norway, Greece, Italy and New Zealand, none of the major market countries listed above has ratified it.[42] While both Conventions are frequently referenced in museum codes such as the ICOM Code of Ethics, the standard-setting impact of 1970 has been more pronounced in the museum sector than the provisions of the UNIDROIT Convention (with the possible exception of the latter's guidelines on due diligence[43]). Although the UNIDROIT Convention was an inspiration, in its draft form, for the first EU Directive on the Return of Cultural Objects in 1993, neither it nor the Directive has had a noticeable impact on direct claims for return, which had been the primary purpose of these instruments to begin with. By contrast, the 1970 Convention's influence has been more subtle and yet also more pervasive, seeping into the mainline of the sector like few other instruments of international stature.[44]

While the 1970 Convention might have appeared inadequate during Nigeria's attempt to recover the stolen Ife Head, the Convention's impact can be felt in the standards it has set as an instrument of 'soft law'. Today, no self-respecting museum in the UK would seek to acquire or borrow an item like the Ife Head where even the most pedestrian provenance research would reveal a past theft. To do so would violate existing codes of ethics and institutional policies, including the UK Government's own guidance from 2005 incorporating the 1970 provenance

[38] See LV Prott, *Commentary on the UNIDROIT Convention*, 1st and 2nd edns (Institute of Art and Law).

[39] See Prott, ibid.

[40] At Art 7(b)(ii).

[41] Arts 3 and 5 of the UNIDROIT Convention.

[42] China ratified the UNIDROIT Convention in 1997. In 2024, China undertook a major revision of its cultural heritage law, with an increased focus on fighting illicit trade and facilitating restitution: Law on the Protection of Cultural Relics of the People's Republic of China (2024), see especially Art 81.

[43] At Art 4(4). This can be used as a clear indication of what due diligence should be undertaken when making an acquisition.

[44] Other examples might be the Washington Principles on Nazi-Confiscated Art (1998) and the UN Declaration on the Rights of Indigenous Peoples (2007).

threshold.[45] And indeed no serious art market player in the UK would transact in the object. According to the British Art Market Federation's Principles of Conduct, adopted in 2000, members of the British art trade must undertake not to purchase, sell or offer any stolen property, regardless of when the theft may have taken place; they must then take 'appropriate steps' if they are in possession of such material, which include contacting law enforcement authorities. Such an ethical approach in the private sector was exemplified in this very case: upon learning of the problematic provenance, the Deputy Chair of the English auction house refused to sell the piece and instead handed it to the police. Even if the Convention does not provide a hard and fast route to recovery, it nevertheless renders stolen objects such as this unsaleable on the market. It effectively freezes them out.

It might even be asked whether the relevant authorities were too timid in the matter. Could they not have intervened more actively, motivated by the spirit of the Convention, to secure the Head's return to Nigeria? Under English common law, an owner is not normally barred from recovering stolen property; and any subsequent or current possessor of the object would bear the onus of demonstrating good title, which for a professional in the art market might be difficult.[46] The Convention, at Article 13, then calls on cooperation to facilitate the 'earliest possible restitution of illicitly exported cultural property to its rightful owner' and to 'admit actions for recovery' of lost or stolen items. Sadly, these factors do not seem to have yet been considered in the case.

The Restitution Paradigm

The most recent text by O'Keefe on the Convention was published in 2017.[47] Since then, the approach to restitution has undergone a radical transformation that goes well beyond anything predicated in the Convention itself. It stems from a new approach to dealing with museum collections acquired in circumstances of historical injustice, such as during military conflicts, occupation or colonial exploitation. The more extreme view has demanded that museums 'decolonise' their collections, which might lead to the restitution of artefacts to once subjugated communities.[48] Even the more moderate approach will ask museums to reflect on past methods of

[45] Department for Culture Media and Sport, *Combating Illicit Trade* (2005).

[46] Under the Limitation Act 1980 (Eng), s 4, art dealers must prove good faith through due diligence: *De Préval v Adrian Alan* (24 January 1997) High Court (QB) (1997) *Art and Antiquity Law Reports* 1; *Kurtha v Marks* (2008) EWHC 336 (Ch) 8, 13, 123, 132. See further below at II (Arts 2, 3, 7(b), 13); and V, ch 5.

[47] Note that O'Keefe entitled this expanded version *Protecting Cultural Objects: Before and After 1970*, but for present purposes it is not being considered a formal edition of the Commentary.

[48] Museums Association (UK), *Supporting Decolonisation in Museums* (2021). D Hicks, *The Brutish Museums* (London, Pluto Press, 2020). F Sarr and B Savoy, *Rapport sur la restitution du patrimoine culturel africain, vers une nouvelle éthique relationnelle* (*The Repatriation of African Cultural Heritage: A New Relational Ethics*), Report to the French President (2018).

acquisition that are today considered illegitimate, even if those methods might not have been deemed unlawful at the time.[49]

This new era reflects a 'restitution paradigm'.[50] In this paradigm, museums in the West have come to recognise that they are not the only natural 'homes' for certain objects. In situations where objects were removed in ways that are viewed as morally illegitimate, and when those objects have great cultural or spiritual significance to a country or community of origin, restitution becomes the preferred ethical outcome.[51] The paradigm exists outside strict legal frameworks, focusing instead on ethical decision-making, especially by museums. A similar approach is used in relation to the restitution of art taken during the Nazi period in Europe (1933–1945). The response to a claim will be based on museum policy or sector guidelines.[52] In several countries restitution panels exist to facilitate ethical outcomes.[53] When the law of a particular country prohibits the ethical return of a Nazi-tainted artwork agreed to by a museum, those laws are in many cases amended to allow the return to take place.[54]

In its preference for ethics over law, this new paradigm may seem a world away from the import restrictions, regulation and law enforcement exemplified by an international treaty like the 1970 Convention. And yet the paradigm has shifted the centre of gravity, offering support to those challenging the status quo, and recognising that, although possession may be nine-tenths of the law, its ethical tally counts for far less. Museums now accept that claimants from outside the institutional walls may sometimes have the stronger moral claim to possession. How museums engage with these matters will become a testament to their ability to discharge their ethical duties.[55]

While the world has, in this respect, changed since 2017 – and changed utterly since 1970 – we need to remain appropriately forensic with our object of study. O'Keefe would expect no less. Change in the wider discourse should not necessarily be mistaken for change in the approach to the Convention. It is possible that the two may share characteristics, but they should not be automatically conflated. This is why a careful textual analysis of the Convention remains more valuable

[49] Germany's *Framework Principles for Dealing with Collections from Colonial Contexts* (2019); Arts Council England, *Restitution and Repatriation: A Practical Guide for Museums in England* (2022).

[50] A Herman, *Restitution: The Return of Cultural Artefacts* (London, Lund Humphries, 2021).

[51] See Arts Council England, *Restitution and Repatriation: A Practical Guide for Museums in England* (2022) 17 and the Decision Aid for the Restitution of Cultural Artefacts (Uehiro Oxford Institute, 2026).

[52] The Washington Conference Principles on Nazi-Confiscated Art (1998) speak of 'just and fair solutions' (Principle 8). These have been updated with the 'Best Practices' of 2024.

[53] Those countries are Germany, Austria, the Netherlands, France, the United Kingdom, Ireland and Switzerland.

[54] In the UK, the Holocaust (Return of Cultural Objects) Act 2009; in France, Law no. 2023-650 of 22 July 2023 on the Restitution of Cultural Goods Spoliated during Anti-Semitic Persecutions between 1933 and 1945.

[55] On the question of a moral obligation to return, see the 'Decision Aid for the Restitution of Cultural Artefacts', produced by the Oxford Uehiro Institute and the Institute of Art and Law (Oxford, 2026), which seeks to support museums in making such determinations: darca.uehiro.ox.ac.uk.

than ever. We must avoid the temptation to whisk this important instrument up with the groundswells around us, some of which may have little to do with the Convention or anything intended by its drafters. This is an important lesson: the Convention remains what it is on paper; no more, and no less. To invest the 'spirit of 1970' with more than what it in fact represents can be somewhat careless. To assume the law fits – or to force it to fit – according to the predilections of the beholder is to ignore what the law was intended to do, and how it was so carefully crafted in the first instance.

That said, we must not turn a blind eye to what is happening in the wider world. The 1970 Convention itself was an attempt to engage with that world: to seek a compromise between interests that would change the way in which cultural artefacts were traded and, ultimately, could move around the globe. It represented a settlement of interests, but not a final settlement, as it incorporated a broader hope of how the world might still change. This hope can serve as both a prod and a reminder that all peoples must respect and recognise the cultural heritage of others, just as they would expect others to respect and recognise their own. In order to secure this mutual respect, nations must be willing to work together, to collaborate and co-operate as the Convention so clearly urges them to do. The international partnerships that result can therefore form the basis – even if only one ingredient – of continued change. As the Convention so clearly put it, 'it is essential for every State to become increasingly alive to the moral obligations to respect its own cultural heritage and that of all nations.'[56]

Alexander Herman, London, February 2026

[56] 1970 Convention, Preamble, para 5.

I

The Convention – Past and Present

Chapter 1
Background to the Convention

This chapter outlines the history of changes in international law relevant to the development of the 1970 Convention.[1] The intent of this study is to show how far back the beginnings of a 'modern' change of outlook actually reach, and to demonstrate the acceleration of change that led up to 1970 – even it if did face significant resistance at times – and how this has all come to bear in the twenty-first century.

Disparate concerns about the protection and location of national cultural objects have impacted, and in some ways confused, the gradual development of any legal principle. One concern was to collect such objects in one place; a second was to ensure that a national treasure remained in its appropriate country; a third was to protect such treasures from looting and destruction in conflict; and lastly, now very significant, was the need to prevent the damage and displacement of undiscovered antiquities of great significance. These will each arise at different moments in the history that predates the Convention.

(i) Before the Twentieth Century: Emerging Principle On Looting in Times of Conflict

In some ways, the care and consideration for what we today call 'cultural heritage' began over 2,000 years ago – at least rhetorically speaking. In the second century BCE, the Greek historian Polybius wrote that to plunder paintings and statues after a conquest brought no glory to the conqueror, and warned victorious armies 'not to make the misfortunes of other peoples the adornments of their own country'.[2] Less than a century later, Cicero in *Against Verres* lambasted Governor Gaius Verres of Sicily for looting the temples of their idols on the territory he was meant to be governing, and by contrast praised the Roman general Marcellus for

[1] A much wider view of this history can be found in AF Vrdoljak, *International Law, Museums and the Return of Cultural Objects* (Cambridge, Cambridge University Press, 2008) 2. See also A Herman, *The Parthenon Marbles Dispute: Heritage, Law, Politics* (Oxford, Hart Publishing, 2023) ch 7 on the importance of the 1815 returns and development of rules in the 19th century.

[2] Polybius, Book 39.

refraining from ransacking the city of Syracuse which he had conquered.[3] As noble and sensible as these writers may have been, however, the practice of armies paid no heed to their high-minded exhortations.

Much later, in Renaissance Europe, artistic creativity began to develop its own form of value, divested in many ways from the purely religious. This meant, amongst other things, that looting of artworks in religious wars, even wars waged for a 'just cause', was not always defensible from a theoretical standpoint. The great Spanish theologian and jurist of the time, Francisco de Vitoria (1492–1546), argued that:

> … it is not justifiable to take anything that they possess from either Saracens or Jews, or other unbelievers. As such, that is because they are unbelievers; but the act would be theft or robbery no less than if it were done to Christians.[4]

No less an author than William Shakespeare celebrated one mighty military man able to restrain from pillaging in times of war – who punished those who breached this principle. Henry V has one of his soldiers executed for looting a church in France during the Battle of Agincourt: 'We would have all such offenders so cut off, and we give express charge that in our marches through the country there be nothing compelled from the villages, nothing taken but paid for.' For, the King explains, 'when lenity and cruelty play for a kingdom, the gentler gamester is the soonest winner.'[5]

Despite the best efforts of theologians and playwrights, it appeared that the age-old rights of victors to *spolia* were still very much in operation into the seventeenth century. The father of international law, Hugo Grotius (1583–1645), wrote in his famous book *The Law of War and Peace* in 1625 that, 'It is observed by legal authorities to be a custom, which has silently gained ground, for either allies or subjects, who engage in war, without pay, and at their own risk and expense, to be rewarded with the captures that they make.'[6] However, he also urged combatants to apply the just principle of 'moderation' to actions on the ground, including when it came to selecting the property to pillage: 'There are some things of such a nature, as to contribute in no way to the support and prolongation of war, things which reason itself requires to be spared even during the heat and continuance of war… such as porticos, temples, statues, and other elegant works and monuments of art.'[7]

In terms of practice, a turning point came at the end of the Thirty Years War (1618–1648), which had ravaged central Europe and involved all major Powers except England. During the war there had been seizure and pillage of movables to an extraordinary extent, especially documents, artworks of all kinds and books from

[3] Cicero, *Against Verres*, Book IV, 120.

[4] F de Vitoria, *De Indis et de jure belli, relectiones* 1532 (*Dissertations on the Indians and the Law of War*) (Washington, Carnegie Institution of Washington, 1917, Nys edn), discussed in PJ O'Keefe and LV Prott, *Law and the Cultural Heritage: Volume III: Movement* (London, Butterworths, 1989) 803, 804, 831.

[5] William Shakespeare, *Henry V*, Act III, Scene 6.

[6] The full text of *The Law of War and Peace* was completed in 1625 but was found after his death in 1645 and first published in English in 1868: ch III, para. XIII.

[7] ibid ch XII ('On Moderation'), para V.

libraries. A particularly heinous example was the pillage by the Catholic League of the Palatinate Library in Heidelberg, a famous repository of the Protestant princes; the contents were shipped by the victors to Rome in honour of the Pope.[8] The Peace of Westphalia which put an end to the conflict in 1648 included three treaties signed in Germany: two at Münster and one at Osnabrück. The Treaty of Osnabrück between Sweden and its allies, on the one side, and the Austrian Habsburg Emperor on the other, included a clause stating that 'Records, Writings and Documents, and other Moveables' were to be restored to their original owners.[9] This seems to be the first legal instrument in post-Mediaeval Europe to include any restitutionary provision of this nature. But at the time there was no community of nations (no League of Nations or United Nations) to oversee the administration of a rule that required restitution.

The next century brought a development of the custom whereby the Powers in general refrained from seizing works of art or religious objects. The Swiss scholar Emmerich de Vattel (1714–1758), who was heir to the tradition of Grotius in developing the law of nations, declared in 1758 the inviolability of certain cultural property, even during armed conflict:[10] 'For whatever reason a belligerent plunders the country, he should spare buildings that are the pride of mankind and do not strengthen the enemy, such as temples, tombstones, public buildings, and all other works of art distinguished for their beauty.'[11]

This gradually developing custom was blown to bits by Napoleon. During his 1796–1797 Italian campaign, important artworks were seized by the French Army, usually on the basis of treaty terms imposed upon defeated city states by Napoleon himself.[12] Quatremère de Quincy argued passionately against this policy designed to establish and embellish the great Museum in Paris, the former Louvre Palace of the French Kings.[13] As a result of the Napoleonic conquests, the Museum obtained treasures from Italy, Prussia, Austria, Bavaria, the Low Countries and Spain – as well as ancient artefacts excavated during the Egyptian campaign. French public opinion was strongly in favour of holding the masterpieces in Paris, seen as the enlightened 'capital' of the world.[14]

The Treaty of Vienna, which put an end to the Napoleonic conflict in 1815, did not lay out the principle of restoration. A proposal to include the words 'guarantee the integrity of museums and libraries', which would have validated French retention of the takings, was rejected. However, the Allies occupying Paris took

[8] See T Scovazzi, 'Un'Importante missione diplomatica di Antonio Canova' in *Scritti in onore di Ugo Draetta* (Naples, Editoriale Scientifica, 2011) 679–83.

[9] Treaty of Osnabrück between Sweden and the Austrian Empire (24 October 1648), Article CXIV.

[10] E de Vattel, *The Law of Nations* (1758). See discussion in Vrdoljak (n 1) 64–65.

[11] de Vattel, *The Law of Nations* (1758) book III, ch IX.

[12] Herman (n 1) 105–108. DM Quynn, 'The Art Confiscations of the Napoleonic Wars' (1945) L *The American Historical Review* 437–60.

[13] Quatremère de Quincy in LV Prott (ed), *Witnesses to History: Documents and Writings on the Return of Cultural Objects* (Paris, UNESCO Publishing, 2009) 19.

[14] See, for instance, the complaints of Stendhal in this regard: DM Quynn, 'The Art Confiscations of the Napoleonic Wars' (1945) L *The American Historical Review* 437–60, 459.

it upon themselves to assist in the return of much of what had been looted.[15] The French museums worked hard to delay the departure of their booty and to prevent returns. Of the Napoleonic acquisitions, a great many were returned – well over half – to the states of Germany and Italy, as well as Austria, Spain and the Vatican.[16] Others were lost, damaged or deliberately hidden by Dominique Vivant, Baron Denon, the Louvre's Director, who had already sent many minor works to French provincial museums.[17] In supporting the practice of return, the British delegation to Paris explained that this was done to right a series of notorious wrongs committed by Napoleon. As Foreign Secretary, Viscount Castlereagh stated: 'In applying a remedy to this offensive evil, it does not appear that any middle line can be adopted… The principle of property regulated by the claims of the territories from whence these works were taken is the surest and only guide to justice.'[18]

Throughout the remainder of the nineteenth century, it did seem as though the custom of restraint, as evoked by Castlereagh, held sway – even if tenuously at times. There are very few examples of European Powers looting one another's art collections during the brief conflicts that took place on the Continent during the period, even if cities and towns were taken by assault and badly damaged.[19] Across the Atlantic, during the American Civil War (1861–1865), President Abraham Lincoln commissioned a Code of War from legal expert Francis Lieber. One of the provisions of the 'Lieber Code' provided that artworks seized during a war must be made subject to the ensuing peace treaty (Article 36). This became the cornerstone of an international rule, committed to a legally enforceable instrument, whereby looting of art or religious items was prohibited in war, and required redress should the rule be violated.

Not to be outdone, the European Powers incorporated the principle into international statements on the rules of war. In Brussels in 1874, 15 State representatives drafted a non-binding Declaration Concerning the Laws and Customs of War, which made clear that pillage and the confiscation of artworks should be

[15] Herman (n 1) 105–108. S Williams, *The International and National Protection of Movable Cultural Property* (Dobbs Ferry, Oceana, 1978) 8–9.

[16] B Savoy, '1815. Année zéro. L'Europe à l'heure des restitutions d'oeuvres d'art', Lecture series (Paris, Collège de France, 19 April 2019) part 9. Through the involvement of two German princes, manuscripts stolen from the Vatican that had been deposited there after the looting of Heidelberg in 1622 were returned not to the Pope but to the German city, a restitution nearly 200 years in the making: see T Scovazzi , 'Evolutionary Trends as regards the Return of Removed Cultural Property' in L Durbán and A Lazari (eds), *El tráfico de bienes culturales* (Valencia, Tirant lo Blanch, 2015) 26.

[17] Quynn (n 14) 437–60 appears to be the most detailed discussion of how much was restored or lost.

[18] Viscount Castlereagh, Note XV delivered to the Allied Ministers respecting the Restitution of the Works of Art, Paris, 11 September 1815.

[19] One example is the taking by Austria of the Crown of the Lombards and the Cup of Queen Theodelina in 1859, only to be restored to Italy by the Treaty of Vienna in 1866, another are the flags and other accoutrements taken by Prussia during the Franco-Prussian War of 1870–71.

forbidden in war.[20] Then in 1880, the Institute of International Law (a congregation of leading jurists) produced the 'Oxford Manual' on the laws of war, which prohibited pillage and the seizure from, inter alia, institutions devoted to arts and science, as well as reprisals.[21] At the end of the century, the Powers at last agreed to a binding series of rules to apply in war, though only as between signatory Powers: the Convention (II) with Respect to the Laws and Customs of War on Land was entered into on 29 July 1899 at The Hague, and the 51 signatories included France, Great Britain, Germany and Russia. Article 47 of the accompanying regulations prohibited pillage, while Article 56 prohibited seizure of (as well as destruction and intentional damage to) 'works of art or science', and required that such action be 'made the subject of proceedings'. These provisions were replicated in the next Hague Convention of 1907 at Articles 46, 47 and 56.[22]

(ii) The First World War and After: Return, Restitution and Reparation

After the cataclysm of the First World War (1914–1918), the Treaty of Versailles of 1919 offered a new legal structure to govern relations between European powers – and indeed States more generally. It set up the League of Nations, the first attempt for general permanent cooperation of States to prevent armed conflict. Also, for the first time since the Treaty of Osnabrück, provisions on the return and replacement of cultural items were specifically included.

Article 245 of the Treaty required the German Government to restore to the French any of the 'trophies, archives, historical souvenirs or works of art' that had been taken from France during the Franco-Prussian War of 1870–71. Article 246 of the Treaty required Germany to restore to the Emir of Mecca (called at the time 'the King of the Hedjaz') a very old Quran taken from Medina by the Ottomans and to transfer the skull of 'Sultan Mkwawa' taken from East Africa to the British.[23] Article 247 required Germany to replace in kind all the manuscripts, incunabula, printed books, maps and other objects as substitutions for those destroyed in the burning of the Library of Louvain in Belgium (a disaster from the first year of the War). It also required Germany to hand over objects held

[20] See the Project of an International Declaration Concerning the Laws and Customs of War ('Brussels Declaration') (Brussels, 27 August 1874): Art 39 prohibits pillage, Art 8 treats property of institutions dedicated to, inter alia, arts and sciences as private property, and Art 38 prohibits confiscation of private property (including ipso facto property listed in Art 8). Under Art 8, if there is any seizure, destruction or wilful damage of 'works of art and science' inter alia this should be made the subject of legal proceedings (perpetrators presumably to be punished and restitution ordered).

[21] Institute of International Law, 'The Laws of War on Land' (Oxford Manual) (Oxford, 9 September 1880): Arts 32, 53 and 85. Note that the earlier 'Brussels Declaration' had been silent on reprisals.

[22] Regulations to the Second Hague Convention: Convention (IV) Respecting the Laws and Customs of War on Land (The Hague, 18 October 1907).

[23] The latter stayed in the hands of the British for quite some time, apparently only transferred to Tanzania in 1954: ntz.info/gen/n00404.html.

in German museums: two leaves of the famous Van Eyck triptych of the 'Mystic Lamb' to St Bavo's Cathedral in Ghent and the leaves of Dierick Bouts' *Last Supper* to St Peter's Church in Louvain. Interestingly, these last items had not in fact been looted during the War, but had come legitimately to German museums during the nineteenth century. These clauses replaced a more general clause which would have stipulated more extensive returns.[24]

Annex II of the Treaty of Versailles set up a 'Reparation Commission', composed of the United States, United Kingdom, France and several other States, providing an agency to supervise the requirements of the Treaty. However, it was recognised in the Treaty that 'the resources of Germany are not adequate, after taking into account permanent diminutions of such resources which will result from other provisions of the present Treaty, to make complete reparation for all such loss and damage' (Article 232).

After the breakup of the Austro-Hungarian Empire there were bitter conflicts concerning contested heritage between the Hungarian National Museum and those in charge of the Austrian museums.[25] Many of the major museums in Europe were adamant that their collections were sacrosanct and had no intention of returning materials taken from other countries before the War.[26] The Treaty of St Germain-en-Laye in 1919 between the Allies and Austria included a special clause dealing with the Austrian collections. Article 196 stated that the new Republic of Austria had to negotiate for 'amicable arrangements' with the relevant successor States by which objects of 'artistic, archaeological, scientific or historic character' once belonging to the Austro-Hungarian Empire were to be transferred to those new States if they 'ought to form part of the intellectual patrimony' of such States. It also ensured that Austria would keep, conserve and not alienate any such material for at least 20 years so that these negotiations could properly take place. Similar provision was made in the Treaty of Trianon in 1920 between the Allies and Hungary (Articles 175, 177).

The negotiations between Austria and Hungary themselves (under the Treaty of Venice of 1921) were fraught and not finally settled until 1932. Austria argued strongly that the collections in Vienna should not be dispersed, insisting on the 'integrity' of these collections.[27] Hungary emphasised the importance of its historical links. Approximately 1,000 artefacts were returned to Hungary from the

[24] Vrdoljak (n 1) 23–29.

[25] H Tietze, 'L'Accord Austro-Hongrois sur la répartition des collections de la Maison des Habsbourgs' (1933) 23–24 *Mouseion* 22; A Jakubowski, *State Succession in Cultural Property* (New York, Oxford University Press, 2015) gives detailed information on the returns after the First World War, 64–83.

[26] See further detailed discussion of these arrangements in Vrdoljak (n 1) 77–84.

[27] Jakubowski (n 25) 76–78 gives details on the Agreement of Austria and Hungary Concerning Museum and Library Objects, with three Protocols and three Annexes, Venice, 1932.

previous Imperial collection. This included the sword of King Ulászló II and the full plate armour of King Louis II from the early sixteenth century.[28]

The Treaties also provided, respectively, for the return of documents and historical material possessed by public institutions and for the restoration of 'objects of the same nature… which may have been taken away since 1 June 1914 from the ceded territories, with the exception of objects bought from private owners.'[29] The Treaties not only provided for the repatriation of objects removed during the war, but (as with the Treaty of Versailles) also for a certain 'cultural compensation' – restitution-in-kind for the lost or destroyed cultural property.[30]

Finally, the 1921 Treaty of Riga between Russia/Ukraine and Poland specifically mentioned that Russia and Ukraine should restore war trophies taken from Poland since 1772 as well as libraries, archaeological collections and archives, collections of works of art, and so on (Article 11, paragraph1). Tracking the extent to which these well-intentioned provisions were fulfilled would be an enormous task.

(iii) The 1920s: Developing Concern for the Displacement of Antiquities

To artworks taken during armed conflicts can be added another problematic category: the countless antiquities excavated during peacetime. Since the eighteenth century, an exuberant enthusiasm for the classical past had resulted in the displacement of a vast number of antiquities from their points of discovery to the great collections of Europe. The earliest systematic archaeological studies began in 1738 with the ancient city of Herculaneum, near Pompeii in Italy. At the end of the century, Napoleon's Egyptian campaign sparked a fascination with Ancient Egypt, and his experts carried many of their finds with them back to France. In 1816, the British Museum acquired from Lord Elgin the controversial sculptures of the Athenian Acropolis.[31] In the 1810s it was Belzoni at Thebes in Egypt, in the 1840s Layard at Nineveh and Botta at Khorsobad, in the 1850s Newton at Halicarnassus, in the 1870s Schliemann at Troy and in the 1880s Humann at Pergamon, and so on. Treasures from these ancient sites would make their way to the European capitals of London, Paris and Berlin.

The great sites of archaeological discovery, especially in Egypt and the Middle East, were not well protected. The main Power controlling this land in the nineteenth century was the Ottoman Empire, which had little to no interest

[28] P Apor, 'The National Museums of Hungary' in P Aronsson and G Elgenius (eds), EuNaMus Report No 1, *Building National Museums in Europe 1750–2010*. Conference proceedings from EuNaMus, European National Museums: Identity Politics, the Uses of the Past and the European Citizen (Bologna 28–30 April 2011), published by Linköping University Electronic Press.

[29] Under Arts 191–92 (St Germain) and Arts 175–76 (Trianon).

[30] Jakubowski (n 25) 64–65.

[31] See Herman (n 1) ch 4.

in civilisations that predated its own, nor indeed for vestiges of the pre-Islamic world.[32] There was no local grounding in scientific archaeology, no funding for digs and little understanding of the significance of the incredible, unexplored sites at its doorstep. The early archaeologists thus took the prerogative to explore such places and export their finds to their own countries. Archaeology became such a passion in Europe that a lively competition between the Great Powers – and their national institutions – inevitably resulted.

As archaeological activity continued into the twentieth century it morphed into a more scientific enterprise. Meanwhile there was a growing realisation in places of origin about the importance of antiquities and the need to police ancient sites.[33] However local legislation was often insufficient to adequately control excavations, whether authorised or clandestine. This was true during the period of the League of Nation mandates: Britain enacted legislation for its mandataries in Iraq in 1924 and Palestine in 1929, while France did the same for its mandataries in Syria and Lebanon in 1933. All of these once represented territories of the defunct Ottoman Empire, which had collapsed at the end of the First World War.

Iraq's first national antiquities law of 1924, for example, came out of the Anglo-Iraqi Treaty at the end of the War. The Antiquities Act required that all antiquity finds be first offered to the appropriate government department and that any export required a licence from that department (Article 3). All excavations had to be licensed by the department (Article 5). When the British mandate ended in 1932, there were 11 expeditions of five different nationalities operating in the country simultaneously.[34] The first non-British Director of Iraqi Antiquities revised the terms applying to removable finds. Although Iraq was now in a position to legislate for activities taking place on its territory, in many cases the State did not have the resources to fully implement the law.[35]

Charles de Visscher, a renowned scholar of international law and future international judge, thought the appropriate regulation of antiquities could be achieved only through domestic legislation.[36] Western archaeologists, on the other hand, wanted international rules to meet their goals: the acceptance of foreign archaeological teams by the host governments; the participation of such teams in excavations and finally the expatriation of finds to fill overseas collections.

[32] See E Eldem, 'From Blissful Indifference to Anguished Concern: Ottoman Perceptions of Antiquities, 1799–1869' in Z Bahrani, Z Çelik and E Eldem (eds), *Scramble for the Past: A Story of Archaeology in the Ottoman Empire, 1753–1914* (Istanbul, SALT, 2011) 285–308.

[33] ibid.

[34] For further discussion on practice in the mandates, see Vrdoljak (n 1) 105–108.

[35] For more information, see PJ O'Keefe and LV Prott, *Law and the Cultural Heritage: Volume I: Discovery and Excavation* (London, Butterworths, 1984) 46–48.

[36] In the 1930s, he worked on the drafts for OIM described below. De Visscher, 'La protection internationale des objets d'art et des monuments historiques' (1935) *Revue de droit internationale de législation comparée* 32; 'La protection des patrimoines artistiques et historiques nationaux; nécessité d'une réglementation' (1938) 43–44 *Mouseion* 19; AR Hall, 'The Recovery of Cultural Objects Dispersed during World War II' (1951) *Department of State Bulletin* (United States) 337, which includes English translations of de Visscher's drafts and his writings on the subject.

The League of Nations also brought into being the International Commission for Intellectual Cooperation (ICIC) and from this body came the Office international des Musées (OIM) in 1926. Six years later, the OIM was tasked with drafting a convention for the protection of antiquities and other objects of cultural value. Clearly the issue was serious enough to be regulated at an international level – or at least for regulation to be contemplated. As we shall see, this activity would lay the groundwork for the 1970 Convention many years later.

(iv) The 1930s: Early Attempts at International Regulation

In 1933, the OIM produced a document with a rather long-winded title (a perennial feature in this area), Draft International Convention on the Repatriation of Objects of Artistic, Historical or Scientific Interest, Which Have Been Lost or Stolen or Unlawfully Alienated or Exported. Though it was largely approved by the members of the ICIC in July of that year, opposition developed amongst several States (the US, UK, Netherlands),[37] considering any accession to the agreement 'undesirable'.[38] Certain States would accept the draft only with amendments (Australia, Italy, Japan, Denmark), while others were ready to adopt it without reservation (Canada, Egypt, India, Ireland). The text built on the experience of returns to countries of origin, such as those that followed the breakup of the Austro-Hungarian Empire, as mentioned above. It provided compensation to bona fide acquirers who had to return a cultural object (Article 3) and for the settlement of disputes through diplomatic, arbitral or judicial procedures (Article 7).[39]

Following comments from States, a new draft was prepared in 1936 to take account of some of the criticisms, with twice as many provisions. The focus was less on 'repatriation' and more on 'protection' of national historic or artistic treasures (a shift demonstrated by the removal of the former term from the title). The objects covered were more limited, as they had to meet the standard of being a 'national treasure', and had to be notified and published (Articles 1(2), 3, 4). There remained a requirement for compensation to be paid to possessors who were required to return objects (Articles 8, 19).

In July 1937 the ICIC and the League of Nations approved the holding of a Diplomatic Conference in 1938 to finalise the draft convention. The majority of interested States were satisfied with the latest version. However, some States were not happy with this version and, because their participation was deemed important for the success of the Convention, it was considered wise to try to meet their particular concerns. The Netherlands, which had a particular interest in the work,

[37] R Goy, 'Le Régime international de l'Importation, de l'Exportation et du Transfert de Propriété des Biens culturels' (1970) 16 *Annuaire français de droit international* 605; Vrdoljak (n 1) 113.

[38] League of Nations, C290 M 1 54, 1935 XII, 58.

[39] For commentary on this text, see Vrdoljak (n 1) 112.

offered to consult with other governments and to host the diplomatic conference and another draft was therefore prepared.

The 1939 draft restricted the reach of the proposed convention to a very narrow band of objects: it applied only to objects owned by a State or public institution (Article 1(1)) and only to objects that had been catalogued individually before their dispossession (Article 1(2)). This draft departed radically from those of 1933 and 1936. It retained provisions on *bona fide* possession and finely-tuned compensation. Article 12 allowed States to decline obligations regarding their colonies, protectorates, overseas territories or mandataries, which for the time would have denuded the instrument of much of its global applicability. This was certainly in the interests of imperial powers, while colonies and mandataries would have had no say whatsoever.[40]

While the third revision was generally accepted by most of the States, before it could be put to a vote the Second World War erupted in Europe on 1 September 1939. The envisaged Diplomatic Conference never took place.

(v) The Second World War and its Aftermath

Acts of wilful destruction, misappropriation and looting were widespread within Nazi-controlled territories during the Second World War (1939–1945). The Allied governments (including of the United Kingdom, the United States, the USSR and the exiled French) issued a statement in 1943 to this effect, known as the London Declaration. It gave a warning that the Allies would do their utmost to undo acts of dispossession practised by Nazi Germany and its allies against 'the countries and peoples who have been so wantonly assaulted and despoiled'. Accordingly, the Allies reserved their rights to declare invalid all transfers/dealings relating to property taking place during occupation, whether these took the form of open looting or plunder or – a remarkably perceptive point – 'of transactions apparently legal in form, even when they purport to be voluntarily effected.'[41]

After the liberation of Europe from the Nazis, the London Declaration was implemented through legal instruments to ensure that the principle of restitution would not be negated by conflicting provisions of national law. France, the United Kingdom and the United States each issued a law on restitution for their respective zones of occupation in Germany. These laws overrode inconsistent provisions of the German Civil Code. In the US zone, for example, this took the form of *Law No. 59 – Restitution of Identifiable Property*, which provided that, 'Property shall be restored to its former owner or to his successor in interest…' (section 3.75(2)). Confiscation was defined as a deprivation resulting from a 'transaction *contra*

[40] For more on the drafts of the 1930s, see PJ O'Keefe, *Protecting Cultural Objects: Before and After 1970*. (Builth Wells, Institute of Art and Law, 2017) 10–12.

[41] Inter-Allied Declaration Against Acts of Dispossession Committed in Territories Under Enemy Occupation or Control (London, 1943).

bonos mores, threats or duress, or an unlawful taking or any other tort' (section 3.76(1)). When the occupation concluded in 1954, the German Government agreed to adopt the same provisions. However, restitution was not forthcoming in many cases, a failure that lingered for many decades to come.[42]

The London Declaration was especially important in recognising the dubiousness of transactions that may have appeared legitimate on their surface, even those 'apparently legal in form, even when they purport to be voluntarily effected'.[43] During the occupation this description covered not only forced loans and donations and those exacted by fear and intimidation, but also sales at unrealistic prices by persons seeking to ensure the safety and security of themselves and their families.[44]

In 1945, immediately after the Second World War, the United Nations (UN) was formed, as well as one of its central agencies, the United Nations Educational, Scientific and Cultural Organization (UNESCO). UNESCO had 37 founding Member States. It set about in the aftermath of the War drafting a convention that would respond to the cataclysm that the world had so recently endured: the Convention for the Protection of Cultural Property in the Event of Armed Conflict was adopted at The Hague in 1954 (called the Hague Convention).

The 1954 Hague Convention introduced the term 'cultural property', which was defined to comprise both movable and immovable property 'of great importance to the cultural heritage of every people' (Article 1). The Convention then required Contracting Parties to protect cultural property during armed conflict, including to refrain from attacking or putting in harm's way any cultural property (unless required by military necessity) and preventing or stopping the theft, pillage or vandalism of cultural property (Article 4). Although the Convention required States to forbid looting, it did not contain restitutionary provisions. This was due to a disagreement at the time amongst States represented at The Hague.[45] Instead, a Protocol to the Convention was passed in parallel, adopted by only some of those present. This Protocol required States to recover and return cultural property that had been exported from an occupied territory, whether directly or indirectly.[46]

In the meantime, an earlier body had been replaced. The OIM, founded after the First World War, was considered moribund and incapable of taking on the challenges posed within the new post-War order. It was replaced in 1946 by the International Council of Museums (ICOM). Needless to say, the draft conventions of the 1930s were neither revived nor discussed by ICOM or UNESCO during this period.

[42] See NE Palmer, *Museums and the Holocaust*, 2nd edn, R Redmond-Cooper (ed) (Builth Wells, Institute of Art and Law, 2020); S Nahlik, 'La Protection des Biens culturels en Cas de Conflit armé' (1967) I *Recueil des Cours de l'Académie de droit international de La Haye* 113.

[43] London Declaration, para 3.

[44] O'Keefe earlier noted that many transactions in the colonial context could arguably fit these same categories: *Protecting Cultural Objects* (Builth Wells, Institute of Art and Law, 2017) 15.

[45] K Chamberlain, *War and Cultural Heritage: A Commentary on the Hague Convention and its two Protocols*, 2nd edn (Builth Wells, Institute of Art and Law, 2013).

[46] 1954 Protocol to the Hague Convention, Art 1.

Chapter 2
The Preparation of the Convention

(i) 1960–1968: Disagreement and Breakthrough

It took until the 1960s for the interest in adopting international rules governing the illicit trade in antiquities to return to the fore. At UNESCO's eleventh General Conference in 1960, a resolution was adopted to appoint a group of experts to study the possibility of a draft convention. Two years later, ICOM submitted a report which examined the technical and legal aspects of possible regulation in this area, including conflicting treatments of *bona fide* acquirers across different jurisdiction and the question of time and prescriptibility, ultimately concluding that any consensus for such regulation would be unlikely.[47]

A Working Party was established, which pushed for further studies and surveys on the matter.[48] At the twelfth UNESCO Conference in 1962, a heated debate took place between States rich in heritage (sometimes called 'source countries') and States with active art markets (often called 'countries of destination' or 'market countries') as to the way ahead.[49] The Director-General of UNESCO during this period was René Maheu (1905–1975), a man of forceful personality[50] with a somewhat 'tempestuous' character.[51] He appeared deeply concerned by the oppositional stance of various countries and he may well have feared that there would be serious consequences for UNESCO were a convention on this topic not delivered.

Mexico and Peru were two of the most insistent Member States urging UNESCO to provide a convention intended to slow the rate of trafficking. Because of its propinquity to the United States, Mexico had become increasingly concerned about the illegal excavation and trafficking of its cultural heritage. Archaeologists in the United States had also become concerned with the state of protection of Mexican heritage. The issue had been raised in a dialogue between the Presidents of Mexico and the United States in 1967.[52] Mexico pointed to two bilateral treaties with the United States, one on migratory birds and the other on stolen motor vehicles, as possible models for a way ahead. It was rightly divined that the most powerful country in the world was much more comfortable with bilateral arrangements than with large international conventions. The Mexicans even made clear

[47] UNESCO/CUA/1 (14 April 1962), Resolution 4.413.

[48] 'Report of the Working Party on International Regulations Designed to Prohibit and Prevent the Illicit Export, Import and Sale of Cultural Property', *Records of the General Conference Twelfth Session*, Unesdoc 283 (Paris, 1962).

[49] ibid 284.

[50] AM M'Bow, 'Address by Director-General of UNESCO at the Ceremony of Tribute to the Memory of René Maheu', Unesdoc DG/76/10.

[51] D Johnson, 'Simone de Sartre' (7 June 1985) 6 *London Review of Books* No 10, 11–12.

[52] J Nafziger, 'The 1970 UNESCO Convention: Insights, Circumspections, and Outlooks' in JA Sánchez Cordero (ed), *The 1970 UNESCO Convention: New Challenges* (Mexico, Instituto de Investigaciones Jurídica, 2014) 211, 214.

that, should cultural heritage threats not be addressed, their cooperation on cross-border law enforcement would by no means be guaranteed.[53]

Director-General Maheu had decided, by early 1968, that a draft convention should be prepared in time to submit to the sixteenth General Conference in October–November 1970. The topic of the Convention was added to the programme of the Executive Board meeting, and then to the Agenda of the General Conference. UNESCO rules for making international standard-setting instruments are unsurprisingly demanding, requiring an appropriate length of time for documents to be prepared, translated and distributed, then for a large number of comments to be received and integrated into the text.[54] They involve the undertaking of preliminary studies, examination by the Executive Board, the preparation of a report and more. In this instance, the persistence and speed of the process was propelled by Maheu.

In January 1968, Maheu quickly authorised the preparation of a 'preliminary study' required by UNESCO rules. The Assistant Director-General (ADG) commissioned Robert Brichet (1915–2002), a member of the French administration with degrees in law, art and archaeology, to prepare a 'preliminary study on the means of prohibiting and preventing the illicit export, import and transfer of ownership of cultural property'. He promptly submitted a draft Convention to UNESCO on 26 February.[55] The UNESCO Legal Adviser was not enthusiastic, indicating that the UNESCO mandate was to show advantages and difficulties of the drafting, not to support one particular view of a text. He stated that the task of the Executive Board was to decide whether to refer the issue to the General Conference, not to settle the text internally.[56]

Meanwhile Brichet's report was sent for review to a group of four appointed experts, seemingly chosen by the Director-General (no trace of their comments could be found in the UNESCO archives). Certain suggestions were made by the Director of the Culture Division on the revised text and returned to Brichet, who then made amendments.[57] The Executive Board, finding it 'desirable' that an international convention be drafted on the subject, authorised Maheu to convene a special committee to commence the formal drafting, according to UNESCO's Rules of Procedure.[58]

[53] MB Feldman, 'Proceedings of the Panel on the U.S. Enabling Legislation of the UNESCO Convention on the Means of Prohibiting and Preventing the Illicit Import, Export and Transfer of Ownership of Cultural Property' (1976) 4 *Syracuse Journal of International Law and Commerce* 97, 133.

[54] 'Rules of Procedure concerning recommendations to Member States and international conventions covered by the terms of Art IV, para 4, of the Constitution 111', Basic texts (Paris, UNESCO, 2014) 111.

[55] O'Keefe called this admittedly 'fast drafting', but explained that Brichet would have found a wealth of useful precedents from the work undertaken at OIM in the 1930s: O'Keefe, *Protecting Cultural Objects* (2017) 20.

[56] Unesdocs 069: 7A 827 Importation-Exportation & Vente illicite des Biens culturels, Part IV – 12/X/64 to 31/III/68.

[57] Unesdoc 78 EX/9: Report on the Possibility of Drafting a Convention Concerning the Illicit Import, Export and Transfer of Ownership of Cultural Property.

[58] Unesdoc 78 EX/9, Decision 4.4.3.

(ii) 1968–1969: Draft Conventions Circulated and Discussed

In August 1968, the Director-General published the 'Preliminary Study',[59] which provided a brief summary of the earlier history of efforts to protect cultural treasures and a draft Convention in the Annex. This was distributed to all UNESCO Member States with a request for comments. Out of more than 100 members, 28 responses were received, with five more coming in after the deadline. In the meantime, the fifteenth General Conference of 1968 had endorsed the adoption of a Convention and expected a text to be presented at the next General Conference in 1970.

In February 1969, a Final Report was distributed which included an Annex with a summary of all comments States had made on the first draft.[60] Ten Member States approved the preliminary draft convention as it was, with six additional States supportive; fourteen submitted observations concerning substantive issues. These issues were varied: concerning the impact on the art and antiquities trade, the difficulty of confirming *bona fide* acquirers, and compensation. Austria opposed the draft, Germany worried about the dispersal of collections, Sweden did not trust the system for import and export controls. Eastern European States noted that the draft seemed to evade the possibilities of collective ownership in a communist economy.[61] The UK found the wording too vague and impractical for national legislation capable of enforcement. Cambodia and China would have wanted to see the convention apply retroactively to objects that had already left their countries of origin, while France took the opposite view.[62] The US recommended alternative arrangements based on less prescriptive text (eg, compulsory import provisions), guided by a strong statement of principle which States could follow as they saw fit.[63] In fact, the US State Department decided to produce its own proposed text. It convened a committee of lawyers in 1969, which produced an alternative draft that substantially diverged from that of UNESCO.

Drafting conventions is generally difficult: if there were broad agreement, there would be little need for a convention. When it is imperative to find a solution, drastic measures may need to be taken to achieve results, which was the approach taken here by Maheu. Challenges were legion. Correspondence was slow before the advent of computers. Many newly independent countries had difficulty funding travel to meetings, or sparing valuable administrators to deal with every new issue that arose. Language barriers posed additional problems. As a result, the drafters might not always have achieved the most accurate meaning for terms, phrases or entire provisions.

The term 'cultural property' was, at the time, a relatively recent legal fabrication. Prior to the mid-twentieth century, international treaties tended to list the

[59] Unesdoc SHC/MD/3.

[60] Unesdoc SHC/MD/5, 2–23.

[61] See eg the comments from Bulgaria: Unesdoc MD 5 Annex II, 2.

[62] For more detail on each of these responses, see O'Keefe, *Protecting Cultural Objects* (2017) 22–23.

[63] Submitted 16 December 1969, this long statement mixed comments on the text with criticisms of the process of drafting, definitions and effects on national law.

intended categories of material when dealing with anything of this nature, as can be seen in the various peace treaties described above, as well as in the earlier Hague Conventions of 1899 and 1907.[64] It was the Hague Convention of 1954 which employed the neat catch-all term 'cultural property', which it defined rather broadly at Article 1. However, the term's first appearance in an international document was slightly earlier: in a July 1946 statement by the Allied governments pertaining to property that had passed through neutral countries during the Second World War.[65] For present purposes, the term was introduced in the UNESCO discussions from about 1964, though as we will see the definition would be somewhat different from that found in the 1954 Hague Convention.

(iii) 1970: Adoption of the Convention

The special committee established by the Executive Board in accordance with the UNESCO Constitution was called the 'Special Negotiating Committee', an indication that there were diverse, perhaps contradictory, views at play. Sixty-one States participated in this committee.

The United States took part at the urging of Mexico, but generally felt that cultural matters should be dealt with by professionals and not dictated by governments. As import controls were a matter for Customs, this came under the banner of administrative law, and so an expert in administrative law, Paul Bator, was added to the delegation. Thankfully, Bator wrote in detail about his experiences in a 1982 article.[66] He called the legislative process 'highly confused and untidy'.[67] Importantly, the US delegation had been surprised to learn that the UNESCO rules prevented the Secretariat text from being replaced at this late stage by any other text, such as the text prepared by the committee of US lawyers convened by the State Department in 1969. The American delegation made clear that the Secretariat draft was unacceptable.[68] They were, however, able to introduce the substance of a number of their clauses into this draft. The reason for this seems to be that the other members were desperate to have at least one major market country sign up to the Convention – Switzerland and the UK were already absent from discussions – so the US demands were heeded, at least in part.[69]

Batorsummarises the strange world he had entered, offering a colourful depiction of the legislative environment of UNESCO at the time:

[64] Andreas Giorgallis calls this style 'periphrasis': A Giorgallis, 'On the Definition of Heritage' (2025) 30 *Art Antiquity and Law* 309.

[65] Full text at AR Hall, 'Recovery' (1951) Annex I.

[66] PM Bator, 'An Essay on the International Trade in Art' (1982) 34 *Stanford Law Review* 275, 373, 374.

[67] ibid 371.

[68] ibid 372.

[69] ibid 373.

> The views of the various delegations did not fall into sharply defined and focused categories. There were a few delegations which were not interested in a convention with any substantive teeth. There were delegations sympathetic to the views of the United States, but with whom negotiation and agreement were nevertheless difficult because of problems of language and different traditions of domestic law regarding this field. A few delegations agreed with the United States almost completely. A large number of countries were conscientiously interested in working out a draft that the United States could accept, but were also genuinely attracted, substantively and politically, to the Secretariat approach. The most important country in this group was Mexico, and the eventual key to the politics of the meeting was the working out of a position that could be sponsored both by the United States and Mexico…
>
> Some delegations appeared well-informed and competent; others appeared to me to be uninterested, uninformed, and confused. All this made the process of delineating and focusing issues and of creating stable and powerful blocks of opinion extremely difficult.[70]

Bator goes on to speak about confused and disorderly proceedings and the different uses of words such as 'ownership', 'dominion' and '*bona fide*', representing widely divergent legal systems, along with the fact that the proceedings were in four languages.[71]

He also concluded that a number of provisions of the Convention 'can be safely ignored because they will have no substantive effect'. He gives one example (Article 3) which he declares to be 'a mysterious provision that will not be operative in the United States.'[72] He is dismissive of certain phrases: the use of the words 'consistent with national legislation' is confusing and so suggests an effort to ignore provisions that include them (Articles 5(a) and 13)). Other phrases are also difficult: 'as appropriate for each country' and 'shall take provisional measures to the extent feasible' (in Articles 5, 9, 10(a)). Despite these reservations, however, the US delegate said he deeply appreciated the spirit of compromise which had prevailed in the debates.[73]

And so, on 14 November 1970, the Convention on the Means of Prohibiting and Preventing the Illicit Import, Export and Transfer of Ownership of Cultural Property was adopted by the sixteenth General Conference of UNESCO. Seventy-seven States voted in favour of adoption, one against, and eight States abstained. It is not known how particular States voted. The vote was by show of hands and no record was made apart from the total figures. Only one State made a public statement (Upper Volta), complaining of the requirement to pay compensation by requesting States (at Article 7(b)). Three days later, on 17 November, the Convention was signed by the President of the General Conference and Director-General Maheu.

UNESCO rules for bringing international instruments into existence, then as now, require that the instrument be adopted at a General Conference. This

[70] ibid 374–75.

[71] ibid 375.

[72] O'Keefe called this reading a 'grave error': *Protecting Cultural Objects* (2017) 34. See commentary on Art 3 below, II.

[73] Unesdoc 16 C/17, Annex II.

differs from the usual practice of specialised agencies of the United Nations. Under UNESCO rules, a convention is adopted by Member States at the General Conference and then signed by the Director-General and the President of the General Conference on behalf of States. These two signatures indicate that the text is the authentic text as adopted.[74] Each Member State is then required to submit the convention to its competent authorities 'within a period of one year from the close of the session'.[75] The instrument then has to be 'ratified', 'acceded to' or 'accepted' by a State in order for that State to become party to it. 'Ratification' and 'acceptance' are the actions used in relation to the 1970 Convention (the ultimate effect in international law is the same).

With these proceedings, the Convention was launched into the world, which ended the first part of a very long process. As we have seen, the Convention did not spring suddenly into being at the tail end of the 1960s. It was preceded by years of effort, beginning with the League of Nations in the 1930s and continuing after the War with UNESCO. The 1960s saw many colonial territories gain independence and demand return of cultural material taken during the preceding decades (in some cases, centuries). Illegal excavation and export were on the rise. These were all factors that bore on the advent of the 1970 Convention. And since its adoption, it has established standards and sought to regulate certain illicit conduct.

The trade in 'cultural property' – relating as it does to rare and beautiful objects – often triggers passion and emotion when regulation is at issue. From the cowherd who discovers a magnificent terracotta statue, to the dealer in a luxurious showroom, to the collector admiring what he alone possesses: all are affected by the circumscription of trade in cultural objects. Those who successfully bring about change in this area are to be applauded for marshalling the opposition to looting and illicit traffic in cultural objects and shifting the international landscape. And any change in this area is best understood in the light of history, international politics, international law and the internal law of States. This is what we will turn to more fully below.

Chapter 3
The Convention Comes into Force

The year 1970 has come to occupy a special place in the consciousness of those engaging in, or affected by, the trade in cultural heritage, particularly antiquities. As we know, that was the year the sixteenth General Conference of UNESCO adopted the Convention. However, in accordance with its terms, the Convention would only come into force three months after the deposit of the third ratification,

[74] Art 14, Rules of Procedure Concerning Recommendations to Member States and International Conventions Covered by the Terms of Art IV, para 4, of the UNESCO Constitution.

[75] Art 4(4), UNESCO Constitution.

acceptance or accession (Article 21). The three States that lodged the necessary instruments were Ecuador (Acceptance on 24 March 1971), Bulgaria (Ratification on 15 September 1971) and – as we saw in the Introduction – Nigeria (Ratification on 24 January 1972), and so the Convention came into force three months thereafter, on 24 April 1972. It applied first only to these States, and would apply to any other State only three months after that State lodged its instrument of ratification, acceptance or accession.

Which States and at what date they became legally bound by the particular obligations of the Convention depends on the date each State ratified or accepted the Convention. Article 7, for instance, will apply only from the date at which the Convention has been brought into force in both of the relevant States (i.e. the source State and the State of destination).[76] That said, there is nothing to prevent a State from going further than the Convention explicitly requires. The definition of a prohibited import is a matter for the State, incorporated in its own legislation and representing its own decision. In fact, there is room for creative use of national legislation, with the 1970 Convention as a starting point. Examples of this are the implementing legislation in Canada, Australia and Germany: all three have introduced more general import restrictions for illicit cultural objects that go well beyond Article 7, for instance.[77]

Confusion often arises about the effect of the Convention. The lines between its strict legal effect and its effect on ethical standards are often blurred. This can have serious consequences for anyone trying to establish rights in relation to a particular item of 'cultural property', as defined under the Convention. It also leads to political complications surrounding the Convention. The adoption of the text in 1970 inspired many concerned professionals (especially archaeologists and museum professionals) to regard 1970 as the cut-off date for the investigation of provenance. That year has become well established as the commencing date for *ethical* provenance research. As one important publication stated: 'the 1970 UNESCO Convention changed forever the ethical landscape of the museum world'.[78]

Codes of practice affecting museums around the world have generally adopted the 1970 date as a line in the sand. The British Museum, for instance, first subscribed to the principles of the Convention in 1998 and formally incorporated the 1970

[76] See for instance the Canadian case of *R v Heller* (1983) 27 Alta LR (2d) 346, in which the Court had to interpret the Canadian law implementing the Convention in this way, relating to imported cultural property from Nigeria (see commentary on Art 7 below, II). In *Protecting Cultural Objects* (2017), O'Keefe expressed disagreement with the Court's interpretation of Art 7 of the Convention and believed instead the Canadian law has a wider scope than the Convention.

[77] Found in Canada's Cultural Property Export and Import Act of 1985, s 37, Australia's Protection of Movable Cultural Heritage Act 1986, s 14, and Germany's Cultural Property Protection Act of 2016, s 28. See further about national implementation below, V.

[78] N Brodie, J Doole and P Watson, *Stealing History: The Illicit Trade in Cultural Material* (Cambridge, McDonald Institute for Archaeological Research, 2000) 9.

date into its Acquisition Policy in 2000.[79] During that same year the archaeologist Professor Colin Renfrew recognised that it was 'widely accepted in Britain that no public institution, such as a museum, should purchase unprovenanced antiquities unless it can be securely documented (for instance by adducing their publication prior to that date) that these have been publicly known since before 1970.'[80] It then became UK Government policy following the country's ratification of the 1970 Convention in 2002. Guidance published by the Department for Culture, Media and Sport provides that museums 'should acquire or borrow items only if they are certain they have not been illegally excavated or illegally exported since 1970'. The reference to 1970 is explained as 'a clear, pragmatic and practicable watershed that is already widely understood and supported. … 1970 is generally accepted as the key point for an ethical approach to museum acquisitions in this area'.[81]

The American Association of Art Museum Directors updated its guidelines, *The Acquisition of Archaeological Material and Ancient Art*, in 2008 to take on board the date of the signing of the Convention, 17 November 1970, referred to therein as 'the most pertinent threshold for the application of more rigorous standards to the acquisition of archaeological materials and ancient art as well as for the development of a unified set of expectations for museums, sellers and donors.'[82] It went on to state that: 'Member museums normally should not acquire a Work unless provenance research substantiates that the Work was outside its country of probable modern discovery before 1970 or was legally exported from its probable country of modern discovery after 1970'.[83]

ICOM adopted a revised Code of Ethics in 2004. Paragraph 7.2 states that the policy of museums should acknowledge the 1970 Convention, amongst others, as 'international legislation which is taken as a standard in interpreting the ICOM Code of Ethics'. This is applicable to all members of ICOM, both individual and institutional, of which there are over 60,000 in nearly 140 countries.[84] The Code has been translated into nearly 40 languages. It is the most influential instrument world-wide for spreading the moral standards associated with museum acquisition, and thus promoting the Convention in the ethical space.

[79] 'Wherever possible the Trustees will only acquire those objects that have documentation to show that they were exported from their country of origin before 1970 and this policy will apply to all objects of major importance' (4.2.3), British Museum Acquisition Policy (2000), as presented to the House of Commons Select Committee for Culture, Media and Sport (2000), Annex II. Reference to the 1970 date continues to the 2018 iteration, though it appears that by 2024 the policy had been shortened to refer to the 1970 Convention only in broad terms.

[80] C Renfrew, *Loot, Legitimacy and Ownership: The Ethical Crisis in Archaeology* (London, Duckworth, 2000) 16.

[81] *Combating Illicit Trade: Due Diligence Guidelines for Museums, Libraries, Archives on Collecting and Borrowing Cultural Material* (2005) 2 (Basic Principles).

[82] *The Acquisition of Archaeological Material and Ancient Art*, as updated in 2013 (relevant text of provisions quoted has remained the same). Note the use of the date of signing, 17 November, rather than adoption, 14 November.

[83] ibid.

[84] See ICOM website: icom.museum/en/get-involved/become-a-member/.

Chapter 4
Implementation and Management of the Convention

The Convention does not explicitly require cultural property to be seized at the border on importation. It is for the State concerned to determine the most practical way to administer the Convention in light of the circumstances of that State. In both the Canadian and Australian implementing legislation, the importation of cultural property illegally exported from another State Party to the Convention is an offence and the property is liable to seizure and recovery or forfeiture.[85] But, unless it is recognised and seized at the point of entry (or following the receipt of information by the authorities), nothing happens until the State has received an official request from the country of origin alleging illegal export.[86] The authorities may then proceed to investigate and, if the property is found, seize it. The responsibility is on the importer to make proper enquiries. This appears to be a convenient and efficient method of implementing the Convention.

Under Article 21 of the Convention, UNESCO has a significant role to play in the management of the Convention. States Parties may call on UNESCO for technical assistance. The Organization may, on its own initiative, conduct studies into the illicit movement of cultural property and make proposals to States Parties for implementing the Convention. However, the Convention does not establish a permanent official forum where States can discuss its effect and make suggestions for improvement[87] – though, as we shall see, certain ad hoc bodies have taken shape over the years, in some ways to fill this gap. Revision of the Convention is technically possible, but complex and unlikely to lead to improvement in the short term.

A fund was established to support the Convention, which grew out of a recommendation from the Third Meeting of States Parties to the Convention in 2015. According to UNESCO, the Fund aims to support States 'in their efforts to fight effectively against the illicit trafficking of cultural property, in particular capacity-building, the awareness and communication, the inventory work and the monitoring of auction houses.'[88] It can also assist developing countries in participating at relevant UNESCO sessions in Paris. The Fund is financed by voluntary contributions and, by the 2024–2025 year, had a total budget of just over $350,000.

[85] The Cultural Property Export and Import Act of 1985 (Canada) provides for recovery 'to ensure the return' at s 37(5) and the Protection of Movable Cultural Heritage Act 1986 (Australia) provides for forfeiture at ss 14 and 34–38. The Australian legislation goes further than that of Canada in that it can theoretically apply to any State, not just a State Party to the 1970 Convention.

[86] At s 37(3) of the Canadian law and s 41 of the Australian law.

[87] In this it differs from other UNESCO Conventions dealing with cultural heritage (eg, the Convention concerning the Protection of the World Cultural and Natural Heritage of 1972 established an Intergovernmental Committee known in short as the 'World Heritage Committee').

[88] See UNESCO website, 'Fight Illicit Trafficking of Cultural Property': www.unesco.org/en/fight-illicit-trafficking/support.

According to the UNESCO website, there were seven State contributors to the Fund, including China, the Netherlands and Turkey.[89]

(i) The Intergovernmental Committee (ICPRCP)

The Intergovernmental Committee for Promoting the Return of Cultural Property to its Countries of Origin or its Restitution in Case of Illicit Appropriation (ICPRCP) is independent of the 1970 Convention.[90] It was created in 1978 by the UNESCO General Conference[91] with the primary task of 'making it possible for countries whose cultural heritage had been dispersed to assemble representative collections of this heritage through the return of at least some of the works that had been lost'.[92] The push came from the UNESCO Director-General at the time, Amadou-Mahtar M'Bow.[93] When the Convention had been adopted, certain States were greatly concerned at its lack of retroactivity, particularly those newly independent States that had hoped it would enable them to recover objects taken by former colonial rulers. As one African commentator noted, 'the colonisers were more concerned with developing the museums of foreign objects in the capitals of their respective mother countries than with building museums in the colonies themselves'.[94]

The UNESCO General Conference established the ICPRCP in order to provide an avenue for States to meet these concerns.[95] It was to be a purely advisory body. A State could request the restitution or return of 'any cultural property which [had] a fundamental significance from the point of view of the spiritual values and cultural heritage of the people of a Member State and which [had] been lost as a result of colonial or foreign occupation or as a result of illicit appropriation'.[96] The

[89] UNESCO website, 'Fund of the 1970 Convention': core.unesco.org/en/project/170GLO4042.

[90] The background and much more detail about the development of the ICPRCP can be found in PJ O'Keefe and LV Prott, *Law and the Cultural Heritage: Volume III: Movement* (London, Butterworths, 1989) 850ff. For later information see AF Vrdoljak, *International Law, Museums and the Return of Cultural Objects* (Cambridge, Cambridge University Press, 2008) 211 and 234 and A Jakubowski, 'Intergovernmental Committee for Promoting the Return of Cultural Property to its Countries of Origin or its Restitution in Case of Illicit Appropriation (ICPRCP)' in AF Vrdoljak, A Jakubowski and A Chechi, *The 1970 UNESCO and 1995 Unidroit Conventions on Stolen or Illegally Transferred Cultural Property* (Oxford, Oxford University Press, 2024). Reports of meetings of the ICPRCP are published by UNESCO online.

[91] Resolution 20 C4/7.6/5.

[92] Taken from the report of the First Session of the Committee, opening address of the Director-General of UNESCO, Unesdoc 21 C/83, 1.

[93] 'A Plea for the Return of an Irreplaceable Cultural Heritage to Those Who Created It', 1978: unesdoc.unesco.org/ark:/48223/pf0000034683.

[94] H Abranches, *Report on the Situation in Africa*, Unesdoc CLT-83 CONF/216.3 (1983) 5. This may be a one-sided view: the development during the colonial period of important public museums in Nigeria and India by the British may be used as countervailing evidence.

[95] Resolution 20 C4/7.6/5

[96] ICPRCP Statute, Art 3(2).

Committee would then act as facilitator in bringing about negotiations between the parties.

To date, UNESCO lists on its website only six successful cases of return or restitution 'under the aegis of the ICPRCP'[97] and the extent of the Committee's role in some of these might be debatable. One of the cases was brought by Tanzania in 2006, concerning the Makonde Mask stolen in 1984 and held since 1985 by the Barbier-Mueller Museum in Switzerland. The dispute had been ongoing for some time before the submission and had already involved an offer to settle by the Museum in 2002, which was eventually accepted by Tanzania seven years later. It is difficult to attribute the return of the mask in 2010 to the ICPRCP; in fact, ICOM and the Swiss Office for Culture seemed to be more instrumental in assuring return under appropriate terms.[98] Turkey's 1986 case against Germany for the Bogazköy Sphinx took 25 years to be settled when, in 2011, the piece was returned under a bilateral agreement between the parties.[99] The most infamous cultural property dispute of all, Greece's claim for the Parthenon Marbles at the British Museum, has been before the ICPRCP since 1984 when Greece first lodged its request against the UK, and remains unresolved.[100] The two other cases currently before the ICPRCP at the time of writing, both also involving the UK, do not appear close to resolution: Zambia's 2018 claim for the Broken Hill Man skull (archaic human remains held at the Natural History Museum in London)[101] and Nigeria's 2020 claim for the Ife Bronze Head (an 800-year-old artefact brought to an English auction house in 2017)[102] – the latter case features on the cover of this book and was discussed in the introduction.[103]

The ICPRCP usually holds meetings every two years. Beginning in 1980, it has referred to the problem of illicit traffic in cultural heritage at almost every session. Mostly this has involved disseminating information on how particular States sought to deal with it and the activities of UNESCO and other international organisations such as INTERPOL, ICOM and the World Customs Organization. Much attention was devoted to programmes on training held by UNESCO and other bodies to counteract trafficking. For a number of years the ICPRCP considered a Declaration of Principles Relating to Cultural Property Displaced in Connection with the Second World War, but it failed to gain support from the General Conference.[104] Rules of Procedure on Mediation and Conciliation were adopted by the ICPRCP in 2010 to give States additional means of 'facilitating bilateral negotiations to improve

[97] www.unesco.org/en/fight-illicit-trafficking/return-and-restitution-under-icprcp.

[98] K Hausler and E Selter, *Beyond Restitution* (Oxford, Hart Publishing, 2025) 158–62, 176–77; F Shyllon, 'Return of the Makonde Mask from Switzerland to Tanzania – A Righteous Conclusion?' (2011) XVI *Art Antiquity and Law* 79, 80.

[99] A personal account of involvement with this case is in LV Prott, 'The Sphinx Within the Wall: A Tale of Two Germanies and Three Sphinxes' (2010) XV *Art Antiquity and Law* 147.

[100] A Herman, *The Parthenon Marbles Dispute: Heritage, Law, Politics* (Oxford, Hart Publishing, 2023) 71–72, 82–83, 152–53.

[101] ICPRCP/18/21.COM 8 (Paris, UNESCO, May 2018).

[102] ICPRCP/21/22.COM 5 (Paris, UNESCO, Sept 2021).

[103] See also below, II (Arts 2, 3, 7(b), 13); V, ch 5

[104] Unesdoc CLT-2010/CONF.203/COM.16/2 Rev.

the restitution or return of cultural property to its countries of origin'.[105] Vrdoljak sees the work of the Committee as evolving over its existence to represent the needs of a broader constituency than was first envisaged. She understands the work of the ICPRCP as increasingly promoting 'cooperation between States, rather than the transfer of knowledge and resources from one State to another'.[106] Jakubowski agrees, calling the body 'crucial to the entire UN system of global governance for the protection of movable cultural heritage' and reminding us not to become overly focused on the low number of cases it has considered.[107]

Through the ICPRCP, a Code of Ethics for Dealers in Cultural Property was drafted and then endorsed by both the ICPRC and the Thirtieth UNESCO General Conference in 1999.[108] This short eight-Article document provided, inter alia, that professional traders will not import, export or transfer ownership of cultural property where they have 'reasonable cause to believe it has been stolen, illegally alienated, clandestinely excavated or illegally exported' (Article 1), without specific mention of the 1970 Convention nor of the 1970 date as a provenance cut-off. Work has been under way for some time to revise this Code, which came to completion in 2026.[109]

Model Provisions on State Ownership of Undiscovered Cultural Objects were also drafted in an attempt to assist States in implementing domestic laws that clarified public ownership of antiquities, with a view to facilitating State claims in foreign courts for the return of looted objects.[110] The provisions were presented at the seventeenth Session in 2011, and, acting on the Recommendation of the Committee, the UNESCO and UNIDROIT Secretariats disseminated them to Member States and promoted their use.[111]

In 1999, the Committee also recommended the establishment of a dedicated fund. That Recommendation was adopted the same year by the UNESCO General Conference at its Thirtieth Session, inviting the Director-General to establish this fund within UNESCO, to be known as the 'Fund of the Intergovernmental Committee for Promoting the Return of Cultural Property to its Countries of Origin or its Restitution in Case of Illicit Appropriation'.[112] By the end of 2023, the Fund's remaining balance was approximately $125,000: initially the main contributor to the fund was Greece (giving approximately $230,000 over the first ten

[105] Unesdoc CLT-2011/CONF.208/COM.17/2REV.

[106] AF Vrdoljak, *International Law, Museums and the Return of Cultural Objects* (Cambridge, Cambridge University Press, 2008) 234.

[107] Jakubowski (n 90) 472.

[108] CLT/CH/INS-06/25 rev. O'Keefe and Prott were integral to the process of drafting and promoting the Code.

[109] See Decision of the ICPRC, 25th Session, ICPRCP26/25.COM 13 (Paris, May 2026).

[110] Provisions like these have indeed assisted in cases in the past: for instance, the criminal prosecution of dealer Frederick Schultz in the United States (*US v Schultz*, 333 F.d 9 (2d Cir. 2002); and the civil claim brought by Iran to recover Bronze Age artefacts held by a London dealer (*Iran v Barakat* [2007] EWCA Civ 1374). See P Gerstenblith, 'Schultz and Barakat: Universal Recognition of National Ownership of Antiquities' (April 2009) XIV *Art Antiquity and Law* 14.

[111] Unesdoc CLT-2011/CONF.208/COM.17/2REV, 2.

[112] 30 C/Resolution 27.

years), but the only contributor since 2012 has been the State of Monaco (having given approximately $35,000 in total).[113]

(ii) Meetings of States Parties

Meetings of States Parties to the 1970 Convention have, since 2015, become a common feature of the UNESCO calendar. This is perhaps surprising, since the Convention itself never expressly set out meetings for States Parties. It did require periodic reports on the operation of the Convention at dates set by the General Conference (at Article 16), but this is quite different. Such reports were tabled in 1970 and then a mere six times in the 40 years that followed. The usual pattern was that only a limited number of States made the effort to report – normally between 20 and 30 – and reports were rather general and not particularly informative. In 2006, the Executive Board prioritised monitoring the 1970 Convention, but only 35 per cent of the membership responded, with little indication of the success of the Convention in practice and what could be done to improve its implementation.[114]

In 2003, an ad hoc meeting was held on the sidelines of the General Conference by particular States with an interest in more frequent reporting under the Convention (fewer than half the States Parties to the Convention took part). The meeting set out Recommendations to Member States of UNESCO designed to counter illicit traffic, inviting UNESCO 'to propose, for consideration and approval by the next meeting of States Parties to the 1970 Convention, guidelines for the appropriate implementation of the 1970 Convention'.[115] This meeting was subsequently referred to as the 'First Meeting of States Parties'.

A second 'Meeting of States Parties' took place in June 2012. The Secretariat presented a paper setting out three possibilities going forward to strengthen the Convention: a revision of the text itself; a Protocol to the Convention; or the establishment of a specific monitoring body, with an amendment 'providing for the frequency of the Meetings of States Parties and the establishment of a subsidiary body (an Intergovernmental Committee)'.[116] The Meeting adopted the third of these options, establishing what it called a 'Subsidiary Committee'. An Extraordinary Meeting of States Parties was then held in July 2013 in order to elect the 18 members of this Subsidiary Committee. The Subsidiary Committee met for the first time the following day and decided to establish an informal working group to draft Operational Guidelines for the implementation of the 1970 Convention.[117]

[113] ICPRC/24/24.COM/7, Report on the use of the ICPRCP Fund, 24th Session (Paris, May 2024) Annex I: Financial Report of the Fund as of 31 December 2023.
[114] Unesdoc 184/EX 20.
[115] Unesdoc CLT-2003/CONF/207/5.
[116] Unesdoc C70/12/2.MSP/6.
[117] Unesdoc C70/13/1.SC/Decisions.

A Third Meeting of States Parties was then held in 2015. The most significant decision at this Meeting was the adoption of the 'Operational Guidelines'.[118] Also adopted was a proposal for the dedicated fund to enhance the implementation of the 1970 Convention. The creation of this Fund was approved by the Director-General of UNESCO and then by the General Conference at its meeting in November 2015 (discussed above).[119]

Subsequent meetings of States Parties to the 1970 Convention have thereafter been held every two years. In general, these meetings result in resolutions that reaffirm support for the Convention, call on the remaining UNESCO States Parties that have not yet ratified the Convention to do so, highlight the tools available to assist in combating the illicit trade and reiterate the importance of better examining the effectiveness of the Convention through State reporting. Since 2019, they have called upon States Parties to contribute voluntarily to the Fund supporting the Convention, often at a suggested minimum of 1% of total contributions to UNESCO, and have thanked those States that have.[120] They have also been used to elect members to the Subsidiary Committee. Latterly, they have proposed, examined and adopted Model Provisions on the Prevention and Fight Against the Illicit Trafficking of Cultural Property, which are meant to assist States Parties with the implementation of the Convention into domestic law.[121]

Previous editions of this book had indicated an inherent contradiction in the system. The monitoring body for the 1970 Convention cannot be the same as for other UNESCO cultural conventions, which specifically provide for such.[122] The Meeting of States Parties to the 1970 Convention therefore cannot operate on the same legislative basis. It is an ad hoc body even if provision was made for it to meet on a regular basis. The same would hold true for a 'subsidiary committee' intended to exist on a permanent basis. Neither body can impose mandatory actions or requirements on States. Nevertheless, both meetings of the States Parties and of the Subsidiary Committee have continued apace since 2015, unhindered it seems by this irregularity.

(iii) Meetings of the Subsidiary Committee

As with meetings of the States Parties, there is no provision in the 1970 Convention for permanent sessions of any 'subsidiary committee', and yet these have been taking place annually for some time now. The first session of the Subsidiary

[118] For more on the Operational Guidelines, see below.

[119] Unesdoc C70/15/3.SC/4, 4.

[120] See, eg, the Meetings of States Parties in May 2023 (C70/23/7.MSP 14) and May 2025 (C70/25/8.MSP 14).

[121] See Item 9 of the Eighth Meeting of States Parties, C70/25/8.MSP/9 (Paris, May 2025). For more on the Model Provisions, see below, IV, ch 3(iii).

[122] For example, the 2001 Convention on the Protection of the Underwater Cultural Heritage provides for regular meetings of States Parties at Art 23.

Committee was established under the Extraordinary Meeting of States Parties in July 2013, with the next one following a year later. A third session was held in September 2015, with the goal of examining reports by States Parties on measures taken to implement the 1970 Convention (some 60 reports were received). State reporting – a requirement under Article 16 – has grown in leaps and bounds since the establishment of this more entrenched body to oversee the process. In 2019, the Committee received and reviewed 69 reports and, in 2023, 91 reports, a remarkable upswing since the early 2000s, representing over 60 per cent of States Parties.[123]

In addition to managing the process of reporting, the decisions of the Subsidiary Committee often focus on urging States Parties to demonstrate support for the Convention and highlighting best practices and the tools available for cooperation in supporting the goals of the Convention. It has also looked at questions around due diligence and updating the voluntary code for dealers.[124]

(iv) Operational Guidelines

Operational Guidelines have become an important component of UNESCO's work in relation to cultural heritage, and separate guidelines exist for the 1972 World Heritage Convention, the 2001 Underwater Heritage Convention, the 2003 Intangible Cultural Heritage Convention and the 2005 Cultural Diversity Convention. They are not international legal agreements and cannot bind States Parties.[125] Normally, they indicate how States might implement provisions of the Convention into their domestic laws, regulations and administrative practices.

Work on Operational Guidelines to the 1970 Convention began in 2013 and the product was adopted by the Third Meeting of States Parties in May 2015. The purpose of the Guidelines is set out in paragraph 8, demonstrating an aim to:

> … strengthen and facilitate the implementation of the Convention, to minimize risks related to disputes over the interpretation of the Convention as well as to litigation, and thus to contribute towards international understanding.[126]

In some ways, the Guidelines have offered useful material for the interpretation of the Convention. For example, they include special mention of 'objects of ethnological interest and items of indigenous communities' (paragraph 12), a significant

[123] The analysis for the 2019–2022 reporting cycle was undertaken by the Subsidiary Committee and produced in June 2023: C70/23/11.SC/7.

[124] See Session of the Subsidiary Committee of the Meeting of States Parties, Item 9, C70/25/13.SC/9 (Paris May 2025).

[125] Such guidelines may influence state practice under international law, but they do not constitute practice themselves.

[126] In *Protecting Cultural Objects* (2017), O'Keefe questioned this purpose, claiming it was doubtful the Guidelines were sufficiently precise and complete to enable decisions to be made on interpretation. He saw it as highly unlikely that issues of interpretation could lead to litigation, making it difficult for him to accept this as a valid premise for the Guidelines.

issue for many indigenous groups and one that has caused concern when return from museum collections has been denied. They also encourage the creation of 'specialized police and customs units' or 'law enforcement agencies' (paragraph 22), which can prove useful, as well as eliciting the engagement of local communities to keep watch over archaeological sites and report interference with them (paragraph 47), which can be an effective tool to dissuade looting and the trade in illicit material. It can be said that, at times, the Guidelines try to achieve goals not provided within the Convention itself, which can be undermined by the fact that the Guidelines do not give rise to legal obligations.[127] The Guidelines also go rather further than the Convention by stating that 'if documentary proof of legal export cannot be provided to the competent authorities for cultural property to which the Convention applies, such cultural property should be retained by such authorities and returned to the State Party concerned, according to the relevant national legal procedures' (Paragraph 64), which is not directly supported by provisions in the Convention itself.[128]

(v) Evaluation Study

UNESCO has an Internal Oversight Service (IOS) charged with 'providing assurance that programmes and plans are delivered efficiently and effectively, that strategic management information is reliable and timely, and that continuous improvements are fostered in methods, procedures and accountabilities so as to enhance the quality and impact of UNESCO's operations'.[129]

In April 2014, the IOS produced an evaluation of UNESCO's standard-setting work and dealt with the 1970 Convention, seeking a 'better understanding about how conventions work in practice'.[130] Some respondents asked for further clarification of the Convention.[131] It was clear that there was still sufficient confusion about its operation and effect to warrant such clarification. An evaluation of the Convention was then undertaken by UNESCO's evaluation section. Three States were visited (Mongolia, Peru, Turkey) and a small number of individuals consulted. A List of Recommendations was produced. The Secretariat reported that: 'The

[127] For instance, they encourage States to designate 'products of archaeological and paleontological excavation' (para 12) and they highlight the concept of 'inalienability' which they state should be 'fully respected' (para 63), even though neither could lead to a legal requirement for return. 'Sales on the Internet' are also referred to (paras 68–70), which of course postdate anything considered at the time of the Convention.

[128] In *Protecting Cultural Objects* (2017), O'Keefe found that this could raise a number of legal issues, particularly if the current holder bought the object after a thorough examination of its provenance and no defects were found: 52.

[129] www.unesco.org/new/en/unesco/about-us/how-we-work/accountability/internal-oversight-service/how-we-work.

[130] Unesdoc IOS/EVS/PI/133REV.

[131] ibid 34.

evaluation offers a strategic orientation for helping the Convention to consolidate its achievements and realize its potential even more fully in the future'.[132]

One key criticism was the lack of funding and how money was being spent. The Evaluation Report stated that 'more than half of the Secretariat's budget is used to cover costs related to the statutory meetings'.[133] This was the subject of an audit by the IOS, which found that 'the current situation is unsustainable as support from the regular programme budget decreases and the workload of the convention secretariats increases.' Certain recommendations included reducing the frequency, duration and agenda of the meetings of governing bodies, synchronising the meetings of the general assemblies and using more sponsors for meeting expenses, including for translation and interpretation. Common platforms for support services should be sought across the culture conventions, the audit suggested, and alternative funding structures investigated.[134]

[132] Unesdoc C70/14/2.SC/4, 2. In *Protecting Cultural Objects* (2017), O'Keefe questioned the effectiveness of this evaluation and the content of its conclusions, which seemed to repeat suggestions that had been made by various commentators over the years without adding much.

[133] Internal Oversight Service, Evaluation of UNESCO's Standard-setting Work of the Culture Sector Unesdoc IOS/EVS/PI/133 REV, 12.

[134] H Purkait, S Douet and N Tabacchi, *Audit of the Working Methods of Cultural Conventions*, Unesdoc IOS/AUD/2013/06, 1: unesdoc.unesco.org/ark:/48223/pf0000223256. In *Protecting Cultural Objects* (2017), O'Keefe considered some of these suggestions unhelpful. For instance, 'synchronising meetings' may sound sensible, but in fact would place too much of a burden on the Secretariat, which is already spread thin. He also noted that streamlining meetings may be difficult for national committees, who may be divided across different national agencies depending on the relevant convention. And lastly, obtaining project-specific sponsors may dilute the power of the Secretariat to act on long-term objectives, if the quite specific wishes of donors need to first be addressed.

II

Article-by-Article Analysis

Preamble

The General Conference of the United Nations Educational, Scientific and Cultural Organization, meeting in Paris from 12 October to 14 November 1970, at its sixteenth session,

Recalling the importance of the provisions contained in the Declaration of the Principles of International Cultural Co-operation, adopted by the General Conference at its fourteenth session,

Considering that the interchange of cultural property among nations for scientific, cultural and educational purposes increases the knowledge of the civilization of Man, enriches the cultural life of all peoples and inspires mutual respect and appreciation among nations,

Considering that cultural property constitutes one of the basic elements of civilization and national culture, and that its true value can be appreciated only in relation to the fullest possible information regarding its origin, history and traditional setting,

Considering that it is incumbent upon every State to protect the cultural property existing within its territory against the dangers of theft, clandestine excavation, and illicit export,

Considering that, to avert these dangers, it is essential for every State to become increasingly alive to the moral obligations to respect its own cultural heritage and that of all nations,

Considering that, as cultural institutions, museums, libraries and archives should ensure that their collections are built up in accordance with universally recognized moral principles,

Considering that the illicit import, export and transfer of ownership of cultural property is an obstacle to that understanding between nations which it is part of UNESCO's mission to promote by recommending to interested States, international conventions to this end,

Considering that the protection of cultural heritage can be effective only if organized both nationally and internationally among States working in close co-operation,

Considering that the Unesco General Conference adopted a Recommendation to this effect in 1964,

> *Having before it* further proposals on the means of prohibiting and preventing the illicit import, export and transfer of ownership of cultural property, a question which is on the agenda for the session as item 19,
>
> *Having decided*, at its fifteenth session, that this question should be made the subject of an international convention,
>
> *Adopts* this Convention on the fourteenth day of November 1970.

Some mistakenly believe that the Preamble to an international convention is insignificant. Bator, for example, referred to the words above as 'conventional … boilerplate'.[1] On the other hand, the Vienna Convention on the Law of Treaties (1969) states that the Preamble is part of the context in which treaties are to be interpreted (Article 31(2)).[2] The Preamble should be seen as establishing general principles to guide interpretation. Blake summarises this Preamble as setting out the philosophical approach of the Convention as a whole; namely, 'that protection of the cultural heritage can only be fully effective if organized both nationally and internationally amongst States working in cooperation'.[3]

In becoming party to the 1970 Convention, States signify that they appreciate certain enunciated principles. The interchange of cultural property in spreading knowledge of other cultures – what has sometimes been called the 'ambassadorial' role of art – is important. But it is not of primary significance. The Preamble points out that an item of 'cultural property' can be properly appreciated and wholly contribute to its civilising mission only when all the information it contains or represents is extracted. There has been a significant development in these views since 1978 when a UNESCO Committee of Experts debated the 'primacy of the object' as well as the 'primary significance' of information and research after vigorous discussion of both points of view.[4] Those connoisseurs who view an object purely from an aesthetic perspective see only part of the whole; as do those archaeologists who ignore aesthetics purely in pursuit of scientific value. Information is of primary importance because it is only this which allows full appreciation of the object and its contribution to the evolution of humankind.

The Preamble states that 'it is incumbent upon every State to protect the cultural property existing within its territory against the dangers of theft, clandestine excavation and illicit export'. These three activities either destroy the information inherent in the object or prevent access to it. Of these, clandestine excavation is arguably the most destructive. Theft can mean that the object is lost to public access but at least knowledge of its existence is preserved and it may – if

[1] PM Bator, 'An Essay on the International Trade in Art' (1982) 34 *Stanford Law Review* 275, 377.

[2] The International Court of Justice has held that Article 31 of the Vienna Convention represents customary international law and applies even though States are not party: *Kasikili/Sedudu Island (Botswana v Namibia)* [1999] ICJ Rep 1045.

[3] J Blake, 'Turkey' in JAR Nafziger and RK Paterson (eds), *Handbook on the Law of Cultural Heritage and International Trade* (Cheltenham, Edward Elgar, 2014) 437, 449.

[4] Committee of Experts on the Establishment of an Intergovernmental Committee concerning the Restitution or Return of Cultural Property, Unesdoc CC-78/Conf.609/6 (Dakar, 1978).

the object is recovered – once again emerge into the light. Illicit traffic can contribute to loss of identity, whether national or indigenous, as well as contributing to destruction. Destruction and clandestine excavation go hand-in-hand. Looters usually have to work in secret or against a deadline in case they are discovered. They pay scant regard for anything that will not return them the maximum financial value. Thus objects or parts thereof may be tossed aside in favour of that which appears valuable: jewels taken by tomb raiders at the expense of less attractive (but culturally significant) metalwork, for instance. Knowledge could have been gained but is discarded because it has no monetary value.[5] They are almost always wrong in making this assessment, as historical or archaeological importance mean nothing to them.

The Preamble correctly observes that States have a moral obligation to prevent these activities and to cooperate with other States in so doing. All States must cooperate to bring about effective measures to prevent theft, clandestine excavation and illicit export. This cannot be done by any one State acting alone. States with many sites and many collections, whether public or private, cannot afford to protect every last one. Nor can borders be sufficiently blocked so as to stop all illicit shipments. In these circumstances, any one State which does not act to prevent inward shipments from its neighbours can become a clearing house for illicit ventures and undermine the endeavours of others seeking to protect cultural property.

But legal obligation is one thing; ethical considerations are quite another. States are not alone in bearing a moral obligation for the preservation of cultural property. Museums, libraries and archives also have to recognise that they are part of the process. In building up and supplementing their collections they must pay attention to the provenance of what they are offered or want to gather in. This is part of acting according to what the Preamble calls 'universally recognized moral principles'. No longer is it sufficient to accept what the holder or dealer says of the origins of what is on offer. Its history must be researched and statements on where it came from, and how it came, verified. Only in this way can the trade in cultural property be cleansed and its destruction, together with the accompanying loss of knowledge, be halted. This is what is meant when museums claim to abide by the principles of the 1970 Convention.

Theft, clandestine excavation and illicit export of cultural property create obstacles to proper cultural understanding between States. States should look to take action at both national and international levels. Collecting institutions must therefore support States by not contributing to such illicit activities either directly (by buying unprovenanced material from dealers) or indirectly (by accepting gifts the history of which is unknown beyond the donor).

The Preamble concludes by laying great stress on cooperation. This cooperation is then achieved – or such is the attempt – in the text that follows.

[5] PJ O'Keefe, *Trade in Antiquities: Reducing Destruction and Theft* (Paris, London, UNESCO Publishing, Archetype, 1997).

Article 1

For the purposes of this Convention, the term 'cultural property' means property which, on religious or secular grounds, is specifically designated by each State as being of importance for archaeology, prehistory, history, literature, art or science and which belongs to the following categories:

a. Rare collections and specimens of fauna, flora, minerals and anatomy, and objects of palaeontological interest;
b. property relating to history, including the history of science and technology and military and social history, to the life of national leaders, thinkers, scientists and artists and to events of national importance;
c. products of archaeological excavations (including regular and clandestine) or of archaeological discoveries;
d. elements of artistic or historical monuments or archaeological sites which have been dismembered;
e. antiquities more than one hundred years old, such as inscriptions, coins and engraved seals;
f. objects of ethnological interest;
g. property of artistic interest, such as:
    i. pictures, paintings and drawings produced entirely by hand on any support and in any material (excluding industrial designs and manufactured articles decorated by hand);
    ii. original works of statuary art and sculpture in any material;
    iii. original engravings, prints and lithographs;
    iv. original artistic assemblages and montages in any material;
h. rare manuscripts and incunabula, old books, documents and publications of special interest (historical, artistic, scientific, literary, etc.) singly or in collections;
i. postage, revenue and similar stamps, singly or in collections;
j. archives, including sound, photographic and cinematographic archives;
k. articles of furniture more than one hundred years old and old musical instruments.

'Cultural Property'

Establishing what is meant by the term 'cultural property' is always going to pose challenges. The definition at Article 1 has not escaped criticism. Bator regarded the description by categories as overbroad; imposing 'no meaningful constraints' on the coverage of the Convention.[1] That said, each State is understandably granted the right to specify the scope and content of its own cultural property.[2] Carducci describes the definition in Article 1 as a 'mixed' definition: one element allowing

[1] PM Bator, 'An Essay on the International Trade in Art' (1982) 34 *Stanford Law Review* 275, 377. M Frigo, *La protezione dei beni culturali nel diritto internazionale* (Milan, Giuffrè Editore, 1986) 198, appears to agree.

[2] G Carducci, *La restitution internationale des biens culturels et des objets d'art* (Paris, LGDJ, 1997) 218–20.

a State to define its own cultural heritage, while the other is imposed – whatever may be designated, it must also be 'of importance' and must fit within the defined categories.[3] As each State has the right to make its own designation, a State's declaration of designation (such as that made by France when ratifying the Convention in 1997) can only circumscribe its own cultural property, not that designated by other States looking to recover cultural property on a foreign territory.[4]

The definition of 'cultural property' is notably different from the definition of the same term found in the 1954 Hague Convention for the Protection of Cultural Property in the Event of Armed Conflict. The latter is illustrative (using the term 'such as' when listing examples of property of great importance in its Article 1)[5] while the 1970 Convention list is exhaustive. The 1954 definition was designed for the general protection of cultural property in times of armed conflict, a principle to which all parties were agreed, and might sensibly be left open to elaboration. The 1970 Convention is dependent on a compromise between exporting and importing States. Its definition therefore describes the ambit *within which* objects are to be selected for export and import control, thus limiting the kinds of property for which States may be obliged to implement export and – more importantly – reciprocal import controls.

However, these terms are subject to interpretation and this can create differences of approach between States. For example, the United States, in its Convention on Cultural Property Implementation Act, defined 'objects of archaeological importance' to which it would apply the provisions of Article 9 as objects which were more than 250 years old.[6] The Canadian Control List designates objects as being those 'recovered from the soil or waters of Canada' without age limitation. The United States' interpretation was seen by Canada as an unwarranted limitation of the obligations under the 1970 Convention.[7] Indeed, for countries such as Australia and New Zealand, a 250-year rule would exclude practically the entire archaeological evidence of early permanent European settlement. Intriguingly, under US domestic law, the Archaeological Resources Protection Act of 1979 applies to objects over 100 years old,[8] unusually at odds with the implementation of international obligations under the 1970 Convention.

Is there any particular relationship between the general descriptive words at the beginning of the definition ('property … of importance for archaeology, prehistory, history, literature, art or science') and the specific categories? Fraoua takes the view that the categories enumerated in Article 1 illustrate the particular nature of

[3] ibid 218–20.

[4] ibid 220.

[5] See below, IV, ch 1(iii).

[6] 19 USC, s 302(2)(1).

[7] IC Clark, 'The Cultural Property Export and Import Act of Canada: An Appraisal Nine Years After Implementation' in LV Prott and J Specht, *Protection or Plunder? Safeguarding the Future of Our Cultural Heritage* (Canberra, AGPS, 1989) 19–20.

[8] 16 USC s 470bb(1).

the cultural property to be protected.[9] For example, he suggests that fauna, flora, minerals and anatomical and palaeontological objects[10] are objects of importance for science, whereas those comprised in Article 1(b), (c) and (d) are of archaeological, historical, prehistoric or artistic interest. However, there is no specific cross-reference from the separate elements of the general definition to particular illustrative categories. The order of the words does not follow the same pattern, as one would expect if this had been the case (eg 'science' is the last element in the general definition, related by Fraoua to the first of the categories). As Fraoua himself acknowledges, an item may belong to more than one category. Finally, 'science' should be read in the widest sense, since antiquities, ethnographic objects and furniture may be of as much interest to the social or evolutionary sciences as a palaeontological object may be to the physical sciences. A fossil may be of importance for the physical sciences, but also for the study of prehistory and archaeology.

The lack of any connection between the order in the general definition and that in the specific categories is also borne out by the history of what became Article 1. The three drafts of the proposed convention in the 1930s[11] had no list of categories. They all referred to general qualifying words such as 'artistic', 'historical', 'archaeological' and 'scientific' – or a combination of these. On the other hand, Brichet's first draft in 1968 did not have general words but contained eight categories, including 'objects of ethnological interest'. The same method of defining cultural property appeared in the final report that UNESCO presented to the Special Committee of Government Experts in April 1970. It was only during the meeting of that Committee that the present design of Article 1 was adopted. There is no evidence of any intention to have particular connections between the general words and the specific categories of cultural property which were considerably expanded compared to Brichet's list. The general categories appear to represent the interests of certain States that wanted to make sure these were specifically represented.

It is worth noting that, in their reporting, States have taken the position that they have, individually, clear definitions of 'cultural property' within their legal systems.[12]

'On Religious or Secular Grounds'

The inclusion of religious grounds for basing a designation is significant. A number of States base their political system on a separation of Church and State, meaning that the administration of one is not to interfere with the other. There are also

[9] R Fraoua, *Convention concernant les mesures à prendre pour interdire et empêcher l'importation, l'exportation et le transfert de propriété illicites des biens culturels* (Unesdoc CC-86/WS/40, 1986) 53.

[10] Art 1(a).

[11] Above, I, ch 2.

[12] For the 2019–2022 reporting cycle, UNESCO noted that, of the 91 States reporting on implementation of the Convention, over 80% reported to have an 'excellent' (31%), 'very good' (34%) or 'good' (17%) national framework providing for a clear definition of cultural property: Subsidiary Committee of the Meeting of States Parties, 11th Session, C70/23/11.SC/7 (Paris, UNESCO, 1–2 June 2023) p 9.

States where the great bulk of cultural property is owned by religious authorities. As this may be considered private property, cultural administrators may have little access to it. Nevertheless, the specific reference to religious grounds for designation means that they have a base in the 1970 Convention for acting to *protect* such property.

'Designated by each State'

From the categories specified in the definition, cultural property is to be 'specifically designated as being of importance for archaeology, prehistory, history, literature, art or science'. The Operational Guidelines stress the significance of specific designation but offer no indication of what is meant by this.[13] Different interpretations of the phrase have been offered by commentators and used by States.

Bator feared that there was an already existing 'tendency in the art-rich countries to embargo all or virtually all art'.[14] By 'art-rich countries' Bator meant the countries from which cultural property is taken for the so-called market States. His comment overstated the case but reflected the fears of market States at the time the Convention was adopted. It formed the important motivation, it seems, for the United States' interpretation that only subjected to import control cultural property stolen from a museum or similar institution or, in cases where cultural patrimony was in jeopardy, certain archaeological or ethnological materials.[15]

There is nothing in the *travaux préparatoires* to indicate that the operation of the 1970 Convention should be restricted by the interpretation of 'specifically designated'. Could 'specifically designated' be interpreted as meaning that each and every item must be individually described? To require this would limit the reach of the Convention quite drastically. Moreover, it could not cover as yet unexcavated archaeological material which, by its nature, cannot be described, let alone included in a national inventory, and would thus exclude control over clandestinely excavated material.

This can be achieved in a variety of ways taking into account the methods commonly used by States in implementing legislation. One is appropriate for legal systems which classify important cultural items. Typically, such systems make all classified items either prohibited exports, or subject to export permits. The list of classified items therefore serves as a list of 'specifically designated' objects. Canada and Australia use a system based on 'Control Lists'. This system operates by descriptions of general categories, in which part of the material in the categories proposed in Article 1 is much more specifically described (eg, by criteria based on value in money, age, local connection) and only that material is subject to export

[13] Paras 11, 12.
[14] See Bator (n 1) 329.
[15] These come, respectively, from Art 7(b) and Art 9 of the Convention. See Bator, ibid 339.

permit. The permit will be granted unless it is decided that its loss would 'significantly diminish' the national cultural heritage.[16] The decision as to the exportability of objects is therefore taken not in advance, but at the time the export permit is sought.

Bator noted that a State choosing to designate virtually all its antiquities and works of art would deprive the 'specifically designated' provision of independent significance.

> There is no objective standard by which we could prove that a designation is insufficiently specific, and the question would inevitably dissolve into a disagreement about the substantive question whether specific material is or is not important.[17]

However, the possibility of some States designating all cultural material as subject to export control should not be completely dismissed: there are some countries which have been so denuded of their cultural property that anything that remains would be of importance to the national cultural heritage. A convention which is designed to cover all sorts of States and situations needs to allow for such cases.

The words 'specifically designated by each State as being of importance' clearly indicate that each State has the right to decide what objects are important to its national heritage.[18] The United States was unwilling to accept the logic and the consequences of the definition. The original Secretariat Draft would have required all Parties to prohibit the importation of any cultural property unless accompanied by a valid export certificate. The United States opposed that prohibition on the grounds that it gave exporting States the power to dictate what importing States could legally allow into their territory, regardless of the latter's substantive interests.[19] The Canadian Government, on the other hand, took the view that property specifically designated by another State as important for archaeology, prehistory, history, literature, art or science would become an illegal import into Canada.[20] Canada regarded it as proper for every State to have the right to designate what it regards as important cultural property.[21] Niec properly pointed out that the right of each State to define its own cultural heritage is based on a fundamental principle:

> The reason for a formal diversity of legal constructions in various States lies in material factors – ie, a great diversity in cultural circles and differences in the standard of cultural

[16] Cultural Property Export and Import Act of 1975, s 8(3) (Canada); Protection of Movable Cultural Heritage Act 1986, s 10(6) (Australia).

[17] Bator (n 1) 381.

[18] Commentators also taking this view include JB Gordon, 'The UNESCO Convention on the Illicit Movement of Art Treasures' (1971) 12 *Harvard International Law Journal* 537, 543; H Niec, 'Sovereign Rights to Cultural Property' (1971) 4 *Polish Yearbook of International Law* 239, 249; Fraoua (n 9) 52; AFG Raschèr, M Bauen, Y Fischer, MN Zen-Ruffinen, *Cultural Property Transfer* (Brussels, Zurich; Bruyland, Schulthess; 2005) 16.

[19] Bator (n 1) 328.

[20] DF Cameron, *An Introduction to the Cultural Property Export and Import Act*, 2nd edn (Ottawa, Department of the Secretary of State, 1980) 22.

[21] Clark (n 7) 19–20.

> resources. For these reasons, the granting to each State the right subjectively to specify the scope and content of the definition of cultural property constitutes a form of practical realization of the principle that in international relations the cultures of individual nations are equal, and as a result of specific conditions and trends of development each nation contributes its own unique share to the cultural heritage of mankind.[22]

The US specialist in international criminal law Bassiouni prepared a draft international criminal code which contained a provision modelled on Article 1 of the 1970 Convention. His comment on that draft provision read:

> … with respect to cultural property within a state's territory, only the state has the authority to declare given cultural property as being important to its cultural heritage. The conclusion that Subsection 1.1 requires the agreement of all Contracting Parties as to which property is within the scope of this Article is impractical and unintended.[23]

It is right, therefore, that certain objects hailing from one State that may seem peculiar or unimportant to others are worthy of protection. For instance, an 'orator's flywhisk' (or *fue*) would likely be considered part of the irreplaceable cultural heritage in Samoa, and thus worthy of protection, although no other State would include such an object within its definition of cultural property.

The Operational Guidelines list three categories of cultural property as posing special challenges in terms of specific designation: (i) products of archaeological and paleontological clandestine excavation; (ii) elements of artistic or historical monuments or archaeological sites which have been dismembered; and (iii) objects of ethnological interest and items of Indigenous communities.[24] The first is mentioned because of the impossibility of producing inventories of such material. To overcome this, the need for State ownership is stressed in the Guidelines together with designation of the protected general category of objects to be found. In respect of the second category, States Parties are invited to define the types of objects that are 'susceptible to pillage'. The third category is of major concern to States such as Australia, Canada, New Zealand and the United States which have significant Indigenous populations. These States seek to recognise and respect the cultures of the Indigenous peoples within their territories. There are many other States with 'First Peoples' such as Japan (the Ainu), China (with 55 'nationalities', some with very ancient roots in the country) and numerous Latin American States with Indigenous minorities. The trend to recognise the rights of these peoples is enunciated in the UN Declaration on the Rights of Indigenous Peoples from 2007. As we have seen, the 1970 Convention is not retroactive and it follows that the Indigenous cultural heritage which was taken during the colonial period cannot be recovered under the Convention.

[22] Niec (n 18) 250.

[23] MC Bassiouni, *A Draft International Criminal Code and Draft Statute for an International Criminal Tribunal* (Dordrecht, Nijhoff, 1987) 168.

[24] Para 12.

When it came to drafting the UNIDROIT Convention on Stolen or Illegally Exported Cultural Objects in 1995, the categories from Article 1 were maintained but the requirement for designation was removed. The preliminary draft of that Convention defined 'cultural object' as 'any material object of artistic, historical, spiritual, ritual or other cultural significance.' Other versions of a general clause were also considered during the negotiations. However, some delegations were suspicious of such a general clause and wanted a more specific definition. At the fourth meeting of governmental experts called to prepare the Convention it was agreed to use the same categories as were used in the UNESCO Convention. While the element of 'importance' was retained, the requirement of 'designation' does not appear. This was to ensure that individual owners whose cultural property had been stolen, but never designated by the State, would have the opportunity to bring an action in another jurisdiction under the UNIDROIT Convention.

'Of Importance'

Article 1 of the 1970 Convention states that property which is specifically designated should be of 'importance' for archaeology, prehistory, history, literature, art or science. How to rate objects for inclusion has been a constant problem. The OIM draft of 1939 referred to such objects as only needing to be of 'interest'; the UNESCO Recommendation of 1964 required them to be of 'great importance'.[25] Article 1 therefore sits somewhere between the two. 'Importance' is a relative matter; what may be important to one State may not be to another. Nevertheless, each State should have the power to decide what is of importance to it as part of its cultural property, within the confines of the categories to come.

The listed categories (a) to (k)

(a) Rare collections and specimens of fauna, flora, minerals and anatomy, and objects of paleontological interest

While paragraphs (b) to (k) relate to objects produced by human endeavour, paragraph (a) includes objects of intrinsic value. Although paragraph (a) arguably could include objects adapted by human hands (eg fossils turned into sculpture), for the most part it may be a stretch to call a natural specimen 'cultural' property in the strictest sense. Indeed, some have questioned including such objects in the first place. Nudds, for instance, does not believe that fossils are relevant as 'fossils are not part of the developed culture of the country in which they happen to have

[25] Para 1.

been preserved'.[26] However, the reason for their inclusion within the definition of 'cultural property' in the Convention will be set out below.

Collections

Article 1 makes three references to 'collections', including in paragraph (a).[27] However, the Convention contains no definition of 'collection'. Usually they are singled out for special treatment because they have a value which transcends that of their component objects. The collection itself can be viewed as a creation – illustrating the ideas and ideals of its creator as conceived in time. Sometimes it becomes an entity of greater importance than its individual parts. When this occurs the collection as a whole becomes an item of cultural property.

But what is a collection? Very broadly, in the current context, it is an assemblage of specified objects having cultural value. For example, section 1.1 of the Heritage Act of 2016 of the Netherlands defines a collection as 'cultural objects that belong together from a cultural-historical or scholarly viewpoint'. This emphasises the requirement that an assembly of objects, to be considered a collection, must have an underlying theme. Provided there is this theme, two objects could constitute a collection. Would they need to be kept in the same place? There seems to be no inherent reason why this should be so.

National laws implementing the Convention do not seem to have paid any special attention to problems posed by collections in the context of theft and illicit traffic, in spite of their inclusion in Article 1. As the UNIDROIT Convention borrows the categories in its Annex from the 1970 Convention, it includes collections in the same context. It also makes special reference to claims for restitution of stolen cultural objects belonging to a 'public collection'[28] which, for the purposes of that Convention, 'consists of a group of inventoried or otherwise identified cultural objects' owned by institutions listed, such as a religious body.[29]

Fauna and Flora

Rare collections and specimens of fauna and flora would almost inevitably relate to 'science' from the beginning of the Article, or else possibly 'history' or 'archaeology'. In the context of the Convention, fauna and flora have been little studied. Is the term 'fauna' intended to cover living creatures? It would be possible to argue that a beast belonging to a rare breed of cattle is a specimen of fauna of importance to science. Similarly, living plants and their seeds could be classified as 'flora'.

[26] JR Nudds, 'Ethics, science and the trade: let's get together' (2001) 7(6) *The Geological Curator* 191, 193; contra J Ulph, 'Acquiring fossils: a complex picture' (2018) 10(10) *The Geological Curator* 657–70.

[27] The others are in paras (h) and (i), see below.

[28] Art 3(4).

[29] Art 3(7).

Considering national implementation may be useful. Regulations under Australia's implementing legislation list as 'natural science objects' any 'type specimen' of present-day fauna and flora.[30] A 'type specimen' is then defined rather scientifically as 'holotype, lectotype, neotype, paratype or syntype, as appropriate' (eg a holotype is the original specimen from which the description of a new species is made). [31] A type specimen could therefore be a dried plant or preserved animal, usually kept in a museum or herbarium. In South Korea, the Cultural Heritage Protection Act of 2007 refers to animals, 'including their habitats, breeding grounds and migratory areas', and plants, 'including their natural habitats'.[32] The Japanese Law for the Protection of Cultural Property has similar definitions.[33] Costa Rica provides for flora and fauna that are *related to* 'cultures prior to or contemporaneous to the establishment of the Hispanic culture in the country'.[34]

In 2010, the connection between culture and 'wild' fauna and flora was emphasised by the Secretary-General of the Convention on International Trade in Endangered Species of Wild Fauna and Flora of 1973 (CITES) during a speech marking the 40th anniversary of the 1970 UNESCO Convention. He quoted the Preamble to CITES where Contracting States indicate their consciousness of 'the ever-growing value of wild fauna and flora from aesthetic, scientific, *cultural*, recreational, and economic points of view' [italics added].[35] Like the 1970 UNESCO Convention, CITES deals with problems brought about by theft and illicit traffic, although it is restricted to wild animals and plants. In appropriate circumstances the two conventions might work together.

Seeds come under the heading of flora and could therefore be considered cultural property. There is an inter-relationship here with intellectual property rights, which control who can exploit the use of such seeds,[36] whereas cultural property rules control ownership and movement of the seeds themselves. These two sets of rights can reside in different entities. Consequently, seeds could be subjected to the same regime regarding theft and illicit traffic as other cultural property.

Minerals

'Minerals' is a general term, though the minerals must of course be 'rare' to be considered cultural property. The Australian Regulations referred to above provide

[30] Protection of Movable Cultural Objects Regulations 1987, SI 1987/149, para 3.4(h).

[31] Para 3.5.

[32] South Korean Cultural Heritage Protection Act 2018, s 3(c).

[33] See Art 2.

[34] Act No 6703 of 1982.

[35] J Scanlon, 'CITES Shares Experience with UNESCO' (15 March 2011).

[36] Generally intellectual property rights (patents) can be obtained for genetically engineered traits, but not for essentially biological breeding processes: see European Patent Convention (2001), Art 53(b). In the US, the patentability reaches much further: *JEM Ag Supply Inc v Pioneer Hi-Bred Int'l Inc*, 534 U.S. 124, 2001 (US Supreme Court). Consider also the Nagoya Protocol on Access to Genetic Resources and the Fair and Equitable Sharing of Benefits Arising from their Utilization to the Convention on Biological Diversity (2010).

significant detail in defining this term, so are worthy of further consideration: they include in their definition 'carving or sculpture created from any mineral, including a polished gemstone', but not 'any ore or concentrate used industrially or intended for industrial use'.[37] Diamonds, opals and sapphires are specifically listed as being protected provided their monetary value is greater than that set out in Regulations, while other gemstones worth more than A$25,000 are protected, as well as any other minerals worth over A$100,000.[38]

Gold nuggets worth more than A$250,000 come within the Australian definition as well. One of these – the 25kg 'King of the West' – came to prominence when it was exported from Australia in 1997 without a permit. It was offered for sale at Sotheby's, New York, in 1999 at which time the Commonwealth of Australia became aware of its export. Following discussion with Sotheby's and the exporter's solicitor, the nugget was returned to Australia. As the exporter had not knowingly attempted to evade Australian export controls, the Minister exercised his discretion to hand the nugget back. An export permit was subsequently denied and the nugget sold to an Australian mining company to remain in Australia. It is now known as the 'Normandy Nugget'.[39]

Certain domestic laws may apply export controls to meteorites as well.[40] Meteorites are composed of a variety of stones and minerals such as iron, which come from space and have survived the fall through the earth's atmosphere and collision with the ground. Some have been considered sacred to certain groups. For example, the 15.5 ton Willamette Meteorite comes from Oregon. It was revered by the Clackomas Indians but was acquired by the American Museum of Natural History as a gift. The donor had bought it from a local commercial company on whose land it had rested. In 2000, the Museum and the Confederated Tribes of the Grand Ronde Community of Oregon entered into an agreement giving the Tribes access for religious and cultural purposes. The Tribe agreed to drop its claim for return of the meteorite. Going forward, if the museum failed to publicly display it, except for temporary periods, the meteorite would be conveyed to the Tribe. A notice describing the history of the meteorite and its scientific importance was displayed next to the stone.[41]

Anatomy

Rare collections and specimens of anatomy are included under paragraph (a), provided of course that they are of importance for 'archaeology, prehistory,

[37] Protection of Movable Cultural Heritage Regulations 1987, para 3.5.

[38] Para 3.4.

[39] 'Giant gold nugget discovered in Australia', 17 January 2013, *The Perth Mint*, referring back to the Normandy Nugget.

[40] For example, Australia (Protection of Movable Cultural Heritage Regulations 1987, para 3.4(g)) and Canada (Canadian Cultural Property Export Control List, CRC, c 448, s 2, Group 1, 2(e)).

[41] American Museum of Natural History, 'Willamette Meteorite Agreement' recognising spiritual relationship of the Grande Ronde Community to the Meteorite, 22 June 2000.

literature, art or science'. There are many connections illustrating this importance. For example, the juncture of art and anatomy has a long history. The Musée Fragonard in France contains works of art derived from bodies preserved in the 1700s. More controversially, the touring exhibition *Body Worlds* rendered human bodies as art objects by a process of plastination for public consumption, beginning in 1995.[42]

Many Indigenous peoples refuse to accept human remains as property. They argue that museums holding human remains cannot have ownership of them, must not display them and must return them to the society they came from for burial.

> … it is very important that the whole process is managed very carefully, from the delicate negotiation with institutions, to the handling of the remains, which are regarded as people not scientific specimens, and as such are accorded the full respect due to revered ancestors.[43]

The importance of human remains to Indigenous groups is underscored by the UN Declaration on the Rights of Indigenous Peoples at Article 12, which speaks of a right to repatriation. Access to these human remains must also be provided through 'fair, transparent and effective mechanisms developed in conjunction with indigenous peoples concerned.'[44] Subsequent to the Declaration, UNESCO also produced its *Policy on Engaging with Indigenous Peoples* (2018) which also highlights access and repatriation matters.[45]

In general, human remains have been displayed for as long as museums have existed. For example, many collections possess Egyptian mummies and place them on exhibition. These remain of great interest to the general public. Remains of Europeans have also been exhibited. For example, the Western Australian Maritime Museum has a skeleton on display of a man who was involved in the *Batavia* mutiny. The ship had run aground on a voyage from the Netherlands to what is now Indonesia. While the captain went to seek assistance, part of the crew and passengers mutinied. The cut which bisected the skull of the skeleton illustrates the extreme nature of the fighting during the clash.[46]

There is nevertheless pressure on museums to withdraw displays of human remains on grounds that they are disrespectful to the people from whom they derive. The Pitt Rivers Museum in Oxford removed its popular exhibition of preserved shrunken heads of the Shuar peoples (tsantsa) in 2020.[47] Consequently, a State will have to decide what human remains it will designate as 'cultural

[42] *Body Worlds* was conceived by Gunther von Hagens and was first displayed in Tokyo in 1995, before touring the world over the following 15 years. A permanent London display continued until the onset of the COVID-19 Pandemic in 2020.

[43] C McCarthy, 'The Practice of Repatriation: A Case Study from New Zealand' in L Tythacott and K Arvanitis (eds), *Museums and Restitution: New Practices, New Approaches* (Farnham, Ashgate, 2014) 71, 75.

[44] Arti12(2).

[45] UNESCO, *Policy on Engaging with Indigenous Peoples* (Paris, 2018) 27.

[46] I Macleod, 'Shipwreck Graves and Their Conservation Management' (2008) 31(1) *AICCM Bulletin*.

[47] See Pitt Rivers statement, 'Shrunken heads' (2020).

property' under the terms of Article 1. It is noteworthy that the Human Tissue Act 2004 in the United Kingdom allows national museums to deaccession remains of a person who died less than 1,000 years before the Act came into force.[48] Remains more than 1,000 years old are still subject to restrictions on deaccessioning under the legislation establishing those museums.

Objects of Palaeontological Interest

The inclusion of paleontological objects (remains of early life preserved in amber, plants, animals, traces of shells, fish and later mammals) as 'cultural property' has not been without controversy. The connection between objects of palaeontological interest and fossils is immediately apparent. But how can these relate to anything cultural; that is, associated with human life? For instance, Nudds has asserted that 'fossils are not part of the developed culture of the country in which they happen to have been preserved'.[49]

Such a view ignores the fact that palaeontological objects have fascinated humans for centuries. At first they were curiosities, the source of marvel and wonder prompting people to imagine the sort of creatures they came from. They have also been scientifically studied. They are also relevant to the history of collecting and museums. They are thus definitely part of that category of 'cultural property' of importance for science set out at the beginning of Article 1.[50] There is a tension between the general requirement of 'importance', on the one hand, and the objects being only of 'interest' in this paragraph.

In Australia, the implementing Regulations of 1987 mentioned above offer a helpful definition of a palaeontological object: 'a vertebrate or invertebrate fossil or plant fossil or a trace fossil specimen', a definition that specifically excludes 'fossil fuels' and 'fossiliferous rock' with an industrial use.[51] However, it includes fossil matter made into a sculpture or 'other object' and 'precious or non-precious opal replacement fossil of a vertebrate or invertebrate animal or of a plant'.[52]

For certain States, the illicit trafficking of fossils has been a major problem. These include China, Argentina and Brazil. In 2003, China (where fossils of feathered dinosaurs have been found) requested Australia's assistance in the return of illegally exported fossils.[53] Fossils, including those of dinosaur eggs, fish and mammals, were seized the following year in response to the request, and were returned to China. The United States returned four tons of fossils to Argentina in 2008. It was alleged these had been exported concealed with minerals to

[48] At s 47.
[49] Nudds (n 26) 191, 193.
[50] See also Ulph (n 26) 657.
[51] Protection of Movable Cultural Heritage Regulations 1987, para 3.5.
[52] Replacement fossils are those where the intricate internal structures of plants and creatures such as snails, fish, birds, and mammals have been preserved by chemical alteration before the cavity was filled by a silica solution.
[53] The Australian Department of the Environment and Heritage Annual Report, 2004–2005.

evade Customs authorities. A tip-off had been received that the mining company involved was offering the fossils for sale at an international fair in Arizona. Experts then determined that these were indeed from Argentina and that their export had been prohibited under Law 25.743 on the Protection of the Archaeological and Paleontological Heritage. The United States seized and returned the fossils following the receipt of letters rogatory from Argentina.[54]

Brazil is another country that has suffered from the illegal excavation and export of fossils. For example, it has been said that '14 of the 24 reference specimens, or holotypes, of pterosaur fossils collected in the Araripe Basin [are] housed by foreign institutions.'[55] This had a significant impact on scientific study in the country. Over the years, there have been successful attempts at recovering specimens. French authorities returned nearly 1,000 fossils taken from Brazil in 2022, while 33 insect fossils were returned from the UK in 2024.[56] The most infamous palaeontological specimen of all – the Ubirajara dinosaur bird fossil taken in 2006 – was returned by the Natural History Museum of Karlsruhe in Germany in 2023.[57]

(b) property relating to history, including the history of science and technology and military and social history, to the life of national leaders, thinkers, scientists and artists and to events of national importance

The category in paragraph (b) is capable of extending to a vast range of objects. It is a matter for each State to decide what is covered. Some States will have much that is of international importance while for others material might only be of mere 'national' importance. For example, 'social history' would cover the accoutrements of a person significant to national history, like Australian outlaw Ned Kelly (1855–1880), who is little known outside his own country. Kelly's armour, used in a shootout with police, is on a list of objects absolutely prohibited from export from Australia.[58] The same would apply to local heroes in other countries.

We must, however, keep in mind that the intent of the 1970 Convention is the prevention of theft and illicit trafficking. Are the objects proposed for inclusion under paragraph (b) likely targets of such activities? There are some objects that must be protected by all means possible. Those that do not fall within this group perhaps should not be dealt with in such legislation. It would be usual for a simple case of theft to be adequately covered by general laws on stealing. Only when it is

[54] US Immigration and Customs Enforcement, 'ICE returns huge cache of rare fossils smuggled into US from Argentina' (10 May 2008). D Schwimler, 'Stolen fossils back in Argentina' (*BBC News*, 4 July 2008).

[55] E Gibney, 'Brazil Clamps Down on Illegal Fossil Trade' (*Nature*, 4 March 2014).

[56] UNESCO, 'French customs return 998 stolen fossils to UNESCO Global Geopark in Brazil' (3 June 2022); A Barton, 'Smuggled fossils found in Yorkshire return to Brazil' (*BBC News*, 4 June 2024).

[57] R Pérez Ortega, 'Rare dinosaur heads home as Germany agrees to return Brazilian fossil' (*Science*, 19 July 2022). See also PP Stewens, 'Ubirajara and Irritator Belong to Brazil: Achieving Fossil Returns Under German Private Law', *International Journal of Cultural Property*, 20 March 2024.

[58] The armour was effective in that body shots from the police bounced off but he was brought down when his unprotected legs were shot.

thought the object may be smuggled out of the country does the implementing legislation for the 1970 Convention become important.

Many States occupy land that was formerly the home of a different race of people or people who worshipped different deities. Sometimes land is shared and one group occupies a superior economic or political position. The dominant group may ignore the cultural heritage of others and, although eminently collectable, it is not protected by any controls on theft or export and denied respect and support. Some would argue that the international community should step in if the State fails to adequately protect such heritage. However, the 1970 Convention provides no basis for giving special protection of this nature. If there are other States that would like to see protection implemented, they would have to rely on diplomatic or political persuasion.

(c) products of archaeological excavations (including regular and clandestine) or of archaeological discoveries

For many States, paragraph (c) represents the most important category for protection in Article 1. The history, purpose and structure of the 1970 Convention are all intimately entwined with objects that have come from illicit excavations. These objects may have been taken explicitly or accidentally. As such, paragraph (c) speaks of excavations both 'regular' (ie officially authorised) and 'clandestine' (ie by persons without authority and contrary to law). To ensure that these distinctions are capable of being appropriately recognised, implementation of paragraph (c) requires the introduction of a system of permits for archaeological excavation and an appropriate entity to manage it (see Article 5).

Paragraph (c) refers to 'products' of archaeological excavations and discoveries. To make sense of this, it must include more than the objects that are excavated or found. In particular, documents recording what has been found; the processes that were used and the results of studies done on and relating to these objects should also be considered as falling under paragraph (c). The 1956 Recommendation on International Principles Applicable to Archaeological Excavations makes special mention of documentation on excavations:

> … the national archaeological services should, as far as possible, make their documentation and reserve collections available for inspection and study to excavators and qualified experts …[59]

The 'Rüschlikon Principles' of 1994[60] also place great emphasis on the role played by documentation:

> Archaeological work and findings, particularly documentary records and primary field data, are of public interest, not commodities to be exploited for personal enjoyment and profit, and not private property. Not only because, as a rule, they are

[59] Para 25.

[60] 'Principles for Partnership in Cross-Cultural Human Sciences Research with a Particular View to Archaeology' (Swiss Academy of Humanities and Social Sciences and the Swiss Liechtenstein Foundation for Archaeological Research Abroad, 1994).

> supported by public funds but especially because they are of public concern since they deal with social, political, and cultural history, and thus with the identity of the respective communities. Archaeologists may withhold their findings for a limited time which, however, must not exceed the period indispensable for sound scientific evaluation.[61]

The extent of a permit system will depend on the nature of land ownership within the State. For example, the owner of the land may also own objects buried in it. The State may have no power to control excavation unless there is legislation to this effect. For example, in England, scheduled monuments are archaeological sites and monuments of national importance protected under the Ancient Monuments and Archaeological Areas Act 1979. Sites on other land may be under the control of the person who owns that land. This has given rise to problems when metal detectorists come onto land at night in search of antiquities (a practice known as 'nighthawking'). They often abscond with the finds, leading to a loss of knowledge about the objects and their context, as well as a loss of the financial value for the owner.[62] Landowners find it difficult to pay for private security to guard sites and the police do not have sufficient resources. The problem of unregulated metal detectorists is not limited to the UK.[63]

When a State comes to implement paragraph (c), consideration should be given to the 'UNESCO/UNIDROIT Model Provisions on State Ownership of Undiscovered Cultural Objects' of 2011.[64] Provision 3 of this document provides that 'Undiscovered cultural objects are owned by the State, provided there is no prior existing ownership.' If an object is therefore removed illegally from the site, State ownership will facilitate an action to have it returned wherever it is located, including in a foreign jurisdiction, or indeed a criminal prosecution for its theft.[65] Such recourses to private law and criminal law are generally outside the scope of the 1970 Convention, although they can be supported by the principles set out in Article 13.

[61] Para 15.

[62] See, eg, the Icklingham Bronzes: J Browning, 'A Layman's Attempts to Precipitate Change in Domestic and International "Heritage" Laws' in KW Tubb (ed), *Antiquities Trade or Betrayed: Legal, Ethical and Conservation Issues* (Archetype, 1995) 145–49. See also Historic England, *The Nighthawking Survey* (2009).

[63] For the 2019–2022 reporting cycle, UNESCO has noted that, of the 91 States reporting on implementation of the Convention, half the respondents indicated that the regulation of metal detectors was either 'poor' (35%) or merely 'satisfactory' (15%): Subsidiary Committee of the Meeting of States Parties, 11th Session, C70/23/11.SC/7 (Paris, UNESCO, 1–2 June 2023) p 12.

[64] Below, IV, ch 3(iii).

[65] For an example of a successful civil claim see the English case of *Iran v Barakat* [2007] EWCA Civ 1374, and for a criminal prosecution see *US v Frederick Schultz* 178 F. Supp. 2d 445 (SDNY 2002), aff'd, 333 F.3d.393 (2d Cir. 2003). For more on these cases, see P Gerstenblith, 'Schultz and Barakat: Universal Recognition of National Ownership of Antiquities' (April 2009) XIV *Art Antiquity and Law* 21. The previous approach, whereby courts would not recognise foreign heritage laws, was exemplified by the English case of *Attorney General of New Zealand v Ortiz* [1982] 1 QB 349; [1982] 3 WLR 571; [1983] 2 WLR 809.

There is a great variety of archaeological sites around the world. Some are less likely to attract thieves: eg trace remains of shelters or temporary camp sites of nomadic peoples. In general there will be no need to distinguish these in legislation relating to theft and illicit traffic. However, underwater cultural heritage, particularly shipwrecks, may well need particular attention. The Convention on the Protection of the Underwater Cultural Heritage of 2001 contains its own provisions on theft and illicit traffic.[66] These are much stronger than those in the 1970 Convention. States would do well to consider this when assessing whether to become party to the 2001 Convention.

(d) elements of artistic or historical monuments or archaeological sites which have been dismembered

Paragraph (d) refers to objects which have been removed from monuments or archaeological sites, for this is the meaning of 'dismemberment'. In many States it is inevitably a crime to remove such objects. When it happens, the consequences can be severe. After studying reports of the looting of decorative and structural elements from temples and sites in Cambodia, Davis and Mackenzie conclude:

> When taken together, these scattered reports paint a picture of a cultural tragedy that reduced Cambodia's temples – some of which had stood for a millennium – from open-air museums to riddled shells within decades.[67]

There were also reports beginning in the 1990s on how the destruction of archaeological sites in Iraq fuelled the market in antiquities. The following report related to looting at the ancient site of Nineveh:

> The process by which large relief slabs were converted into small marketable fragments is noteworthy. In cases where the surrounding relief surface was not well preserved, these parts were broken away to create a well-preserved fragment… A similar case is a fragment […] that shows small figures behind a city wall. The large figures directly above the city were completely broken away, evidently so that their large scale would not distract from the interest of the miniature scene below.[68]

Paragraph (d) refers to monuments that are 'artistic or historical'. Although the popular perception of the word 'monument' may conjure up a very large edifice, in reality it can be a term used in domestic law to describe a wide variety of types of buildings and their surrounds, in use or in ruin. Elements of such buildings can – sadly – be removed by looters with enough time and patience.

Decorative features are often designed for a particular building. These include features such as ceilings, panelling, frescoes, doors, windows, fireplaces and even

[66] For instance, Art 14. Discussed below in V, ch 2.

[67] T Davis and S Mackenzie, 'Crime and Conflict: Temple Looting in Cambodia' in JD Kila and M Balcells (eds), *Cultural Property Crime: An Overview and Analysis of Contemporary Perspectives and Trends* (Leiden, Brill, 2015) 292, 293.

[68] JM Russell, *The Final Sack of Nineveh: The Discovery, Documentation, and Destruction of King Sennacherib's Throne Room at Nineveh, Iraq* (New Haven, Yale University Press, 1998) 48.

furniture. At first glance there would appear to be a significant difference in the degree of mobility of these features. However, with modern techniques and a greater or lesser degree of effort, all decorative features can be removed. A visitor to the Hearst Castle at San Simeon in California can see how decorative features from European buildings were removed and taken half-way around the world to be reassembled in a radically different context. The building left behind, if it survives at all, is but an empty shell, devoid of all that gave it meaning.

The dismemberment of a French chapel by the removal of frescoes gave rise to significant legal proceedings on the meaning of 'immovable' and 'movable' in the Civil Law. The case of *Fondation Abegg v Ville de Genève*[69] concerned important eleventh-century frescoes in Catalan style which had been discovered in an abandoned chapel in southern France, then being used by local farmers for wood storage. In 1954 the frescoes were detached from the walls and sold by a dealer. When exhibited in a Swiss museum, the chapel owners sued for their return in the French courts. The case turned on whether they were movables or immovables. The possessor, the City of Geneva, argued that the frescoes had come into its hands as movables and that, under a Franco-Swiss Treaty, only the Swiss had jurisdiction.[70] The French court of first instance held that, under French law, they were immovable by nature; the Court of Appeal of Montpellier also held that they were immovable, though by intention. The Cour de Cassation overturned these findings, holding instead that they were movables. Nevertheless, the Swiss decided to return the frescoes as a loan, and subsequently the City of Geneva converted this transfer into a donation in 2003.[71]

The dismemberment of a monument can give rise to conflict between the owner of the building and the cultural authorities. A church, for example, may have been used as a place of worship for many hundreds of years. Changing views of faith and worship may have wrought alterations in its fabric. To strip it of elements that illustrate these events is to destroy it, not only as a witness of the past, but arguably as part of a living culture as well. Following the Second Vatican Council of the Roman Catholic Church, many churches were denuded of their interior features to present a more austere public face. There were arguments as to whether this was allowed under the relevant State legislation on historic preservation.[72] What then was the status of objects that had been so removed?

It has long been held that the scope of a 'monument' extends to the surrounds of the structure which forms its core. As set out in the 'Venice Charter' on conservation

[69] *Ville de Genève et Fondation Abegg v Consorts Margail*, D.1985.208, note Maury; *Fondation Abegg v Ville de Genéve* D.1988.325.

[70] LV Prott, 'Movables and Immovables as Viewed by the Law' (1992) 1 *International Journal of Cultural Property* 389.

[71] M Cornu and M-A Renold, 'New Developments in the Restitution of Cultural Property: Alternative Means of Dispute Resolution' (2010) 17 *International Journal of Cultural Property* 1, 11, 21.

[72] J Bernard, 'Church and State Disagree over Management of Religious Heritage' *The Art Newspaper* (July–August 1996), p 28.

and restoration, adopted by The International Council on Monuments and Sites (ICOMOS) in 1964:

> The concept of a historic monument embraces not only the single architectural work but also the urban or rural setting in which is found the evidence of a particular civilization, a significant development or a historic event. This applies not only to great works of art but also to more modest works of the past which have acquired cultural significance with the passing of time.[73]

The more extensive the setting, the more susceptible it will be to the removal of significant objects placed in that setting. The form of dismemberment might be particularly prevalent where the setting is a garden. ICOMOS has a committee dedicated to the protection and preservation of historic gardens. Its Charter on gardens starts with the statement:

> A historic garden is an architectural and horticultural composition of interest to the public from the historical or artistic point of view. As such, it is to be considered as a monument.[74]

Theft is a significant problem for monuments of this nature. For example, statuary is often a target particularly if it was carved by a famous artist or has a special relationship with the garden. And in cemeteries, for example, architectural features such as carvings on tombs and decorative metal railings can be targeted. Once removed they can be spirited out of the country to a market where they will be unrecognisable.

It will be obvious from the above that paragraph (d) has a very broad coverage. Prevention of theft and illicit traffic would of course reduce the demand for objects flowing from dismemberment, especially at the international level. Effectively dealing with this aspect when implementing the 1970 Convention is essential.

(e) antiquities more than one hundred years old, such as inscriptions, coins and engraved seals

The terminology in paragraph (e) is somewhat confusing. An 'antiquity' is defined as being over 100 years old. However, the general understanding of 'antiquity' is that it relates to the ancient past. Legislation from around the time of the 1970 Convention often defined an antiquity as an object 'produced or modified by human agency' more than 100 years old.[75] The Nigerian law of 1978 uses a fixed cut-off date of 1918 for 'antiquities',[76] while the Antiquities Law of Qatar from 1980 requires antiquities to be over 40 years of age.[77] There may thus have been an understanding at the time that 'antiquity' did not mean an object of particularly great vintage.

[73] ICOMOS, International Charter for the Conservation and Restoration of Monuments and Sites (The Venice Charter 1964), Art 1.

[74] ICOMOS, Historic Gardens (The Florence Charter 1981).

[75] For example, s 2 of the Antiquities Act 1976 of Malaysia.

[76] Decree No 77 of 28 September 1978 of the National Commission for Museums and Monuments.

[77] Qatari Law Number 2 of 1980 on Antiquities, Art 1.

Paragraph (e) lists three examples of what the drafters considered 'antiquities': 'inscriptions, coins and engraved seals'. This is a strange list of illustrations. Of all the thousands of objects from earlier times, there is no indication of why these particular examples were selected. First, an inscription is not an antiquity. It must be carved onto material, such as a stone, before it can have permanence and truly be an 'antiquity'. Engraved seals fall within a rather niche field with limited interest amongst the general public. Coins, of course, do hold great interest for collectors.

Let us therefore consider coins in further detail. It must be remembered that to qualify the coin must be of 'importance for archaeology, prehistory, history, literature, art or science'. Many coins are found in the course of archaeological investigation. Although it is easy to legislate controls on coins, such controls are very difficult to implement. Coins are easily portable and susceptible to both theft and illicit traffic:

> … there was no possibility of establishing a paper-trail for the coins and certainly no way of repatriating them; to which of the half-dozen contemporary countries that contained various of the places of minting would we return them? In general this is why coins are often actually or tacitly ignored in considerations of illegal traffic.[78]

In 2009, China entered into a Memorandum of Understanding with the United States regarding the imposition of restrictions on the import into the US of certain categories of cultural property, including coins. These included early Zhou Dynasty objects of exchange, tool-shaped and disc-shaped coins, Qin Dynasty square-holed coins, Han-Sui era coins and Tang Dynasty coins.[79] An association of coin collectors challenged the restrictions but this was ultimately rejected by the Fourth Circuit Court of Appeals.[80] This exemplifies the complexities involved in trying to regulate the trade in ancient coins.

Coins have featured in legal proceedings as well. Usually these concern dealers who have been caught holding illicitly traded coins. Other permutations can exist as well. Renold refers to Swiss proceedings where India claimed the restitution of two seventeenth-century coins from Hyderabad against the Crédit Agricole Indosuez in Geneva. These coins were pledged to the Bank in 1988 to secure a loan granted to financial companies controlled by the descendant of the last ruler (Nizam) of Hyderabad. India considered itself the owner of these coins following the unification of the country in 1950, claiming that the coins had been exported in violation of Indian legislation.[81] The Swiss Supreme Court held that the Bank had taken the necessary steps to ensure that the creator of the pledge had ownership of the coins.

[78] JM Fossey, 'Illicit Traffic in Antiquities: Some Canadian Experiences' in JD Kila and M Balcells (eds), *Cultural Property Crime: An Overview and Analysis of Contemporary Perspectives and Trends* (Leiden, Brill, 2015) 206, 215.

[79] Federal Register, Vol 79, No 8, (13 January 2014): Rules and Regulations, 2092.

[80] *Ancient Coin Collectors Guild v US Customs and Border Protection, et al* 698 F 3d (4th Cir 2012), 899 F 3d 295 (4th Cir 2018).

[81] MA Renold, 'The International Protection of Archaeological Heritage: Questions of Private International Law and of Legal Harmonization' in JA Sánchez Cordero (ed), *The 1970 UNESCO Convention: New Challenges* (Mexico City, Instituto de Investigaciones Jurídica, 2014) 297, 300.

(f) objects of ethnological interest

Ethnology is the branch of anthropology dealing with the comparative and analytical study of cultures. Objects produced by those cultures would be of 'interest' – using the term from paragraph (f) – to those engaged in such studies. These will usually relate to living cultures within States. There will often be two interests at play: the State will want to keep these objects within its borders in order to preserve the culture that produced them; but there will be an interest in seeing the objects distributed as broadly as possible and brought to the attention of other peoples in order to illustrate the abilities of their makers. To achieve these conflicting goals, the State may well want to impose some form of export control.

The Republic of Korea has done this in respect of what it calls 'folklore materials'. These include the clothing, implements and houses which are indispensable for understanding changes in the life of the people, as well as their manners and customs regarding food, clothing and shelter, occupation, religious faiths and annual rites.[82] The export of such objects is prohibited.[83] Malaysia forbids the export of 'historical objects' which include any 'ethnographic material such as household or agricultural implements, decorative articles, personal ornaments; works of art such as carvings, sculpture, paintings, architecture, textiles, musical instruments, weapons and any other handicraft; manuscript, coin, currency note, medal, badge, insignia'.[84] Fiji prohibited the export, among other things, of all Fijian weapons including clubs, spears, bows, arrows and slings and 'forks of bone, ivory or wood made for the eating of human flesh'.[85]

The inclusion of ethnological material elsewhere in the 1970 Convention should be noted. In fact, the two other provisions referring to such material do so in somewhat conflicting ways. First of all Article 4, in setting out what categories of material can form part of the cultural heritage of the State, includes cultural property acquired by ethnological missions (as well as archaeological and natural science missions), provided this was with the consent of the authorities of the country of origin.[86] This implies that much material of this nature is indeed outside its country of origin and presumably in institutions or archives in the West; therefore it is not intended to be returned to its homeland since, as stated, it forms 'part of the cultural heritage' of the State where it is currently located. Later in the Convention, at Article 9, States may take resolute action, which can include adding export and import controls, if the cultural patrimony of a State is 'in jeopardy from pillage of archaeological or ethnological materials'. This is one of the two provisions implemented by the United States, which often does list specific types of ethnological material in its bilateral agreements with requesting States under the

[82] Art 2(4), Cultural Heritage Protection Act 2007.
[83] Art 35.
[84] Malaysian Antiquities Act 1976.
[85] Fijian Preservation of Objects of Archaeological and Palaeontological Interest Act 1940.
[86] Art 4(c).

Convention on Cultural Property Implementation Act.[87] The inclusion of objects of ethnological interest within a State's definition of 'cultural property' can have a wider impact – even an indirect one – that goes beyond Article 1.

In defining the modern parameters of 'ethnological' objects, it is worth considering the more finely tuned explanation offered in the Convention's 'Operational Guidelines' adopted at the Meeting of States Parties in 2015.[88] These provide a helpful outline of the importance of stemming the increased traffic in ethnological and anthropological items, linking these specifically to material taken from indigenous groups.[89] This is then taken further with the Model Provisions on the Prevention and Fight Against the Illicit Trafficking of Cultural Property, approved at the Meeting of States Parties to the 1970 Convention in 2025, which include in the definitional provision the specific inclusion of 'property of spiritual or cultural interest, recognized by Indigenous Peoples as part of their cultural heritage'.[90] This of course goes beyond what is set out in the Convention itself – a fact noted by the drafters of the Model Provisions – but can be useful as a reminder of the importance of indigenous material within the wider national heritage of a State.

There is a possible link too between ethnological material and what we now call 'intangible cultural heritage'. In 2003, UNESCO adopted the Convention for the Safeguarding of the Intangible Cultural Heritage, which in its definition of 'intangible cultural heritage' includes 'instruments, objects, artefacts' associated with that heritage.[91] The 'safeguarding' of these may well require a prohibition on their export, which could supplement the goals and purposes of the 1970 Convention.[92]

The United Nations Declaration on the Rights of Indigenous Peoples, adopted by the UN General Assembly in 2007, also bears on the desirability of prohibiting the export of ethnological objects of interest.[93] In the Declaration, States undertake to 'provide redress through effective mechanisms, which may include restitution, developed in conjunction with indigenous peoples, with respect to their cultural, intellectual, religious and spiritual property taken without their free, prior and informed consent or in violation of their laws, traditions and customs'.[94] Subsequent to the Declaration, UNESCO also produced its *Policy on Engaging with Indigenous Peoples* (2018) which reaffirms many of these points.[95]

[87] For instance, in the Bilateral Agreements with Colombia, Bolivia and Afghanistan.

[88] 'Operational Guidelines for the Implementation of the Convention on the Means of Prohibiting and Preventing the Illicit Import, Export and Transfer of Ownership of Cultural Property', as adopted at the Third Meeting of States Parties to the Convention (Paris, UNESCO, 2015).

[89] See p 7.

[90] Model Provisions on the Prevention and Fight Against the Illicit Trafficking of Cultural Property, as adopted by the Eighth Meeting of States Parties to the 1970 Convention (Paris, UNESCO, 19–20 May 2025).

[91] Art 2.

[92] Art 2.

[93] PJ O'Keefe and LV Prott, *Cultural Heritage Conventions and Other Instruments: A Compendium with Commentaries* (Builth Wells, Institute of Art and Law, 2011) 334.

[94] Art 11(2).

[95] *Policy on Engaging with Indigenous Peoples* (Paris, UNESCO, 2018) 27.

(g) property of artistic interest, such as:

- *(i) pictures, paintings and drawings produced entirely by hand on any support and in any material (excluding industrial designs and manufactured articles decorated by hand);*
- *(ii) original works of statuary art and sculpture in any material;*
- *(iii) original engravings, prints and lithographs;*
- *(iv) original artistic assemblages and montages in any material;*

Paragraph (g) covers 'property of artistic interest'. What is of artistic interest to one person may not be at all interesting to another. Moreover, the examples given in paragraph (g) are not exclusive but merely illustrative ('such as…'). States have a wide scope to include numerous works that they consider important cultural property in terms of their own history, literature or art. For the most part, many of the objects covered under this paragraph will be uncontroversial: an oil painting by Rembrandt, a watercolour by Turner, a sculpture by Bernini would of course all fit comfortably within the definition. But consider violins, which might also fall under paragraph (k), but could be included here if of sufficient 'artistic interest' (a Stradivarius, for example).

Paragraph (g) places great emphasis on originality. However, this attribute is often difficult to establish for many of the objects listed. For example, an original print is made from a matrix – stone, wood or metal – on which the artist has produced a design by hand. The image is transferred to paper, strictly speaking by ink, although there are variations in the way this is done and the way the paper responds to the ink.[96] However, there are reproductions such as those produced by photomechanical processes that are very difficult to distinguish from an original print. More recent are those made by modern printers. In Australia, for instance, the Protection of Movable Cultural Heritage Regulations 1987 simply refer to 'prints, posters, photographs or similar works of art with potential for multiple production.'[97] To qualify for export controls, prints must be worth more than A$10,000.

The difficulty of establishing originality is described by Glatthard, in the context of trade in Chinese artworks. For instance, he explains how it is usually difficult to distinguish between archaic and forged jade objects, thus authentication requires an analysis of chemical composition, including the interior.[98]

(h) rare manuscripts and incunabula, old books, documents and publications of special interest (historical, artistic, scientific, literary, etc.) singly or in collections

The objects listed in paragraph (h) – manuscripts, incunabula, old books, documents and publications of special interest – have often been the target of thieves

[96] B Gascoigne, *How to Identify Prints* (New York, Thames and Hudson, 1988).
[97] See para 5.3.
[98] N Glatthard, 'China, Switzerland and the Transfer of Cultural Goods: On the Agreement Regarding the Illicit Import, Export and Restitution of Cultural Goods', *Jusletter* (22 June 2015).

and subject to illicit traffic. However, they are often overlooked when considering the implications of the 1970 Convention: attention is concentrated more on archaeological objects and artistic works that capture public attention. Books and the other objects listed here are seldom on show – and incunabula (books printed before 1500) are barely known beyond expert circles. Often the library or museum housing them does not know what is held. In these circumstances, it is easy for thieves to take what they can. Indeed, they may not want the entire book or set of documents, but might slice out one particular part or page. These objects may be of great interest to scholars who need access for lengthy periods to do their research. While users could be subject to constant supervision in libraries, this would seem to be an intrusion on privacy rights and the honour of scholars, not to mention an obvious drain on public resources.

Several cases can be mentioned to demonstrate the ease with which perpetrators were able to act. In 1996, Anthony Melnikas, an art history professor from Ohio State University, was sentenced to fourteen months in prison for theft from the Vatican Library. He had removed leaves from a treatise with a penknife, then offered these for sale to a book dealer in the United States. The book was identified by a professor of art history at Princeton University.[99] In 2007, Cesar Gomez Rivero, a Uruguayan national and frequent visitor to the Spanish National Library in Madrid, used a razor blade to cut pages from a rare edition of *Cosmographia*, a German work published in 1482. The theft was not noticed until another scholar consulted the work some time later and noticed that pages were missing. No one is above such nefarious activity. The Head of Manuscripts at the Royal Library of Sweden, Anders Burius, had been stealing manuscripts for a decade, with a haul that totalled over 60 books. He would take his loot to Germany and sell it at auction there, since German law allowed title to pass to good faith buyers in this way.[100] He was found out in 2004.[101]

Such cases illustrate the ease with which parts of books can be taken; moved from country to country seemingly without problem. As we see with Burius, the lure exists even for members of staff who are, in many cases, poorly paid while surrounded by objects of great beauty and value. The temptation to take from the collection, particularly when it may be badly catalogued and stored, can be great. More brazen thefts can also take place, such as the 2017 theft of over 200 rare books from a warehouse near Heathrow Airport in London, where thieves abseiled in through a hole in the roof. The books were recovered three years later, buried under a house in rural Romania.[102] Ultimately recovery efforts require cooperation between States for thefts to be noticed, registered and communicated, then for objects to be returned – insofar as this is possible.[103]

[99] 'Mystery Over Vatican Pages', *Times Higher Education Supplement* (9 June 1995).
[100] Art 935(2) of the German Civil Code.
[101] When Burius was being investigated, he took his own life.
[102] 'Stolen books worth £2.5m found under floor of Romanian house' *BBC News* (18 September 2020).
[103] In the Burius case, the Swedish Royal Library undertook to recover as many manuscripts as could be located and have so far (at 2026) reportedly recovered 17 out of 60.

Another interesting example of book theft concerns the manuscript of 'The 120 Days of Sodom' composed by the Marquis de Sade in 1785 on small pieces of paper smuggled into the Bastille in Paris and glued together into a scroll. Immediately before the destruction of the prison in the French Revolution, it was saved and, in 1982, it was in the hands of the de Sade family. However, it was lent to a bookseller who sold it to a Swiss erotic books collector. A court in France put it on the Interpol list of stolen artefacts, but a Swiss court ruled in favour of the Geneva collector, saying he had bought it 'in good faith'. Requests by the French National Library to purchase it were rebuffed.[104] It was only after the death of the collector that the manuscript was 'recovered'. This was not achieved using restitutionary processes: it was bought by a French company for 7 € million and returned to France, where it was put on display at a private museum.

(i) postage, revenue and similar stamps, singly or in collections

To qualify under Article 1, the material listed in paragraph (i) – 'postage, revenue and similar stamps' – must be of importance for 'archaeology, prehistory, history, literature, art or science'. For example, a postage stamp may qualify as important for history if it depicts a person or event that has played a significant historical role. Some stamps are of obvious importance as cultural property. A prime example of this would be the 'Penny Black' issued in the United Kingdom in 1840. It was the world's first adhesive stamp and meant that the postage would be paid by the sender before the letter or parcel was put in the mail. The same is true of other countries when the stamp issued is relevant to a local event of importance.

'Revenue' stamps are attached to documents and other objects, eg beer kegs to show that government taxes have been paid. Often they were destroyed when the object was used, such as when it was opened.

Certain States extend the definition beyond the stamps themselves. Canada includes 'a pre-production proof of a Canadian postage stamp' under its category of applied and decorative art, provided it was made outside Canadian territory, is over fifty years old and has a fair market value of more than C$3,000.[105] Australia qualifies the inclusion as 'a postal marking, or postage or revenue stamp, that is in mint condition or is attached in any way to a document'. But it also goes further to specifically list 'any material used in the design, production, usage or collection of stamps'.[106]

(j) archives, including sound, photographic and cinematographic archives

Archives are records kept by individuals, families, commercial companies, public bodies or governments. Historians look to them to build or clarify the historical record. It is usually quite essential that they be kept together and

[104] T Perrottet, 'The Marquis de Sade Crimes of Passion' (2015) 45(10) *Smithsonian* 72, 76.
[105] Canadian Cultural Property Export Control List, Group IV, s 5 (1)(d).
[106] Protection of Movable Cultural Heritage Regulations (Australia), Part 8, 8.3.

whole. The 1970 Convention can assist when there is danger of theft of, and/or illicit traffic in, archives. Are archives at risk of theft or loss due to illicit traffic? Cuba, for one, lists 'documents from the early days of the Revolution', 'historical documents from the wars of independence' and 'deeds of land' as being at risk.[107] The demand for such material appears to come from the United States, Mexico and Spain.

Implementing legislation will have to specify the specific archives intended to be included. The term is very broad and will catch millions of individual objects if there has been no careful assessment. Official archives, ie those recording the operations of government, are usually established and controlled by legislation. But that leaves many that are privately owned and subject to the wishes of the owner. Commercial companies may seek to move their centre of operations from one State to another and may wish to take their archives with them. Should their removal be prohibited and subject to forced return?

Paragraph (j) specifically mentions 'sound, photographic and cinematographic archives'. These do not have to be of great artistic value. A film can have historic value. Consider the film, *The Story of the Kelly Gang*, made in 1906 purely as entertainment. This is largely recognised as the first commercial secular narrative film ever made. It tells the story of Ned Kelly, an Australian outlaw who was captured in the Siege of Glenrowan and hanged in 1880. The film was immediately popular although banned by authorities in Victoria. It was believed to have been lost. However, segments were found beginning in the 1970s. A digitally restored version has been made, but the original pieces are kept in the Australian National Film and Sound Archive.[108] The film played a key role in developing the significance of the Kelly Gang and its enduring influence on Australian culture. Needless to say, its removal from Australia would be a significant loss to local heritage.

(k) articles of furniture more than one hundred years old and old musical instruments

Furniture can have a close connection to the history, literature or art of a State. For example, it may have been used by a person prominent in its history, or even internationally. It may be part of a complex which, taken as a whole, shows the development of a particular fashion. It may have been designed by a person who greatly influenced the form and function of furniture. In all cases the State must decide if it is necessary to prevent its export. The 100-year rule is intended to preserve the rights of creators to enjoy the fruits of their genius by allowing them and their descendants to export the furniture to buyers in other countries.

[107] LM Almeida Luis and M Ramos Díaz, 'Control in Cuban Customs' in H Hooff (ed) *Culture & Development: Stop the Illicit Traffic of Cultural Property* (Havana, UNESCO Regional Office, 2013) 70, 72.
[108] National Film and Sound Archive, 'The Story of the Kelly Gang' *Australian Screen*.

The second part of paragraph (k) deals with 'old musical instruments'. This is a somewhat strange way of expressing a category of objects intended to be protected. Just what is meant by old? Certainly there have been numerous examples of theft of certain types of musical instrument:

> Rare instruments of the violin family, easily concealed and highly portable, have often been targeted for theft, and when they go missing they all too often are lost to their owners for many years.[109]

The instrument would have to be of such value as to come under the general qualifications of importance found at the beginning of Article 1.

[109] C Shapreau, 'The Purloined Stradivari' (2015) 16(3) *IFAR Journal* 19, 21.

Article 2

1. The States Parties to this Convention recognize that the illicit import, export and transfer of ownership of cultural property is one of the main causes of the impoverishment of the cultural heritage of the countries of origin of such property and that international co-operation constitutes one of the most efficient means of protecting each country's cultural property against all the dangers resulting therefrom.
2. To this end, the States Parties undertake to oppose such practices with the means at their disposal, and particularly by removing their causes, putting a stop to current practices, and by helping to make the necessary reparations.

There are many causes for the impoverishment of the cultural heritage. For example, natural disasters, decay and war. Illicit traffic has certainly been one of the most significant for countries of origin. It is particularly damaging when archaeological remains are at issue, for traffickers have so often masked the stripping of sites to ensure that prized relics are scattered around the world before the authorities of the source country realise what has happened. States Parties to the Convention patently recognise this through the inclusion of Article 2, by which the Parties agree to oppose illicit traffic with the means at their disposal. However, the significance of the Article lies in the notion that this cannot be achieved by States individually. There must be a cooperative effort that involves both source and market States.

To begin, source States need to have adequate legislation: implementing the Convention, providing for appropriate protection of antiquities and setting up proper administration. But ratification and passing legislation is not enough. Funding has to be provided for protection and preservation of sites and collections, for the training of people to care for the sites, for police and for the passing of information to the general public. Overall, there must be education on a continuous basis. There is much that source States can do to help themselves. Scovazzi and Ferri state that:

> Many of the problems posed by the illicit traffic in archaeological objects lie with the States of origin. The appropriate preservation of archaeological sites and contexts is essential to prevent the illegal trafficking of archaeological objects.[1]

However, source States can only do so much. When they are beset by war, control of archaeological sites and traffic in cultural property becomes implausible. For many, funding and personnel are restricted by the need to provide essential services to their citizens. Sites in many developing countries are unknown until looting takes place. For example, Iraq has over 10,000 known archaeological sites and many more not yet listed. Prevention of clandestine excavation and trafficking is therefore best prevented, as Article 2 reminds us, by cooperation between source States and market States.

[1] T Scovazzi and PG Ferri, 'Recent Developments in the Fight Against the Illicit Export of Archaeological Objects: The Operational Guidelines to the 1970 Convention' (2015) XX *Art Antiquity and Law* 195, 202.

Consequently, market States must be proactive, having legislation to effectively implement the Convention. They should be prepared to act when requested to seize objects flowing from illicit traffic and either return them to the State making the request or hold them within the legal system while the courts determine the rightful owner. Police and Customs officers should be made aware of the illicit traffic in cultural property, particularly archaeological material. Above all, market States should not only do the minimum under the Convention, but seek to cooperate with source States even if this has a detrimental effect on the art market and collectors in their own territory.

Is this a legal or a moral obligation on the part of States Parties?

Fraoua states that Article 2(1) creates no obligation on States Parties, but draws attention to the seriousness of the problem of illicit traffic.[2] Added to this restrictive view should be the point that authorities in a State Party to the 1970 Convention should not be able to expressly deny the deleterious effects of the illicit trade on cultural heritage, even if dealers and collectors from its own territory argue otherwise. Fraoua then considers Article 2(2) as requiring States to lend assistance in the return of illicitly exported goods, though there may be questions as to how the ambiguous phrase 'make the necessary reparations' in English could be read in quite this way. It could be asked, for example, how reparations could be due if Article 3 (in Fraoua's reading) does not itself impose direct obligations on States. Where then would the obligation to make reparations come from?[3]

Bator dismisses Article 2 as 'clearly rhetorical …; it closes with an empty undertaking to put a "stop to current practices, and … [help] to make necessary reparations"'.[4] But the undertaking is perhaps empty only if one chooses to make it so. Article 2 could instead be regarded as the dominant principle of the entire Convention, one which should restrain States from minimising their overall Convention obligations. The Operational Guidelines, for instance, refer to Articles 2 and 3 'as stating the fundamental principles of the Convention'.[5] With this reading, in case of ambiguity in other provisions of the Convention, Article 2 could be used to scope the ambit of those commitments. Article 31(1) of the Vienna Convention on the Law of Treaties should be recalled:

> A treaty shall be interpreted in good faith in accordance with the ordinary meaning to be given to the terms of the treaty in their context and in the light of its object and purpose.

[2] R Fraoua, *Convention concernant les mesures à prendre pour interdire et empêcher l'importation, l'exportation et le transfert de propriété illicites des biens culturels* (Unesdoc CC-86/WS/40, 1986).

[3] The only possible explanation for Fraoua's interpretation might be a reliance on the French text to resolve the ambiguities of the English text (eg the latter used 'particularly' rather than 'in particular' for 'notamment' and 'make the necessary reparations' for 'effectuer les réparations qui s'imposent'): PJ O'Keefe, *Protecting Cultural Objects: Before and After 1970* (Builth Wells, Institute of Art and Law, 2017) 132–33.

[4] PM Bator, 'An Essay on the International Trade in Art' (1982) 34 *Stanford Law Review* 275, 377.

[5] Operational Guidelines for the Implementation of the Convention, Adopted at Third Meeting of States Parties to the Convention (Paris, 2015), para 13.

It should be considered how persons involved in the actual implementation of the 1970 Convention have interpreted Article 2. Chamberlain, an adviser to the UK Government during the UK's adoption of the Convention in 2002, stated that Article 2's provisions are 'essentially rhetorical' and the undertakings of a political nature, but nevertheless concluded that 'they form part of the object and purpose of the Convention in the light of which the Convention needs to be interpreted'.[6] In the context of Switzerland's adoption of the Convention in 2005, Raschèr et al included the obligation of States 'to oppose with the means at their disposal the illicit import, export and transfer of ownership of cultural property' as one of the provisions of the Convention which, while not legally binding, require States to do everything in their power to enable implementation within their legal systems.[7]

The phrase 'undertakes to oppose' at Article 2(2) could be read to invoke a legal obligation on States, even if the precise content is left somewhat imprecise. Although the provision does not specifically require statutory implementation, it could nevertheless be said that the principle should guide State activities. For example, if authorities of the State had in their possession cultural property which they knew had been stolen or illegally exported from another State Party, would Article 2(2) not prompt the State to secure its restitution or repatriation? Such a situation arose when the Ife Bronze Head, featured in the Introduction and on the cover of this book, was handed over to the UK authorities in 2017 by an English auction house.[8] The object was known to have been stolen from a Nigerian museum in 1987 and had been registered as such with UNESCO. The only countervailing factor might be the private law rights of third parties, but these would not normally have a bearing on a State's obligations under international law. Would returning the head to Nigeria not be within the 'means at [the UK's] disposal'?

Writers such as Chamberlain and Raschèr et al, who do not go so far in their interpretation, accept there is an obligation to adopt a policy which will minimise illicit import, export and transfer of ownership of cultural property. Article 2(2) requires States Parties to remove the 'causes' of these activities. One significant cause is the collecting of cultural property without provenance (or with incomplete provenance). Campaigns can therefore be conducted to make collecting such material anathema. Market States could reduce collecting by requiring, for example, a person seeking a taxation advantage through a museum donation to provide the provenance of the object since 1970. Another cause is the attractiveness of clandestine excavation to local populations in source States. Alternative income flows could thus be examined. States could educate local people on the value of archaeological sites for tourism, if properly excavated, and stress their importance

[6] K Chamberlain, 'UK Accession to the 1970 UNESCO Convention' (September 2002) VII *Art Antiquity and Law* 231, 242.

[7] AFG Raschèr, M Bauen, Y Fischer and MN Zen-Ruffinen, *Cultural Property Transfer* (Brussels, Zurich; Bruyland, Schulthess; 2005) 15.

[8] See above, Introduction, p *.

for the history of the region. People could be shown how little they get for looted objects compared with dealers in market States.

Article 2 sets out three means by which States may oppose 'illicit import, export and transfer of ownership of cultural property'. The qualifying words 'particularly by' indicate that these are examples only and that the true extent of the provision is established by the phrase 'with the means at their disposal'. One of the most effective means at the disposal of a State is to decree import of an object into that State to be unlawful if it has been unlawfully exported from another State Party. This was the approach adopted, for example, by the Explanatory Memorandum on the Bill for legislation implementing the 1970 Convention in the Netherlands.[9] Discussing the implementation of the Convention, the Dutch Memorandum states that:

> … the Convention allows the States Parties wide discretion in respect of the manner of implementation. However, this discretion must be used in such a way as to create an effective system of protection for cultural property. Effective protection of this kind should exist even when the Convention does not provide any definite rules on a specific point. It is therefore inevitable that the present implementing legislation contains rules that do not appear as such in the Convention, but are necessary in order to give full effect to the general provisions of the Convention.[10]

Basing an import prohibition on Article 2(2) would thus be a perfectly legitimate means of implementing obligations under that Article, even though there is no express mention of it.

[9] Explanatory Memorandum to the 1970 Convention on the Illicit Import, Export and Transfer of Ownership of Cultural Property (Implementation) Act 2009.

[10] ibid.

Article 3

> The import, export or transfer of ownership of cultural property effected contrary to the provisions adopted under this Convention by the States Parties thereto, shall be illicit.

Article 3 is one of the most difficult provisions of the 1970 Convention to interpret, but that does not mean it can be ignored. To understand it, we must first turn to Article 31 of the Vienna Convention on the Law of Treaties, by which an interpretation which gives a provision some meaning is preferred to one which renders it meaningless. It is obvious that if the provision had no meaning whatsoever, it would not be in the Convention text at all. The Preamble must also be considered: it emphasises that the true value of cultural property 'can be appreciated only in relation to the fullest possible information regarding its origin, history and traditional setting'.

Among commentators, Goy in 1970 had regarded Article 3 as obliging States Parties to regulate both imports and exports.[1] Fraoua considered that it made unlawful in international law acts which were unlawful under national law 'adopted under this Convention'.[2] He specified the provisions of the Convention on which national laws may base their legislation. Such legislation may therefore declare as unlawful: export without an export certificate (Article 6(b)), import of property stolen from a museum or other institution (Article 7(b)(i)) or transfers of ownership likely to promote illicit import or export (Article 13(a)). These acts then become unlawful in international law and should be treated as illicit transactions by other States Parties to the Convention.

Chamberlain considered Article 3 essentially an interpretative provision but noted that, if it did have 'more substance in the sense that it requires States Parties to ensure that their civil and criminal law suitably deters persons from undertaking the acts referred to in the Article, then the principles of English civil and criminal law… can be pointed to as having this effect'.[3] Bator regarded the provision as 'mysterious' without saying why nor what its impact might be.[4]

Article 3 governs 'import, export and transfer of ownership' that are 'contrary to provisions' in the Convention. And we know that Article 2(2) requires States Parties to oppose 'illicit import, export and transfer of ownership' with the means 'at their disposal'. But what do these mean together? One answer is for a State to impose a simple prohibition on the import of objects unlawfully exported from

[1] R Goy, 'Le régime international de l'importation, de l'exportation et du transfert de propriété des biens culturels' (1970) 16 *Annuaire français de droit international* 605, 621.

[2] R Fraoua, *Convention concernant les mesures à prendre pour interdire et empêcher l'importation, l'exportation et le transfert de propriété illicites des biens culturels* (Unesdoc CC-86/WS/40, 1986) 57.

[3] K Chamberlain, 'UK Accession to the 1970 UNESCO Convention' (September 2002) VII *Art Antiquity and Law* 231, 242. One might wonder how this interpretation by a legal adviser to the UK Government would have been considered some years later when the Ife Bronze Head was handed over to the Metropolitan police (it had been stolen in 1987 from a museum in Nigeria): see above, Introduction.

[4] PM Bator, 'An Essay on the International Trade in Art' (1982) 34 *Stanford Law Review* 275, 377.

another State. Another might be to impose more restrictive bans on objects lacking the export certificates required by Article 6. Otherwise, a State might choose to read this provision quite minimally and to only impose import bans on cultural property stolen from a museum, monument or similar institution, as is explicitly set out at Article 7(b)(i) of the Convention.

While a good number of States Parties to the Convention have fallen back on the last of these three options, there remains a compelling argument that Article 3 in fact empowers States to do more than this. Certain States have implemented a broader interpretation of the import restrictions, though not necessarily with a direct reference to Article 3. Canada bans the import of cultural property exported contrary to the laws of fellow States Parties to the Convention.[5] Germany has had a similar import ban in place since its implementing law of 2016.[6] Australia goes further by applying its import restriction to the unlawfully exported movable cultural heritage of a State whether or not that State is party to the Convention.[7] New Zealand prohibits the import of protected foreign objects exported in contravention of the laws of the foreign State.[8] Certain States in the Middle East give an equally broad remit to import restrictions on antiquities: Qatar and the United Arab Emirates, for instance, though the extent of the use of such restrictions in practice may be somewhat uncertain.[9]

In previous editions, this commentary has argued for an interpretation of Article 3 whereby States Parties are required in their national law to render imports unlawful when they are unlawfully exported from another State. The position is based on reading Article 3 in conjunction with the export restrictions States may impose under Article 6. By this reading, one cannot split the State obligations: they must mirror one another. Accordingly, it may not be entirely sufficient for States to implement only the import restrictions enunciated at Article 7(b), since Article 3 can create obligations in its own right.[10] One commentary on the provision by Franca has adopted the same view: the author explains how an unlawful export of cultural property must be viewed as 'contaminated' on import and therefore

[5] Cultural Property Export and Import Act 1985, s 37.

[6] German Cultural Property Protection Act 2016, s 28 (and definitions). For commentary, see R Peters, 'Preventing Trafficking in Cultural Property: Import and Export Provisions as Two Sides of the Same Coin' (2019) 2 *Santander Art and Culture Law Review* 95, 101.

[7] Protection of Movable Cultural Heritage Act 1986, ss 3, 14. See the interpretation provided by the High Court of Australia in *Palmanova v Commonwealth of Australia* [2025] HCA 35.

[8] Protected Objects Act 1975 (as amended), ss 10A, 2 (definitions).

[9] See Qatari Law No 2 of 1980 on Antiquities, Art 29; Abu Dhabi Law No 4 of 2016 on the Cultural Heritage of Abu Dhabi, Art 15; United Arab Emirates Law No. 11 of 2017 on Antiquities, Arts 7(2) and 16.

[10] For more detail, see the 2017 text: PJ O'Keefe, *Protecting Cultural Objects: Before and After 1970* (Builth Wells, Institute of Art and Law, 2017) 135.

illegal according to the domestic laws of the importing State.[11] This has also been supported by Gerstenblith.[12]

It is worth noting that other international instruments have sought to render unlawful the import of cultural property illegally exported from another State (eg without a valid export licence). The Operational Guidelines for the Implementation of the 1970 Convention, introduced by UNESCO in 2015, indicate that the prohibition of export from one State Party 'should make illicit the import of that cultural property into another State Party'[13] – though this is intended as guidance only and so does not have force of law for States Parties. In the European Union, however, the principle has been made law by Regulation 2019/880 on the Introduction and the Import of Cultural Goods. Article 3(1) of that Regulation prohibits the introduction into the territory of listed cultural goods that were removed from their place of origin in breach of the laws and regulations of that place.[14] While this has no direct bearing on interpretations of the 1970 Convention text, it does align with the broad goals of the Convention.

It is understood that obligations flowing from Article 3 would not be 'self-executing'.[15] Franca calls them instead 'doubly articulated' 'end-norms', calling these 'rules that define a specific end to be reached but leave the means or ways to reach that goal at the discretion of the addressees of the norm'.[16] In deciding how to implement the obligations, a State might determine which transactions are to be dealt with, and whether they are to be regarded as void or voidable. In terms of a prohibition of imports, this could mean: fining, imprisoning or extraditing a person importing prohibited cultural property; a State Party suing the importer for its return; or rendering a transaction involving illegal import either a nullity (ie no legal effect) or voidable (ie prima facie valid, but subject to court determination).

[11] M Franca, 'Article 3 of the 1970 UNESCO Convention: Definition of "Illicit"' in AF Vrdoljak, A Jakubowski and A Chechi, *The 1970 UNESCO and 1995 Unidroit Conventions on Stolen or Illegally Transferred Cultural Property* (Oxford, Oxford University Press, 2024) 82.

[12] P Gerstenblith, 'Evolving Implementation of the 1970 UNESCO Convention', *Essays in Cultural Heritage in Honour of Francesco Francioni*, forthcoming. See also P Gerstenblith 'The 1970 UNESCO Convention: Past Present and Future' in S Vigneron and J Ulph, *Research Handbook on Art, Culture and Heritage Law* (London, Edward Elgar, 2026) 232–40.

[13] Operational Guidelines for the Implementation of the Convention on the Means of Prohibiting and Preventing the Illicit Import, Export and Transfer of Ownership of Cultural Property, adopted at the Third Meeting of States Parties (Paris, UNESCO, 2015) para 58. See commentary in T Scovazzi and PG Ferri, 'Recent Developments in the Fight Against the Illicit Export of Archaeological Objects: The Operational Guidelines to the 1970 Convention' (2015) XX *Art Antiquity and Law* 195, 222.

[14] This prohibition applies to 'Part A' cultural goods, which are listed in the Appendix to Regulation 2019/880 and effectively replicate the categories from Art 1 of the 1970 Convention.

[15] S von Schorlemer, *Internationaler Kulturgüterschutz: Ansätze zur Prävention im Frieden sowie im bewaffneten Konflikt* (Berlin, Duncker & Humblot, 1992) 440–43. On the view that none of the Convention is self-executing: see KG Siehr, 'Globalization and National Culture: Recent Trends Toward a Liberal Exchange of Cultural Objects' (2005) 38 *Vanderbilt Journal of Transnational Law* 1067, 1076; Z Veres, 'The Fight Against Illicit Trafficking of Cultural Property: The 1970 UNESCO Convention and the 1995 UNIDROIT Convention' (2014) 12(2) *Santa Clara Journal of International Law* 4, 97; Franca (n 11) 82–84.

[16] Franca (n 11) 90.

Canada and Australia have taken the view that those transactions may give rise to litigation, ie that perpetrators simply risk having the property claimed back as 'illegally imported' (Canada) or as an 'unlawful import' (Australia).

Otherwise, a State might not render imports illegal per se, but might otherwise seek to stifle the practice of importing or otherwise dealing in 'illicit' material: for instance, by ensuring that museums and art dealers do not acquire such material, either through legislation[17] or through codes of practice and due diligence guidance.[18] It could also be said that a State which has foreign cultural property in its possession that had been, without doubt, taken unlawfully from another State Party after the Convention came into force should deem that property 'illicit' and work towards restituting it.[19] The possible effect of such a purposive reading of Article 3 is that one barrier to return – non-retroactivity – can be partially collapsed: if the import, export or transfer occurred in a State that had adopted the Convention, then that property should always be deemed 'illicit', even to a State that only subsequently adopted the Convention.

During the meeting of the Special Committee of Experts in 1970, the United States delegation queried the legal effect of this provision. A legal officer of the Secretariat responded 'that it was perhaps redundant of the substantive provisions of the Convention. Several delegates of civil law countries expressed the view that this provision could have juridical consequences, but no specific explanation was given.'[20]

Nahlik notes that the experts were not agreed in the Committee of Experts, called in 1983 to consider the Convention, as to how far the obligations imposed by the Convention on the importing States referred only to stolen property, and how far they also covered cultural property which had been exported in contravention of export regulations.[21] He considers the Convention ambiguous. Sandrock takes the view that Article 3 requires a State Party to hold void any contract that might involve cultural property still within the State of origin whose export would breach that State's regulations.[22] Where the property is

[17] Switzerland, for instance, has legally mandated due diligence requirements for the art trade: see Cultural Property Transfer Act 2005, s 6 (Arts 15–16), and below V, ch 4.

[18] The UK, for instance, has adopted policy around museum acquisitions: Department for Culture, Media and Sport, *Combating Illicit Trade* (2005).

[19] This could have been a route considered by the UK in relation to the Ife Head discussed in the Introduction. The Head deemed 'illicit', UK authorities could have co-operated in 'facilitating the earliest possible restitution' of the object to Nigeria, as per Art 13(b) of the Convention.

[20] Report of the United States Delegation to the Special Committee of Governmental Experts to Examine the Draft Convention on the Means of Prohibiting and Preventing the Illicit Import, Export and Transfer of Ownership of Cultural Property (Paris, UNESCO, 13–14 April 1970) 11.

[21] SE Nahlik, 'International Co-operation to Prevent Illicit Traffic of Cultural Property' (1981–83) 51–53 *Annuaire de l'Association des Anciens Auditeurs de l'Académie de La Haye* 73, 78–79.

[22] O Sandrock, 'Foreign Laws Regulating the Export of Cultural Property: the Respect Due to them by the Judge of the Lex Fori' in P Lalive (ed), *International Sales of Works of Art* (Paris, Institute of International Business Law and Practice and Faculté de Droit de Genève, 1988) 457, 460, 464, 478.

already outside the State of origin when the contract is made, he considers the Convention ambiguous.

The provision makes clear that import, export and transfer of ownership contrary to the Convention 'shall be illicit'. 'Illicit' is not generally used in English language statutes: the terms 'unlawful' and 'illegal' are usually preferred. That said, it can have a wider scope beyond what is proven to be unlawful, as shown in the field of criminology. Mackenzie explains:

> The criminological perspective … encourages us … to be more nuanced in our approach, and to develop terms and concepts which can capture the uncertainty which the justice system has obscured with its harsh binary distinction. 'Illicit' antiquities is the term which has developed in the research literature to convey the perceived suspect origins of artefacts which cannot be, or have yet to be, proven illegal.[23]

Mackenzie considers that the possession of objects could be considered 'illicit' even though by law it is no longer illegal. Consider an object which has been stolen from a State but acquired in another State by a person in circumstances where, by the laws of that State, the purchaser obtains good title. Legally that person is the 'owner', but Mackenzie would consider that title tainted by the illicit nature of the earlier transaction.[24]

Similar wording is found in Article 11 of the Convention which provides that the export and transfer of ownership of cultural property under compulsion arising from the occupation of a country by a foreign power is to be regarded as 'illicit'. Bator states that Article 11 'prohibits compelled exports from 'occupied territories''[25] without explaining why this provision amounts to a prohibition while (according to him) Article 3 does not. The word 'illicit' also appears in the 1999 Protocol to the Hague Convention,[26] defined as 'under compulsion or otherwise in violation of the applicable rules of the domestic law of the occupied territory or of international law'.[27]

One final point should be made about Article 3. It may be arguable, following Franca, that the provision evokes a rule of customary international law.[28] This would mean that it reflects a generalised practice amongst States and that those States act according to a sense of being bound. Owing to the still conflicting approach taken by States to Article 3, this might be difficult to affirm with a sense of overwhelming conviction. However, some of the more recent developments outside the strict bounds of the Convention (such as the coming into force of import prohibitions under European Union Regulation 2019/880) may indicate that a customary rule is not far off.

[23] S Mackenzie, 'Illicit Antiquities' from the *Trafficking Culture* website: traffickingculture.org.

[24] Such might be his interpretation of an English case like *Winkworth v Christie, Manson & Woods* [1980] 1 Ch. 496.

[25] Bator (n 4) 378.

[26] Arts 9 and 21.

[27] Art 1. See R O'Keefe, *The Protection of Cultural Property in Armed Conflict* (Cambridge, Cambridge University Press, 2006) 287.

[28] Franca (n 11) 91–92.

Article 4

The States Parties to this Convention recognize that for the purpose of the Convention property which belongs to the following categories forms part of the cultural heritage of each State:

a. cultural property created by the individual or collective genius of nationals of the State concerned, and cultural property of importance to the State concerned created within the territory of that State by foreign nationals or stateless persons resident within such territory;
b. cultural property found within the national territory;
c. cultural property acquired by archaeological, ethnological or natural science missions, with the consent of the competent authorities of the country of origin of such property;
d. cultural property which has been the subject of a freely agreed exchange;
e. cultural property received as a gift or purchased legally with the consent of the competent authorities of the country of origin of such property.

Article 4 defines cultural property as that which may be considered part of a national 'cultural heritage' through connecting factors. It is obvious that this is not an exclusive definition. The Article begins by stating that the definition is 'for the purpose of the Convention'. There may be property which is part of the cultural heritage of a State which is not listed in Article 4. This Article must be read in conjunction with Article 1 which, as we have seen, sets out categories of objects that may be considered 'cultural property' for the purposes of the Convention. There is no clear indication as to how the two terms relate. One proposition is to take the categories of Article 1 and combine them with the idea of an 'inheritance'.[1]

Article 4 is not concerned with issues of ownership. Its purpose is to set the reach of the Convention by establishing what cultural property States may choose to protect through the procedures of the Convention. Some such property may be privately owned, some owned by the State, some ownerless. How these are treated depends on the internal law of the State and recognition by other States. But this is not the business of Article 4. Switzerland, for instance, uses Article 4 as the basis for defining the term 'cultural heritage': cultural property owned by the Confederation 'of essential importance to cultural heritage' can be listed on the Federal Registry.[2]

Paragraph (a) refers to that which has been created by nationals, or, where important, by non-nationals within the territory.[3] Fraoua interprets 'important' cultural property created by non-nationals to cover only that which is made by non-nationals with a close relationship to the country concerned.[4] He therefore

[1] See LV Prott and PJ O'Keefe, 'Cultural Heritage or Cultural Property?' (1992) 1 *International Journal of Cultural Property* 307.

[2] Swiss Law on the International Transfer of Cultural Property (2005), Art 2 (defining 'cultural heritage') and Art 3 (establishing the Federal Register).

[3] Art 4(a).

[4] R Fraoua, *Convention concernant les mesures à prendre pour interdire et empêcher l'importation, l'exportation et le transfert de propriété illicites des biens culturels* (Unesdoc CC-86/WS/40, 1986) 60.

considers a cultural object created by an artist who lived only briefly in the country as 'not important'. This may be an artificial restriction, since temporary residents can indeed produce objects which are very significant for the culture of that country, eg the Welsh landscapes of Alfred Sisley or early scenes of Indigenous life by a visitor to Australia can be key historical documents to the UK and Australia respectively. Commissioned portraits of persons of state or royalty may be artistically important as well.

Care has to be taken in implementing the Convention so that it does not adversely impact the work of creators. If the work of living artists, for example, is to be included in the cultural property of the State under Article 4 then a decision has to be made as to what restriction will be placed on its movement. Artists need to be able to sell their production, including abroad, in order to make a living; they need to be able to have their work seen by a wide audience. Any restriction will reduce their market. Some countries, such as Canada, only impose export controls on artworks created by artists who are no longer alive,[5] while the UK does not limit its controls in this way.[6]

Paragraph (b) lists as national cultural heritage cultural property 'found within the national territory'. This would cover, for example, archaeological remains of neighbouring or extinct cultural groups found within a territory now occupied by a different cultural group. Nafziger considers two possible interpretations:

> The controlling verb 'found' has been interpreted variously to include, on the one hand, undiscovered material that may be found in the future but has not yet been actually discovered, or, on the other hand, only material that has been physically found in the sense of having been discovered or has otherwise specifically come to light.[7]

It would seem logical to opt for the first of these interpretations. Otherwise, it might be necessary to introduce a commencement date and there is none which would be sensible. Once again, Article 4 indicates only categories of cultural property which States can consider as falling under the Convention. It makes perfect sense to include objects which have not yet been found that, once found, become part of the cultural heritage.

Paragraph (c) lists cultural property acquired by archaeological, ethnological or other scientific teams with the 'consent' of the host country. Such provisions were common in laws regulating archaeological research going back some way.[8] More recently, this practice has been restricted owing to exploitation by certain

[5] Cultural Property Export and Import Act, s 4(3).

[6] See the 1997 export block of an early work by then still alive Lucien Freud: *Art Newspaper*, No 69, April 1997, 7.

[7] JAR Nafziger, 'The 1970 Convention: Insights, Circumspections, and Outlooks' in JA Sánchez Cordero (ed), *The 1970 UNESCO Convention: New Challenges* (Mexico City, Instituto de Investigaciones Jurídica, 2014) 211, 221.

[8] cf Art 23 of the 1956 Recommendation on International Principles Applicable to Archaeological Excavations.

foreign teams on the one hand and, on the other, the creation of better national facilities for undertaking archaeological research.

Paragraph (d) lists cultural property which has been 'the subject of a freely agreed exchange' as part of a State's cultural heritage. Care has to be taken that the transaction really is 'a freely agreed exchange'. The Rüschlikon Principles emphasise this point:

> Archaeologists engaged in cultures other than their own should work for international exchange and short-term or long-term loans of cultural objects, provided this is helpful for education, mutual understanding, historic and aesthetic enjoyment, or scientific purposes, and on condition that conservation requirements are fulfilled.[9]

At paragraph (e) are included gifts and that which has been legally purchased 'with the consent of the competent authorities of the country of origin of such property'. The question of 'consent' is one that may give rise to controversy where the material concerned comes from a community and authorisation to transfer was or is challenged.

The Preliminary Draft Convention[10] and the Revised Draft[11] both contained an additional provision, paragraph 4(f), which would have included:

> Cultural property acquired by a State or one of its nationals before this Convention entered into force for the State in question.

A number of States objected to this provision because, in the words of the Mexican reply, '...it would imply waiving the right to recuperate cultural property which has been removed from the country illicitly'.[12] The Special Committee of Experts deleted this clause without giving reason. Its omission suggests that the mere fact of possession of cultural property by a State does not of itself determine whether it is part of the cultural heritage of that State. Such property may be the subject of claims for restitution or return, even if these are outside the Convention itself (see Article 15, which allows for such agreements).

There may be overlap between any of these sections: ie more than one State may claim the same object as part of its cultural heritage, though direct conflicts are most likely to arise in relation to paragraphs (a) and (b). It is important to recall that Article 4 does not deal with ownership, but with what could be called 'heritage value'. It is neither necessary nor desirable to accept one claim to the exclusion of others where a cultural object has played an important part in the cultural life of several communities – though this may of course give rise to problems of sharing or determining priorities between such communities. For instance, the original manuscripts of the works of Thomas Mann might be

[9] Principles for Partnership in Cross-Cultural Human Sciences Research with a Particular View to Archaeology (Rüschlikon, 1994), reproduced in PJ O'Keefe, *Trade in Antiquities: Reducing Destruction and Theft* (Paris, London, UNESCO, Archetype, 1997) 123–32.

[10] Unesdoc SHC/MD/3 Annex, 2.

[11] Unesdoc SHC/MD/5 Annex III, 2.

[12] Unesdoc SHC/MD/5 Annex I, 14.

claimed as part of the cultural heritage of the United States and of Germany: he wrote in both places, was a national of each and had great influence on both cultures. Or consider two paintings by the English artist George Stubbs that are of iconic Australian animals – one of a kangaroo and the other of a dingo – the first ever paintings made of each species. However, Stubbs never visited Australia and made the paintings from a description given to him by Joseph Banks who accompanied Captain Cook on his voyage to Australia in 1770. The paintings were privately owned in England until 2012 when they were sold to a foreign buyer. The UK Government placed an export stop and they were eventually acquired 'for the nation' to be displayed at the National Maritime Museum in Greenwich.[13] The National Gallery of Australia had wanted to acquire the paintings as important illustrations of Australian history. A representative of the gallery was quoted as saying that the episode 'forever deprives Australian audiences of permanent access to two of the most historically significant works of art in the story of our nation's visual heritage'.[14]

Other cultural property of foreign origin in accordance with paragraphs (c), (d) and (e) may be relevant to more than one country. Canada includes in its national cultural heritage objects which have been in the country for more than 35 years or have been associated with an important Canadian figure or are part of a known Canadian collection. Thus it has held a 1612 Dutch atlas,[15] papers of Rudyard Kipling[16] and a painting by Renoir[17] to be part of Canada's cultural heritage. It is in fact common practice to include works not made by nationals but which have been in the country so as to have become influential in that culture as part of the national cultural heritage. Brazilian legislation includes as part of its cultural heritage Portuguese objects of early date,[18] and most colonised and immigrant countries whose culture derives from outside the boundaries of their present territory have similar provisions.

Niec suggested, in cases of conflicting claims, using the criterion of the 'effective link', similar to that established by the International Court of Justice in the 'Nottebohm Case' for the nationality of individuals.[19] In that case, Nottebohm had become a national of Liechtenstein although he had been born in Germany and was resident in Guatemala. The Court held that Guatemala was not bound to recognise a nationality which was tenuous and not based on a social fact of attachment, a genuine connection of existence, interests and sentiments. Although

[13] 'Stubbs's Kangaroo and Dingo Paintings Saved for the Nation', *Heritage Fund* (6 November 2013).

[14] D Passmore, 'Australia Loses Out as George Stubbs Painting of Kangaroo Stays in UK' (*News.Com.AU*, 7 November 2013).

[15] Department of Communications (Canada), *Annual Report 1979–1980*, 18–20.

[16] *Annual Report 1982–1983*, 20–22.

[17] *Annual Report 1983–1984*, 25–27.

[18] Law No. 4845 of 19 November 1965 prohibiting the removal from the country of artistic works and handicrafts produced in the country up to the end of the monarchic period, art 2.

[19] *Liechtenstein v Guatemala* (1955) ICJ Reports, 4. See H Niec, *Ojczyzna Dzieta Sztuki* (Warsaw-Krakow, Panstwowe Wydawnictwo Naukowe, 1980) reviewed by SE Nahlik, *Polish Yearbook of International Law* (1981) 258, 261.

Niec's suggestion is helpful, there may still be more than one State with an 'effective link'.[20] It would not appear to dispose of the argument therefore in the kind of cases indicated above.

The Convention does not provide rules to regulate competing interests of States.[21] The wisdom of this reticence has been justified by the increasing practice of accepting what is sometimes called a 'shared heritage'. This implies an understanding of the interests of countries which are now prepared to exchange exhibits, return some cultural objects, respect diverse interests in the same material and learn from their respective curators, all with the goal of increasing knowledge and exchanging best practices.

It is interesting to note that Italy, in a case before the European Court of Human Rights,[22] raised the argument that Italy had a compelling State interest founded on Article 4 to monitor and control the trade in important artworks on its territory, even when those artworks were by foreign nationals and had not been created in Italy. That case involved a Van Gogh owned by the Swiss dealer Ernst Beyeler but held in Italy. By implication, Italy must have considered the Van Gogh 'freely traded' according to paragraph (d) and thus a legitimate part of its cultural heritage. The European Court of Human Rights did not find Italy's argument referencing the 1970 Convention particularly helpful, but did in the end support Italy's argument on this point for more general reasons:

> in relation to works of art lawfully on its territory and belonging to the cultural heritage of all nations, it is legitimate for a State to take measures designed to facilitate in the most effective way wide public access to them, in the general interest of universal culture.[23]

Though outside the context of Article 4 of the 1970 Convention, this statement by the Court (and the rousing reference to 'the general interest of universal culture') seems to align with the overall principles underpinning the provision, especially in relation to the 'shared heritage' mentioned above.

Bator found Article 4 'particularly unintelligible' and stated that it would 'seem to have no operative effects'.[24] The United States has made no legislative effort to define its own cultural heritage and this may explain why a lawyer from that country could not see the point of such a provision. Bator also stated that this attempt

[20] A Müller-Katzenburg, *Internationale Standards im Kulturgüterverkehr und ihr Bedeutung für das Sach- und Kollisionsrecht* (Berlin, Duncker & Humblot, 1996) 142–54.

[21] See the discussion by Müller-Katzenburg, ibid 149ff.

[22] *Beyeler v Italy* [2000] ECHR 462. The case is discussed in M-A Renold, 'A Landmark Decision in Art Law by the European Court of Human Rights: Beyeler v. Italy' (2000) V *Art Antiquity and Law* 73. In the end, the claimant Mr Beyeler won his human rights claim against Italy since, although the State had a legitimate interest in protecting cultural property within its territory, it had not acted proportionally with Mr Beyeler and so violated his right to peacefully enjoy his possessions (Article 1, Protocol to the European Convention on Human Rights).

[23] ibid para 113.

[24] PM Bator, 'An Essay on the International Trade in Art' (1982) 34 *Stanford Law Review* 275, 377.

to define the cultural heritage of a State is 'for purposes which are themselves obscure'. The wording of the Article commences:

> The States Parties to this Convention recognize that for the purpose of the Convention property which belongs to the following categories forms part of the cultural heritage of each State …

This means that, in the operation of the reciprocal obligations under the Convention, a State is entitled to expect other Parties to recognise its right to protect cultural property falling into such categories. Thus the argument could be mounted that the American legislation extending protection in bilateral agreements to archaeological objects that are more than 250 years old[25] does not properly respect Article 4 since, as we have seen, that limit might be quite inappropriate for the cultural property of certain States. That said, the United States did not implement any article apart from Articles 7(b) and 9 of the Convention, so it might argue (as indeed Bator did) that Article 4 had no purchase whatsoever.

[25] Convention on Cultural Property Implementation Act (1983) 19 USC 2601, ss 2601(2)(C)(i)(II), 2602(a)(1)(A).

Article 5

To ensure the protection of their cultural property against illicit import, export and transfer of ownership, the States Parties to this Convention undertake, as appropriate for each country, to set up within their territories one or more national services, where such services do not already exist, for the protection of the cultural heritage, with a qualified staff sufficient in number for the effective carrying out of the following functions:

a. contributing to the formation of draft laws and regulations designed to secure the protection of the cultural heritage and particularly prevention of the illicit import, export and transfer of ownership of important cultural property;
b. establishing and keeping up to date, on the basis of a national inventory of protected property, a list of important public and private cultural property whose export would constitute an appreciable impoverishment of the national cultural heritage;
c. promoting the development or the establishment of scientific and technical institutions (museums, libraries, archives, laboratories, workshops . . .) required to ensure the preservation and presentation of cultural property;
d. organizing the supervision of archaeological excavations, ensuring the preservation "*in situ*" of certain cultural property, and protecting certain areas reserved for future archaeological research;
e. establishing, for the benefit of those concerned (curators, collectors, antique dealers, etc.) rules in conformity with the ethical principles set forth in this Convention; and taking steps to ensure the observance of those rules;
f. taking educational measures to stimulate and develop respect for the cultural heritage of all States, and spreading knowledge of the provisions of this Convention;
g. seeing that appropriate publicity is given to the disappearance of any items of cultural property.

On one reading, Article 5 may seem to have a very limited application today. The phrase 'where such services do not already exist' might be understood to limit the scope to a very small number of States or to none at all, since practically all States will now have services of one form or another. The situation was very different in 1970, a time when ex-colonial territories and other successor States were still in the process of setting up their own administrations to deal with cultural property.

A more logical reading of Article 5, however, would interpret it to apply when services do exist but may not cover one or more of the listed functions, or not cover them adequately. It can be persuasively argued that filling the gap is in effect making provision for services that do not already exist. There is no point in setting up a service to carry out functions unless the capability exists to carry them out. This will also need funding, as is set out at Article 14. Article 5 requires qualified staff 'sufficient in number for the effective carrying out' of the functions. Often the ministry responsible for heritage is relatively low down in the structure of government, with a lack of political clout when finances are allocated. Article 5 therefore puts pressure on States Parties by basing the level of funding on the need to effectively carry out the listed functions.

The obligations in Article 5 are qualified by the words 'as appropriate for each country'. Some take the view that the phrase converts what would otherwise be legal obligations into moral ones.[1] Although the inclusion of this phrase has undoubtedly given States wide discretion,[2] it has not eliminated all legal obligation. It would be appropriate not to act, for example, if a State already had national services of this kind, or took the view that certain functions were not at issue, perhaps because illicit excavation was not a problem in that particular State. However, in a situation involving overwhelming evidence of cultural property deterioration, coupled with the inadequacy of existing services, a State Party that failed to act would be in breach of the obligations of this Article. Fraoua takes the sensible view that the words 'as appropriate for each country' relate only to the legal and financial resources of the country concerned.[3] He considers that every State has an obligation to create a national service for the protection of cultural property, but need not require it to perform tasks which would demand resources disproportionate to its capacity.[4] In practice, most States reporting on implementation indicate the existence of national services in their respective jurisdictions.[5]

Above all, there must be adequate consultation and flow of information between parts of the national administration. The service responsible for protection of cultural property cannot possibly cover all aspects of this alone. The police, Customs, finance and other specialised agencies must be aware of how their operations will affect cultural property and co-ordinate with the agency directly charged with responsibility for protection. In several States it may be necessary for religious authorities to be involved as well.

Article 5 requires, self-evidently, a reciprocal trust between the national service responsible for cultural property and the public. The former can easily come to see itself as the sole guardian of that property due to its technical expertise. But that is only part of the job of keeping heritage safe. The public also needs to have an emotional attachment to the cultural heritage supported by a belief that the national service will act to support that heritage.

Paragraph (a) speaks of drafting laws and regulations. In principle of course this may be a difficult task for hard-pressed cultural services. For it to be done effectively, the draftsperson must have experience and be able to translate into legal language the policy goals as set out. To facilitate the process, UNESCO and UNIDROIT produced in 2011 the Model Provisions on State Ownership of

[1] RD Abramson and SB Huttler, 'The Legal response to the Illicit Movement of Cultural Property' (1973) 5 *Law and Policy in International Business* 932, 962.

[2] PM Bator, 'An Essay on the International Trade in Art' (1982) 34 *Stanford Law Review* 275, 377.

[3] R Fraoua, *Convention concernant les mesures à prendre pour interdire et empêcher l'importation, l'exportation et le transfert de propriété illicites des biens culturels* (Unesdoc CC-86/WS/40, 1986) 62.

[4] O'Keefe agreed wholeheartedly with Fraoua's view: see *Protecting Cultural Objects* (2017) 143.

[5] For the 2019–2022 reporting cycle, UNESCO has noted that, of the 91 States reporting on implementation of the Convention, nearly 70% responded that their national services were established at a level that was 'excellent' (15%), 'very good' (29%) or 'good' (25%): Subsidiary Committee of the Meeting of States Parties, 11th Session, C70/23/11.SC/7 (Paris, UNESCO, 1–2 June 2023) p 10.

Undiscovered Cultural Objects[6] and, more recently, UNESCO approved Model Provisions for implementing the 1970 Convention itself.[7] Where adequate legislation already exists at the time the State becomes Party to the Convention, the provision would seem to require the State to periodically assess and revise such legislation to ensure that it remains effective. It is interesting to note that the clear majority of States Parties, in their reporting, indicate the existence of adequate legislation in implementing the Convention.[8]

Paragraph (b) then refers to a list of important public and private cultural property whose export would constitute an appreciable impoverishment of the national cultural heritage. This list is to be established 'on the basis of a national inventory of protected property'. Some discussion has taken place as to the relationship of this inventory to the requirement, in Article 1, that cultural property of importance be specifically designated. The French authorities, for example, made the following comments on the draft Convention:

> An inventory of this sort is in fact kept in France, apart from the cataloguing of items or collections of outstanding interest. The authorities do not, however, consider it possible to make use of this inventory which is extremely bulky and prepared with a strictly scientific intention, for purposes of the supervision of dealings in the property in question.[9]

In commenting on this section of the Article, the Secretariat stated:

> The inventory is not established for the purpose of the customs, but for scientific purposes which will encourage the study and classifying of the various items that make up the cultural heritage and determine those objects which should be preserved and subject to export prohibition and those the legal transfer of which from the country can be authorized.[10]

Such an inventory should reveal, for example, the rarity and quality of objects of a particular type and allow judgements to be made as to their need for protection. The making of such an inventory places a large burden on States poor in resources. However, the inventory need not, as pointed out by the Secretariat, be a single volume: '… each museum, town or region can establish the sections relating to their respective cultural property.'[11]

Bákula is highly critical of the role of inventories as set out in Article 5. She states that the Convention's reference to a 'national inventory of protected

[6] Model Provisions on State Ownership of Undiscovered Cultural Objects (2011).

[7] Model Provisions on the Prevention and Fight against the Illicit Trafficking of Cultural Property (Paris, UNESCO, May 2025). See below at IV, ch 3(iii).

[8] For the 2019–2022 reporting cycle, UNESCO has noted that, of the 91 States reporting on implementation of the Convention, over 70% did so by a special law either alone or in combination with civil and/or criminal law, while 66% reported a change in legal framework as a result of ratification: Subsidiary Committee of the Meeting of States Parties, 11th Session, C70/23/11.SC/7 (Paris, UNESCO, 1–2 June 2023) pp 6–7.

[9] Unesdoc SHC/MD/5 Annex I, 8.

[10] Unesdoc SHC/MD/5 Annex II, 5.

[11] Unesdoc SHC/MD/5 Annex II, 5.

property' implies selecting only 'part of each country's movable cultural heritage'.[12] Certainly it does that, but selection of what may be considered 'heritage' is an integral part of any logical system of cultural property management. Not everything can be considered heritage and, particularly for controlling illicit trafficking in a national context, there must be an element of selection. It is true that undiscovered archaeological objects cannot be on an inventory, but legislation providing for State ownership of such material, as suggested by UNESCO and UNIDROIT, can fill the gap.[13]

Inventories can, of course, be assembled with the help of NGOs and civil society. For example, the International Foundation for Art Research (IFAR) worked in Peru with the National Institute of Culture and the Catholic Church to organise, provide staff for and fund the making of an inventory of paintings in selected churches.[14] In Ukraine, following Russia's full-scale invasion in 2022, a Digital Museum Fund Register was set up to record all data on the country's museum artefacts, a project funded by USAID, UK Dev and Switzerland, carried out by the Eurasia Foundation, EGAP and the East Europe Foundation, a Ukrainian NGO.[15]

Certain States have a very clear inventory of national heritage: Switzerland is a prime example with its 'Inventory of Cultural Property of National and Regional Importance'.[16] In fact, of the States Parties reporting on their implementation of the Convention, a clear majority have indicated the existence of a national inventory of cultural property.[17]

Other States might apply a 'listing' approach, but only when it comes to the export of objects of national importance. In this way, Canada created an export 'Control List' which sets out categories of important material for which an export permit will in the first instance be required,[18] later taking account of whether the export would 'significantly diminish the national heritage' (words similar to those in paragraph (b), ie 'an appreciable impoverishment of the national cultural heritage').[19] Australia has its own type of Control List, which is split into two categories:

[12] C Bákula, 'Combating Trafficking in Cultural Property: The 1970 Convention: Evaluation and Prospects' background paper for participants in the Second Meeting of States Parties to the 1970 Convention (Paris, UNESCO, 20–21 June 2012) 3.

[13] See the UNESCO-UNIDROIT Model Provisions on State Ownership of Undiscovered Cultural Objects (2011) Art 3.

[14] FJ Truslow, 'The IFAR Inventory of Cuzco Churches and Its Lessons' (2013) 14 *IFAR Journal* 28.

[15] Digital State UA (Ministry of Digital Transformation of Ukraine), 'How Ukraine's Digital Museum Fund Protects Cultural Heritage in Wartime' (5 August 2025): this project of the Ministry of Digital Transformation was carried out by the Eurasia Foundation with assistance from USAID and UK Dev, as well as others such as Switzerland.

[16] The inventory was created in 1988 and has been updated in 1995, 2009 and 2023.

[17] For the 2019–2022 reporting cycle, UNESCO has noted that, of the 91 States reporting on implementation of the Convention, nearly 70% have indicated the existence of a national inventory of cultural property that is excellent (13%), very good (32%) or good (23%): Subsidiary Committee of the Meeting of States Parties, 11th Session, C70/23/11.SC/7 (Paris, UNESCO, 1–2 June 2023) pp 6–7. On these national inventories, 70% said that all, almost all or most protected cultural property was inventoried: p 17.

[18] Cultural Property Export and Import Act 1975, s 8(3).

[19] ibid s 11(1).

Class A objects that cannot be permanently exported (listing specific objects such as Victoria Crosses and Ned Kelly's armour) and Class B objects which can be exported only by permit.[20] The UK does not have a formal government listing system, not even a 'control list' for exports; it relies instead on criteria for protection, namely the three 'Waverley criteria' (importance to history/national life, outstanding aesthetic importance and outstanding importance for scholarship), to be applied by the export authorities.[21] The view was taken at the time of the UK's ratification of the 1970 Convention that this export licensing system was sufficient to comply with Article 5. As the Ministerial Advisory Panel set out in its advice at the time:

> We are convinced that the UK's current export licensing system, with its list of categories of the type of objects that will qualify, satisfy this requirement. Australia and Canada, both of which have acceded to the UNESCO Convention, have broadly similar export control systems.[22]

It should also be noted that, according to paragraph (b), the list has to be kept 'up to date', so must not be treated as a static document. It also applies equally to public and private ownership, reflecting the general philosophy of the Convention which is concerned with heritage value irrespective of ownership. States may need to encourage private owners to register important cultural objects by tax or other incentives.

What impact might the inventory have on achieving the principal aim of the Convention, namely to curb illicit trade? Many years ago, Chatelain pointed out that a scientific inventory may not contain the information needed to easily and quickly identify a stolen or unlawfully traded object.[23] In 1993, the Getty Information Institute initiated a collaborative project with government administrations, museums, dealers, police, Customs, the insurance industry and appraisers to develop an international documentation standard for the information needed

[20] Protection of Movable Cultural Heritage Act 1986, ss 8,10, and accompanying Protection of Movable Cultural Heritage Regulations 2018, Schedule 1 (7.3), (9.2A).

[21] See DCMS Statutory Guidance, 'Export Controls on Objects of Cultural Interest' (London, DCMS, December 2020) para 12. The export authorities consist of the Export Licensing Unit at Arts Council England, the Expert Advisers, the Reviewing Committee on the Export of Works of Art and the DCMS. The Secretary of State makes the ultimate decision on whether to defer an export licence on the basis of the three 'Waverley criteria' (history/national life, aesthetic significance, significance for study).

[22] Advisory Panel on the Illicit Trade (2000) para 56. It should be noted that the Australian and Canadian systems are in fact somewhat different, since they each operate an export Control List set out in legislation, unlike the UK. Subsequent to this, Parliament passed the Export of Objects of Cultural Interest (Control) Order 2003 under the Export Control Act 2002, which requires a licence for any 'object of cultural interest' manufactured or produced over 50 years before export, with limited listed exceptions like postage stamps and birth, marriage or death certificates (ss 1–2, Schedule 1). This operates in conjunction with various date and value thresholds as set out by the Secretary of State from time to time under Article 2 of the 2003 Order. It might therefore be argued that the UK's equivalent of a 'control list' includes cultural objects in the relevant categories that are above the thresholds, though it is not a list of specific objects per se.

[23] J Chatelain, 'Means of Combating the Theft of and Illegal Traffic in Works of Art in the Nine Countries of the EEC' (Commission of the European Communities, Doc.XII/920/79-E, 1976) 48.

to identify specific items of cultural property.[24] Out of this came the 'Object ID' standard which was endorsed by the thirtieth General Conference of UNESCO in November 1999, following a Recommendation by the ICPRCP, and has now been widely adopted around the world.[25] The 'Object ID' is the international standard for recording data on movable cultural property which should be used to the fullest extent possible by all States. The Object ID entry requires photographs as well as other important information about the relevant object, such as type, material and date.[26]

Photographs, in particular, are hugely valuable in the hunt for illicitly trafficked objects, especially used in conjunction with other indicators. For example, it was the cache of photographs discovered in the Swiss warehouse used by trafficker Giacomo Medici in 1995 that helped uncover the vast smuggling network that had brought looted Italian artefacts to museums around the world.[27] Mattern explains how among the evidence was a striking pair of photographs:

> The first image was that of 'two dirt-encrusted fragments of a terra-cotta figure,' which the Italian prosecutors maintained was taken after the fragments were excavated from the earth; it was noted that signs of smoke damage were visible on the fragments. The second was an image of the same terra-cotta figure, bearing the same signs of smoke damage, but intact and now part of the J. Paul Getty Museum collection.[28]

Mattern concludes that the 'international community views photography as a form of documentation that can help to deter illicit trade and aid in identification and recovery should the need arise'.[29] Photographs should therefore be seen as part of an object's essential documentation as set out in paragraph (b), as well as in the wider Convention.

Inventories provide extra protection for collections at times when that protection is needed most. After civil war broke out in Syria in 2011, for instance, much reliance was placed by the international community on officially documented collections from Syrian institutions. For instance, the European Union prohibited the importation, export or transfer of Syrian cultural property, particularly goods forming 'an integral part of either the public collections listed in the inventories of the conservation collections of Syrian museums, archives or libraries, or

[24] See R Thornes with P Dorrell and H Lie, 'Introduction to Object ID: Guidelines for Making Records that Describe Art, Antiques and Antiquities', Getty Information Institute (Los Angeles, J Paul Getty Trust, 1999).

[25] Supported, for instance, by ICOM, Interpol, ICCROM, UNESCO and the World Customs Organisation. ICOM holds the licence rights to promote the use of the standard among museum professionals.

[26] The 'Object ID' checklist lists the following information to be entered, along with photographs: type of objects, materials and techniques, measurements, inscriptions and markings, distinguishing features, title, subject, date, period and maker, as well as a short description.

[27] For more on this infamous case, see P Watson and C Todeschini, *The Medici Conspiracy: The Illicit Journey of Looted Antiquities* (New York, Public Affairs, 2007).

[28] E Mattern, 'The Role of Photography in the Protection, Identification, and Recovery of Cultural Heritage' (2012) 19 *International Journal of Cultural Property* 133, 144.

[29] ibid 146.

the inventories of Syrian religious institutions'.[30] After Russia's full-scale invasion of Ukraine in 2022, documented collections were relied upon to demonstrate the extent of Russian looting of Ukrainian institutions,[31] with the Ukrainian Government creating the 'Digital Museum Fund' for this very purpose.[32] And in situations of natural disaster, inventories are essential in recovery efforts: in the midst of the fire at Notre-Dame Cathedral in Paris in April 2019, the inventory allowed firefighters to recover valuable objects from the treasury, including the famous 'Crown of Thorns' relic.[33]

Paragraph (c) requires the national services to promote development or establishment of institutions (museums, libraries, archives etc.) to ensure the preservation and presentation of cultural property. This does not require the national service to actually establish such institutions, only to 'promote' their development or establishment; a less onerous activity.

Paragraph (d) asks national services to organise the supervision of archaeological excavation, ensure the preservation *in situ* of certain cultural property, and protect certain areas for future archaeological research. The first part of this provision is clearly directed at clandestine excavation, which severely damages archaeological heritage. Ensuring preservation *in situ* and preserving areas for future research are both widely accepted in archaeological practice for sites on land. For example, they were included in UNESCO's 1956 Recommendation on International Principles Applicable to Archaeological Excavations.[34] Likewise, the European Convention on the Protection of the Archaeological Heritage (Revised) of 1992 requires that States Parties undertake to implement measures 'for the conservation and maintenance of the archaeological heritage, preferably *in situ*' (Article 4). The 2001 Convention on the Protection of the Underwater Cultural Heritage shows a preference for preservation of shipwrecks *in situ* at Article 2(5):

> The preservation *in situ* of underwater cultural heritage shall be considered as the first option before allowing or engaging in any activities directed at this heritage.

Note that this remains the 'first option'. It is not an absolute undertaking, but will depend on circumstances.

[30] Council Regulation (EU) No 36/2012 of 18 January 2012 concerning restrictive measures in view of the situation in Syria (as amended), Article 11c.

[31] An example is the looting of the Kherson Art Museum by Russian occupying forces in 2022, with many of the works being brought to occupied Crimea, where they remained after Kherson's liberation by the Ukrainians. The director of the museum claims that more than 10,000 artworks (out of a collection of 14,000) were stolen in this way: S Kishkovsky, 'These are Terrible Crimes: A Ukrainian Museum Director's Fight to Recover Art', *The Art Newspaper* (16 July 2024).

[32] Digital State UA (Ministry of Digital Transformation of Ukraine), 'How Ukraine's Digital Museum Fund Protects Cultural Heritage in Wartime' (5 August 2025).

[33] S Asaf, 'Crown of thorns returns to Notre-Dame Cathedral after fire' (*BBC News*, 13 December 2024).

[34] Articles 21, 9.

Protecting archaeological areas is no easy task, particularly if they are large and remote or difficult to access. Guards may be hired to protect a site from looters and other intruders. In many countries, whether this is effective often depends on how enthusiastic the guards are and how much they are paid.[35] The Operational Guidelines for the 1970 Convention recommend that local communities should be encouraged to protect sites as well.[36] This is of course sensible, but will require a dedicated team to oversee it to ensure it is self-sustaining over time.

According to paragraph (e), the national service must also establish ethical guidelines for collectors and curators, amongst others. The Preliminary Study on the draft Convention text of the late 1960s stated that:

> It is essential that the new rules to be worked out for acquisitions shall place collectors and dealers on the same footing as curators; otherwise museums would be restrained for the sole benefit of illicit trade in cultural property.[37]

The United States, at least initially, made ethical acquisition a matter of choice for museums and placed no restraint at all on private collectors. This could arguably benefit the least scrupulous collectors. In order to fight the inertia amongst dealers, UNESCO developed an International Code of Ethics for Dealers in Cultural Property which was adopted in 1999.[38] An update was endorsed in 2026.

Paragraph (f) requires States Parties to take educational measures to stimulate and develop respect for the cultural heritage of all States and to spread knowledge of the provisions of the Convention.[39] The Preliminary Study mentioned above had stated that:

> Strong action must be taken against carelessness, ignorance, to say nothing of political or religious fanaticism, which influence the fate of cultural property.[40]

Education must of course benefit the wider public, but there is also an element of 'specialist' education required in order to truly serve the goals of the Convention. For example, police, lawyers, prosecutors and judges all need to be aware of the special problems posed by clandestine excavation, theft and illicit trafficking.[41] A prosecutor may treat the clandestine excavation of a site as relatively minor compared to capital crimes such as murder. A judge may see the illicit export of a pot as a white-collar crime deserving only a minor penalty. Education is therefore

[35] S Dural, *Protecting Çatalhöyük: Memoir of an Archaeological Site Guard* (Walnut Creek, Left Coast Press, 2007).

[36] Para 47.

[37] Unesdoc SHC/MD/3, 7. See further above, I, ch 2(ii).

[38] See above, IV, ch 3(iv).

[39] Art 5(f).

[40] Above (n 37). See also I, ch 2(ii).

[41] See, eg, the Port Vila declaration for Melanesia, 7 August 2015: UNESCO, *Workshop on the Fight Against the Illicit Trafficking of Cultural Property in Melanesia*, Port Vila, Vanuatu, 5–7 August 2015, p 38.

needed amongst such groups to demonstrate the larger consequences of cultural property crime.[42]

In order to be effective, specialists in the field in many countries will need to be given viable career paths.[43] A career path does not mean that officials spend their entire working life dealing with matters of cultural property. They should nevertheless be encouraged to specialise, given credit for the work they have done and promoted accordingly.

Lastly, paragraph (g) requires that 'appropriate publicity' be given to the disappearance of items of cultural property.[44] What is 'appropriate'? The Preliminary Study is helpful once more:

> The disappearance of any cultural object should, at the request of the State claiming that object, be brought to the knowledge of the public by means of appropriate publicity … If such publicity should not lead to the immediate recovery of the cultural object, it would have the merit of drawing the attention of the public, specialist circles in particular, to the object in question. The latter would then be unmarketable, with the result that the holder, to avoid serious trouble, might be induced to restore it to its owner.[45]

In the 1980s, Fraoua suggested that 'appropriate publicity would be that which would bring the loss to the attention of the greatest number of people', such as publication in specialist journals dealing with the sale and purchase of cultural objects.[46] Of course, we have moved on significantly since then, and most of the publicity or registration of thefts would now be done online.

While there is no centralised list on which States can register looted property, INTERPOL has a list of some 57,000 stolen objects, used to assist law enforcement,[47] while the Art Loss Register keeps its own list of some 700,000 objects, which can be consulted by subscribers, including art market professionals.[48] ICOM has over 20 'Red Lists' of antiquities at risk, designed to assist police, Customs, dealers and parties acquiring objects from countries or regions with particularly problematic histories of looting (eg Iraq, Syria, Afghanistan, Mexico, Peru, Brazil, Ukraine), though these only list *types* of objects, not actual stolen pieces.[49] UNESCO initiated a campaign called 'The Real Price of Art' in 2020, which sought

[42] As an example of sensitivity displayed by a judge to cultural heritage value, in the English case of *R v Hakimzadeh* [2009] EWCA Crim 959, the offender cut out pages from Persian manuscripts at two important libraries and the sentencing judge recognised that damage to such material 'can diminish the intellectual and cultural heritage of the nation', thus prompting a higher sentence, affirmed by the Court of Appeal: see case note by K Warner, 'Theft of Cultural Heritage: *R v Hakimzadeh*' (April 2010) XV *Art Antiquity and Law* 95.

[43] See this in relation to Andean heritage: F Berrios, 'Lessons Learned in the Andean Region and Central America' in H van Hooff (ed), *Culture & Development: Stop the Illicit Traffic of Cultural Property* (Havana, UNESCO Regional Office, 2013) 42, 43.

[44] Art 5(g).

[45] Unesdoc SHC/MD/3, 7. See also I, ch 2(ii).

[46] Fraoua (n 3) 67.

[47] See Interpol website, 'Stolen Works of Art database': www.interpol.int/en/Crimes/Cultural-heritage-crime/Stolen-Works-of-Art-Database.

[48] See Art Loss Register website: www.artloss.com.

[49] ICOM Red List Database: icom.museum/en/resources/red-lists/.

to highlight the risks of dealing in certain types of looted cultural objects.[50] Then, in 2025, it launched a much bigger project, at a reported cost of over $2 million: 'The Virtual Museum of Stolen Cultural Objects'.[51] This online database included several hundred looted or stolen objects from the world over, based on entries from the INTERPOL database. The visually-impressive website is clearly meant to increase publicity for such objects – furthering the goals of Article 5(g) of the 1970 Convention.

From a legal perspective, it can also be said that the publicity provision goes some way towards solving the complex problems associated with the *bona fide* purchaser. In fact, during the drafting process of the Convention, UNIDROIT was of the opinion that an international publicity campaign relating to a lost cultural object would make it possible, in a civil lawsuit, to 'cast doubt on the good faith' of any future acquirer of such property so as to preclude the use of a defence related to the good faith purchase or possession, facilitating the object's eventual return.[52]

To conclude, it should be clear by this point that Article 5 of the Convention goes well beyond the mechanics of import and export, outlining the broader responsibility of States for national protection of the cultural heritage. That protection could be called one of the more effective means of preventing illicit traffic. A State not only has a responsibility to its own people in that respect, but also to humanity.[53]

[50] UNESCO, 'The Real Price of Art, International UNESCO campaign reveals the hidden fact of art trafficking' (20 October 2020). There has been criticism of this campaign: N Kenney, 'UNESCO under fire for using Met objects in anti-trafficking campaign', *The Art Newspaper* (13 November 2020).

[51] UNESCO, 'Virtual Museum of Stolen Cultural Objects' (Oct 2025). For cost, see A Schrader, 'UNESCO has teamed up with Interpol to Build a Virtual Museum of Stolen Cultural Artifacts' (*artnet*, 13 October 2023).

[52] As relayed in the Preliminary Study on the draft, Unesdoc SHC/MD/3, 7.

[53] In this way, compare statements in the preambles to other international conventions which speak of the common heritage of humanity: cf Hague Convention of 1954, para 2; World Heritage Convention of 1972, para 2; and the Convention on the Protection and Promotion of the Diversity of Cultural Expression of 2001, para 2.

Article 6

The States Parties to this Convention undertake:

a. to introduce an appropriate certificate in which the exporting State would specify that the export of the cultural property in question is authorized. The certificate should accompany all items of cultural property exported in accordance with the regulations;
b. to prohibit the exportation of cultural property from their territory unless accompanied by the above-mentioned export certificate;
c. to publicize this prohibition by appropriate means, particularly among persons likely to export or import cultural property.

Article 6 requires parties to introduce an export certificate for cultural property, to prohibit export unless accompanied by such a certificate and to publicise this prohibition. An assumption might be that these obligations are intended primarily for source States, in order to ensure they have appropriate schemes in place to monitor what is leaving, though the provision of course applies to all States Parties. Noticeably absent from the provision is any mention of provenance checks at the point of export, checks that have been considered more recently by certain market States.[1]

Bator called the provision an 'unfortunate holdover' from an earlier draft.[2] Abramson and Huttler state that, because import controls were restricted to property stolen from public institutions (at Article 7(b)(i)), any other cultural property, even if stolen from private collections or otherwise illegally exported, is not specifically protected by the Convention:

> In essence, illegally exported property can be legally imported, and will not be subject to the Convention's forfeiture provisions.[3]

As such, they argue, Article 6 has been 'emasculated … and it retains only minimal significance'.[4] This interpretation can of course be made only if Article 3 is held to have no substantive effect. If that is the case, then why include Article 6 at all? Since both provisions must have been intended to mean *something*, it could instead be argued that Article 6 must ensure that States that set up export controls in accordance with the Convention can expect to have them recognised and supported by other States Parties – one way to do so would be through Article 3.[5] Frigo, for one,

[1] Switzerland requires exporters to indicate in a Customs Declaration where an archaeological or paleontological object was found: see below, V, ch 4. The UK has investigated provenance in export licensing: Institute of Art and Law, *Research Report: Export Licensing and Provenance* (London, Department for Culture, Media and Sport, 3 June 2025).

[2] PM Bator, 'An Essay on the International Trade in Art' (1982) 34 *Stanford Law Review* 275, 377.

[3] RD Abramson and SB Huttler, 'The Legal response to the Illicit Movement of Cultural Property' (1973) 5 *Law and Policy in International Business* 932, 961.

[4] ibid.

[5] This view has been forcefully set out in previous editions of this book, as well as in PJ O'Keefe, *Protecting Cultural Objects: Before and After 1970* (Builth Wells, Institute of Art and Law, 2017) 135–38, 151.

emphasises that Article 6 is no less important than the other provisions of the Convention.[6]

Raschèr et al interpret Article 6 in relation to Article 3:

> … exporting a country's cultural property requires official authorization eg each export must be accompanied by the aforementioned certification. The export is considered illegal in terms of Article 3 UNESCO Convention 1970 without the export certificate. This type of certificate as well as publicizing legal regulations governing export are primarily intended to promote the legal certainty for the transfer of cultural property.[7]

There seems, moreover, to be some misapprehension as to what Article 6 actually requires by way of the imposition of export controls. Bator, for example, says that 'the United States could not and would not give up the right to decide for itself whether and when to apply export controls over works of art'[8] and that 'almost every country in the world restricts and regulates the export of cultural property; the outstanding exception is the United States of America'.[9] This position was set out in the United States' Reservation under the Convention, regarding export controls.[10] However, the United States does restrict the export of certain categories of material (such as certain Native American material and pieces taken from national monuments).[11] It would therefore not be giving up that right in accepting Article 6 of the Convention. All it would be undertaking, in addition to its normal practice, would be some use of an export certificate. This need not be in respect of all cultural material, but only such as has been designated as protected. Under the Canadian system, only cultural property listed in the Control List needs an export permit; the rest does not. Assuming that every piece of cultural property from any State Party to the Convention requires an export certificate would not be a sensible interpretation of Article 6. The suggestion that it does, coupled with the United States' interpretation of what is required by way of Customs control, imparts to the Convention an air of impracticality which it does not merit.

The Committee of Experts studying the implementation of the Convention in 1983 suggested that it would be of assistance to developing States to establish model export certificates which would be universally accepted, thus indicating their espousal of the interpretation suggested here.[12] In 2005, UNESCO and the World Customs Organization (WCO) published just such a model certificate.[13] In the Certificate, the exporter must provide the expected sort of information

[6] M Frigo, *La protezione dei beni culturali nel diritto internazionale* (Milan, Giuffrè Editore, 1986) 212.
[7] AFG Raschèr, M Bauen, Y Fischer and MN Zen-Ruffinen, *Cultural Property Transfer* (Brussels, Zurich; Bruyland, Schulthess, 2005) 20.
[8] Bator (n 2) 377.
[9] ibid 314.
[10] See below, V, ch 6.
[11] See below, ibid, for more.
[12] Unesdoc 22 C/93, 5.
[13] CLT-2005/WS/5.

(name, address, details on the exporter, etc), as well as details about the object itself (dimensions, weight, inventory number, etc) and any relevant dating, geographical origin, attribution and so forth. This should be accompanied by photographs and catalogue references. The completed application must be endorsed by a Customs export office.

It is worth noting that States themselves, in their reporting, tend to indicate the overwhelming existence of legislation or regulation to control the export of cultural property from their respective territories.[14]

[14] For the 2019–2022 reporting cycle, UNESCO has noted that, of the 91 States reporting on implementation of the Convention, over 90% reported legislation and/or regulations in place to control the export of cultural property: Subsidiary Committee of the Meeting of States Parties, 11th Session, C70/23/11.SC/7 (Paris, UNESCO, 1–2 June 2023) p 10.

Article 7

The States Parties to this Convention undertake:

a. To take the necessary measures, consistent with national legislation, to prevent museums and similar institutions within their territories from acquiring cultural property originating in another State Party which has been illegally exported after entry into force of this Convention, in the States concerned. Whenever possible, to inform a State of origin Party to this Convention of an offer of such cultural property illegally removed from that State after the entry into force of this Convention in both States;

b. i. to prohibit the import of cultural property stolen from a museum or a religious or secular public monument or similar institution in another State Party to this Convention after the entry into force of this Convention for the States concerned, provided that such property is documented as appertaining to the inventory of that institution;

   ii. at the request of the State Party of origin, to take appropriate steps to recover and return any such cultural property imported after the entry into force of this Convention in both States concerned, provided, however, that the requesting State shall pay just compensation to an innocent purchaser or to a person who has valid title to that property. Requests for recovery and return shall be made through diplomatic offices. The requesting Party shall furnish, at its expense, the documentation and other evidence necessary to establish its claim for recovery and return. The Parties shall impose no customs duties or other charges upon cultural property returned pursuant to this Article. All expenses incident to the return and delivery of the cultural property shall be borne by the requesting Party.

The complex and highly detailed Article 7 was based on a provision proposed to the drafting committee by the United States in the leadup to 1970.[1] It replaced a draft provision which complemented the export control provision in Article 6 by requiring importing States to treat cultural property illegally exported from its State of origin as an illegal import.[2] The existing provision, it will be seen, is far more limited than this.

Some argue that Article 7 is the core of the 1970 Convention. For example, Pavoni states: 'As is well known, the restitution obligation envisaged by the 1970 Convention only covers property stolen from museums and religious or public monuments and institutions',[3] ie those mentioned in Article 7(b)(i). Previous editions of this commentary considered this a limited interpretation

[1] Above, I, ch 2(ii).

[2] RD Abramson and SB Huttler, 'The Legal Response to the Illicit Movement of Cultural Property' (1973) 5 *Law and Policy in International Business* 932, 951.

[3] R Pavoni, 'Sovereign Immunity and the Enforcement of International Cultural Property Law' in F Francioni and J Gordley (eds), *Enforcing International Cultural Heritage Law* (Oxford, Oxford University Press, 2013) 79, 81.

of the Convention and instead proposed that Article 7 be read as subsidiary to Article 3, which sets out the guiding principle of the Convention: that illicitly exported cultural property should be regarded as an illicit import.[4] Nevertheless, we will consider the provision in detail, first paragraph (a) applying to acquiring institutions, then paragraph (b)(i) relating to import restrictions and finally paragraph (b) (ii) relating to restitution and compensation.

Paragraph (a)

The obligation imposed by this subsection is:

> to take the necessary measures, consistent with national legislation, to prevent museums and similar institutions within their territories from acquiring cultural property originating in another State Party which has been illegally exported …

At the request of the US delegation to UNESCO in 1970, the words 'consistent with national legislation' were inserted into an earlier provision, and it was stated that the section would be interpreted so as to confine the effect of this measure to museums whose acquisition policies are controlled by the State. This interpretation appears to have almost vitiated the provision as far as the United States is concerned, since there appear to be only two – at most three or four – such institutions in that country.[5] Some US commentators feel certain that this was the intended effect of the amendment,[6] although it seems to remove one of the most important steps in stemming illicit traffic, especially in light of the minimalist view taken of Articles 5(e), 5(f), 5(g) and 10, which imply a duty to encourage responsible acquisition policies in collecting institutions.

A more sophisticated view of Article 7(a) has been developed by Nafziger, who points out that the present provision was a compromise between a 'weak' amendment, which would have required parties, *inter alia*, (1) to transmit to museums and other institutions the text of the Convention and (2) to make every effort to obtain the support of such museums and institutions for the principles of ethical acquisition;[7] and a 'strong' amendment, which would have prohibited acquisition of cultural property by any museum within the territory of a State Party unless accompanied by an export certificate from its State of origin.[8] If the compromise

[4] See as well PJ O'Keefe, *Protecting Cultural Objects: Before and After 1970* (Builth Wells, Institute of Art and Law, 2017) 135–38, 153.

[5] Only two if the National Archives and Library of Congress, possibly more if the Smithsonian Institution and National Gallery of Art are included, though their status is somewhat complicated.

[6] Abramson and Huttler (n 2) 965–66; PM Bator, 'An Essay on the International Trade in Art' (1982) 34 *Stanford Law Review* 275, 380.

[7] Note the apparently similar requirement on States in the European Convention on the Protection of the Archaeological Heritage (Revised) 1992, Art 10(iv).

[8] JAR Nafziger, 'Article 7(a) of the UNESCO Convention' in LD DuBoff, *Art Law: Domestic and International* (South Hackensack, Fred B. Rothman & Co., 1975) 387, 388–89.

was between these two positions, Article 7(a) cannot be logically interpreted to be weaker than the 'weak' position,[9] which at least required transmission of information to the appropriate institutions and encouragement of ethical acquisition policies. Nafziger argues that, while almost all museums cannot be considered instrumentalities of the United States Government, they are subject to control, because of the tax advantages and outright support that accrue to US museums from all levels of government. Government regulation of acquisition policies, he suggests, might be tied, as a sort of *quid pro quo*, to further support of museums by the government.[10]

This has happened in the United Kingdom where adherence to the 1970 Convention and the ethical code adopted by the UK Museums Association are conditions of museum accreditation for funding purposes.[11] Similarly, the Swiss Working Group stated in 1999:

> A ban on acquisition of stolen cultural objects can be implemented by directive for museums with public funding without a formal legislative basis. This applies at the federal level as well as at the cantonal and community levels. Museums with important joint financing by public funds or private cultural institutions can be called upon to comply with the ban: if subsidies are provided, related conditions can be linked to their use.[12]

Interestingly, the Swiss implementing legislation, enacted in 2005, introduced a *legislative* ban on Federal institutions acquiring – or even exhibiting – stolen, unlawfully excavated or unlawfully exported cultural property, thus taking this provision even further.[13] Similarly, Denmark has a legislative ban on its museums acquiring cultural objects illegally exported from a State Party to the Convention.[14]

While today in the United States curatorial consensus has supported the Convention and ethical acquisition policies have been adopted by many institutions, there remain outliers whose principles and practice do not reach these standards. It might not be unfairly expected of a government to draw the attention of such outliers to the desirability of ethical practice and the standards established by the Convention and to make any further government assistance dependent upon the adoption of ethical policies.

[9] See the European Convention on the Protection of the Archaeological Heritage (Revised) 1992, which makes a 'weak' requirement for ethical practice aimed at museums not under State control, at Art 10(iv); a much stronger requirement exists regarding museums under State control at Art 10(iii) of that Convention.

[10] Nafziger (n 8) 391–92.

[11] The Museums Accreditation Scheme is managed by Arts Council England: see Arts Council England, *Collections development policy template* (2014) paras 6.1, 9.3. Para 9.3 specifically requires museums to include in their acquisition policies a statement that, with reference to the 1970 Convention, they will 'reject any items that have been illicitly traded.'

[12] Working Group, *International Transfer of Cultural Objects: UNESCO Convention of 1970 and UNIDROIT Convention of 1995* (Berne, Federal Office of Culture, 1999) 31–32.

[13] Swiss Act on International Transfer of Cultural Property (2005), Art 15.

[14] Danish Law on Museums No 358 of 8 April 2014, s 33.

Paragraph (b)(i)

Article 7(b)(i) requires States to prohibit import of cultural property stolen from a museum, religious or secular public monument or similar institution in a State Party to the Convention, provided that the property is documented in the inventory of the institution. The paragraph could be seen to have a relatively limited application, since it does not require import restrictions on other illicitly removed cultural property, such as cultural property illegally excavated, stolen from a private home or indeed illegally exported though not necessarily stolen. The requirement that it be documented on an inventory is also very restrictive.

It is difficult to know exactly what sort of institutions may be covered. Many focus their analysis solely on museums. But what exactly is a 'religious public monument'? This may cover a major cathedral, especially one listed by the State, but would it apply to a village church, temple or mosque? Villagers may not consider a place of private worship to be a 'public monument' as such. What of small shrines in Asian villages? Would a monastery be a religious public monument or perhaps a 'similar institution'? What of the burial caves of Tana Toraja in Indonesia, the contents of which were looted in the 1970s and ended up in Western museums?[15] Or consider the Miho Museum in Japan, housing a private collection of antiquities, acquired by the Shumei organisation, a spiritual movement.[16] The wording of Article 7(b)(i) is clearly designed to meet Western expectations and its full application to other types of scenarios begs further investigation.

Because the object must pertain to an inventory, Article 7(b)(i) has no relevance to the argument whether cultural property which has been clandestinely excavated and unlawfully exported is 'stolen'.[17] By its very nature such property will not have been documented and, even if it came from the grounds of a religious institution (such as the Chola bronze in *Union of India v Bumper Development Corp.*[18]), it would still not be covered. Even objects stolen from a collection may be difficult to document as 'appertaining' to that collection. A remote church; a rural Buddhist shrine in Laos;[19] an ancient temple in India – all these are very unlikely to have an accurate

[15] E Crystal, 'Rape of the Ancestors: Discovery, Display, and Destruction of the Ancestral Statuary of Tana Toraja' in PM Taylor (ed), *Fragile Traditions: Indonesian Art in Jeopardy* (Honolulu, University of Hawaii Press, 1994) 29, 31.

[16] S Melikian, 'A Splendid Art Collection Goes on Display in Japan', *International Herald Tribune* (6 November 1997). It has been alleged that the Miho Museum collection contains a number of illicitly trafficked objects.

[17] PJ O'Keefe and LV Prott, *Law and the Cultural Heritage: Volume III: Movement* (London, Butterworths, 1989) 373.

[18] [1991] 4 All ER 638.

[19] B Egloff and K Kelly, *Sacred Caves of Tam Ting (Pak Ou). Luang Prabang, Laos: Mystery, Splendor, and Desecration* (Bangkok, White Lotus, 2015) 76. Though the Tam Ting caves of Laos were 'inventorised' in the 1990s, by 2011 they had been denuded of all their Buddhist sculptures, over 600 in total. As the authors bemoan: 'Unfortunately, it is all but impossible to relate the missing objects precisely to the existing object descriptions without doing an object by object cataloging of the figures, as many of the remaining figures have moved or have been replaced by others. However, it is painfully obvious that all of the life-size Buddha figures in the upper cave are missing'.

inventory, or indeed *any* inventory, of the sacred objects they hold; they remain, however, objects that may well capture the attention of collectors and dealers. Even the British Museum, the last place anyone might expect to be devoid of inventories, was revealed in 2023 to have had over one million undocumented objects in its collection.[20] This came after the revelation that a senior member of staff had been pilfering items from the collection over a period of a decade or more.[21] Overall, States reporting on their implementation of the Convention have largely indicated the existence of specific inventories for museums and monuments.[22]

The precise wording around inventories – 'documented as appertaining to the inventory' – is interesting. This appears to suggest that the stolen object need not have been listed on an official 'inventory' of the institution, provided there was some external evidence that it belonged to the institutional inventory.[23] The issue may arise in relation to the British Museum thefts mentioned above. Since the theft scandal broke in 2023, a recovery team established by the institution has been piecing together external evidence of what was in the collection and at what time (including notes and drawings made by scholars over the years of gemstones, coins and the like).[24] This may become pertinent if the UK tries, through diplomatic means, to trigger the restitutionary mechanism of Article 7(b)(ii) to recover stolen material that had not been on the official museum registry.

One of the reasons for the limited scope of Article 7(b)(i) was the fear amongst many in the market States that to impose broader import controls would be unworkable. Bator thought it:

> … would entail the creation of an enormously elaborate, expensive, and intrusive regime of border controls. It is easy to say that illegally exported art may not be imported. But effectuating such a policy, in a society in which millions of people cross the borders every year, and into which art objects numbering hundreds of thousands are brought, would be a nightmare … Imagine … the customs process as applied to a B747 planeload arriving at JFK or Los Angeles, each person armed with a document in foreign tongue [*sic*] applicable to each art object bought abroad.[25]

The somewhat misguided assumption behind Bator's surreal illustration is that a certificate would be required for every cultural object and that every passenger

[20] M Bailey, 'British Museum to digitise collection as one million objects are found to be undocumented', *Art Newspaper* (19 October 2023).

[21] See K Razzall, 'Thief at the British Museum' (*BBC*, 2024) www.bbc.co.uk/programmes/m001zrbs.

[22] For the 2019–2022 reporting cycle, UNESCO has noted that, of the 91 States reporting on implementation of the Convention, 77% indicated the existence of specific inventories at museums and religious or secular public monuments: Subsidiary Committee of the Meeting of States Parties, 11th Session, C70/23/11.SC/7 (Paris, UNESCO, 1–2 June 2023) p 17.

[23] C Woodhead, 'Article 7(b)(i) of the 1970 Convention: Prohibition of Import of Inventoried Cultural Property' in AF Vrdoljak, A Jakubowski and A Chechi (eds), *The 1970 UNESCO and 1995 UNIDROIT Conventions on Stolen or Illegally Transferred Cultural Property: A Commentary* (Oxford, Oxford University Press, 2024) 226, 234.

[24] J Lawson-Tancred, 'British Museum Seeks Treasure Hunter to Recover Stolen Antiquities' (*ArtNet News*, 5 January 2026). And see British Museum press statement, 'An update on the progress of the recovery programme' (London, British Museum, 26 September 2023).

[25] Bator (n 6) 329–30.

would be carrying objects from States Parties to the Convention; this is likely never to transpire. But, for similar reasons, the Netherlands had initially balked at imposing import controls under the Convention, calling checks by Customs officials 'impractical, if not impracticable':

> Controls, in order to be effective, should imply factual examinations of all transports upon importation, with the purpose of checking whether they contain any goods noted on a world base as stolen property. In fact, examining shipments on such a large scale as to allow for a deterring effect is regarded neither practically possible nor desirable, because it would considerably hamper the flows of trade. Moreover, the breaking off of tariff and non-tariff barriers between a large number of countries in Western Europe … goes along with the desire to simplify or even abolish customs formalities in the relations between these countries, and consequently goods, today, are in fact only examined at random, if at all.[26]

While it is true that effective prevention of import of illicitly exported goods at the point of entry to another country (by inspection of luggage, etc.) would place an enormous additional burden on the Customs services of most countries and one which would far exceed their present capacity, this approach is no more required by the Convention than by other laws on illegal imports. Customs services have devised other ways of policing illegal imports beside inspection at point of entry. Even for crimes regarded by all governments as being of the most serious kind, such as the illegal importation of arms, currency and narcotics – even for illegal immigration – reliance is placed on a combination of other methods, such as exchanges of information, the use of profiles and spot-checks. Canada, which shares the Western approach to international trade and freedom of travel, planned its implementing legislation so as not to rely on border controls:

> It is not intended … to set up elaborate checks on imports at Ports of Entry to enforce this law. First, it is up to the importer to know whether or not the cultural property being imported has legally left its country of origin … Second, the Act provides only for action to be taken when a reciprocating State requests in writing the recovery and return of cultural property illegally imported into Canada.[27]

The US delegation to the Special Committee of Government Experts reported on Article 7(b) that:

> The import prohibition is to be understood as creating a juridical basis for later actions to recover the cultural property involved. As several delegations commented, it is not expected that illicit cultural property ordinarily could be caught by customs authorities at the frontier.[28]

[26] Quoted in Unesdoc 22 C/93 at p 3.

[27] DF Cameron, *An Introduction to the Cultural Property Export and Import Act*, 2nd edn (Ottawa, Department of the Secretary of State, 1980) 22. Canada, *Cultural Property Export and Import Act* 1975, s 31(3). Australia takes a similar approach in the Protection of Movable Cultural Heritage Act 1986, s 41(1).

[28] Report of the United States Delegation to the Special Committee of Governmental Experts to Examine the Draft Convention on the Means of Prohibiting and Preventing the Illicit Import, Export and Transfer of Ownership of Cultural Property (Paris, UNESCO, 13–14 April 1970) 14.

In their preparations for acceding to the 1970 Convention, some Customs services suggested that implementation of Article 7(b)(i) would require delivery of a detailed list of specific objects stolen from each and every institution in each and every State Party to the Convention. Unless a State chooses to apply this provision to objects stolen before the entry into force of the Convention and imported after that date, such a list would have no purpose. There is no necessity for a complete inventory of every such stolen object to be delivered before an import restriction can be made. The contrary view was taken only by Japan.[29] The practical solution for thefts after entry into force of the Convention would be for a State to supply the full inventory details when seeking information on the whereabouts of the object or when seeking its return.

Since legal proceedings for the return of stolen property exist in most, if not all, legal systems, one might ask what additional benefits flow to parties to the Convention by prohibiting its import, especially since Article 7(b)(i) does not even apply to all forms of stolen cultural property. The answer is, in substance, very little. In terms of simplified procedure, which is provided according to Article 7(b)(ii), however, there is some advantage. It may also be useful, says Bator, in cases where civil proceedings are barred by lapse of time.[30] In respect of the United States, however, it seems that action under the National Stolen Property Act would be available for a wider group of stolen objects than action under Article 7 of the 1970 UNESCO Convention and its implementing legislation.[31]

By contrast, the UNIDROIT Convention of 1995 extends its coverage to illegally excavated objects, and does not invite similar agonies over inventories. In that Convention, restitution is available for stolen cultural objects, defined to include at Article 3(2), 'a cultural object which has been unlawfully excavated or lawfully excavated but unlawfully retained'. And under Article 5 of the UNIDROIT Convention, illegally exported cultural objects can be subjected to return to the State of origin, whether or not they have been stolen.

Paragraph (b)(ii)

'take appropriate steps'

Because, under Article 7(b)(i), a narrowly defined subset of cultural property has become a prohibited import, the onus can now justifiably be put on the State of import to 'take appropriate steps to recover and return' such property. The concept of 'appropriate steps' is relative. The authorities may seize the object in reliance on

[29] Below, V, ch 3.

[30] Bator (n 6) 383.

[31] ibid 354–55. Examples of the National Stolen Property Act being used to seize and recover stolen property that would never have been covered by the 1970 Convention are the cases involving 'Portrait of Wally' and antiquities dealer Frederick Schultz.

their Customs power, as has been done in the United States on the basis of bilateral treaties, or on the basis of special seizure provisions in legislation implementing the 1970 Convention, as in the case of Australia.[32] The State may prosecute the importer, as did Canada in respect of the Nok sculpture in *R v Heller* (although ultimately without success).[33]

For the UK, Chamberlain has explained that for criminal matters, the police would be empowered to seize the object as evidence and then apply to the court seeking an order to return the object to its rightful owner.[34] In less obvious circumstances, appropriate steps may mean advising the requesting State to take legal proceedings; for example, where there are complex questions of title. As Chamberlain explains:

> It can be argued that ensuring that our courts have jurisdiction to resolve disputes of this kind, together with effective remedies, constitute the 'appropriate steps' in terms of Article 7(b)(ii).[35]

This would be the very minimum required by the Convention. Additional measures might include administrative assistance, such as the use of police and Customs officials in tracking down the location of the object, liaising between the holder and officials of the requesting State in an effort to resolve the dispute, and providing advice as to appropriate legal representation if required. The legislation in Norway, for example, specifically provides that Norwegian authorities will assist the requesting States in tracing and recovery.[36] It would be prudent for the requested State to have the power of seizure or at least a legal means to hold the disputed object pending a decision by a competent authority, if no resolution can be achieved by the parties. On this point it must be realised that it could well take months to locate the proper representative of the claimant and for this representative to initiate a claim. That said, the requested State should treat the matter with some urgency such that its ratification is not construed as mere lip service to the Convention.

In terms of the speed and cost of litigation, Article 7(b)(ii) may be an advantage to poorer States, though it does put something of a burden on requested States, which will not usually have budgeted for such actions. It should be noted, however, that the requested State is required to act only 'at the request' of the State Party of origin. This means that an institution from which cultural property had been stolen cannot assume that a claim will be processed; it depends on the commitment and competence of its own national government, as well as an appreciation of international politics in such bilateral requests (eg the strength of diplomatic

[32] Protection of Movable Cultural Heritage Act 1986, s 14(1). This was used very effectively by the Commonwealth in seizing the Shiva Nataraja from the National Gallery of Australia in 2014, in order to return it to India, and a Bolivian artefact from the Palmanova gallery in 2021: *Palmanova v Commonwealth of Australia* [2025] HCA 35.

[33] *R v Heller* (1983) 27 Alta LR (2d) 346; appeal decision (1984) 51 AR 73.

[34] This would be under the Powers of Criminal Courts (Sentencing) Act 2000 or the Police (Property) Act 1897: see Chamberlain, VII *Art Antiquity and Law* (September 2002) 231, 247.

[35] ibid 248.

[36] Norway's Act Concerning the Cultural Heritage of 1978, as amended, s 23c.

relations at the time). The internal political calculation may well be for the State to refrain from bringing a claim so as not to upset the status quo.

The problem of course may be that the property claimed falls outside the strict scope of Article 7(b). In 1981, Ecuador brought a case to the ICPRCP at UNESCO alleging that illegally exported Ecuadorian material had been taken to Italy in 1974, complaining of 'the extremely slow pace of the judicial process' in the civil courts in Italy.[37] Unfortunately for Ecuador, Italy had only become a State Party in 1978 and so did not have any direct obligations under the Convention.[38] Likewise, in the case mentioned in the Introduction, Nigeria brought a claim against the UK before the ICPRCP in 2020 for the return of an Ife Bronze Head stolen from a Nigerian museum in 1987, currently in the possession of the UK authorities after its confiscation from a Belgian dealer in 2017. Before the ICPRCP, the UK argued that the Head fell outside Article 7(b) because the theft had occurred before the UK acceded to the Convention (in 2002), and so the UK did not have any obligation in this respect.[39] While neither case may have triggered the application of Article 7(b)(ii), it might nevertheless be said that Italy and the UK should have acted more helpfully to the respective claimant States, in line with other provisions of the Convention,[40] as well as the overall spirit of the Convention.

While the 1939 draft Convention spoke only of actions by States,[41] the original Secretariat draft for the 1970 Convention would have allowed actions by 'the owner of the cultural property in question, his authorized agent or the State of which he is a national'.[42] This was not adopted, although the principle did find its way into the 1995 UNIDROIT Convention on Stolen or Illegally Exported Cultural Objects (at Article 3).

'after the entry into force'

There is a non-retroactivity element to paragraph (b)(ii), just as there were under paragraphs (a) and (b)(i), namely that the import must have taken place after the Convention entered into force 'in both States concerned'. This would seem obvious, since it would be hard to imagine the provision applying to imports that had occurred before such a date. However, because paragraph (b)(i) is limited to thefts occurring after the Convention's entry into force, this further limits the recovery mechanism in (b)(ii). For example, the Ife Head mentioned in the Introduction had certainly been brought into the UK after the UK's ratification of the Convention in 2002, but the initial theft from the Jos Museum in Nigeria had occurred well before that date (in 1987); and so Article 7(b)(ii) could not apply.

[37] Unesdoc CC-81/CONF.203/10, 5.
[38] Unesdoc CC-81/CONF.203/10, 6.
[39] 24th session of the ICPRCP (Paris, UNESCO, May 2024).
[40] Such as Arts 2(2), 3 and 13.
[41] OIM 102-1939, Arts 4, 5 and 7.
[42] Unesdoc SHC/MD/3 Annex, 4, Art 10(c).

The High Court of Australia interpreted Article 7(b)(ii) in a somewhat more expansive way in the 2025 case *Palmanova v Commonwealth of Australia.*[43] Quoting commentary on the provision,[44] the Court found that 'the only temporal limitation in Article 7(b)(ii) concerns the date of import of the cultural property', and used this interpretation to support its conclusion that Australia's Protection of Movable Cultural Heritage Act 1986 restricted the import of foreign cultural property regardless of when that property was exported from its State of origin (the case involved an artefact illegally exported from Bolivia in the 1950s).[45] With respect, this interpretation by the Court seems to ignore the fact that Article 7(b)(ii) is limited in its scope by Article 7(b)(i) – although the point the Court was making about Australian implementation stands on other grounds.[46]

'just compensation to an innocent purchaser or to a person who has valid title'

An important feature of Article 7(b)(ii) is that the requesting State must pay just compensation to an innocent purchaser or a person who has valid title to the property. Here the Convention reaches into domestic rules regarding the transfer of property. It is somewhat unfortunate that more detailed consideration was not given to this problem when the Article was drafted, for it has given rise to difficulties. The *bona fide* possessor is protected, in most Civil Law systems, after a certain lapse of time. In France, for example, goods which have been stolen or lost can be reclaimed only within three years against a *bona fide* purchaser.[47] In such cases, where a good title is obtained under domestic law, there may be constitutional requirements that compensation be paid. It is also possible that in such a system the good faith purchaser might be entitled to retain the goods, on payment of their value; this would be clearly unsatisfactory, since the whole purpose of the exercise is to ensure the return of the object.

[43] [2025] HCA 35.

[44] SK Urice and GA Levy, 'Article 7(b)(ii) of the 1970 UNESCO Convention: Cooperation for the Return of Cultural Property' in AF Vrdoljak, A Jakubowski and A Chechi (eds), *The 1970 UNESCO and 1995 UNIDROIT Conventions on Stolen or Illegally Transferred Cultural Property: A Commentary* (Oxford, Oxford University Press, 2024) 245, 256. The Court also quoted Arts 28, 31 and 32 of the Vienna Convention on the Law of Treaties (1969) 1155 UNTS 331.

[45] *Palmanova* at paras 13 and 53: the relevant provision of the Australian law was section 14, which applies to unlawful exports of protected cultural objects from another State brought into Australia after 1987 (the date the law came into effect).

[46] Thank you to Emily Gould, Assistant Director of the Institute of Art and Law, for first raising this point, in correspondence with the author, 2025. A view critical of the High Court's interpretation of Article 7(b)(ii) can also be found in P Gerstenblith, 'Evolving Implementation of the 1970 UNESCO Convention', *Essays on Cultural Heritage in Honour of Francesco Francioni*, forthcoming.

[47] Civil Code, Art 2276 (formerly Art 2279); C de Visscher, 'La protection internationale des objets d'art et des monuments historiques' (1935) *Revue de droit international et de législation comparée* 32, 49ff.

Provision for this eventuality had been expressly covered in the 1939 draft Convention:

> A *bona fide* purchaser shall be ordered to surrender an object only against compensation to be paid in advance by the claimant State when the domestic law of the country to which the claim is addressed allows the said possessor either to retain the object or to demand compensation.[48]

The Secretariat draft for the 1970 Convention was much clearer on the point, since it required States:

> to make provision in their respective national laws for the possibility of dispossessing, for reasons of public utility, and with an advance payment of fair compensation corresponding to the purchase price, *bona fide* possessors of cultural property illicitly imported since the entry into force of this Convention and claimed by the State of origin, the cost of compensation to the possessor to be borne by that State.[49]

Such a provision was clearly drafted with the Civil Law rules in mind; it would, for example, have extended the prohibition of prescription[50] for classified movable cultural objects in French law to all cultural objects covered by the Convention.

The provision, difficult as it is for these reasons, clearly did not have the benefit of adequate consideration from common law lawyers at the time, for the good faith purchaser has no special protection in most common law systems, although a not dissimilar protection is achieved through statutes of limitation after a certain number of years. Rules as to market overt, which used to protect purchasers, have been abolished in England[51] and many other common law jurisdictions. The United States did not wish to alter its domestic law in this respect[52] and accordingly lodged an 'understanding' to this provision when presenting its document of acceptance to UNESCO. Frigo commented that unless action is taken to modify and unify national laws in this regard, the effect of the Convention on illicit traffic will remain limited.[53] Such modifications were indeed made in the quite sophisticated provisions of the UNIDROIT Convention on Stolen or Illicitly Exported Cultural Objects of 1995.[54]

Gordon,[55] with whom Williams agrees,[56] considers that Article 7(b)(ii) can be used only where a possessor has valid title against the owner. This would be

[48] OIM 1939, Art 8(1)(a).

[49] Unesdoc SHC/MD/3 Annex, 4, Art 10(d).

[50] Acquisition of good title after lapse of time.

[51] By the Sale of Goods (Amendment) Act 1994.

[52] JB Gordon, 'The UNESCO Convention on the Illicit Movement of Art Treasures' (1971) 12 *Harvard International Law Journal* 537, 550–51.

[53] M Frigo, *La protezione dei beni culturali nel diritto internazionale* (Milan, Giuffrè Editore, 1986) 27.

[54] Arts 3 and 9, which enable a common law country to retain its rules giving better protection to the original owner of the object and hence to the object in its original context. See LV Prott, *Commentary on the 1995 UNIDROIT Convention*, 2nd edn (Builth Wells, Institute of Art and Law, 2021).

[55] Gordon (n 52) 550–51.

[56] SA Williams, *The International and National Protection of Movable Cultural Property: A Comparative Study* (Dobbs Ferry, Oceana, 1978) 184.

in a situation where the requesting State cannot effect recovery using the property laws of the requested State, if those laws protect good faith possessions. He states that recovery provisions should be read as supplementing, not replacing, existing methods of returning stolen property to rightful owners. This view can be questioned, since Article 7(b)(ii) clearly places the onus on the requested State to act at the request of the requesting State; refusal to act on the ground that other options are open to the dispossessed owner could conceivably be a breach of the Convention. This last point is explained very forcefully in previous editions of this book.[57] Fraoua also interprets this article as allowing an option to proceed under local property laws or by this special procedure.[58] Frigo takes the view that the remedy in Article 7(b)(ii) is supplementary to existing national procedures.[59]

The quantum of compensation may also be controversial. The amount may be difficult to assess:

> Considering the rapid inflation in the value of cultural objects, it is significant whether the purchase price or the value at time of recovery is to be the measure of compensation.[60]

Both the original and the revised draft included the words 'fair compensation corresponding to the purchase price'.[61] This was dropped at the Special Committee of Governmental Experts and the phrase 'just compensation' was substituted. No comment was made by the Special Committee. However, the Canadian 'Introduction' to its implementing legislation points out that, in the Canadian legislation, compensation is to be determined by a court and is not fixed by the price paid, or fair market value, but is an amount 'the court considers just in the circumstances'.[62] The Australian legislation is silent on the question of payment of compensation, consistent with the common law position that no compensation is owed when an object is returned to its rightful owner. However, the Minister has discretion to consider compensation where the acquirer was in possession without any wrongdoing or lack of adequate provenance research.[63] Fraoua considers 'just compensation' to be the purchase price paid by the *bona fide* purchaser.[64] This interpretation would compensate a *bona fide* purchaser for actual outlay.

It would seem most logical if 'just compensation' meant the purchase price: the actual costs of the transaction (including legal fees, etc.) and expenditure necessarily made on preservation. For instance, the Swiss bilateral agreements on the import and repatriation of cultural property require compensation 'for the purchase price paid and any necessary and useful expenses for the protection and preservation

[57] O'Keefe (n 4) 159.

[58] R Fraoua, *Convention concernant les mesures à prendre pour interdire et empêcher l'importation, l'exportation et le transfert de propriété illicites des biens culturels* (Unesdoc CC-86/WS/40, 1986) 78-79.

[59] Frigo (n 53) 224.

[60] Abramson and Huttler (n 2) 953.

[61] Unesdoc. SHC/MD/3, Annex, 4, Art 10(d).

[62] Cameron (n 27) 22; *Cultural Property Export and Import Act* 1975, s 31(6).

[63] This discretion might be implied by s 38 of the Australian Act, though under that provision the Commonwealth can equally claim transportation and disposal costs from the owner.

[64] Fraoua (n 58) 75.

of the cultural property'.[65] The alternative, namely to require a requesting State to compensate at international art market values, would encourage speculation in cultural heritage items and act as a further disincentive to purchasers to make all possible enquiries prior to purchase. Moreover, such an amount may make it impossible for a requesting State, particularly a poor one, to retrieve material. The appreciation in value between purchase and claim can be substantial.[66]

Another consideration is the notion of 'innocent purchaser'. The Secretariat draft used the phrase *bona fide*, but this is not a term of art in the common law, and perhaps for that reason the vernacular adjective 'innocent' was used instead. At the same time the phrase *de bonne foi*, rather than *bona fide*, was used in the French version. The Report of the Special Committee of Experts that finalised the text spoke of just compensation being paid 'to a *bona fide* purchaser',[67] so it seems that 'innocent' should be seen in that sense. The original provision would have corresponded precisely to the scheme of *bona fide* possessors in French Civil Law, for instance. The present phrase does not appear to address precisely the scheme existing in any system of law.

The very slippery concept of *bona fide* tends to be interpreted to the advantage of the purchaser/possessor by a number of presumptions which make it difficult to disprove good faith. For this reason compensation may be required in more cases than not. When the original draft of the 1970 Convention was circulated for comment, there was a clear divergence of views by States as to the incidence of good faith among purchasers. Sweden commented:

> It is obvious that the draft convention is based on a conception that purchasers of illicitly imported cultural property would seldom be in good faith … The Ministry of Justice … finds it more realistic to believe that the cases of *bona fide* possession will be rather numerous.[68]

France commented:

> It is important not to hamper lawful business and not to throw suspicion on *bona fide* merchants, collectors or exhibitors who, by their discovery of such objects or through their appreciation of them, have often themselves largely contributed to giving them a cultural as well as a commercial value.[69]

[65] Taken from the Swiss/Cypriot agreement, Article V(2).

[66] In the case of the Taranaki panels dug up in New Zealand in 1972, they were sold to a dealer for $6,000 that year, then sold promptly to a collector for $65,000 before being offered for sale at auction five years later for £150,000; by 2014 they were estimated at $4.5 million: RR Cater, 'The Taranaki Panels – a case-study in the recovery of cultural heritage' (1982) 34 *Museum* 256; *Attorney-General of New Zealand v Ortiz* [1982] 1 QB 349; [1982] 3 WLR 571; [1983] 2 WLR 809; H Harvey, 'Motunui panels returned to Taranaki', *Taranaki Daily News* (20 March 2015); the podcast *Stuff the British Stole* features an in-depth story on the matter called 'The Abductions' hosted by Marc Fennell (Australian Broadcasting Corporation, 19 Oct 2021). A Shiva Nataraja was bought from the person who found it in 1976 for the equivalent of £12 and later valued in London at around $250,000 when offered for sale six years later: *Bumper Development Corp Ltd v Comr of Police* [1991] 4 All ER 638.

[67] Unesdoc 16 C/17 Annex II, 5.

[68] Unesdoc SHC/MD/5 Annex I, 16.

[69] Unesdoc CUA/123, 6.

On the other hand, Syria had pointed out in respect of the 1964 Recommendation that, in its opinion:

> the concept of a *bona fide* purchaser should be kept within very narrow limits. Once this recommendation has been published, the cultural property of every country should cease to be regarded as a major source of material profit.[70]

It may be that today buyers of rare and valuable cultural property will find it increasingly difficult to claim that they are *bona fide* if they make no enquiries as to provenance or export status. See for instance longstanding case law from Switzerland[71] and England[72] in this regard.

But Article 7(b)(ii) does not limit the right to compensation simply to an innocent purchaser of stolen cultural property; it extends this to 'a person who has valid title to that property'. Fraoua interprets 'innocent purchaser' (*acquéreur de bonne foi*) as meaning a person who obtains title by acting contrary to law without realising the legal flaw[73] and 'a person who has valid title' (*personne qui détient légalement la propriété*) as a person who has acquired rights by prescription, by lapse of the time limit for restitution actions or by other methods which allowed title to pass in stolen goods. These interpretations appear to fit with French law and most other Civil Law systems; their appropriateness in common law contexts is more problematic. In the United States, the Convention on Cultural Property Implementation Act incorporates Article 7(b)(i) at 19 USC 2607. In the 1999 forfeiture of a manuscript stolen from the Mexican State Archive, the purchaser was not entitled to compensation since the manuscript had the archival stamp and so any argument of being innocent or having valid title fell away.[74]

Firmer rules on the due diligence required to obtain compensation were adopted in Article 4(4) of the UNIDROIT Convention on Stolen or Illegally Exported Cultural Objects of 1995:

> In determining whether the possessor exercised due diligence, regard shall be had to all the circumstances of the acquisition, including the character of the parties, the price paid, whether the possessor consulted any reasonably accessible register of stolen cultural objects, and any other relevant information and documentation which it could reasonably have obtained, and whether the possessor consulted accessible agencies or took any other step that a reasonable person would have taken in the circumstances.

[70] Unesdoc CUA/123 Add I, Annex I, 21.

[71] BGE/ATF 122 III 1 (Federal Court Lausanne, 5 March 1996) also reported in *Neue Zürcher Zeitung* (6/7April 1996) 41. Certain categories of goods have a higher risk of theft (ie antiquities) and so good faith will have to be demonstrated.

[72] *De Préval v Adrian Alan Ltd* (24 January 1997, unreported): the court held that the buyer of two unique candelabra (stolen in 1986) was not in good faith because, being a dealer with experience in the area, he should have been alerted that their provenance might be doubtful. See also R Redmond-Cooper, 'Good Faith Acquisition of Stolen Art' (1997) II *Art Antiquity and Law* 55, and *Kurtha v Marks* [2008] EWHC 336 (QB).

[73] Fraoua (n 58) 75.

[74] *United States v An Original Manuscript*, 1999 US Dist LEIS 1859 (SDNY 1999). The author would like to thank Patty Gerstenblith for alerting him to this forfeiture proceeding and for explaining its importance in the US system.

It might be appropriate, with this understanding of what constitutes due diligence in relation to the acquisition of cultural objects, to interpret the UNESCO provisions in a similar way. UNIDROIT provided a compromise between different national systems with the conditions of proving due diligence for acquisitions absolutely clear.

'documentation and other evidence'

Article 7(b)(ii) also requires the requesting State to furnish, at its expense, documentary and other evidence necessary to substantiate the claim. In some countries, short as they are on cultural and legal experts, and often with a minimal hard-pressed foreign affairs staff, meeting this requirement will be far more difficult than for those with a more advanced administration.

'expenses incident to the return and delivery'

Expenses incident to the return and delivery of such cultural property are to be borne by the requesting State. This again may be burdensome, particularly if the material is fragile. Full payment of transport, preparation, packing and insurance could use up a substantial proportion of the annual budget of some collecting institutions in developing countries. The phrase used in the Article, 'expenses incident to the return and delivery of the cultural property', does not make clear which expenses would need to be met. The requesting State may, therefore, have to rely on the assistance of cultural professionals in requested States in the preparation of the claim and in the care of the cultural property prior to and in preparation for its return. Note, however, that the importing State is not to charge customs or other duties on the return of such property.

Article 8

> The States Parties to this Convention undertake to impose penalties or administrative sanctions on any person responsible for infringing the prohibitions referred to under Articles 6(b) and 7(b) above.

Article 8 provides the only specific reference to general crimes in the 1970 Convention, prescribing penalties or administrative sanctions for violations of any prohibition on export (Art. 6(b)) or import of material stolen from a museum, monument or similar institution (Art. 7(b)). General prohibitions are not mentioned elsewhere in the Convention.

The nature of the penalty is not indicated in the Convention. Canadian and Australian practice give an indication of what may be appropriate and the administrative procedures involved. Canada's Cultural Property Export and Import Act prohibits the export from Canada of 'any object included in the Control List except under the authority of and in accordance with a permit issued under this Act'.[1] Australia's Protection of Movable Cultural Heritage Act 1986 is somewhat more refined in that it allows for the total prohibition of the export of certain objects ('Class A') while others may be exported subject to a permit ('Class B').[2] Both pieces of legislation apply to attempted export as well as actual export. Both also provide that breaches of the prohibition may be punished by fines and/or imprisonment. The Canadian Act gives all officers the necessary powers that they have under the Customs Act, including that of forfeiture.[3] In Australia, a policy decision was taken at the time of drafting the law to make it 'all inclusive' in that no reference is made to other legislation. Forfeiture is thus dealt with in the Act itself.[4] When an Australian protected object is unlawfully exported 'the object is forfeited', whereas in the case of attempted export it is merely 'liable to forfeiture'.[5]

Under the Canadian law, the illegal import or attempted import of property under s 37 is prohibited by s 43. The offender may be fined or imprisoned[6] and forfeiture of the property may occur under the same provision as for exports, as indicated above. This forfeiture provision was not used for many years. In

[1] Cultural Property Export and Import Act, s 40. The Canadian Cultural Property Export Control List consists of objects divided into specified classes, the export of which is deemed necessary to control in order to preserve the national heritage of Canada.

[2] Protection of Movable Cultural Heritage Act 1986, s 9. Persons who want to bring either category of object into Australia (eg for sale or exhibition) may first apply for a certificate authorising their later export.

[3] Cultural Property Export and Import Act, s 51.

[4] Contrariwise, the Australian Customs legislation contains no provision for offences committed in respect of cultural property. Under s 23T of the Customs Act, which was inserted by the passage of the Protection of Movable Cultural Heritage Act 1986, Customs officers taking possession of heritage material are required to pass it forthwith to an inspector under the latter Act. While Customs officers might use other provisions of their legislation to hold heritage material for limited periods, during which investigations are conducted, the seizure of such material with a view to forfeiture can only take place under the Protection of Movable Cultural Heritage Act 1986. For criticism of this see C Forrest, 'Australia's Protection of Foreign States' Cultural Heritage' (2004) 27 *University of New South Wales Law Journal* 605, 622.

[5] Protection of Movable Cultural Heritage Act 1986, s 9.

[6] Cultural Property Export and Import Act, s 45.

Attorney General of Canada v Karin Knappstein,[7] the importer had not committed any Customs offence as the objects were properly declared. Proceedings for recovery were thus commenced under s 37(3) of the Cultural Property Export and Import Act and went uncontested. The Court found that the importer was not due any compensation and the two stone figures involved were returned to Colombia.

Under the Australian law, the import of prohibited cultural material into Australia renders the object *liable* to forfeiture.[8] It requires a decision by the Australian Government to forfeit the object.[9] This is precisely what happened in two cases involving illegally imported Indian artefacts acquired by Australian institutions, both of which were forfeited to the Commonwealth in 2014: the Shiva Nataraja from the National Gallery of Australia and the Ardhanarishvara voluntarily handed over by the Art Gallery of New South Wales (after considerable pressure).[10] In *Palmanova v Commonwealth of Australia*, the Commonwealth was successfully able to forfeit a Bolivian artefact that had been imported into Australia in breach of the Act.[11] Under the law, if the importer knows that the object was a protected object of a foreign country and that the export had been prohibited, that person may be fined or imprisoned.[12] This did not happen in the examples mentioned, which only resulted in forfeiture – no fines or imprisonment.

The problem with fining the offender is that what may be a major sum in one jurisdiction can be insignificant in another; just a cost of doing business. Becerril described a situation in Mexico where 'the fines established in the Federal Monuments Law were updated and now the amount goes from less than a penny to less than $5 USD.'

> In other words, the illicit trafficking of cultural property is a safe business in Mexico: laws are not very clear regarding the objects that must be protected, criminal regulation allows the release on bail and the amount of fines is ridiculous.[13]

There may be other techniques for taking action against criminals such as seizing equipment used in the illicit trafficking or income made from sales of the cultural property concerned.[14]

[7] (2003, unreported).

[8] Protection of Movable Cultural Heritage Act 1986, s 14.

[9] JF Ley, *Australia's Protection of Movable Cultural Heritage: Report on the Ministerial Review of the Protection of Movable Cultural Heritage Act 1986 and Regulations* (Canberra, Australian Government Publishing Service, 1991) 125.

[10] 'Dancing Shiva: National Gallery of Australia to Return Allegedly Stolen Statue to India' (*ABCNews*, 26 March 2014); the AGNSW then returned three more sculptures to India in 2022: 'Provenance project: works from Art of the Past Gallery' (Art Gallery of New South Wales, 2022).

[11] [2025] HCA 35.

[12] Protection of Movable Cultural Heritage Act 1986, s 14(2).

[13] E Becerril, 'The Necessary Evolution of the Mexican Law Under the New Paradigm of the 1972 UNESCO Convention in Order to Strengthen the Fight Against the Illicit Trafficking of Cultural Property' in JA Sánchez Cordero (ed) *The 1970 UNESCO Convention: New Challenges* (Mexico City, Instituto de Investigaciones Jurídica, 2014) 45, 52.

[14] This could be done, depending on the country, using legislation relating the proceeds of crime or money laundering.

Article 9

> Any State Party to this Convention whose cultural patrimony is in jeopardy from pillage of archaeological or ethnological materials may call upon other States Parties who are affected. The States Parties to this Convention undertake, in these circumstances, to participate in a concerted international effort to determine and to carry out the necessary concrete measures, including the control of exports and imports and international commerce in the specific materials concerned. Pending agreement each State concerned shall take provisional measures to the extent feasible to prevent irremediable injury to the cultural heritage of the requesting State.

In his review of the Convention, Bator explained that Article 9 was a 'direct descendant of the 'crisis' provision contained in the United States alternative draft'.[1] Certainly it fits ill with the wording of the rest of the Convention. For example, for the first time the term 'cultural patrimony' is used; elsewhere in the Convention the terms have been 'cultural property' or, at times, 'cultural heritage'.[2] The exact significance of this change in terminology is unclear. It could be regarded as simply a drafting blunder which was not rectified in the final text. Since the other official texts in Spanish, French and Russian all continue to use the same term ('*patrimonio*', '*patrimoine*' and '*nacledie*' respectively), it could be argued that no change of meaning was intended. It is perhaps worth noting that the term 'patrimony' seems to be particular to the United States, possibly as a translation of the Spanish 'patrimonio' from Latin-American legislation. It has in English a flavour of property[3] whereas 'heritage' has a more general connotation. The use of 'patrimony' does reflect the general tendency of the US commentators to treat objects of cultural significance *prima facie* as property, rather than as one element of a more general cultural legacy. Somewhat ironically, the implementing legislation in the United States defines the term 'cultural property' but not 'cultural patrimony'.[4]

The protection of the Article extends only to 'archaeological and ethnographical materials'. It is therefore of little use to countries which may wish to protect a rich heritage of other forms of art. A country such as Italy, for example, will never be able to call for assistance to protect the paintings and sculptures of the Renaissance under Article 9. Moreover, in its implementing legislation, the United States has attempted to restrict those categories even further. The Convention on Cultural Property Implementation Act provides that only objects 'of cultural significance', over 250 years old and 'normally discovered as a result of scientific excavation, clandestine or accidental digging, or exploration' will be covered.[5]

Kaplan implied that the purpose of Article 9 is 'the deterrence of a situation of pillage threatening the cultural heritage, not just of a single State, but of all

[1] PM Bator, 'An Essay on the International Trade in Art' (1982) 34 *Stanford Law Review* 275, 379.
[2] Arts 1, 2, 3, 4, 5, 6 and 7 for 'cultural property'; Art 4 in relation to 'cultural heritage'.
[3] Oxford English Dictionary (OED): 'property inherited from one's father or ancestors'.
[4] Convention on Cultural Property Implementation Act, s 302(6).
[5] Convention on Cultural Property Implementation Act, s 302(2).

mankind'.[6] It is hard to see why this should be so when the phrases used in Article 9 refer to a State 'whose cultural patrimony is in jeopardy' and to 'irremediable injury to the cultural heritage of the requesting State'. The exact relationship between national cultural heritages and the universal cultural heritage is difficult to plot. While one interpretation would see every national cultural heritage as part of the universal cultural heritage, another would consider only the highest achievements, or at any rate only some of the achievements of a national culture, to be part of the universal cultural heritage. If the latter view is taken, Kaplan's approach would limit the cases in which a requesting State could seek help to those where the threat to the national cultural heritage also involved a threat to universal cultural heritage. There is little evidence to support that view in the words of Article 9. Furthermore, Müller-Katzenburg points out that, since the removal of cultural heritage from one country leads to the deterioration, if not extinction, of that particular country's culture, the protection of national cultural heritage must inevitably be in the long-term interest of *all* humanity.[7]

Because many of the terms used are unique to Article 9, definitions are unavailable and so much is left to conjecture. As a result, any precise meaning of the provision as a whole remains uncertain. Disagreement exists especially around the terms 'pillage' and 'in jeopardy'. Regarding 'pillage', Kaplan took the view that, for example, damage done to particular archaeological sites in Canada (at the time he was writing) did not amount to 'pillage', while the crisis involving looted Mayan art 'brings context to the term'.[8] As an example, the United States imposed import restrictions on a wide range of materials – ceramic vessels, figurines, and other objects, as well as stone sculptures – from the Cara Sucia region of El Salvador on evidence that looters had dug more than 5,000 pits damaging or destroying burials, structural remains and other archaeological features; threatening to destroy irreplaceable chapters in El Salvador's archaeological record and amounting to 'intensive pillage'.[9]

As to cultural patrimony being 'in jeopardy', there have been questions as to whether this is equivalent to a 'crisis'.[10] Bator described the provision as 'an umbrella for and encouragement of action to contain crisis situations where some category of archaeological object becomes, in effect, an endangered species'.[11] Feldman, on the other hand, refrained from equating it with crisis situations, saying instead that, 'What is meant is situations that are serious in the sense that there is jeopardy from

[6] W Kaplan, 'Assistance Under the 1970 Unesco Cultural Property Convention: Canada's Request to the United States' (1986) 22 *Stanford Journal of International Law* 123, 146.

[7] A Müller-Katzenburg, *Internationale Standards im Kulturgüterverkehr und ihr Bedeutung für das Sach- und Kollisionsrecht* (Berlin, Duncker & Humblot, 1996) 156.

[8] ibid 146.

[9] United States Information Agency Facts on Protection of El Salvador's Cara Sucia Archaeological Region (Washington, 1987), Doc 9, 1.

[10] JB Gordon, 'The UNESCO Convention on the Illicit Movement of Art Treasures' (1971) 12 *Harvard International Law Journal* 537, 552.

[11] Bator (n 1) 344.

the pillage of archaeological or ethnological material'.[12] Fraoua took the view that pillage and jeopardy of cultural heritage occur where the remains of a particular civilisation are threatened with destruction or extensive movement abroad or when the sale of certain archaeological objects on the international market sets off a broad campaign of clandestine excavation leading to the destruction of important archaeological sites.[13] In an earlier work, Fraoua had noted the possibility of restrictive interpretations of Article 9 and concluded that it should not be considered open to a State Party to refuse to act on the ground that, in its opinion, the pillage complained of was not in fact putting the cultural heritage of the requesting State in danger.[14] He considered that the Article was against illicit traffic in cultural objects, and that the requesting State should not, therefore, be required to produce evidence as to the degree of damage or volume of the illicit trade in these objects.

How States 'may call upon' others for assistance is also left to the interpretation of each State. The US legislation requires a bilateral agreement to be made on the basis of which further action can be taken. Under the Convention on Cultural Property Implementation Act, the United States has entered into some 30 bilateral agreements with other States, including Mexico, Colombia, Algeria, Greece, Cambodia, Egypt, India and Nigeria. However, there is no reference in Article 9 of the Convention to any need for further agreement. Canada imposes import controls on cultural materials which had been illegally exported from other States Parties to the Convention,[15] thus no additional agreement is required. Australia does not even require the other State to be a party to an international convention.[16]

'Parties affected' is left somewhat open-ended, but seems directed at market States who would be in a position to do something to restrict trade. 'Concerted international effort' would also seem clearly designed for market States and is not restricted to 'States Parties'. It may be possible, for example, to persuade other market States who are not, and perhaps have no intention of becoming, parties to the Convention to restrict imports in certain critical situations.

Pending agreement on concerted action, each State concerned is to take provisional measures 'to the extent feasible' to prevent irremediable damage to the cultural heritage of the requesting State. None of the commentators to date gives any suggestion as to what might constitute 'irremediable injury' except Bator who quotes from the United States Senate Report in which two types of case are contemplated:

> (1) the case in which the remains of a particular civilisation are threatened with destruction or wholesale removal, as may be true of certain pre-Columbian monuments, and

[12] Kaplan (n 6) 124–25.

[13] R Fraoua, *Convention concernant les mesures à prendre pour interdire et empêcher l'importation, l'exportation et le transfert de propriété illicites des biens culturels* (Unesdoc CC-86/WS/40, 1986) 80.

[14] R Fraoua, *Le traffic illicite des biens culturels et leur restitution* (Fribourg, Editions Universitaires, 1985) 105.

[15] Cultural Property Export and Import Act (1975), s 31.

[16] Protection of Movable Cultural Heritage Act 1986, s 14.

(2) the case in which the international market for certain items has stimulated widespread illegal excavations destructive of important archaeological resources.[17]

Bator has spoken of some categories of archaeological object becoming, in effect, an 'endangered species'. This seems far too narrow an approach. Destruction of the stratigraphy of a site by clandestine diggers may well cause irremediable damage, as a result of the brisk trade in multiple objects from that site. This happened, for instance, at Ban Chiang in Thailand, a site discovered in 1967 and substantially looted in the early 1970s.[18] A general trade in unprovenanced objects from various sites in a country or countries of the same region may well destroy any national effort to properly survey, date and verify the development of national culture. Other instances could undoubtedly be supplied by archaeologists and ethnologists of damage which is 'irremediable'.

Apart from the United States, Switzerland is the only other State that uses bilateral agreements with other States in order to comply with certain Convention obligations, as set out in its implementing law of 2005, though this is not done on the basis of Article 9.[19] The Swiss have entered into bilateral agreements with ten other States, including Greece, Colombia, Egypt and China. However, these agreements are not limited to situations of 'pillage' or 'jeopardy', and require only that they are of 'essential importance to the cultural heritage' of the reciprocating State, that their export is controlled and that reciprocal rights are granted by the State to Switzerland.[20] The Article 9 language is employed instead in situations where Switzerland in extreme situations may impose 'temporary measures', which can include restrictions on import, transit and export: such situations arise only if the 'cultural heritage of a State… is endangered due to exceptional events'.[21]

North American commentators have noted the 'flexibility' of Article 9.[22] Countries such as Canada and Australia that have taken a broader view of the Convention have not found it necessary to take special legislative steps to implement Article 9, there being already sufficient flexibility (and rather less vagueness) in their implementing legislation. Seriously endangered categories would clearly be subject to export bans and hence would constitute prohibited or unlawful imports. A State whose cultural patrimony is in jeopardy might of course seek additional assistance under Article 9, eg an educational campaign within the

[17] Senate Committee on Foreign Relations (United States of America) Convention on Ownership of Cultural Property, S Exec Rep No 29, 92nd Congress, 2nd Session (1972), p 5.

[18] See S Mackenzie, *Going, Going, Gone: Regulating the Market in Illicit Antiquities* (Leicester, Institute of Art and Law, 2005) 17.

[19] Swiss Federal Act on the International Transfer of Cultural Property (2005), Art 7.

[20] ibid Art 7.

[21] ibid Art 8. Restrictions on unlawfully removed cultural property from Iraq, Syria and Ukraine all appear to have been introduced through separate ordinances entered into by the Swiss Federal Council.

[22] Gordon (n 10) 552; SA Williams, *The International and National Protection of Movable Cultural Property: A Comparative Study* (Dobbs Ferry, Oceana, 1978) 186; RD Abramson and SB Huttler, 'The Legal Response to the Illicit Movement of Cultural Property' (1973) 5 *Law and Policy in International Business* 962.

importing country on the particularly threatened cultural heritage or increased vigilance 'to the extent feasible'.

Kevin Chamberlain, a senior British legal official at the time the UK was studying the implications of becoming party to the 1970 Convention, indicated how the UK might respond if assistance were requested under Article 9:

> Pending agreement the United Kingdom would be obliged to take provisional measures to prevent irremediable injury to the cultural heritage of the requesting State 'to the extent feasible'. Precisely what measures the United Kingdom would take would depend on the circumstances at the time but they could include imposing some form of import controls, using the powers that the United Kingdom currently has under the Import, Export and Customs Powers (Defence) Act 1939, or, in the case of export controls, using existing powers under the United Kingdom's export licensing system… It might also be possible to seek injunctive relief to prevent cultural objects being removed out of the country.[23]

[23] K Chamberlain, 'UK Accession to the 1970 UNESCO Convention' (September 2002) VII *Art Antiquity and Law* 231, 249.

Article 10

The States Parties to this Convention undertake:

a. to restrict by education, information and vigilance, movement of cultural property illegally removed from any State Party to this Convention and, as appropriate for each country, oblige antique dealers, subject to penal or administrative sanctions, to maintain a register recording the origin of each item of cultural property, names and addresses of the supplier, description and price of each item sold and to inform the purchaser of the cultural property of the export prohibition to which such property may be subject;
b. to endeavour by educational means to create and develop in the public mind a realization of the value of cultural property and the threat to the cultural heritage created by theft, clandestine excavations and illicit exports.

The two paragraphs of Article 10 oblige States Parties firstly to restrict 'by education, information and vigilance' and, by special obligations imposed on 'antique' dealers, the movement of cultural property illegally removed from another State, and secondly to take certain general educational measures. The provision is not without some difficulties which will be discussed below, and the running together of a paragraph on education with antique dealers is rather puzzling. The provision on antique dealers originally appeared, in much stronger form, in Article 7(h) of the Secretariat draft.[1] It was relegated to Article 10 when the new form of Article 7 was adopted.

Paragraph (a)

The first part of Article 10(a) requires States:

> to restrict by education, information and vigilance, movement of cultural property illegally removed from any State Party.

Bator comments that this is an 'unenforceable undertaking'.[2] That said, there is a provision for 'good offices' by UNESCO in case of dispute which applies generally to all obligations under the Convention (Article 17). Apart from that, the only recourse would be to procedures outside the Convention, such as to the International Court of Justice or to arbitration agreed by the parties – both unlikely for undertakings in Article 10(a). This paragraph does seem to provide the type of obligation often found in international treaties where parties wish to impose broad objectives but not bind each other to specific forms of implementation.

Raschèr et al comment:

[1] Unesdoc SHC/MD/3 Annex, 3; RD Abramson and SB Huttler, 'The Legal response to the Illicit Movement of Cultural Property' (1973) 5 *Law and Policy in International Business* 932, 953.

[2] PM Bator, 'An Essay on the International Trade in Art' (1982) 34 *Stanford Law Review* 275, 378.

> Implementation of Article 10 UNESCO Convention 1970, is intended to prevent cultural property of questionable origins from being fed through the illicit art trade in order to cloud its true origins.[3]

States Parties are required to take at least some steps to carry out their obligations under Article 10, although what precisely these would be depends on the circumstances. 'Education, information and vigilance' would mean such measures as encouraging journalists, cultural professionals and local communities to circulate information about goods currently in illicit trade; and educating the public (eg those touring heritage-rich countries about the damage done by scavenging important sites and the need to respect local laws). Fraoua suggests the use of films, visits to archaeological sites, and programmes in educational institutions.[4] Certainly States Parties to the Convention should follow the advice of their own cultural professionals on the best means of restricting illicit traffic – some of the strongest comments on this trade have come from cultural professionals in importing countries.[5]

Education and provision of information also apply to persons involved in supervising the flow of trade between countries. One commentator explained the early training of Customs officers in the Netherlands:

> Customs clearly had specialist skills in widely divergent fields, but less experience relating to cultural heritage. A programme was set up to acquaint Customs officials with these matters. This programme included training courses for the cultural experts at Customs (with several training days each year); the production of a video on controlling the export of cultural goods for screening at Customs offices; and pilot projects with targeted inspections at important events, such as the autumn sales at large auction houses, and art fairs.[6]

Next, paragraph (a) requires States to:

> as appropriate for each country, oblige antique dealers, subject to penal or administrative sanctions, to maintain a register… and to inform the purchaser of the cultural property of the export prohibition to which such property may be subject

The provision on 'antique dealers' has received more comment. The term 'antique dealers' appears only in this provision and it is somewhat difficult to understand why dealers in antiques should be singled out for special treatment. 'Antiques' is, in general usage, customarily employed when describing the *near* past, rather than the ancient past (cf 'antiquities'). The majority of 'antique dealers' are sellers of furniture rarely more than 400 years old. 'Dealers in antiquities' on the other hand may sell Mayan grave goods, Classical sculpture, Byzantine relics and Asian

[3] AFG Raschèr, M Bauen, Y Fischer and MN Zen-Ruffinen, *Cultural Property Transfer* (Brussels, Zurich; Bruyland, Schulthess; 2005) 23.

[4] R Fraoua, *Convention concernant les mesures à prendre pour interdire et empêcher l'importation, l'exportation et le transfert de propriété illicites des biens culturels* (Unesdoc CC-86/WS/40, 1986) 83.

[5] For instance, Colin Renfrew (later Lord Renfrew of Kaimsthorn), professor of Archaeology at Cambridge University and author of *Loot, Legitimacy and Ownership* (London, Duckworth, 2000).

[6] M van Heese, 'The Fight Against Illicit Traffic in Cultural Goods – The Dutch Approach' (2006) XI *Art Antiquity and Law* 85, 87–88.

Bronze Age objects, having generally a wide range in both subject matter and date. As Gordon observes:

> It seems legitimate to wonder, however, why the requirement is limited to antique dealers instead of covering all businessmen who regularly deal in cultural property, such as art dealers and merchants who specialize in liquidating estates. Such an extension of the requirement would have provided more protection against illicit dealings.[7]

Since the word 'antiques' is not used anywhere else in the Convention, it may be that it is simply a clumsy translation of the French word 'antiquités'. French, the original language of the draft, has only one word 'antiquité' for both categories. Fraoua simply states that Article 10 requires States to control dealers in antiquities and 'all other dealers in cultural goods' to keep a register.[8] While this may have been the intention of the drafter, it does not appear in the text. As the terms are undefined, it would be possible to interpret the term broadly but, as the obligation imposed is a fairly onerous one, it seems more likely that it will be interpreted restrictively by States with powerful dealer lobbies.

The obligation in respect of antique dealers has caused some problems for federal States. It is expressed to be 'as appropriate for each country': this would cover the situation where local legislation (eg from component units in a federation) already regulates the matter. Bator called this obligation to regulate dealers a 'nuisance provision', while Abramson and Huttler take the view that 'failure to regulate antique dealers would not constitute a breach of the Convention upon a determination that no regulation would be most appropriate for that country.'[9] They base their argument on 'the broad loophole' which was inserted in the provision: the familiar phrase 'as appropriate for each country'. But such a phrase would not allow a party to ignore the provision altogether.[10] At the very least it would seem necessary for a State Party to make some inquiry into existing laws regulating dealers and to draw the attention of the appropriate level of government to this obligation. 'As appropriate for each country' seems more suitably to recognise the great variety of ways in which legal systems around the world control internal trade and leaves a wide discretion as to how they implement this obligation; particularly as regards the penal or administrative sanctions that are to be applied.

Reporting to UNESCO has not indicated a high uptake for this particular obligation. An Evaluation Report in 2014 found that only 52 per cent of State respondents reported that dealers were required to register their sales,[11] while a 2023 report indicated that only 32 per cent of reporting States responded

[7] JB Gordon, 'The UNESCO Convention on the Illicit Movement of Art Treasures' (1971) 12 *Harvard International Law Journal* 537, 553.

[8] Fraoua (n 4) 83.

[9] Abramson and Huttler (n 1) 963.

[10] See also Fraoua (n 4) 84.

[11] Above, I, ch 4.

positively on this matter.[12] However, there are a number of countries, particularly in the Middle East, which have had a great deal of experience of trafficking in cultural objects and which have quite detailed legislation regulating the activities of dealers: Turkey and Egypt for example.[13] Such detailed regulation of dealers is often very difficult to enforce even where the penalties are severe and the cultural authorities diligent. When Germany became party to the 1970 Convention in 2007 its implementing legislation contained a provision dealing specifically with the requirement for record keeping by the art and antique trade; this has held true in the subsequent German legislation from 2016.[14] There were objections from the trade but the Report on the implementation by the Federal Government recorded that 'the additional burden on the German art and antiques trade that was feared in 2007 as a consequence of the statutory recording obligations in respect of the purchase and sale of cultural property has failed to materialise'.[15] Switzerland, in its implementing law, imposes strict legal requirements on 'persons active in the art trade', including a requirement for due diligence and the keeping of records.[16]

The United Kingdom took the view, when adopting the Convention, that dealers registered for Value Added Tax are already required to keep records containing the specified information. Failure to keep these records would be an offence under the tax legislation. Customs would have a right to access the records and the police can do so when they have a search warrant.[17] Whether in practice this is effective in deterring the illicit trade is debatable. *ArtWatch UK* has reported in the past on the systematic plundering of churches in England and Wales, which went largely unnoticed for years:

> Treasures ranging from masonry to tapestry to stained glass have been taken from isolated churches, often in the notably rural counties of Devon and Herefordshire, feeding a trade in ecclesiastical objects facilitated by art dealers' failure to carry out due diligence.

[12] For the 2019–2022 reporting cycle, UNESCO has noted that, of the 91 States reporting on implementation of the Convention, only 32% responded 'excellent', 'very good' or 'good' on the requirement to register, while 31% responded 'poor' and 26% merely 'satisfactory': Subsidiary Committee of the Meeting of States Parties, 11th Session, C70/23/11.SC/7 (Paris, UNESCO, 1–2 June 2023) p 14.

[13] J Blake, 'Turkey' in JAR Nafziger and RK Paterson (eds), *Handbook on the Law of Cultural Heritage and International Trade* (Cheltenham, Edward Elgar, 2014) 437, 444.

[14] Act on the Protection of Cultural Property, 2016, ch 4 ('Requirements related to the placing on the market of cultural property'), including record keeping requirements (s 45). For commentary, see R Peters, 'Preventing Trafficking in Cultural Property: Import and Export Provisions as Two Sides of the Same Coin' (2019) 2 *Santander Art and Culture Law Review* 95.

[15] German Federal Government, 'Report of the Federal Government on the Protection of Cultural Property in Germany' (Berlin, 2013) 4.

[16] Swiss Law on the International Transfer of Cultural Property (2005), Art 16.

[17] See K Chamberlain, 'UK Accession to the 1970 UNESCO Convention' (September 2002) VII *Art Antiquity and Law* 231, 250 and the Advisory Panel on Illicit Trade Report (London, Department for Culture, Media and Sport, 2000), para 59. Note also that the more recent Regulations applying anti-money laundering rules to the UK art market might serve this purpose as well: Money Laundering Regulations 2017 (applying to art market participants from January 2020).

The reporting quotes a senior police officer from West Mercia police saying that while:

> … most collectors would have bought items in good faith, the dealers involved were not doing enough to ensure that objects were on the market legitimately. He said: "Our general consensus is that their records are woefully inadequate. They say they comply with the law and they probably do – just – but do they turn a blind eye? I would say, yes they do."[18]

If this is the situation in England, how much more difficult will it be to have dealers maintain detailed records in less wealthy and less organised countries with a less informed population?

The motive behind Article 10(a) was for records on the origin of goods being traded to be used to assist in the tracing of property illicitly acquired and to enable its return before it became untraceable. Dealers are also to notify purchasers of relevant export restrictions. This can be an explicit legal requirement in certain States, for instance in Switzerland under its implementing legislation.[19] The United Kingdom adopted an interesting approach to this requirement. According to Chamberlain at the time:

> The UK could give effect to this obligation through the system of implied warranties under the Sale of Goods Act 1979, in particular the implied warranty that the property was free from encumbrance, of satisfactory quality and reasonably fit for its purpose.[20]

The art trade commonly argues that its dealings should be secret; that no details of the seller or buyer should be revealed. A number of reasons are given: knowledge of the location of an object could assist thieves; a seller may want to avoid tax, keep his or her assets hidden from a spouse, etc. Most of these reasons do not stand up to analysis. Other fields such as share trading transactions cannot be kept secret. There is no valid reason why the art trade should enjoy complete secrecy. As Elsen states, 'anonymity for sellers to museums is an archaic, unjustified, and outrageous anomaly'.[21] Besides, art market professionals have more recently fallen within the regime of Anti-Money Laundering regulations, forcing them to disclose and do far more than they had ever done in the past.[22]

Registration of dealers on the terms set out in this Article would go a long way towards solving this problem of secrecy.

Over the years, the importance of Article 10(a) has been stressed by the Subsidiary Committee to the Meeting of States Parties[23] and the ICPRCP.

[18] F Hallett, 'Does the Art Trade Turn a Blind Eye to Church Thefts?' (*ArtWatch UK*, 2015).

[19] Swiss Law on the International Transfer of Cultural Property (2005), Art 16(2).

[20] Chamberlain (n 17) 250.

[21] A Elsen, 'An Outrageous Anomaly' originally published in *ARTNews*, reprinted in (1992) 1 *International Journal of Cultural Property* 129, 131.

[22] In the European Union, for example, this was introduced with the 5th Anti-Money Laundering Regulations, which covers 'art market participants' (begun January 2020).

[23] For instance by the Subsidiary Committee, C70/21/9.SC 9 (Paris, 2021) and C70/22/10.SC 9 (Paris, 2022); and by the Intergovernmental Committee, ICPRCP/22/23.COM 12 (Paris, 2023).

Paragraph (b)

The obligation to develop public concern for cultural property and threats to cultural heritage is undertaken in many countries by museums and other heritage bodies. UNESCO itself has promoted the cause with projects such as the 'Real Price of Art' campaign of 2020[24] and 'The Virtual Museum of Stolen Cultural Objects' of 2025.[25]

One of the most effective means of spreading information on the 1970 Convention and its role is through the education of children. For example, in the United Kingdom a lot of attention has been given to putting information into local communities and schools, particularly on the damage done by treasure-hunting and metal detecting, using archaeologists and local historical societies to provide manpower, and setting up informational digs as holiday activities for schoolchildren.[26] It is expected that an interest generated at a young age will survive into adulthood and support the necessary governmental action for the protection of cultural property.

[24] UNESCO, 'The Real Price of Art, International UNESCO campaign reveals the hidden fact of art trafficking' (20 October 2020). There has been some criticism of this campaign: N Kenney, 'UNESCO under fire for using Met objects in anti-trafficking campaign', *The Art Newspaper* (13 November 2020).

[25] UNESCO, 'Virtual Museum of Stolen Cultural Objects', October 2025. For cost, see A Schrader, 'UNESCO has teamed up with Interpol to Build a Virtual Museum of Stolen Cultural Artifacts' (*artnet*, 13 October 2023).

[26] 'Pioneering Programme Using Archaeology to Empower Young People', *Historic England* (28 May 2023), as well as the latter's creation of 'Heritage Watch' groups associated with local police forces.

Article 11

> The export and transfer of ownership of cultural property under compulsion arising directly or indirectly from the occupation of a country by a foreign power shall be regarded as illicit.

Article 11 is the third of four Articles in the 1970 Convention dealing with illicit export.[1] It covers situations where the occupying power demands that cultural property be exported or compels an owner to transfer possession. But what if the owner is in a position where he or she has to sell the object in order to survive because of economic conditions created by the occupation? It could be said that this is indirect compulsion arising from an occupation. There is of course an analogy to be drawn with forced sales that occurred in Nazi-controlled territories of Europe during the Second World War, many of which have been re-examined as a result of latter-day restitution claims.[2]

What is the effect of the export or transfer being 'illicit'? Import is not mentioned, although perhaps import into another State Party would by default be illicit according to Article 3. Bator saw the phrase 'shall be regarded as illicit' as amounting to a prohibition, although he found similar wording in Article 3 'mysterious' and falling short of a real prohibition.[3] Fraoua goes further: he considers that the effect of the provision is to make transfers of goods removed contrary to the wishes of their true owners as void and ineffective.[4] Chamberlain considers it likely that an English court would refuse to recognise such transfer of title on grounds of public policy.[5] Once again, whether a transaction is 'illicit' is difficult to establish and the effect of its interpretation would depend on the legal system being asked to implement this provision. At the very least, the transaction of export or transfer of ownership should not stand and the position prior to occupation should be reinstated.

This interpretation echoes the 1954 Hague Convention for the Protection of Cultural Property in the Event of Armed Conflict and, in particular, its Protocols of 1954 and 1999.[6] The 1954 Protocol set out, first, that the export of cultural property from an occupied territory shall be prevented by Contracting Parties and, second, that Contracting Parties must take into custody cultural property imported into their territories either directly or indirectly from an occupied territory.[7] The 1999 Protocol expands on this by requiring occupying Parties to prohibit and prevent

[1] The others being Arts 3, 9 and 13(d).

[2] While the Washington Conference Principles on Nazi-Confiscated Art (1998) did not specifically provide for 'forced sales', the Best Practices (2024) incorporate forced sales and sales under duress as being equivalent to 'Nazi-confiscated' or 'Nazi-looted': *Best Practices for the Washington Conference Principles on Nazi-Confiscated Art* (Washington DC, 5 March 2024) endorsed by over 30 countries.

[3] PM Bator, 'An Essay on the International Trade in Art' (1982) 34 *Stanford Law Review* 275, 378.

[4] R Fraoua, *Convention concernant les mesures à prendre pour interdire et empêcher l'importation, l'exportation et le transfert de propriété illicites des biens culturels* (Unesdoc CC-86/WS/40, 1986) 85.

[5] K Chamberlain, 'UK Accession to the 1970 UNESCO Convention' (Sept 2002) VII *Art Antiquity and Law* 231, 250.

[6] See below, IV, ch 1(iii).

[7] Protocol (1954) at Art I(2).

illicit export, other removal or transfer of cultural property, as well as archaeological excavations (unless required for safeguarding, recording or preservation).[8]

Article 11 of the 1970 Convention is an important adjunct to these instruments, since it could apply in States Parties to the 1970 Convention which are not party to the 1954 Convention or its Protocols. There are, for instance, some 15 more States Parties of the 1970 Convention than the Hague Convention, 35 more than the First Protocol and 60 more than the Second Protocol.[9] Consequently, there will be situations where Article 11 is the only international provision governing traffic from an occupied country. Under the 1954 Convention, UNESCO may render assistance and under the 1970 Convention it may provide various services (see Article 15): these provisions could be usefully applied where the States concerned are not all Parties to one or other of the Conventions.

However, Article 11 can be applied only where there has been occupation by a 'foreign power' ie another State. It cannot be used in a situation of non-international armed conflict, whereas the 1954 Hague Convention does apply in such circumstances (see Article 19 of the 1954 Convention). An example from the 1990s can help to illustrate this distinction. As the former Yugoslavia was disintegrating, the town of Vukovar in Croatia was hotly contested and fell to the Federal Yugoslav forces in November 1991. The contents of the Vukovar museum were removed to Novi Sad in Federal Yugoslav territory. Croatia argued that this was an illegal export from occupied territory, Yugoslavia being party to both the 1954 and 1970 Conventions. Although Yugoslavia had not then recognised Croatia as an independent State, the 1954 Hague Convention can apply to non-international conflicts through Article 19. Article 11 of the 1970 Convention, on the contrary, would not apply to such situations. The Federal Government argued that it had acted to protect the cultural property concerned. On behalf of the Council of Europe, an art expert examined the collection and found it was being well cared for.[10]

Croatia was recognised as an independent State on 15 January 1992 by all States of the Council of Europe. In 1994, part of the 'Vukovar treasure' was sent to Paris for exhibition by the Federal Republic of Yugoslavia. Croatia protested, seeking its return to Croatia, and the exhibition was cancelled. France returned the collection to the Federal Republic. It was said to be contrary to France's obligations under the First Protocol to the Hague Convention for France to allow the import of cultural property exported from an occupied territory in this way.[11] Only in 2001 were some of the treasures returned to Croatia – but, as usually happens during armed conflicts, the rest had been destroyed or had otherwise gone missing.[12]

[8] Art 9.

[9] Such numbers are subject to change, though perhaps not dramatically since all four instruments have reached plateaus in terms of ratifications (marked at January 2026).

[10] For the entire Vukovar episode, see A Jacobowski, *State Succession in Cultural Property* (Oxford, Oxford University Press, 2015) 229–32.

[11] LV Prott, 'Repatriation of Cultural Property', *University of British Columbia Law Review* (1995) special issue, 229–40, 236.

[12] Jacobowski (n 10) 229–32.

Article 12

> The States Parties to this Convention shall respect the cultural heritage within the territories for the international relations of which they are responsible, and shall take all appropriate measures to prohibit and prevent the illicit import, export and transfer of ownership of cultural property in such territories.

The obligation to extend the Convention to dependent territories at Article 12, when drafted in 1970, could have covered a still important number of areas. However, the major States which then administered territories – France, the United Kingdom, the United States and even Australia (re Papua-New Guinea) – did not become party for some time, at which point most of those territories had become independent. Former metropolitan powers often have substantial cultural material relating to the history of former dependent territories, in the form of archives and ethnological collections. The obligations in the 1970 Convention to protect the cultural heritage of these areas by export control (Article 6), education (Article 10) and administrative action (Article 8) had a special significance at a time when territories were becoming independent, as they often did not have the resources to care for large amounts of cultural property and were often dependent for some time on expertise and resources in the former metropolitan State. Special agreements were appropriate in such situations, and return of cultural property could become a lively issue.

Another sensitive issue is the question of cultural property in areas which are no longer regarded as 'dependent territories' but integrated into the former colonising power. Examples from the Pacific include Easter Island (Chile), Hawaii (United States), Tahiti and New Caledonia (France). The overseas part of the integrated State may have important and different cultural property which the inhabitants wish to protect for their own descendants' better access. Some States are accepting the different cultural needs of the groups that compose them, even groups on the same territory, and are entering into return arrangements to allow them to recover objects – as well as human remains – located in national museums. Both Australia and Canada control the export of Indigenous material and have made numerous internal returns since the 1980s.[1] The United States has important legislation requiring internal repatriation to Native American peoples[2] and has subsequently adopted legislation to prevent export.[3]

A related issue is the return of cultural property from museums in the capital of a Federation which has disintegrated or of a unitary country which has split apart. Important cultural property originating from the States which emerged

[1] For Canada, see the Canadian Cultural Property Export Control List (CRC 448), Group II, and for Australia the Protection of Movable Cultural Heritage Act 1986, ss 7(b) and 8.

[2] Native American Graves Protection and Repatriation Act, 25 USC ss 3001-13. The term includes native inhabitants of Hawaii.

[3] Safeguarding Tribal Objects of Patrimony Act (2022), known as the 'STOP Act'.

from the former Soviet Union remained within the Russian Federation.[4] Likewise, cultural property was contested in the breakup of Czechoslovakia, the dissolution of Yugoslavia and the separation of Eritrea from Ethiopia in the early 1990s.[5] Lingering issues between new States of this nature are not settled by the 1970 Convention and have to be dealt with by applying the laws of State succession or through other international procedures, such as UNESCO's Intergovernmental Committee (ICPRCP).[6] States seem to be reluctant to use arbitration or the International Court of Justice to settle these kinds of dissolution disputes. Many of them have been resolved by negotiation between the dissolved units (former Czechoslovakia) or by conflict or political pressure from other concerned States (former Yugoslavia).[7]

[4] Pertinent examples include parts of the Scythian Treasure, Bronze Age artefacts from the Black Sea area (present-day Ukraine), excavated in the 19th and early 20th centuries and today kept at the Hermitage Museum in St Petersburg, and the Pamiri Ismaili manuscripts from central Asia (including present-day Tajikistan), currently held in Russian state archives. On the latter, see G Lalbekova, 'Imperial Legacies and Displaced Heritage: The case for repatriation of Pamiri Ismaili manuscripts from Russian State Archives', LLM dissertation (Queen Mary University of London, 2025), unpublished.

[5] See A Jacobowski, *State Succession in Cultural Property* (Oxford, Oxford University Press, 2015) chs 6 and 7.

[6] See above, I, ch 4(i).

[7] See Jakubowski (n 5) ch 6.

Article 13

The States Parties to this Convention also undertake, consistent with the laws of each State:

a. to prevent by all appropriate means transfers of ownership of cultural property likely to promote the illicit import or export of such property;
b. to ensure that their competent services co-operate in facilitating the earliest possible restitution of illicitly exported cultural property to its rightful owner;
c. to admit actions for recovery of lost or stolen items of cultural property brought by or on behalf of the rightful owners;
d. to recognize the indefeasible right of each State Party to this Convention to classify and declare certain cultural property as inalienable which should therefore ipso facto not be exported, and to facilitate recovery of such property by the State concerned in cases where it has been exported.

Article 13 reflects provisions of the Secretariat draft which Bator considered 'complex', 'potentially far-reaching' and 'confusing'.[1] He dismissed their importance, however, on the ground that the undertakings were:

> drained of significance by the fact that they are all made subject to the phrase "consistent with the laws of each State": this was put in to insure that no action inconsistent with or going beyond existing domestic laws of the parties would be required.[2]

The Article should not, however, be so lightly dismissed. In becoming a Party to the Convention, a State must use its best efforts to perform the undertakings. At the very least, a thorough examination of the existing law, its full use towards the purposes of the Convention, and the use of appropriate administrative procedures appear to be required. The difficulties with Article 13 stem from the fact that, like Article 6, it was retained in substantially the same form as in the revised Secretariat draft although related provisions in Article 7 were subsequently changed. Bator stated that, because the Articles were dealt with one by one, the earlier ones were agreed to without wide appreciation of their relationship to later provisions.[3] While this may be true of Article 3, which was adopted before Article 7, it could not be true of Article 13, which was considered subsequently. There is certainly no reason for 'reading down' the provisions of Article 13 to the limited class of goods specified in Article 7.

Paragraph (a)

Paragraph (a) contains the only standalone reference to 'transfer of ownership' in the whole Convention, despite its inclusion in the Convention's title. The original

[1] PM Bator, 'An Essay on the International Trade in Art' (1982) 34 *Stanford Law Review* 275, 378.
[2] ibid 378.
[3] ibid 374.

draft included significant controls on the acquisition of illegally exported goods by museums in importing States (now replaced by the much weaker provision in Art 7(a)). Since there is no indication of what kind of transfer is likely to promote illicit traffic, States have considerable freedom of action in deciding how best within their own legal systems to hinder transfers of ownership likely to promote illicit traffic, and there may therefore be considerable variation between States. For example, in Cyprus private collections must be declared to the Department of Antiquities and inventoried by archaeologists contracted by the Government.[4] Egypt and Jordan prohibit all trade in antiquities.[5] In its 1930 legislation, the former Republic of China took the drastic step of forbidding any foreigner from acquiring cultural property.[6] Such a provision today would almost certainly be contrary to international instruments for the protection of human rights which forbid discrimination on the basis of race or nationality. Nonetheless, a State may clearly decide to regulate all transfers of cultural objects above a certain value; or of acquisitions without certain kinds of documentation (export certificates or statements of provenance). In New Zealand there are strict rules on the sale or other disposal of a *taonga tuturu* with connections to Māori culture.[7] These can be passed only to a registered collector, a public museum or through the offices of a licensed auctioneer or licensed secondhand dealer.[8]

Each State will need to assess which kinds of transfer are 'likely to promote' illicit traffic within that country. Fraoua considers that the paragraph relates primarily to exporting States which have not already taken steps such as classification or registration,[9] but this seems too restrictive, since the paragraph also relates to transfers of ownership likely to promote illicit import – hardly a matter within the competence of exporting States.

Paragraph (b)

The requirement that States ensure that their competent services co-operate in facilitating the earliest possible restitution of illicitly exported cultural property to its 'rightful owner' is a difficult provision to implement. Who is the 'rightful owner'? In some cases of illegal export, the property in the object does not change,

[4] UNESCO, 'Implementation of the Convention on the Means of Prohibiting and Preventing the Illicit Import, Export and Transfer of Ownership of Cultural Property (1970): Reports by Member States and Other States Parties on the Action They Have Taken to Implement the Convention', Unesdoc 32 C/24 (31 July 2003) p 6.

[5] Egyptian Law No 117 of 1983 Promulgating the Protection of Antiquities Law (as amended by Law No 3 of 2010), Art 7; Jordanian Law of Antiquities, 1988, s 24.

[6] Chinese Law on the Preservation of Ancient Objects, 1930, Art 6.

[7] New Zealand's Protected Objects Act 1975, s 2 (definitions).

[8] ibid ss 13–16.

[9] R Fraoua, *Convention concernant les mesures à prendre pour interdire et empêcher l'importation, l'exportation et le transfert de propriété illicites des biens culturels* (Unesdoc CC-86/WS/40, 1986) 88.

although the exporter (who may indeed be the 'rightful owner') is liable to legal sanctions within the State of export. For example, in an early English case, *King of Italy and Italian Government v Marquis de Medici and Christie's*,[10] the papers Christie's were preparing to auction in London had been collected by the Medici family and dated from the eleventh to the eighteenth century, including the letters of Lorenzo the Magnificent and others belonging to the City of Florence. About half the 800 lots were State papers, while the other half were family papers, though still of historical interest. The export had been forbidden and the Italian State had a right of pre-emption. The English judge granted an injunction, pending the trial of the action, to prevent the sale of the State papers, on the basis that there was a *prima facie* case that the action would succeed, since the Italian government was entitled to prevent the disposition of its property by someone who was not entitled to it, but not in respect of the family papers, on the ground that the court would be unlikely to grant an order requiring their return to Italy. Those papers were subsequently sold at auction, despite the judge's warning that this might expose the vendors and the purchasers to an action for damages. A decision on the merits was never given.

The provision as to 'rightful owner' clearly also refers to practice in a number of Civil Law jurisdictions where important cultural property is in public hands and cannot legally be transferred. In the Italian case of *Republic of Ecuador v Danusso*,[11] it was shown that the State of Ecuador had a special right of dominion, a sort of co-ownership, with the holders of archaeological material.

If property has been exported by someone other than the rightful owner (eg after theft from a private owner), then remedies would already seem to be open in respect of the theft, either through prosecution or a civil claim for recovery. Article 13(b) could mean rendering assistance by indicating the appropriate procedures to be undertaken, or, where possible, by direct action by the importing State itself, as was taken by the United States in *United States v Hollinshead*.[12] There the defendants had been charged by the United States with conspiracy to transport stolen property in interstate commerce under the National Stolen Property Act. It was alleged they had cut a Mayan stela from an immovable monument in Guatemala and exported it to California in boxes marked 'personal effects'. Under Guatemalan law, the stela was State property and it was found that the defendants knew this. The court held that it was 'stolen' within the terms of the Act.

Article 13(b) could also require the earliest possible return of material which, if unlawfully exported, becomes the property of the State (eg by forfeiture). The provision would, on that interpretation, justify special vigilance by Customs, or notices being sent to collecting institutions, at the request of the exporting country, regarding particularly important items of cultural property which are missing and suspected to be in transit, especially if information suggests that they are still

[10] (1918) 34 TLR 623.
[11] District Court of Turin, 4410 (1979); Court of Appeal of Turin, 593 (1982).
[12] 495 F.2d 1154 (1974).

in the hands of the wrongdoer. This leads into the issue of criminal networks. Here Interpol, Europol, the World Customs Organization and UNODC play an important role. Operation Pandora, for instance, a series of annual actions by law enforcement inaugurated in 2016, has resulted in the seizure of some 200,000 cultural objects, and the arrests of over 500 individuals.[13] As Campbell states: 'viewing antiquities trafficking as a network, criminal interactions can be anticipated and law enforcement can conduct safe, preventive measures like removing convergence settings'.[14]

States Parties are to ensure that their competent services co-operate with other bodies within their national administrative structures and with foreign services to further the work of restitution. Some may find this difficult to achieve. For example, in 2014 Musteaţă referred to a case involving a dealer in Usingen, Germany, who was alleged to hold antiquities from Moldova. An attempt by Moldovan authorities to regain them failed:

> I have the impression that the Moldovan police and prosecutors have little interest in such cases. The Moldovan branch of the International Criminal Police Organization ICPO – INTERPOL – is very passive too. At the moment, it seems to me that we cannot say that all institutions working in the field of fighting illegal antiquities trade are supporting each other. As a result, metal detecting, illegal excavation and the antiquities trade is flourishing in the Republic of Moldova. It is possible that Moldovan authorities do not prioritise this type of crime, as it may not be a politically popular move.[15]

On the situation in Cyprus, Hardy wrote in 2014 that:

> Heritage crime policing is also constrained by a combination of the law enforcement agencies' non-cooperation and the Greek Cypriot police's own regulations. Undercover police investigations into illicit antiquities smugglers and dealers are legal in the north but illegal in the south. Greek Cypriot police appealed for the legalization of undercover police work on '[i]llegal trading in cultural goods, including antiquities and artefacts'; but the Greek Cypriot parliament 'unanimously rejected' the request.[16]

The services to which the 1970 Convention refers must include, or have access to, experts in the relevant laws and procedures concerning restitution and return. Even non-specialist members of staff should be able to recognise when a problem is developing and when it is necessary to involve experts. There is an added advantage if the experts know their counterparts in other States. Workshops organised by UNESCO can play a significant role.

[13] The 'Operation Pandora' project is run as a partnership between Interpol, Europol and the World Customs Organization. See latest numbers from Interpol press release, '80 arrests and more than 37,700 cultural goods seized in major art trafficking bust' (22 May 2025).

[14] PB Campbell, 'The Illicit Antiquities Trade as a Transnational Criminal Network: Characterizing and Anticipating Trafficking of Cultural Heritage' (2013) 20 *International Journal of Cultural Property* 113, 139.

[15] S Musteaţă, 'Archaeological Heritage Crimes in Romania and Moldova: A Comparative View' in L Grove and S Thomas (eds), *Heritage Crime: Progress, Prospects and Prevention* (New York, Palgrave Macmillan, 2014) 71, 76.

[16] S Hardy, 'Threats to Cultural Heritage in the Cyprus Conflict' in Grove and Thomas, ibid 92.

Paragraph (c)

The obligation here to 'admit actions for recovery' of lost or stolen items of cultural property brought by or on behalf of the rightful owners seems to offer very little, since actions of this kind are a cornerstone of any modern legal system. This paragraph, like the others, requires action 'consistent with the laws of each State', which makes it clear that the Convention does not require any extraordinary or uniform action, but only that consistent with the normal procedural rules of that system. The United States delegation to the Special Committee of Government Experts regarded:

> the obligation of this Article as procedural, ie, to provide a judicial remedy for the vindication of a property right if one exists.[17]

Although the view has been expressed that the words 'consistent with the laws of each State' ensure that 'no action inconsistent with or going beyond existing domestic laws of the parties would be required',[18] this is clearly not the case if such actions do not already exist in the legal system of the State Party.

Apart from the limited circumstances of Article 7(b)(i), this is the only provision in the 1970 Convention dealing specifically with 'stolen' cultural property. The concept of 'stolen' is not defined, thus leaving its scope of application to be decided by each national legal system where the question is raised.

Paragraph (c) refers not only to stolen items of cultural property but also to those that have been 'lost'. This is a strange conjunction. Theft is the taking of property by someone other than the owner – an action generally regarded as morally repugnant and legally actionable. Loss occurs when an item of property cannot be found because of misadventure, negligence or similar circumstances. The moral issues between the two are very different and so is the law. Theft is a punishable offence whereas there is no notion of this in relation to a 'loss'. But once again there are various procedures for recovering ownership of lost objects which might be available in the terms of paragraph (c). 'Loss' may be suggested for items which have disappeared long ago and may surface 20, 30 or 50 years later. They may have been stolen, but the evidence may be impossible to find after such a lapse of time. They may have been retrieved from a destroyed building after a natural disaster or conflict. Whether or not theft can be proven, it should be possible for the former owner to claim back the item. Where the exact trail of possession cannot be ascertained, negotiation seems the best option to settle such a claim.

Of great significance will be the situation of clandestinely excavated archaeological objects. The UNIDROIT Convention treats unlawfully excavated or

[17] Report of the United States Delegation to the Special Committee of Governmental Experts to Examine the Draft Convention on the Means of Prohibiting and Preventing the Illicit Import, Export and Transfer of Ownership of Cultural Property (Paris, UNESCO, 13–14 April 1970) 18.

[18] Bator (n 1) 378.

unlawfully retained cultural objects as 'stolen'.[19] Such is also the position in the United States following the 2002 case of *United States v Schultz* and in England following *Iran v Barakat* in 2007 regarding antiquities taken from a foreign State which holds title to them.[20]

Paragraph (d)

An 'indefeasible' right is one which cannot be lost or surrendered. States Parties are therefore being asked in paragraph (d) to recognise the permanent, non-forfeitable right of any other State Party to declare certain cultural property 'inalienable'. Such a permanent right may be seen as parallel to the right of permanent sovereignty over natural resources established by United Nations General Assembly Resolution 1803 of 1962.[21] The 1970 Convention thus requires parties to the Convention to recognise other States Parties' permanent right to certain *cultural* resources.

The concept of inalienability has a long history, going back to Roman law,[22] and is applied generally in continental European legal systems, but not in common law jurisdictions.[23] In France, for example, public collections belong to the State (or to departments and communes, also public bodies). Those which belong to the public domain are classified, inalienable and imprescriptible.[24] 'Inalienable' means that they cannot legally be transferred. 'Imprescriptible' means that ownership of them cannot be acquired merely by adverse possession, 'good faith' acquisition, or other rights, such as lien or mortgage, which give a right over the goods if the owner does not pay the amount due on them. These objects can always be reclaimed by the State.[25] The important consequence of this is that the State will disregard any transactions which occurred in another State that would normally

[19] UNIDROIT Convention on Stolen or Illegally Exported Cultural Objects (1995), Art 3(2).

[20] *US v Frederick Schultz* 178 F. Supp. 2d 445 (SDNY 2002), aff'd, 333 F.3d.393 (2d Cir. 2003); *Iran v Barakat* [2007] EWCA Civ 1374. For more on these cases, see P Gerstenblith, 'Schultz and Barakat: Universal Recognition of National Ownership of Antiquities' (April 2009) XIV *Art Antiquity and Law* 21. Attention should also be directed to the Model Provisions on State Ownership of Undiscovered Cultural Objects, UNESCO/UNIDROIT: above, IV, ch 3(iii).

[21] General Assembly Resolution 1803 (XVII) of 14 December 1962: 'Permanent sovereignty over natural resources'.

[22] M-A Latournerie, 'L'inaliénabilité: histoire d'un concept' and J-M Leniaud, 'Les fondements de la règle d'aliénabilité dans le droit du patrimoine culturel' in Cornu et al (eds), *L'Inalienabilité des collections, performances et limites?* (Paris, L'Harmattan, 2012) 11–30; 31–52.

[23] LV Prott, 'Inalienability and Other Modes of Protection in Current Legal Systems' in Cornu et al, ibid 75–120.

[24] *Code du Patrimoine*, Art L451-5, and *Code général des propriétés des personnes publiques*, Art L2112-1.

[25] C de Visscher, 'La protection internationale des objets d'art et des monuments historiques' (1935) *Revue de droit international et de législation comparée* 32, 39.

be recognised as valid according to the *lex situs* (the law of the place where the last transfer of ownership occurred).[26]

A not dissimilar effect may be achieved if property regarded by the exporting State as 'forfeit', notwithstanding that the forfeiture has not been recognised by other States, arrives in a State of destination. One interpretation of this provision would be that a State Party simply admits the right of another State Party to ignore all intermediate transactions and reclaim the property whenever it is found again within that State's frontiers. Another interpretation is that an importing State would *recognise* the inalienability placed on the object by the exporting State and would enforce, in its own jurisdiction, the title of the exporting State against the holder's acquisition following any transactions subsequent to the imposition of inalienability. An 'understanding' lodged by the United States at the time of its accession avoids this latter interpretation for its own purposes. In the early French case of *Frias c Pichon*,[27] a silver ciborium, recognised as inalienable under Spanish law, had been taken from Spain and sold to Pichon in France. Frias sued in France to recover the ciborium but the Tribunal de la Seine held that only French rules as to inalienability would be applied and, as the goods were not inalienable by French law, the title of the French purchaser was recognised.

Chamberlain advises that, in England, the 'recovery of such objects could be through the criminal law (the powers that the police have under PACE [Police and Criminal Evidence Act 1984] and the Police Property Act) or through the civil law by allowing an action for conversion by the State asserting ownership'.[28] With respect to the Ife Bronze Head discussed in the Introduction to this book – stolen from a Nigerian museum in 1987 and shipped to England by a dealer in 2017 – it could be argued that these avenues should have been given more appropriate consideration by the UK Government, such that inaction in the case did not flout international commitments under Article 13 of the Convention.

The issue of inalienability was a major one in the negotiations leading up to the UNIDROIT Convention on Stolen or Illegally Exported Cultural Objects in 1995. The result was to allow States to declare certain time limitations on actions relating to material that may otherwise be considered 'inalienable' to another State (see Article 3(5)). Prott comments:

> At the Diplomatic Conference the Committee of the Whole voted for the recognition by all Contracting States of the inalienability of an object from a monument, archaeological site or public collection. This was quite unacceptable to certain States (in particular,

[26] ibid 48. For example, in *Winkworth v Christies Ltd.* [1980] 1 Ch. 496 a collection of Japanese miniatures was stolen in England; sold to a *bona fide* purchaser in Italy and then sent back to London for auction. The English court held that the matter of title was to be settled by reference to Italian law in this case – the *lex rei sitae* – though there can be exceptions to this principle (eg if it would contradict public policy).

[27] *Duc de Frias c Baron Pichon*, Trib Civ de la Seine, Journal de Droit International, E Clunet (ed) (1886) 593.

[28] K Chamberlain, 'UK Accession to the 1970 UNESCO Convention' (September 2002) VII *Art Antiquity and Law* 231, 251.

the Netherlands and Switzerland, which were active members of the working group, and the United Kingdom, which was not). They insisted that inalienability would render the Convention impossible to accept in their countries. The working group therefore developed this provision allowing a State to establish an absolute limit of 75 years to claims for public collections, although it was, for political reasons, expressed as an exception to the general rule in Article 3(4). Nonetheless its substance was crucial in the negotiations.[29]

[29] LV Prott, *Commentary on the 1995 UNIDROIT Convention*, 2nd edn (Builth Wells, Institute of Art and Law, 2021) 60.

Article 14

> In order to prevent illicit export and to meet the obligations arising from the implementation of this Convention, each State Party to the Convention should, as far as it is able, provide the national services responsible for the protection of its cultural heritage with an adequate budget and, if necessary, should set up a fund for this purpose.

The granting of an adequate budget to the national services responsible for managing the cultural heritage sufficient for them to prevent export contrary to local laws and meet the obligations required by the Convention is the substance of this provision. It is rather strangely placed and would more logically follow Article 5 which sets out the functions of those services.

The prevention of illicit export, including the payment of an adequate budget to the services involved, is, as we have seen, beyond the capacity of many developing States. The adequacy of budgets in wealthier States is, however, also suspect. Canada is a wealthy State with developed legislation and a highly competent administration. Yet Fossey, as late as 2015, in relation to Canada's ability to control illicit imports, observed that 'inadequate funding and insufficient personnel rendered the task overwhelming'.[1]

Some services are left to local or private bodies to fund without any inquiry as to whether these funds are adequate. In some cases such specialised services do not exist and the functions concerned are dispersed among various offices. This makes planning and adequate budgeting difficult and may lead to inadequate funds and unrealistic expectations. This is especially true in federal systems of government, which may need to make special arrangements to ensure that there is some overview and co-ordination of dispersed services, and that they are adequately funded.

Article 14 also mentions the setting up of a fund 'if necessary' for the same purposes. The 1964 Recommendation suggests the use of such a fund for the purchase of exceptionally important cultural property, and it is an integral part of export control in some countries. Canadian and Australian legislation, for example, each provides for a Fund to assist in the purchase of cultural property which is not given an export permit, in order to allow a museum to acquire it.[2] In the UK, several funds serve to support the acquisition of national treasures during export deferral – especially the Art Fund, the National Lottery Heritage Fund and the National Heritage Memorial Fund – though the funding route is not set out in legislation. Over the years, these funds have succeeded in supporting a long list of acquisitions. In 2023, the Art Fund and National Heritage Memorial Fund helped

[1] JM Fossey, 'Illicit Traffic in Antiquities: Some Canadian Experiences' in JD Kila and M Balcells (eds), *Cultural Property Crime: An Overview and Analysis of Contemporary Perspectives and Trends* (Leiden, Brill, 2015) 206, 207.

[2] In Canada, this is the Canadian Heritage Preservation Endowment Account: Cultural Property Export and Import Act (1985), s 36. In Australia, it is the National Cultural Heritage Account: Protection of Movable Cultural Heritage Act 1986, s 25B.

support the National Portrait Gallery's co-acquisition of Joshua Reynolds' *Portrait of Mai* (an astonishing £25 million was raised to purchase a half-share in the work, with the other half acquired by the Getty Museum in California).[3]

The original draft of the 1970 Convention suggested much more specifically the setting up of a fund:

> to finance the compensation …, to ensure publicity for lost cultural property and to purchase for public collections certain items of cultural property of special importance. Such a fund could also be used for rewarding those who make archaeological discoveries or trace cultural property which has disappeared, by a payment proportional in value to that of the property discovered or traced.[4]

The commentary to the Secretariat's draft[5] made it clear that the fund or other appropriate financial measures should place the national services for the protection of cultural property 'in a position as necessary to take financial steps to prevent the export of an item of cultural property':

> The fund in question might be used particularly for the acquisition by the competent authorities, on behalf of a public collection, of a particularly important privately-owned item of cultural property which its owner wishes to put on the market.

This has never eventuated. The 'Fund of the 1970 Convention' established by UNESCO through the Third Meeting of States Parties in 2015 is something altogether different: it is aimed at fighting the illicit trade, rather than supporting individual States in making acquisitions.[6]

[3] Department for Culture Media and Sport, *Export of Objects of Cultural Interest 2023–24* (November 2024) 34.

[4] Unesdoc SHC/MD/3 Annex, 4, Art 12.

[5] SHC/MD/3, 12.

[6] See above, I, ch 4.

Article 15

> Nothing in this Convention shall prevent States Parties thereto from concluding special agreements among themselves or from continuing to implement agreements already concluded regarding the restitution of cultural property removed, whatever the reason, from its territory of origin, before the entry into force of this Convention for the States concerned.

International agreements already in existence are not affected by the coming into force of the 1970 Convention. The 1970 Treaty between the United States and Mexico, for example, providing for recovery and return of 'Stolen Archaeological, Historical and Cultural Properties' was not affected by the entry into force of the Convention at a later date for both parties. Similarly, multilateral Conventions such as the 1976 Convention on the Protection of the Archeological, Historical, and Artistic Heritage of the American Nations, remained in force for the parties, even where those States subsequently acceded to the 1970 Convention.

The text of this article also makes clear that States Parties are free to make bilateral agreements among themselves in relation to cultural property removed before the Convention came into force. The logic here is that the 1970 Convention should not be seen as precluding such a bespoke arrangement for particularly contentious material (eg colonial-era removals or spoils of war). It seems that this provision seeks to satisfy those States who would have preferred the 1970 Convention to have a retroactive effect in this regard.[1] The Operational Guidelines to the Convention adopted at the Third Meeting of States Parties in 2015 went further: States Parties should be 'encouraged to find a mutually acceptable agreement' relating to illegally exported, illegally removed or stolen cultural property imported before the Convention's entry into force, especially one that is 'in accordance with the spirit and the principles of the Convention'.[2]

The use of regional agreements is also a suitable way of supplementing the UNESCO Convention with provisions which may be appropriate to a specific region or grouping of States but which could not be universalised.

During the drafting process one delegation also pointed out that Article 15 does not restrict the rights of States to conclude bilateral agreements for the restitution of cultural property removed from the territory of *another* State before or after the entry into force of the Convention.[3] In South East Asia, Thailand has occupied a pivotal position in the illicit trade involving items of cultural property taken from neighbouring States. In 2002, Nagashima recorded artefacts being smuggled from Thailand to Singapore so as to avoid being caught on the land route but then

[1] See above I, ch 3. It was suggested in previous editions of this work that the provision might be read to extend to all special agreements, beyond those relating to pre-implementation removals: PJ O'Keefe, *Protecting Cultural Objects: Before and After 1970* (Builth Wells, Institute of Art and Law, 2017) 184.

[2] Operational Guidelines for the Implementation of the Convention, Adopted at Third Meeting of States Parties to the Convention (Paris, 2015) para 103.

[3] Unesdoc 16 C/17, 6.

being shipped back to Bangkok because of the city's status as the centre of 'genuine stolen works of art'.[4] Recognising the vast outflow of material from Cambodia, in 2000 Thailand and Cambodia signed a bilateral Agreement on Co-operation to Combat Illegal Border Trafficking of Movable Cultural Assets to be Returned to Their Countries of Origin. This allowed for recovery of stolen or illegally exported cultural objects found in the other State. Although much was made of a truckload of antiquities caught crossing the border at the time the Agreement was made, the illicit trade between those two countries does seem to have subsided since then.[5]

The words 'whatever the reason' qualifying the removal also leave it open to States to deal with any situation, not only those concerning colonisation and foreign occupation which were at the origin of subsequent claims for restitution and return. Despite having implemented the Convention in 1979, Peru has bilateral agreements with over a dozen States, each looking to prohibit and prevent illicit trade respectively between them.[6] One such agreement, signed with Egypt in 2005, was resorted to in 2013 when two Peruvian antiquities were detected by Egyptian postal officials, bought by an Egyptian national online from a dealer in Colorado, USA, and were returned to Peruvian officials.[7] China has over 25 bilateral agreements. China's agreement with Italy from 2006, to prevent looting and provide for the return of antiquities, is said to reinforce both the 1970 Convention and the 1995 UNIDROIT Convention in both countries.[8] Twenty years later, this has certainly borne fruit: one major restitution in 2024 involved over 50 artefacts returned from Italy.[9] China's Memorandum of Understanding with Greece, from 2008, reinforces the 1970 Convention, while providing an undertaking to collaborate on the return of important cultural objects, even in cases that fall outside the Convention.[10] In 2015, Egypt and Jordan signed a Cooperation Agreement that

[4] M Nagashima, *The Lost Heritage: The Reality of Artifact Smuggling in Southeast Asia* (Bangkok, Post Books, 2002) 108.

[5] N Brodie, J Doole and P Watson, *Stealing History: The Illicit Trade in Cultural Material* (Cambridge, McDonald Institute for Archaeological Research, 2000) 12.

[6] This includes many South and Latin American countries, but also Austria, China, Egypt and Turkey: J Batievsky and J Velarde, 'The Protection of Cultural Patrimony in Peru' in B Hoffman, *Art and Cultural Heritage: Law, Policy and Practice* (New York, Cambridge University Press, 2006), 104.

[7] B Alva Guerrero, 'Peru in Egypt: Archaeological Recovery' in H van Hooff (ed), *Culture & Development: Stop the Illicit Traffic of Cultural Property* (UNESCO Regional Office, Havana, 2013) 48.

[8] Memorandum of Understanding between the Italian Republic and the People's Republic of China on the Prevention of Theft, Clandestine Excavations, Illicit Import, Export, Trafficking and Transit of Cultural Property and on the Promotion of Restitution (Beijing, 20 January 2006).

[9] See State Council of the People's Republic of China (press release), 'China Appreciates Italy's Cultural Heritage Protection, Lost Relics Return Work: Spokesperson' (11 November 2024), celebrating the return of 56 Chinese artefacts, which were viewed by Chinese President Xi Jinping along with Italian President Sergio Mattarella: 'It demonstrates Italy's respect for China's cultural heritage and is a vivid example of China-Italy friendship'.

[10] EN Moustaira, 'Greece' in JAR Nafziger and RK Paterson (eds), *Handbook on the Law of Cultural Heritage and International* Trade (Cheltenham, Edward Elgar, 2014) 176, 188.

concerned the protection and restitution of stolen cultural property, as well as the fight against illicit trade in antiquities.[11]

Interestingly, Article 15 has been swept up as one of three key Articles in the Convention that can serve to facilitate the return or restitution of illicitly exported cultural property: States Parties were called upon during the seventh session of the Subsidiary Committee to the Meeting of States Parties in 2019 to take the necessary measures to facilitate such returns 'in accordance with articles 7, 13 and 15'.[12] This decision by the Subsidiary Committee was then welcomed, both in 2021 and 2024, by no less a body than the UN General Assembly.[13]

In relation to cultural property illegally removed before the entry into force of the 1970 Convention, the General Assembly also expressed its 'grave concern' regarding this issue in 2024, specifically in relation to objects 'which are part of museums and collections'; it called on Member States to take the appropriate steps for their 'return or restitution to the countries of origin'.[14] This was the first time any such statement had been made at the General Assembly level. It seemed to target controversial holdings in museums such as the Parthenon Marbles at the British Museum in the UK or the Bust of Nefertiti at the Neues Museum in Germany (though no specific collections were mentioned). The General Assembly went on to express its recognition that 'most of these objects constitute an essential part of the spiritual, ancestral, historical and cultural heritage of their countries of origin' and underscored the importance of 'ensuring access to these artefacts for preserving cultural identity and continuity for present and future generations'.[15]

[11] Model Provisions on the Prevention and Fight Against the Illicit Trafficking of Cultural Property (2025), 19.

[12] Seventh session of the Subsidiary Committee of the Meeting of States Parties to the 1970 Convention (Paris, May 2019).

[13] UN General Assembly Resolution 11, 76th session (6 December 2021) and Resolution 13, 79th session (6 December 2024).

[14] Resolution 6, 79th session (6 December 2024).

[15] ibid.

Article 16

> The States Parties to this Convention shall in their periodic reports submitted to the General Conference of the United Nations Educational, Scientific and Cultural Organization on dates and in a manner to be determined by it, give information on the legislative and administrative provisions which they have adopted and other action which they have taken for the application of this Convention, together with details of the experience acquired in this field.

Obligations are placed by Article 16 on States Parties to inform UNESCO of their implementing legislation or regulations, the actions they have taken and any experience acquired in its application. At its nineteenth session (1976), the General Conference, by Resolution 4.122, requested that Member States submit reports on implementation of the 1964 Recommendation on the means of prohibiting and preventing the illicit export, import and transfer of ownership of cultural property and the 1970 Convention for consideration at its twentieth session.[1] The General Conference in 1978 requested the Secretariat to ask States for the reasons why they found difficulty in acceding to the 1970 Convention.[2] Reports were subsequently requested and published at regular intervals as is required by the UNESCO Constitution. However, not all States reported. For a while, State practice and particular developments were discussed from time to time at the ICPRCP. But this practice was strongly criticised by a number of European States, who wanted a clear separation between the ICPRCP and the work of implementing the 1970 Convention.

Since Meetings of States Parties to the 1970 Convention were established more concretely and regularly in 2012, and since the 'Subsidiary Committee' was established with regular meetings in 2013,[3] these issues now have more appropriate forums to be discussed.[4] Reviewing national reports has been made part of the remit of the Subsidiary Committee.[5] Since 2015 the Subsidiary Committee has been reminding States Parties of their 'obligation to report' under Article 16.[6] This has greatly improved the uptake amongst States: 27 States first reported in 1978, and the number dipped to a meagre eight in 1995, but it has grown impressively to 91 in 2023, representing over 60 per cent of States Parties to the Convention for the first time ever.[7]

These reports are made available online. A Culture Monitoring Platform was introduced in 2025, which has been able to gather data through periodic reporting mechanisms of the 1970 Convention.[8]

[1] Unesdoc 20 C/84.
[2] Unesdoc 22 C/93.
[3] Above, I, ch 4(iii).
[4] Unesdoc C70/15/3.MSP/5B March 2015.
[5] Rules of Procedures, paragraph I.b, as introduced by Resolution 6.MSP 15 of the Sixth Meeting of States Parties (Paris, 25–26 May 2021).
[6] Third Meeting of the Subsidiary Committee (Paris, 28–30 September 2015).
[7] Subsidiary Committee of the Meeting of States Parties, 11th Session, C70/23/11.SC/7 (Paris, UNESCO, 1–2 June 2023).
[8] Resolution 8.MSP 12, Eighth Meeting of the States Parties to the 1970 Convention (Paris, 19–20 May 2025).

Article 17

1. The States Parties to this Convention may call on the technical assistance of the United Nations Educational, Scientific and Cultural Organization, particularly as regards:
   (a) Information and education;
   (b) consultation and expert advice;
   (c) co-ordination and good offices.
2. The United Nations Educational, Scientific and Cultural Organization may, on its own initiative conduct research and publish studies on matters relevant to the illicit movement of cultural property.
3. To this end, the United Nations Educational, Scientific and Cultural Organization may also call on the co-operation of any competent non-governmental organization.
4. The United Nations Educational, Scientific and Cultural Organization may, on its own initiative, make proposals to States Parties to this Convention for its implementation.
5. At the request of at least two States Parties to this Convention which are engaged in a dispute over its implementation, UNESCO may extend its good offices to reach a settlement between them.

UNESCO has long been active in providing Parties to the Convention with technical assistance in information and education, consultation and expert advice as well as co-ordination and good offices, at the request of the parties. Beginning in the 1980s, it published national laws on cultural heritage,[1] a study on the workings of national controls,[2] the 'Handbook of National Regulations Concerning the Export of Cultural Property',[3] an early commentary on the 1970 Convention[4] and a resource handbook for the implementation of the 1970 Convention.[5] In the early 2000s, it set up an electronic database of national legislation forwarded by States and supplied expertise for the drafting of national legislation. Since 2015, many activities of this nature have been taken up by the Subsidiary Committee of the Meeting of States Parties to the Convention.[6]

Since 1986, UNESCO has conducted, with the close cooperation of INTERPOL and ICOM, regional workshops on fighting illicit traffic, thus enabling States to compare national practice and learn of other possible means of improving implementation. For instance, a series of workshops were organised in Africa

[1] Unesdoc CLT-85/WS: the 'red leaflet' series on national legislation.

[2] LV Prott and PJ O'Keefe, 'Implementation of the 1970 UNESCO Convention on the Means of Prohibiting and Preventing the Illicit Import, Export and Transfer of Ownership of Cultural Property', Unesdoc CLT-83/WS/16 (1983).

[3] LV Prott and PJ O'Keefe, *Handbook of National Regulations Concerning the Export of Cultural Property* (Paris, UNESCO, 1988).

[4] R Fraoua, *Convention concernant les mesures à prendre pour interdire et empêcher l'importation, l'exportation et le transfert de propriété illicites des biens culturels* (Unesdoc CC-86/WS/40, 1986) 53.

[5] P Askerud and E Clément, *Preventing the Illicit Traffic in Cultural Property* (Paris, UNESCO, 1997).

[6] See, eg, Decisions of the Subsidiary Committee of the Meeting of States Parties, Thirteenth Session, C70/25/13.SC/Decisions (Paris, May 2025).

beginning in 2023 in order to encourage the more effective implementation of the Convention amongst African States.[7] A significant side benefit of regional workshops is that they enable people to meet their counterparts in the administrations of other States. Having established a personal relationship, it is much faster and easier to make contact if it is necessary to deal quickly with a theft or a case of illicit export. It is also more efficient if one official wishes to alert his or her counterpart that a suspected illicit import has occurred.

By Article 17(2), UNESCO may, on its own initiative, research and publish studies on the illicit trade. O'Keefe, for instance, published a report in 1997 on the trade in antiquities.[8] UNESCO has now published Model Provisions on the Prevention and Fight Against the Illicit Trafficking of Cultural Property, approved at the Eighth Meeting of States Parties to the 1970 Convention in 2025.[9]

It has been suggested that UNESCO could document and publish violations of the Convention and thus bring pressure to bear on the States responsible for such violations.[10] However, in light of the varying interpretations given the Convention, this would have been almost impossible to implement as no State would likely agree to the future possibility of being criticised. Suggestions are also made from time to time that individuals alleged to be involved in theft and/or illicit trafficking should be named. However, this could give rise to charges of defamation by the persons concerned, or at least a violation of privacy rights. In 2019, the UNESCO General Conference had suggested the Director-General issue public statements condemning sales of illicitly-traded cultural objects when petitioned to do so by affected States.[11] This proposal was studied by UNESCO bodies, looking into whether such a statement would indeed comply with UNESCO's role under Article 17.[12]

The ICPRCP has also been active in promoting technical assistance: in 1999, the General Conference of UNESCO established a Fund at the request of the ICPRCP to assist in the recovery of objects, endorsed the International Code of Ethics for Dealers in Cultural Property and supported the 'Object-ID' identification system to help trace missing objects.[13] In 2011, it adopted the UNESCO/UNIDROIT Model Provisions on State Ownership of Undiscovered Cultural Objects.

The provision in Article 17(3) for cooperation with non-governmental bodies reflects the close cooperation with bodies such as ICOM and ICOMOS, which are both directly concerned with instances of theft and illicit traffic concerning

[7] See Eighth Meeting of States Parties to the 1970 Convention, Item 7 – Report on the Activities of the Secretariat, C70/25/8.MSP/7, 'Support for UNESCO's Global Priority Africa' (Paris, 19-20 May 2025), paras 13–20.

[8] PJ O'Keefe, *Trade in Antiquities: Reducing Destruction and Theft* (Paris, UNESCO Publishing, Archetype, 1997).

[9] See above, I, ch 4.

[10] RD Abramson and SB Huttler, 'The Legal response to the Illicit Movement of Cultural Property' (1973) 5 *Law and Policy in International Business* 932, 963.

[11] Resolution 42-II(5) of the 40th General Conference of UNESCO (November 2019) 40C.

[12] Subsidiary Committee of the Meeting of States Parties, 12th Meeting, C70/24/12.SC (Paris, May 2024).

[13] See above, I, ch 4.

museums, sites and monuments.[14] The International Centre for the Study of the Preservation and Restoration of Cultural Property (ICCROM), founded in 1956, complements that work through training, information, research, cooperation and advocacy for the cultural heritage.[15] Although not mentioned in Article 17, there is close coordination between UNESCO and other international governmental organisations, such as UNIDROIT, WIPO and the World Customs Organization, and regional organisations such as the Council of Europe.

Under Article 17(4), UNESCO, on its own initiative, may make proposals to States Parties on the implementation of the Convention. Examples of this are the Recommendation of the Committee of Experts in 1983 and the Final Report into the Evaluation of UNESCO's Standard-setting Work of the Culture Sector in 2014.[16]

Finally, under Article 17(5), UNESCO may extend its good offices to reach a settlement between States Parties engaged in a dispute on the implementation of the Convention. So far it has not been called on to do so, although the seeds of such a dispute were clearly present early on between Mexico and the United States after the rejection by Mexico of the form of the United States' implementation of the Convention.[17] Similarly, a difference of opinion existed for more than ten years between the United States and Canada as to the application of the Convention to the pillaged material for which Canada was seeking an import ban from the United States.[18] It is noteworthy that UNESCO can offer its services to resolve disputes only if requested to do so by at least one of the parties.

There is no other mechanism indicated to resolve disputes arising from the Convention. This is quite surprising since the dispute settlement clause in a treaty is usually one of substance – not the fifth paragraph in a provision relating to technical assistance. In other Conventions specific reference is often made to the International Court of Justice as the appropriate body to resolve disputes. In any event, where parties are subject to the compulsory jurisdiction of that Court,[19] or wish between themselves to submit a dispute concerning the Convention to that Court, there is no reason why this should not be done. It would seem wise, however, to start with the expertise in cultural matters of UNESCO, since the International Court of Justice has very little experience in this field and its one final decision which involved cultural matters was not, in respect of those matters, particularly well handled.[20]

[14] ICOM Code of Ethics (2004), ss 2.2, 2.3 and 2.4 (this version was rebranded in 2017 and has undergone a series of new drafts, towards a final approval in 2026); ICOMOS, International Charter for the Conservation and Restoration of Monuments and Sites (The Venice Charter 1964), Arts 7, 8 and 15.

[15] See website at www.iccrom.org.

[16] See above, I, ch 4(v).

[17] See above, I, chs 2–3.

[18] See above, Art 9.

[19] This must be accepted by States in advance: Statute of the International Court of Justice, Article 35.

[20] *Temple of Preah Vihear, Merits, Judgment (Cambodia v Thailand)* ICJ Reports, 1962, p 6.

UNESCO, as a specialised agency of the United Nations, may request advisory opinions from the International Court of Justice on legal questions arising within the scope of its activities.[21] There have been suggestions at times that this could be an avenue for certain cultural property disputes involving historically removed antiquities (ie the Parthenon Marbles) to find their way before the International Court of Justice, with the support of UNESCO, but this has never been taken up.[22]

[21] Charter of the United Nations, Art 96; Constitution of UNESCO, Art V.

[22] International human rights barrister Geoffrey Robertson has made such a suggestion regarding the Parthenon Marbles at the British Museum: see A Herman, *The Parthenon Marbles Dispute: Heritage, Law, Politics* (Oxford, Hart, 2023) ch 7, pp 115–18.

Article 18

This Convention is drawn up in English, French, Russian and Spanish, the four texts being equally authoritative.

Article 18 provides that the languages of the Convention are English, French, Russian and Spanish. All four texts are equally authentic and no single one is to be taken as automatically prevailing over the others. Equally authoritative texts may assist where the phrasing appears particularly clumsy. Difficulties with some of the English text have been indicated above. Where ambiguity occurs in the text of any of these languages, recourse may be had to the others to assist in its resolution. However, where a comparison of the texts does not resolve the problem, the Vienna Convention on the Law of Treaties, Article 33(4), lays down the residual rule that the meaning must be adopted which best reconciles the texts, having regard to the object and purpose of the treaty. Aust points out that:

> … this does not mean that the most restrictive interpretation, or the lowest common denominator must be adopted. Nor does it mean that each language text will carry the same weight.[1]

Currently UNESCO uses the six official languages of the United Nations system, adding Arabic and Chinese to the authoritative languages for those conventions drafted after the official adoption of these additional languages.

[1] A Aust, *Modern Treaty Law and Practice*, 3rd edn (Cambridge, Cambridge University Press, 2013) 226.

Article 19

1. This Convention shall be subject to ratification or acceptance by States Members of the United Nations Educational, Scientific and Cultural Organization in accordance with their respective constitutional procedures.
2. The instruments of ratification or acceptance shall be deposited with the Director-General of the United Nations Educational, Scientific and Cultural Organization.

The words 'ratification' and 'acceptance' simply represent different State linguistic practice in becoming party to international conventions. Since the 1970 Convention is already signed on behalf of Member States of UNESCO – as seen in the attestation at the very end of the Convention – the only action States can then take is the deposit of an instrument indicating their full acceptance of the obligations of the Convention.

Since the first edition of this book was published in 2000, some 60 additional States have become party to the Convention. These include States such as Austria, Belgium, Chile, Germany, Netherlands, New Zealand, Norway, the UK and the United Arab Emirates – all States very significant in one way or another in the illicit trade in cultural property. In early editions, O'Keefe took pains to indicate those that had not then ratified, calling on them to do so.[1] Today, this still includes, in Asia: Indonesia, Malaysia, Thailand, the Philippines and Singapore; in Africa: Mozambique, Namibia and Uganda; and in the Pacific: Fiji, Papua New Guinea, Tonga and Vanuatu, amongst others. Thailand and Singapore are especially problematic, having been recognised as transit States many years ago.[2] At every meeting of States Parties to the 1970 Convention, the remaining UNESCO Member States that are not yet States Parties to the Convention are invited to ratify it.[3] UN Member States have also been encouraged by the General Assembly to ratify the Convention each time the General Assembly considers the matter.[4]

The withdrawal of a State from UNESCO itself does not legally affect the status of a State Party to the 1970 Convention. For example, in 1983 the United States withdrew from UNESCO. During their period of withdrawal, the United States was still party to the 1970 Convention. Under the Trump administrations, the United States again formally withdrew from UNESCO – twice: in 2018, then again, after a brief re-entry, in 2026. This would not affect the United States' obligations under the 1970 Convention, unless further action is taken to formally withdraw the United States from the Convention as well.

[1] See PJ O'Keefe, *Commentary on the 1970 Convention*, 2nd edn (Builth Wells, Institute of Art and Law, 2007).

[2] *Heritage Watch UK* press statement (November 2005).

[3] Eighth Meeting of States Parties to the 1970 Convention, C70/25/8 (May 2025).

[4] For example, at the 76th General Assembly meeting, 76/16/21 (8 December 2021), Resolution 7.

Article 20

1. This Convention shall be open to accession by all States not members of the United Nations Educational, Scientific and Cultural Organization which are invited to accede to it by the Executive Board of the Organization.
2. Accession shall be effected by the deposit of an instrument of accession with the Director-General of the United Nations Educational, Scientific and Cultural Organization.

Any State Member of UNESCO may accede to the Convention. Other States may do so only if invited by the Executive Board of UNESCO. Article 20 is of little relevance at present, since 195 States are Members of UNESCO. It was only significant when the Convention was adopted in 1970, a time when States were still coming into existence through decolonisation and the breakup of existing States. They may have been more willing to become party to the 1970 Convention than join UNESCO itself. However, that time is now past. What is now more important are those States which are Members of UNESCO but not party to the Convention (see Article 19 above).

Article 21

> This Convention shall enter into force three months after the date of the deposit of the third instrument of ratification, acceptance or accession, but only with respect to those States which have deposited their respective instruments on or before that date. It shall enter into force with respect to any other State three months after the deposit of its instrument of ratification, acceptance or accession.

The Convention came into force on 24 April 1972 – three months after the third ratification, by Nigeria, on 24 January 1972 – and for each subsequent acceding State the Convention enters into force three months following the deposit of its instrument of ratification or acceptance.

A State's ratification or acceptance may be challenged. Mexico challenged the participation of the United States[1] but, in light of the passage of time and lack of any further action, this became a dead issue.

[1] See above, I, chs 2–3.

Article 22

> The States Parties to this Convention recognize that the Convention is applicable not only to their metropolitan territories but also to all territories for the international relations of which they are responsible; they undertake to consult, if necessary, the governments or other competent authorities of these territories on or before ratification, acceptance or accession with a view to securing the application of the Convention to those territories, and to notify the Director-General of the United Nations Educational, Scientific and Cultural Organization of the territories to which it is applied, the notification to take effect three months after the date of its receipt.

Article 22 requires parties to apply the Convention to their non-metropolitan territories where possible and to consult their governing bodies where necessary. This provision is a particularly important one in the Pacific and Caribbean areas which have a history of problems of illicit traffic in cultural property and a number of 'non-metropolitan territories' (in the Pacific these include American Samoa, Guam, Pitcairn, Tokelau and Easter Island; in the Caribbean, Bermuda, the Cayman Islands, Puerto Rico and Curaçao).[1] Neither France nor the United Kingdom mentioned their non-metropolitan territories when they respectively became party to the Convention in 1997 and 2002.

Islands which are considered by metropolitan States to be legally component parts of that State (and not dependent territories) such as Hawaii (United States), New Caledonia (France) and French Polynesia (France) also have active concerns in the prevention of illicit traffic.

[1] The ambit of the obligation in respect of territories is also discussed above in regards to Art 12.

Article 23

1. Each State Party to this Convention may denounce the Convention on its own behalf or on behalf of any territory for whose international relations it is responsible.
2. he denunciation shall be notified by an instrument in writing, deposited with the Director-General of the United Nations Educational, Scientific and Cultural Organization.
3. The denunciation shall take effect twelve months after the receipt of the instrument of denunciation.

No denunciation of the 1970 Convention has yet occurred. Denunciation is a specific legal act. It does not occur through withdrawal from UNESCO. The fact that a State is not a member of UNESCO does not in any way change its rights and obligations under the Convention, an independent legal instrument. Thus the departure of the United States from membership of UNESCO cannot affect its rights and obligations under the Convention and it will continue to apply its implementing legislation, unless it undertakes a major reform to repeal it.

Article 24

> The Director-General of the United Nations Educational, Scientific and Cultural Organization shall inform the States members of the Organization, the States not members of the Organization which are referred to in Article 20, as well as the United Nations, of the deposit of all the instruments of ratification, acceptance and accession provided for in Articles 19 and 20, and of the notifications and denunciations provided for in Articles 22 and 23 respectively.

As depository of the instruments concerning State membership of the 1970 Convention, the Director-General of UNESCO circulates the text and any comment by other States Parties (if this occurs), as well as publishing a list, regularly updated, of parties to the Convention, and available on the UNESCO website. This site also includes reservations and declarations lodged by States in relation to the Convention.

Article 25

1. This Convention may be revised by the General Conference of the United Nations Educational, Scientific and Cultural Organization. Any such revision shall, however, bind only the States which shall become Parties to the revising convention.
2. If the General Conference should adopt a new convention revising this Convention in whole or in part, then, unless the new convention otherwise provides, this Convention shall cease to be open to ratification, acceptance or accession, as from the date on which the new revising convention enters into force.

Revision of the Convention is permitted by Article 25. The Committee of Experts which was considering implementation of the Convention in 1983 had before it views as to the revision of the Convention. Some considered that the Convention was too broad to be implemented in any liberal legal system; others that the Convention was too narrow in its reach. The Committee reached the consensus that that it would not be opportune to revise the Convention at that stage, especially since there were over 50 States Parties to it and more participations were being prepared.

Forty years later, with some 100 additional States now party to the Convention, revision seems entirely improbable. It would seem preferable to encourage participation in the existing text, rather than seek to modify it. Revision would complicate the net of reciprocal obligations since the revision would become binding only on States which became party to the revised Convention. Agreement on substantive changes would require a new degree of commitment by importing and market States.

Of course, for States keen on incorporating additional rights of international recovery and return, the UNIDROIT Convention on Stolen or Illegally Exported Cultural Objects of 1995 would be the easily available option. There have been attempts – mostly academic – to draw the two Conventions together and conflate the obligations of States, but these have mostly remained internal to UNESCO and have not necessarily impacted the actions of States.[1]

[1] See, eg, the early draft of the Model Provisions on the Prevention and Fight against Illicit Trafficking in Cultural Property (11 July 2022).

Article 26

> In conformity with Article 102 of the Charter of the United Nations, this Convention shall be registered with the Secretariat of the United Nations at the request of the Director-General of the United Nations Educational, Scientific and Cultural Organization.

The provision at Article 26 for registration of the Convention with the United Nations is a standard provision included in most international agreements, and certainly all those drafted under the auspices of international organisations. It first appeared in the Charter of the League of Nations to implement the policy against 'secret treaties', although this policy is hardly needed in respect of a Convention which has been publicly debated and negotiated over many years.

Article 102 of the United Nations Charter requires the Secretariat of UNESCO to publish treaties registered with it in the United Nations Treaty Series. This was done for the 1970 Convention which is published in Volume 823 of the Series.[1]

[1] 823 UNTS 231, p 231.

III

Interpreting the Convention

Chapter 1
Principles of Interpretation

There are three main sources for interpretating conventions: (i) preliminary documents, (ii) actions by States and (iii) opinions of commentators. But, as we will see, each of these is of relatively limited use when it comes to the 1970 Convention. And, while decisions by dispute-resolving bodies can at times provide significant guides for interpretation, courts – whether domestic or international – have not had occasion to rule directly on the bearing of the 1970 Convention.[1] There have been decisions applying legislation implementing the Convention,[2] but these have not thrown particular light on what individual Articles of the Convention require States to do in fulfilling their obligations.

(i) Preliminary Documents

This source for interpretation comprises the documents used in the lead-up to the adoption of a convention, also known as *travaux préparatoires*. As already noted, the 1970 Convention incorporated elements of the US draft into the Secretariat draft. Part I above outlined the events leading up to the final meeting of experts in 1970.[3] Certain documents relating to that meeting are missing and could not be found despite an extensive search made by Professor Prott with invaluable assistance from the UNESCO Archives staff.

[1] This is quite unlike the 1972 Convention concerning the Protection of the World Cultural and Natural Heritage, which has been considered by the High Court of Australia and, on occasion, by arbitral tribunals in investor-State disputes: PJ O'Keefe, 'Foreign Investment and the World Heritage Convention' (1994) 3 *International Journal of Cultural Property* 259; *Southern Pacific Properties (SPP) v Arab Republic of Egypt* (ICSID Case No. ARB/84/3) (1992); *Thomas Gosling and others v Republic of Mauritius* (ICSID Case No ARB/16/32) (2020).

[2] For example, the Canadian cases of *R v Heller* (1984) 51 AR 73 and *R v Yorke* [1998] NSCA 58, and the Australian case of *Palmanova v Commonwealth of Australia* [2025] HCA 35.

[3] See above, I, ch 2(ii).

(ii) Actions by States

The second source – actions by States – includes the way in which States have incorporated the Convention into their legislation. Many States have specific implementing legislation: for example, Australia, Canada, Czech Republic, Germany, Japan, the Netherlands, Switzerland and the United States. This and the documentation surrounding national legislation – parliamentary debates, press releases, explanatory material for guidance – give valuable indications as to how a particular State sees its obligations. Implementing legislation in specific States (Australia, Japan, Switzerland and the United States) will be considered below in Part V. The United Kingdom, on the other hand, did not enact specific legislation for this purpose, believing that its existing legal system was capable of fulfilling its obligations under the Convention.[4] Whether this is correct or not is a matter for legal experts and courts in the jurisdiction, but it cannot ultimately assist us in interpretation until a case arises and the legal system is tested.

It could be said that the Operational Guidelines prepared by the Subsidiary Committee in 2015 and adopted by the General Conference should be consulted.[5] However, it should be borne in mind that the Operational Guidelines are not an authoritative statement of the meaning of the Articles in the Convention. They are intended as a guide to States implementing the Convention. As a result, they contain references to sources outside the Convention and material that the drafters of the Guidelines thought would be useful to States. They did not appear to be subject to the usual analysis of an international legal instrument intended to be used for interpretative functions.

(iii) Opinions of Commentators

The third source – opinions of commentators – has to be treated with some caution in that the value of a commentator's opinion will depend on the status that person has in the field, and whether he or she is an independent expert or presenting a government opinion or the view of the market.

As already noted, one significant early commentator was the US legal academic Paul Bator.[6] He wrote a 1982 article entitled 'An Essay on the International Trade in Art'[7] drawing on his experience as a member of the US delegation to the negotiations in 1970. He freely admitted that that he was not familiar with such negotiations and was shocked by many of the procedures which did not resemble those he was accustomed to in the US Congress. He argued strongly for a position

[4] It did supplement its accession with a criminal statute, the Dealing in Cultural Objects (Offences) Act 2003.

[5] Above, I, ch 4(iv).

[6] Above, I, ch 2(ii).

[7] PM Bator, 'An Essay on the International Trade in Art' (1982) 34 *Stanford Law Review* 275.

which would see only Articles 7 and 9, 'the heart of the Convention', have any substantive effect. Other provisions he considered 'boilerplate', standard provisions of little or no substantial value in US law-making.[8] Other provisions are referred to as 'ceremonial, rhetorical, and ineffective'. Various other commentators have followed Bator without considering the issues involved.

However, the world has changed greatly since Bator was writing. What Bator saw as a definitive interpretation by the United States has been substantially rejected by other States. For example, in 2009, the Netherlands included in its Explanatory Memorandum to the Bill implementing the Convention the following statement:

> An observation should also be made about the interpretation of the Convention, which is often formulated in vague or ambiguous terms. Differing views are therefore held on its interpretation. It is often assumed, particularly in the United States, that most of the provisions are of a 'ceremonial, rhetorical and ineffective' nature and thus do not have any legal significance and that Articles 7 and 9 therefore form the essence of the Convention. It is accordingly argued that these are the only provisions that need to be implemented. They are derived from proposals made by the United States at a late stage.
>
> The Bill is based on a more balanced interpretation. As such, it is in keeping with the authoritative book entitled 'Commentary on the UNESCO 1970 Convention on Illicit Traffic' by Patrick J. O'Keefe (Institute of Art and Law, Leicester 2000) (see pp 26-31), which sets out to give as much meaning as possible to the provisions of the Convention, in accordance with Article 31 of the Vienna Convention on the Law of Treaties.[9]

Chapter 2
Common Law and Civil Law Perspectives on the Convention

Different systems of law treat the drafting and interpretation of legal instruments differently. Lawyers are intimately involved in the drafting and implementation of international conventions into national law, so their basic understanding of how this is done is heavily influenced by their individual training. It is still relatively rare to find lawyers at home in more than one national legal system.

Predominant in continental Europe, the civil law tradition involves a series of written rules (usually included in a Civil Code) based on Roman law principles. It is entirely appropriate for legislation in these jurisdictions to contain statements of broad principle. Judges in such systems are generally regarded as the servants of the law-givers and duty bound to give effect to those principles in specific cases before them. Under Article 4 of the French Civil Code, for example, judges are forbidden to refuse a case on the ground that the law is lacking, unclear or insufficient.

[8] ibid 377.

[9] Ministry of Education, Culture and Science Explanatory Memorandum, Implementation of the Convention on the Means of Prohibiting and Preventing the Illicit Import, Export and Transfer of Ownership of Cultural Property adopted in Paris on 14 November 1970, 12.

The common law, by contrast, was developed by English judges from the twelfth century onwards. It is based on decisions in specific cases. Common law judges are suspicious of general statements of policy, generally preferring to restrict their pronouncements to the narrowest form required to decide the case before them. Furthermore, because of the development of judicial protections of the individual against the other branches of government, judges often regard themselves as needing to read general statements of principle (whether in legislative instruments or elsewhere) as restrictively as possible. The common law developed as a law of remedies, rather than of rights: 'No right without a remedy' was long accepted as the definition of the system.[10] It is the legal system in England and Wales, Ireland, America, Australia, India, New Zealand, Singapore and Canada (apart from Quebec), amongst other jurisdictions.

The common law dislike of general statements of principle is reflected in Bator's interpretation of the Convention. As already noted, he stated that 'only a small fraction of the Convention was intended to have serious operative consequences' and has described many of the provisions of the Secretariat draft as ceremonial, rhetorical and ineffective, including Articles 1 to 6. On the other hand, Articles 7 and 9 – which came from the United States' draft – he characterised as 'the heart of the Convention' and 'its major substantive provisions'.[11] Lawyers trained in a civil law tradition might well regard Articles 1 to 6 as important statements of agreed principle which should apply to more specific provisions, like Articles 7 and 9, and should not simply be brushed aside.[12]

Many international instruments, influenced by the civil law, are drafted in terms of general principle. This is particularly appropriate where the instrument has to be adapted by modern States to the peculiarities of their own national legal systems; many national lawyers do not have to draft such a flexible scheme. Used as they are to precise language, domestic lawyers dislike the wide scope of treaty provisions which give participant States broad avenues for implementation. This is particularly true of draftsmen in common law systems for the reasons indicated. Bator's dismissal of Article 2 as 'clearly rhetorical', and of Article 10 as unenforceable,[13] reflect these common law tendencies. His view that the 'central premises' of the earlier draft 'had been rejected and excised' can be questioned by the retention, in particular, of Article 3. Arguably the more modern and nuanced view is that statements of principle such as those in Articles 2, 3 and 10 refer to and govern all other provisions adopted by the States Parties.

It thus gives those States discretion as to the action they take on condition that such action does not contravene the provisions of the Convention and that

[10] See Browne-Wilkinson V-C in *Kingdom of Spain v Christie, Manson & Woods Ltd* (1986) 1 WLR 1120, 1117: 'In the pragmatic way in which English law has developed, a man's legal rights are in fact those which are protected by a cause of action… [In] the ordinary case to establish a legal or an equitable right you have to show that all the necessary elements of the cause of action are either present or threatened.'

[11] Bator (n 7) 376.

[12] The perspective from developing countries tends to put great emphasis on general principles as well: see G Abi-Saab comment in A Cassese (ed), *The New Humanitarian Law of Armed Conflict – Proceedings* (Naples, Editoriale Scientifica, 1980) 250.

[13] Bator (n 7) 377.

the express obligations contracted under the Convention are met. However, it is difficult to see how a State Party to the Convention can refuse to acknowledge the validity of a principle embodied in the Convention or refuse to take any positive action in respect of it. The importance of international obligations of this nature was highlighted by Mason J of the High Court of Australia in *Commonwealth of Australia v State of Tasmania*. Although it related to a different UNESCO Convention (the 1972 World Heritage Convention), the words are worth repeating for what they say about the role of conventions generally:

> The absence of precision does not, however, mean any absence of international obligation. In that regard, it would be contrary to both the theory and practice of international law to... deny the existence of international obligations unless they be defined with the degree of precision necessary to establish a legally enforceable agreement under the common law ... However loosely such obligations may be defined, it is apparent that Australia, by depositing its instrument of ratification, bound itself to observe the terms of the Convention and assumed real and substantive obligations under them ... Unless one is to take the view that over 70 nations have engaged in the solemn and cynical farce of using words such as 'obligation' and 'duty' where neither was intended or undertaken, the provisions of the Convention impose real and identifiable obligations and provide for the availability of real benefits ...[14]

Article 31(1) of the Vienna Convention on the Law of Treaties (1969) provides that:

> A treaty shall be interpreted in good faith in accordance with the ordinary meaning to be given to the terms of the treaty in their context and in the light of its object and purpose.

For the 1970 Convention there is much to be said for allowing a degree of freedom of interpretation, provided this does not dilute the meaning of the Convention to the extent that it becomes ineffective or inoperative and does not try to remove all meaning from statements of principle. States have very different interests in the trade in cultural property. What is seen as unlawful by one may not be so regarded by another. The development of common attitudes takes time. Differences in interpretation does not mean that an obligation intended to guide States does not exist.

Chapter 3
Additional Issues with Interpretation

(i) Retroactivity

The normal rule of international law as represented by international custom and Article 28 of the Vienna Convention on the Law of Treaties is that international agreements are not retroactive. There is no provision on retroactivity in the 1970

[14] 46 ALR 625, 807–808.

Convention. The Special Committee in 1969 discussed the possibility of including a non-retroactivity clause but decided it was unnecessary.[15]

Not all States were happy with this approach. In their comments on the original draft, a number of States wanted the 1970 Convention to cover items that had been unlawfully exported before its entry into force.[16] This was in the late 1960s when demands for restitution of cultural property taken by the dominant powers during colonial times were at the fore. Some States feared that any degree of retroactivity would throw doubt on the legal status of cultural objects already in their territory.[17] During the negotiations, it was clear that, while there was some prospect of getting agreement to apply import controls to future transactions, this would be jeopardised by trying to extend the scope of the Convention to objects which had previously left their countries of origin. The outcome will have left certain States frustrated.

In spite of the clear understanding both in law and practice that the Convention is not retroactive, this issue still causes problems. Nagashima once stated that the failure of Thailand, a hub of unlawful trade in Southeast Asia, to ratify the Convention was based on a fear that 'if the provision of Article 11 were applied retroactively, some cultural assets possessed by Thailand would have to be returned'.[18] Borders between Thailand and its neighbours have changed historically and there may be material in Thailand that could be connected to those neighbours, for instance Cambodia.[19]

The non-retroactivity of the Convention does not mean that a State cannot apply principles retroactively in its domestic law if it so wishes. For example, political reasons or sheer altruism may mean a State is more generous than it is required to be in applying the Convention. It is open to (but not obligatory on) a State Party to the Convention to declare illegal all future imports of cultural property which have been illegally exported at any time, or at a particular time chosen by the State Party.[20] Whether national legislation does so or not is clearly a matter for the local judicial authorities to determine if the legislation is silent on the issue. The question though is not resolved by reference to the Convention.

The Australian Protection of Movable Cultural Heritage Act 1986 provides at s 14(1) that where: (a) a protected object of a foreign country has been exported from that country; (b) the export was prohibited by a law of that country relating to cultural property; and (c) the object was imported after the Act's entry into force, the object will be liable to forfeiture. This provision has been interpreted by the Australian Attorney-General's Department as meaning that 'the Act applies

[15] See above, I, ch 2(ii).

[16] For instance, Cambodia and China: see above, I, ch 2(ii).

[17] For instance, France: see above, I, ch 2(ii).

[18] M Nagashima, *The Lost Heritage: The Reality of Artifact Smuggling in Southeast Asia* (Bangkok, Post Books, 2002) 160. See II at Article 11, which relates to cultural property displaced during occupation.

[19] See the dispute in *Temple of Preah Vihear, Merits, Judgment (Cambodia v Thailand)* ICJ Reports, 1962, p 6.

[20] Though unrelated to the 1970 Convention, the European Union introduced just such a prohibition in its Regulation 2019/880/EU on the Introduction and the Import of Cultural Goods, Art 3(1).

to objects imported after 1 July 1987, but which were previously exported from another country at any time when there was a cultural heritage protection law in force, contrary to the provisions of that law'.[21] The view has since been supported by the High Court of Australia in *Palmanova v Commonwealth of Australia*.[22] In that case, an artefact unlawfully exported from Bolivia in the 1950s was nevertheless caught by s 14(1) because its entry into Australia post-dated 1 July 1987; it was therefore forfeited to the Commonwealth (to be returned to Bolivia). A provision of this nature puts a prospective importer on notice that, if the history of the object is not known to be clear of illicit trafficking, it could be liable to seizure.

(ii) Reservations and Declarations

As set out in the Vienna Convention on the Law of Treaties, reservations and declarations are statements made by a State on becoming party to a convention which purport 'to exclude or modify the legal effect of certain provisions of the treaty in their application to that State'.[23] Consequently, if certain clauses are excluded by an express reservation by one State, all the other States Parties are bound by all the provisions of the legal instrument except the State which has made the reservation. In practice, if a State uses reservations to avoid a number of the obligations set out in a particular convention, even if comparatively minor ones, it could mean that the State will not be considered a party to that convention at all.

It is common international practice, where it is considered that participation should be broadly based, to allow reservations. As explained by Aust in one of the leading texts on treaty law:

> There is nothing inherently wicked or even undesirable in formulating a reservation to a multilateral treaty. … In many, if not most, cases the purpose of the reservation is merely to adjust the reserving state's obligations under the treaty to conform to its domestic law where, for political, cultural or social reasons, it is not feasible or desirable to change the law.[24]

The original draft Convention included a provision prohibiting reservations.[25] The Special Committee of Governmental Experts in 1970, in deciding to make reservations possible, clearly accepted the view that there would be varying degrees of implementation.

Regarding Article 10 of the 1970 Convention, Australia formulated a reservation at the time of acceptance, since it was not in a position to oblige antique

[21] JF Ley, *Australia's Protection of Movable Cultural Heritage: Report on the Ministerial Review of the Protection of Movable Cultural Heritage Act 1986 and Regulations* (Canberra, Australian Government Publishing Service, 1991) 125.

[22] [2025] HCA 35.

[23] Art 2(1)(d).

[24] A Aust, *Modern Treaty Law and Practice*, 3rd edn (Cambridge, Cambridge University Press, 2014) 121.

[25] Unesdoc SHC/MD/3 Annex, 5, Art 15.

dealers to maintain registers of the origin of each item of cultural property in their possession (this being a power reserved to the individual states in Australia).[26] In contrast, the United States made no reservation to Article 10 and left its operation to its constitutive states, though very few of them seem to have dedicated legislation to satisfy the provision. Nor did the UK make a reservation under the Article, despite the fact that no such obligation exists for British dealers, apart from the normal record-keeping requirements relating to sales tax.[27]

The Vienna Convention sets out that States may limit, by reservation, their obligations under an international treaty where reservations are not explicitly prohibited by the terms of that treaty.[28] However, every treaty contains certain core content which parties must accept if they wish other States to acknowledge them as parties to the treaty at all.[29] Other States Party to the Convention may object to a reservation even if reservations are permissible. Aust writes:

> No reasons for an objection have to be given, though they often are. Even if the basis for the objection is pure policy, it will have the same effect as an objection on legal grounds. By formulating a reservation, the reserving State is consenting to be bound subject to a condition laid down by it. It makes an offer that is subject to acceptance by the other contracting states. It will not, therefore, be legally effective in relation to another contracting state unless that state has accepted it either expressly or by necessary implication.[30]

A declaration, on the other hand, may be made by a State to show how it interprets a provision of the Convention or it may be purely political, expressing that State's views on the subject matter of the Convention or status of another Party.

A State may also use a declaration to disguise a reservation. That may be the case in relation to what are called 'understandings'. The precise effect of these is unclear: some consider that they actually amount to reservations and must be treated in the same way; others that, if a tribunal were to hold the interpretation unwarranted by the text of the treaty, the Party making it is still bound by the text of the treaty and cannot maintain its interpretation without breach of its obligations under the treaty.

Reservations and Understandings appear in an interesting early episode involving the Convention. The United States accompanied its acceptance of the Convention by one Reservation and six Understandings. It 'reserved' the right to determine whether or not to impose export controls over cultural property, while it 'understood' the Convention to be neither self-executing nor retroactive. Its further Understandings related to specific Articles of the Convention (Articles 3, 7(a), 7(b), 10(a) and 13(d)) and how the United States interpreted these.[31]

[26] See letter LA/Depositary/1989/20 (10 January 1990).
[27] See Report of the Illicit Trade Advisory Panel (December 2000) para 59.
[28] Vienna Convention on the Law of Treaties (1969), Art 19.
[29] *Advisory Opinion on Genocide Convention*, ICJ Reports (1951) 15, 29.
[30] Aust (n 24) 125.
[31] Unesdoc Doc. LA/Depository/1984/3 Annex III. See also below, V, ch 6.

The instrument of acceptance by the United States was further accompanied by a statement which read that the Convention was binding on the United States 'subject to' its Reservation and Understandings, as well as to the provisions of its implementing law, the Convention on Cultural Property Implementation Act (CCPIA).[32] After questions from UNESCO, the United States explained that:

> … the terms of the Convention are implemented domestically, within the United States legal and constitutional framework, by the [CCPIA], and therefore, subject to such legislation. The Government of the United States … request that its acceptance be effective in accordance with the relevant articles of the Convention.[33]

The UNESCO Secretariat appears to have accepted that this clarification amounted to an acceptable 'declaration' rather than a 'reservation'. This would seem correct with reference to the last sentence of the passage quoted above, although it must be said that in that case the words 'subject to' are being used in a rather unusual sense.

When the document under discussion was circulated, the Mexican Government responded that the comments and reservations of the United States were 'not compatible with the purposes and aims of the Convention', and could lead to cultural property being imported into the United States and then re-exported to other countries, possibly harming the cultural heritage of Mexico.[34] Considering the early history of the adoption of the Convention in 1970, Mexico must have been disappointed that its efforts to arrive at a compromise with the United States had seemingly led to a fictitious acceptance of the Convention. A State Party to a convention, which objects to a reservation which it considers to be incompatible with the object and purpose of the convention, may consider the reserving State not to be a State Party.[35] Was this then the effect of Mexico's objection? Nafziger concludes that it probably was not: 'It is important, however, to understand that this statement was of a political nature, not a legal nature'.[36]

No other Parties to the Convention have lodged an objection to the United States' Reservation and Understandings. In practical terms, it did not significantly affect Mexico which already had a separate bilateral treaty with the United States on return of stolen cultural objects.[37] In fact, the passage of time seems to have reduced the statement of the United States to an historical footnote. No reference seems to have been made to it in many years.

Should a dispute ever arise as to whether or not the United States is a true Party to the 1970 Convention, it would not be possible for UNESCO to resolve the issue under Article 17(5) since it can deal only with a dispute over implementation

[32] Unesdoc LA/Depository/1984/3 Annex 1.

[33] Unesdoc LA/Depository/1984/3 Annex VI.

[34] Unesdoc LA/Depository (1985) 40.

[35] *Advisory Opinion on Genocide* (n 29) 29.

[36] JAR Nafziger, 'The 1970 Convention: Insights, Circumspections, and Outlooks' in JA Sánchez Cordero (ed), *The 1970 Convention: New Challenges* (Mexico City, Instituto de Investigaciones Jurídicas, 2013) 211, 220.

[37] *Treaty of Cooperation between the United States of America and the United Mexican States Providing for the Recovery and Return of Stolen Archaeological, Historical and Cultural Properties (1970).*

and at the request of States Parties – it cannot determine the *status* of a Party. If both Parties agreed expressly, or were subject to the compulsory jurisdiction of the International Court of Justice, the issue could be taken there for resolution. This is unlikely to ever occur.

Japan ratified the Convention in 2002. It did so with no reservations or declarations although, as we shall see, it has passed legislation that accounts for only the bare minimum of Convention obligations (and arguably may not even meet these).[38] Its membership has not been questioned by other States Parties, although many of the matters it failed to take into account were similar to those the United States covered in its Reservation and Understandings. Most probably the lack of objection meant that States Parties were not alerted to the specific nature of Japan's implementation law which would have required a detailed analysis of the legislation.

Several States, when depositing their instrument of ratification or accession, have included a statement of the cultural property affected by their ratification. This is then listed by UNESCO in its list of 'Declarations and Reservations'. It is unclear whether this should be viewed as a reservation affecting the range of cultural property as defined in Article 1 of the Convention or as a declaration of how the State interprets Article 1. The practice was used, for example, by two Scandinavian States (Denmark and Sweden) in order to clarify the cultural property specifically designated under their respective domestic legislation. It was also used by three EU States (France, Belgium and the United Kingdom) in order to align their obligations under the Convention with those under EU legislation.[39] However, the relevant EU Directive was updated in 2014[40] making the necessity of maintaining such statements questionable; and the United Kingdom withdrew its declaration and reservation after leaving the EU in 2021.[41]

(iii) Limitation Periods

In the context of illicit trade, limitation periods will measure the time within which the holder of an object can have his or her possession challenged by legal action. There is nothing in the 1970 Convention on this matter. National laws exhibit great variation in how they treat limitation or prescription periods. Under the limitation

[38] Below, V, ch 3.

[39] Council Regulation (EEC) No 3911/92 of 9 December 1992 on the Export of Cultural Goods; Council Directive Council Directive 1993/7/EEC of 15 March 1993 on the Return of Cultural Objects Unlawfully Removed from the Territory of a Member State.

[40] The above 1993 Directive was recast, removing the list in the Annex: Directive 2014/60/EU on the Return of Cultural Objects Unlawfully Removed from the Territory of a Member State. The 1992 Export Regulation has also been updated, but the Annex thresholds remain: Council Regulation No 116/2009.

[41] See 'Withdrawal of a Declaration and a Reservation by the United Kingdom of Great Britain and Northern Ireland', deposited at UNESCO, LA/DEP/2021/006 (16 June 2021).

law of England and Wales, for instance, a claim to recover stolen goods must be brought within six years of a first *bona fide* purchase.[42] At the time of its acceptance of the Convention in 2002 the United Kingdom declared that:

> The United Kingdom interprets Article 7 (b)(ii) to the effect that it may continue to apply its existing rules on limitation to claims made under this Article for the recovery and return of cultural objects.[43]

No other State Party has seen it necessary to make such a reservation. In its implementing legislation Switzerland bars actions for recovery if more than 30 years have passed since the object was unlawfully exported,[44] though it did not include a reservation to that effect. In Japan, claims arising from theft of specified foreign cultural property must be brought within 10 years of the theft.[45]

It should be noted that limitation periods were part of the 1995 UNIDROIT Convention, but had been a controversial issue during negotiations and ended up the subject of compromise. As Prott explains:

> While the substance could have been expressed much more economically and elegantly, it was in fact hammered out in such a way as to include key phrases which would make it acceptable to national governments. The complicated text was the price of general acceptance at the conference.[46]

In the end, the UNIDROIT Convention did include its own limitation periods: the general rule that recovery must be undertaken within three years of the claimant discovering the location of the object and the identity of the possessor, to a maximum of 50 years from theft or export[47] – though there is a possibility for longer limitation periods for objects displaced from a monument, archaeological site or public collection.[48] EU Directive 2014/60 on the Return of Cultural Objects has a similar limitation period, though the general rule is three years to a maximum of 75 years.[49]

Often States are concerned that international instruments could override their domestic limitation periods. However, the fact that the 1970 Convention does not mention limitation periods as such means States Parties can apply whatever period is relevant under their local law. Reservations or declarations on this issue (such as the UK's) therefore may not be necessary. On the other hand, very short periods will attract adverse international attention. Japan had a short two-year period for

[42] Limitation Act 1980, s 4. A different rule applies in Scotland under the Prescription and Limitation (Scotland) Act 1973: a 20-year prescription generally, but imprescriptible rights exist against a thief or anyone privy to the stealing (s 8 and Sch 3).

[43] Declarations and Reservations to the 1970 UNESCO Convention, United Kingdom, LA/Depositary/2002/31.

[44] Below, V, ch 4.

[45] Below, V, ch 3.

[46] LV Prott, *Commentary on the UNIDROIT Convention*, 2nd edn (Builth Wells, Institute of Art and Law, 2021) 56.

[47] Arts 3(3) and 5(5).

[48] Art 3(4)–(5).

[49] Directive 2014/60, Art 8.

the bringing of claims to recover foreign stolen property, which was criticised, resulting in the Japanese legislation implementing the 1970 Convention increasing the period, as noted above, to 10 years.[50]

(iv) Public Policy

The 1970 Convention has sometimes been interpreted in contexts well beyond the remit of its text. This has occurred when recourse has been made by domestic courts to 'public policy', a concept which is notoriously difficult to establish in a way that is universally satisfactory. Resort to such policy is often a reaction to a situation where a particular outcome is seen as desirable but cannot be attained by normal means. It enables the 1970 Convention to be used in circumstances where, on its own terms, it would not be applicable.

An early example of this was the 1972 German case of *Allgemeine Versicherungsgesellschaft v EK*.[51] A German Federal Court held that a prohibition in the German Civil Code against contracts which were contrary to public policy included 'international public policy'. In that case, a Nigerian company had entered into an insurance contract with a German company covering the transport by sea of three cases of African masks and statues from the port at Harcourt, Nigeria, to Hamburg. The contract was in breach of a Nigerian prohibition on the export of cultural objects. The plaintiff was seeking damages for the loss of six bronze statues. German law will not enforce a contract contrary to public policy. The Court considered the 1970 Convention and found that it represented emerging international public policy on the issue. Therefore, even though the then Federal Republic of Germany was not a Party to the Convention, the Court held that the contract was unenforceable in Germany since:

> … the export of cultural property contrary to a prohibition of the country of origin for that reason merits, in the interest of maintaining proper standards for the international trade in cultural objects, no protection from the civil law.[52]

Furthermore, it held that the disregard, which was both customary and tolerated in earlier times, of the desire of other nations to keep their cultural treasures, could not be regarded as the contemporary standard for public policy on the enforcement of contracts.

In 1994, the Court of Grasse in France, in connection with criminal proceedings in that country, requested the return from Switzerland, under the European Convention on Laundering, Search, Seizure and Confiscation of the Proceeds of Crime from 1990, of a stolen painting. In June 1996, the examining magistrate in Geneva ordered its return. An appeal for review of this order was eventually made

[50] See below, V, ch 3.
[51] BGHZ 59, p 83.
[52] ibid 80–87.

to the Swiss Federal Court on the basis that the request for mutual assistance was null and void under the Swiss federal law as to mutual assistance on international penal matters. The painting had been sold in each of Switzerland, France, Italy and the United Kingdom – all Parties to the abovementioned European Convention.

In the course of its decision,[53] the Swiss Federal Court said that the plaintiff was the proper owner of the painting and he did not have to wait for the result of the criminal procedure in France before claiming return of the painting. Moreover, there was no ground arising from the protection of fundamental rights which prevented the return of the painting to the owner based on the mutual assistance procedure. The Court emphasised the underlying role played by international public policy in reaching this decision, saying that:

> Where the claim relates to the return of cultural property, the judge giving mutual assistance *must ensure* that he takes into account the international public interest relating to the protection of this property which is common to Switzerland and France.[54] (italics added)

Besides the European Convention mentioned above, the Court related this conclusion to Articles 1(g), 2, 3, 13 and 15 of the 1970 Convention for France and Articles 3(1), 4, 5(1), 6, 8 and 9 of the UNIDROIT Convention for France and Switzerland (neither is party to this Convention). The Court stated:

> These rules, which are based on a shared purpose, constitute as such the expression of international public policy either existing or emerging. … These rules, embodying the need to fight against illicit traffic in cultural property, allow, among other things, for the necessary procedural guarantees to protect the legitimate interests of the good faith possessor.[55]

In the United States, the Seventh Circuit Court of Appeals in *Autocephalous Greek-Orthodox Church of Cyprus v Goldberg and Feldman Fine Arts* made reference to the desirability of following the underlying principles of the Convention:

> While the UNESCO Convention seems to contemplate primarily measures to be implemented by the executive branch of a Government through its import and export rules and policies, the judicial branch should certainly attempt to reflect in its decision making the spirit as well as the letter of an international agreement to which the United States is a party.[56]

This was said in the course of a decision to return mosaics to the Autocephalous Greek-Orthodox Church of Cyprus. They had been ripped from the apse of the Church of the Panagia Kanakaria in the village of Lythrankomi sometime between

[53] *L v Chambre d'accusation du canton de Genève*, BGE 123 II, 134. The case is referred to in AFG Raschèr, M Bauen, Y Fischer and M-N Zen-Ruffinen, *Cultural Property Transfer* (Brussels, Zurich, Bruyland, Schulthess, 2005) 16.

[54] ibid 143.

[55] ibid 144.

[56] 917 F.2d 278 (1990) 296.

1976 and 1979 following the partition of Cyprus.[57] They were imported into the United States by an art dealer in Indiana, who had bought them in Europe, taking possession in the freeport area of the Geneva airport. At that time there was no bilateral agreement between Cyprus and the United States.

The English case of *Islamic Republic of Iran v Barakat Galleries*[58] involved an action by Iran to recover antiquities almost 5,000 years old alleged to have been unlawfully excavated from the Jiroft region of the country. Barakat claimed to have bought them in France, Germany and Switzerland under laws bestowing good title. Iran had never had possession of the objects but had legislation the general effect of which was to give the State title to them. The issue then was whether this was an Iranian 'public law', otherwise unenforceable in England. The Court of Appeal took the view that not all foreign laws were unenforceable as a general principle:

> In our judgment, there are positive reasons of policy why a claim by a State to recover antiquities which form part of its national heritage and which otherwise complies with the requirements of private international law should not be shut out … Conversely, in our judgment it is certainly contrary to public policy for such claims to be shut out.[59]

In reaching this conclusion the Court referred to 'the international recognition that States should assist one another to prevent the unlawful removal of cultural objects including antiquities'.[60] The 1970 Convention was listed among those instruments leading to the decision.

> A refusal to recognise the title of a foreign State, conferred by its law, to antiquities unless they come into the possession of such State, would in most cases render it impossible for this country to recognise any claim by such a State to recover antiquities unlawfully exported to this country.[61]

These cases, reflecting as they do the considered opinion of superior courts in four States, show that the 1970 Convention has a role much wider than its specific terms would suggest: namely, it represents international public policy by which cultural property taken out of a State contrary to its law should be returned, subject only to explicit overriding factors. This finding as to international public policy can guide courts and administrations in their interpretation of the obligations of States under the 1970 Convention. On the other hand, too much reliance should not be put on public policy for interpretation of the 1970 Convention. It must first be formulated from the terms of the Convention itself and be supported by extensive opinion as to the aims and objectives of the Convention. The argument must also be strong enough to persuade the adjudicator (or the other side in the dispute) that it should be recognised as a correct interpretation of the Convention in the widest sense.

[57] The Church is situated in Northern Cyprus.
[58] [2007] EWCA Civ 1374.
[59] ibid 154.
[60] ibid 155.
[61] ibid 163.

IV

The Wider Context

The 1970 Convention does not sit in a vacuum. While it is the pre-eminent agreement between States dealing with illicit traffic in, and theft of, cultural property, it exists within a wider context that has a bearing on how the Convention is interpreted and, ultimately, how it operates. These include other conventions between States, recommendations and resolutions adopted at meetings of international organisations, voluntary model provisions, declarations, codes of ethics and so on. Such instruments cover a wide variety of subjects, such as archaeology, armed conflict, underwater cultural heritage, human rights, trade, intangible cultural heritage and cultural diversity. The bodies responsible for administering them are mainly international organisations, whether worldwide, such as UNESCO or the United Nations more broadly, or regional, such as the European Union or the Council of Europe.

Anyone concerned with problems of illicit traffic or theft of cultural objects must be aware of these other instruments and how they may be relevant. The 1970 Convention may not apply to a particular situation, but one or more of these other instruments might nevertheless be relevant. The following analysis will deal firstly with international conventions and agreements, binding as they are on the States that are party to them (Chapter 1), then with Resolutions and Declarations from bodies of the United Nations (Chapter 2), then with specific UNESCO statements and instructive documents (Chapter 3) and, finally, with codes of ethics and the like which might have a soft law or persuasive effect on how the Convention can be understood (Chapter 4). The order followed is generally by relevance to combating the illicit trade in cultural objects.

Chapter 1
International Conventions and Other Agreements

(i) 1995 UNIDROIT Convention

The UNIDROIT Convention on Stolen or Illegally Exported Cultural Objects was adopted by States in 1995 and brought into force on 1 July 1998.[1] It was developed by the International Institute for the Unification of Private Law (UNIDROIT), an

[1] The drafting history and an analysis of the UNIDROIT Convention can be found in LV Prott *Commentary on the UNIDROIT Convention*, 2nd edn (Builth Wells, Institute of Art and Law, 2021).

agency that works to harmonise areas of private law across jurisdictions. Its genesis, however, occurred much earlier under the aegis of UNESCO, with the specific intention of filling certain gaps left by the 1970 Convention.

The 1970 Convention's limits had long been recognised. A 1982 Report commissioned by UNESCO had looked at how to control the illicit traffic in cultural objects, considering the protection afforded to *bona fide* purchasers within national legal systems.[2] It was well understood that the 1970 Convention did not deal adequately with good faith acquisitions made without knowledge of a prior theft or unlawful export. Nor did it mention the limitation period within which a diplomatic claim for recovery should be brought, thereby defaulting to normal national limitation or prescription rules. Another difficulty was that the 1970 Convention did not expressly prevent the import of cultural property removed from a State through unlawful excavation.[3]

The UNIDROIT Convention therefore sought to fill these gaps. Chapter II deals with the restitution of stolen cultural objects, identifying a larger pool of potential objects than the 1970 Convention. For instance, Article 3 of the UNIDROIT Convention begins with an unimpeachably direct rule:

> (1) The possessor of a cultural object which has been stolen shall return it.

This places a very clear obligation on the possessor, something which the 1970 Convention fails to do. The provision then proceeds to clarify the scope of what may be considered 'stolen':

> (2) For the purposes of this Convention, a cultural object which has been unlawfully excavated or lawfully excavated but unlawfully retained shall be considered stolen, when consistent with the law of the State where the excavation took place.

By contrast, Article 7(b) of the 1970 Convention does not cover unexcavated material in this way, limited as it is to cultural property stolen from a museum, monument or similar institution, and any 'right' of recovery is reserved to the State of origin through diplomatic channels. The UNIDROIT Convention makes it clear that a theft victim shall be able to recover, but so too shall a State for unearthed antiquities. Responsibility will therefore lie with the law of the State where excavation took place. If it wishes to gain the benefit of this provision it must ensure that

[2] LV Prott and PJ O'Keefe, *National Legal Control of Illicit Traffic in Cultural Property* commissioned by UNESCO and discussed at a Consultation of Experts on Illicit Traffic, Unesdoc CLT/83/WS/16 (UNESCO, Paris, 1983). See also J Chatelain, *Means of Combating the Theft of and Illegal Traffic in Works of Art in the Nine Countries of the EEC* (Commission of the European Communities, Doc XII/920/79-E(1976) and S Rodotà, 'The Civil Law Aspects of the International Protection of Cultural Property' in *International Legal Protection of Cultural Property* (1984) 99: 'Explanatory Memorandum' in Council of Europe, *The Art Trade* (1988) 1.

[3] Of course, O'Keefe's view has always been that States Parties to the 1970 Convention should impose such a restriction pursuant to Article 3: see above, II, Article 3.

its laws on theft adequately support a claim in this way, usually by providing for State ownership of newly unearthed antiquities.[4]

Chapter III of the UNIDROIT Convention then deals with the return of illegally exported cultural objects. In this regard, it is much broader than the 1970 Convention. The normal procedure under the UNIDROIT Convention would be that requests for return are made by a State Party to a court in the State Party where the object is located (Article 5(1)). If certain conditions are established, the court has no option but to order return of the object. The requesting State has to establish that the 'removal of the object from its territory significantly impairs one or more of the following interests': physical preservation, integrity, preservation of information, traditional/ritual use or significant cultural importance (Article 5(3)). The inclusion of the last interest has been criticised by those who oppose the Convention because, they allege, it gives the requesting State the opportunity to raise matters that cannot be refuted. For example, one US legal critic has argued that:

> Clearly any claiming country can find some expert that would claim that virtually any object is important to the culture of the claiming country.[5]

Criticisms of this nature seem to overlook the fact that it would be up to the judge of the court in the requested State to make a determination as to whether a particular object is of 'significant cultural importance'. It should also be noted that neither the right of restitution or return applies to removals that pre-dated the Convention's coming into force (Article 10).

For an object restituted or returned under the UNIDROIT Convention, compensation is due only to a possessor who, before acquiring the object, neither knew nor ought reasonably to have known the object was stolen or illegally exported, as the case may be (Article 4(1) for stolen objects and Article 6(1) for illegally exported objects), with an additional requirement regarding stolen objects to show a diligent search. This resolved a longstanding conflict between common law and civil law legal systems that had been left unresolved by the 1970 Convention.[6] Specific guidance is provided in the UNIDROIT Convention regarding the factors a purchaser must take into account in order to be regarded as having exercised 'due diligence', such as the price paid and the degree of consultation with databases of stolen material (Article 4(4)). This provision limits the number of possessors who can be compensated by eliminating those who cannot prove that they have made every effort to ensure that the acquisition was legal.

Careful consideration was given to the compatibility of the two Conventions. For example, care was taken to ensure that the categories of cultural objects listed

[4] See further UNESCO/UNIDROIT Model Provisions on State Ownership of Undiscovered Cultural Objects, below.

[5] JF Fitzpatrick, 'Cultural Property and Art Theft: The Misguided Quest: The Clear Case Against UNIDROIT' (1996) 4 *Journal of Financial Crime* 54, 57.

[6] cf 1970 Convention, Art 7(b)(ii).

in the UNIDROIT Convention were the same as those in Article 1 of the 1970 Convention so that the two Conventions could work together and States could become party to both. Prott declared:

> … UNESCO is satisfied that the new Convention will be complementary to the UNESCO Convention and that its precise and hard-won text should reassure States which remained aloof from the UNESCO Convention because they felt some of its provisions to be ambiguous.[7]

The complementarity of the two Conventions was also emphasised by the Swiss Working Group on the International Transfer of Cultural Objects:

> The two conventions function independently but supplement each other by achieving a common purpose with different means.[8]

(ii) 2001 Underwater Cultural Heritage Convention

The remains of shipwrecks may come from areas of the ocean floor where no State has jurisdiction to ensure they are excavated according to strict archaeological standards. In an attempt to resolve this and other issues, the 31st UNESCO General Conference in 2001 adopted the Convention on the Protection of the Underwater Cultural Heritage. This came into force on 2 January 2009 – 20 States Parties being required to bring that about. There are currently over 80 States Parties.[9] The Convention has provisions bearing directly on theft and illicit trade.

The whole thrust of the Convention is to ensure that any activity directed at underwater cultural heritage complies with the 'Rules Concerning Activities Directed at Underwater Cultural Heritage' set out in the Annex.[10] As the actual activity may lie outside the jurisdiction of States (eg, on the deep seabed), it was necessary to devise a means of control within the power of States. Accordingly, Article 14 provides:

> States Parties shall take measures to prevent the entry into their territory, the dealing in, or the possession of underwater cultural heritage illicitly exported and/or recovered, where recovery was contrary to this Convention.

The more widely the Convention is implemented, the greater will be the impact of Article 14 on trade in underwater cultural heritage. Each State will have to decide what measures it will take to prevent the entry of such material into its territory.

Article 14 refers to 'illicit' export. This term also appears in Article 3 of the 1970 Convention where it might be considered as meaning 'contrary to law', as

[7] LV Prott, 'UNESCO and UNIDROIT: A Partnership Against Trafficking in Cultural Objects' (1996) *Uniform Law Review* 59, 70.

[8] Working Group *International Transfer of Cultural Objects: UNESCO Convention of 1970 and UNIDROIT Convention of 1995* (Berne, Federal Office of Culture, 1999) 10.

[9] As at February 2026.

[10] Art 33.

the French text suggests. The same meaning would be appropriate in the context of Article 14. 'Export' implies that an object is taken out of the territory of a State, although the precise moment of export may need to be defined by legislation.[11] There is no requirement in Article 14 that the heritage in question has to have been illicitly exported from a State Party to the Underwater Convention – only that it be recovered contrary to the Convention. On the other hand, there is no obligation in the Underwater Convention for a State to have such export control laws. It is conceivable that the implementation of the 1970 Convention in certain States may satisfy their obligations under Article 14 of the Underwater Convention, since the definition of 'cultural property' at Article 1 of the 1970 Convention would in most cases cover heritage found underwater.[12]

Article 14 also requires States Parties to prevent dealing in or possession of underwater cultural heritage contrary to the Convention, ie not in accordance with the Rules of the Annex. If States were required only to prevent the entry into their territory of material that had been newly raised from parts of the ocean seabed such as the continental shelf there would be few problems.[13] But Article 14 does not appear to be so limited. The measures taken are to apply in general to underwater cultural heritage whenever and wherever it later goes. It need not be 'illicitly exported'.

The Convention requires States Parties to impose sanctions and provide for seizure where the recovery has not been in accordance with the Underwater Convention.[14] States should be aware that it may be preferable to use this avenue, if available, to recover looted cultural objects, rather than the 1970 Convention.[15]

(iii) 1954 Hague Convention and its Protocols

The 1954 Convention for the Protection of Cultural Property in the Event of Armed Conflict (Hague Convention) and its two Protocols apply to cultural property removed from a territory during a time of armed conflict or occupation. The Convention itself includes only a minimal obligation on States Parties to restrict the theft, pillage and misappropriation of cultural property in such contexts.[16] It applies not only to international conflicts but also to those 'not of an international

[11] For example, in Australia's Protection of Movable Cultural Heritage Act 1986 export is broadly defined to occur when the object is placed on the means of transport taking it to another country (s 9(4)).

[12] This would be true for States that have chosen a broader scope of import restrictions than required by the 1970 Convention, such as Canada, Australia, Germany and Qatar.

[13] The Area is the seabed and ocean floor beyond the limits of national jurisdiction, defined in the United Nations Convention on the Law of the Sea (Montego Bay, 10 December 1982).

[14] PJ O'Keefe, '"Commercial Exploitation": Its Prohibition in the Unesco Convention on Protection of the Underwater Cultural Heritage 2001 and Other Instruments' (2013) XVIII *Art Antiquity and Law* 129.

[15] The only detailed study of the Convention is in PJ O'Keefe, *Shipwrecked Heritage: A Commentary on the UNESCO Convention on Underwater Cultural Heritage*, 2nd edn (Builth Wells, Institute of Art and Law, 2014).

[16] Art 4(3) requires States Party to 'prohibit, prevent, and, if necessary, put a stop' to these actions.

character'.[17] The more significant provisions on illicit traffic are found in the 1954 Protocol to the Convention. There was extensive debate among States at the time of the Convention over how to treat this issue which some saw as involving private law concerns only. In brief, the solution for the Convention was to retain 'only the aspects of public international law, the private law aspects having been abandoned' and for these to appear in a separate legal instrument, ie the Protocol.[18]

States Parties to this First Protocol are required to prevent the exportation of cultural property from territories that they have occupied during an armed conflict. There are approximately 20 fewer States Parties to this Protocol than to the Hague Convention itself. All States Parties must seize cultural property imported from such occupied territories and return it at the 'close of hostilities'. If property is returned, holders in good faith are entitled to an indemnity from the former occupying State. This Protocol has potentially far-reaching effects but has been rarely used.[19]

This may be because there are difficult practical issues in applying the Protocol. For example, when is a territory occupied in the case of conflict 'not of an international character'? When have hostilities 'closed', so as to allow return? How are seized objects to be cared for while awaiting return? How is the holder in good faith to get an indemnity from an occupying power which may not be part of the process?

Certain States, including Canada, Germany, the Netherlands, Switzerland and the United Kingdom, have passed legislation to implement the First Protocol.[20] Others may believe that the principles of the Protocol are already the law of the land in their jurisdictions. The case of the Netherlands is instructive. Although it ratified the Protocol in 1958, it did not initially implement it through domestic legislation. Four decades later, a claim was brought against a Dutch national who had purchased four religious icons in the 1970s that had been looted from a church in Northern Cyprus following the territory's occupation by Turkey. The Autocephalous Greek Orthodox Church commenced legal proceedings in Rotterdam in 1998, arguing that under the First Protocol the buyer could not become the owner, even if he had acted in good faith.[21] The Court held that the Protocol operated only between States and had no binding legal force upon any individual person in the Netherlands. The State therefore appeared to be in breach of its obligations under Article I(3) of

[17] Hague Convention, Art 19.

[18] J Toman, *The Protection of Cultural Property in the Event of Armed Conflict* (Dartmouth, Aldershot, 1966) 344.

[19] The Protocol is discussed in detail in PJ O'Keefe, 'The First Protocol to the Hague Convention Fifty Years On' (2004) IX *Art Antiquity and Law* 99.

[20] CLT-13/8.COM/CONF.203/9 Paris (4 December 2013) 50–52. The United Kingdom's implementation took the form of the Cultural Property (Armed Conflicts) Act 2017, which also implements the Second Protocol.

[21] *Autocephalous Greek Orthodox Church in Cyprus v Lans* (District Court of Rotterdam, 4 February 1999, unreported). The case is discussed in more detail in S Matyk, 'The Restitution of Cultural Objects and the Question of Giving Direct Effect to the Protocol to the Hague Convention for the Protection of Cultural Property in the Event of Armed Conflict 1954' (2000) 9 *International Journal of Cultural Property* 341.

the Protocol. Legislation to remedy the situation was adopted in 2007 and the four icons in question were returned to the Church in 2013.[22]

In the 1990s, Israel returned antiquities to Egypt that had been excavated in the Sinai Peninsula when the territory was occupied by the Israeli army following the Six Day War (1967). Egypt had refused a request by Israel to continue to exhibit these at the Israel Museum on a loan basis. Although they were actually returned under a bilateral agreement, it appears as though this might not have happened had Israel not already been bound under the First Protocol.[23]

A Second Protocol to the Hague Convention was adopted in 1999 and came into force on 9 March 2004. There are approximately 50 fewer States Parties to this Protocol than to the Hague Convention itself. Article 9 requires an occupying party to prohibit and prevent certain activities in the territory concerned. The use of the word 'prevent' indicates that positive action must be taken by the occupying State to stop the activities. The activities listed are:

a. Any illicit export, other removal or transfer of ownership of cultural property;
b. Any archaeological excavation, save where this is strictly required to safeguard, record or preserve cultural property;
c. Any alteration to, or change of use of, cultural property which is intended to conceal or destroy cultural, historical or scientific evidence.

States Parties are obliged to adopt legislative, administrative or disciplinary measures to suppress intentional acts of 'illicit export, other removal or transfer of ownership of cultural property from occupied territory in violation of the Convention or this Protocol'.[24]

The Second Protocol makes it an offence for any person to intentionally, and in violation of the Convention or the Protocol, cause extensive destruction of protected cultural property or cause acts of theft, pillage, misappropriation of, or vandalism directed against such property. States Parties are required to make these into offences in their national law 'punishable by appropriate penalties'.[25]

These two Protocols, taken together, form an effective legal framework for the protection of cultural property in an occupied territory. In practice it will depend on whether States Parties have the necessary will to take action and whether the resources to do so are sufficient. However, if cultural property is taken out of the territory, and ends up in a State Party, the situation is quite clear: it must be seized and returned following hostilities. Anything less is a breach of State responsibility. In this respect, the Protocols in theory operate more effectively than the 1970 Convention in ensuring recovery and return. They do not conflict with the Convention but complement it by providing a more efficient remedy for this important subset of material.

[22] Cultural Property Originating from Occupied Territory (Return) Act (Bulletin of Acts and Decrees, 2007) 123.

[23] T Einhorn, 'Israel' in JAR Nafziger, and RK Paterson (eds), *Handbook on the Law of Cultural Heritage and International Trade* (Cheltenham, Edward Elgar, 2014) 221.

[24] Art 21(b).

[25] Art 17.

(iv) 2003 Intangible Cultural Heritage Convention

Adopted through UNESCO in 2003 and brought into force on 20 April 2006, the Convention for the Safeguarding of the Intangible Cultural Heritage has an impressive number of States Parties, significantly more than the 1970 Convention and the other Conventions discussed above.[26] In spite of its name, the Convention does have a relationship to *tangible* heritage as well. Its definition of 'intangible heritage' specifically includes the 'instruments, objects, artefacts' associated with that heritage.[27] Consequently, the safeguarding provisions of the Convention arguably apply to those objects as well.[28] 'Safeguarding' is stated to mean 'measures aimed at ensuring the viability of the intangible heritage and includes preservation and protection'.[29] Any action that affects the relevant instruments, objects and artefacts would be subject to this regime. For example, the export of a musical instrument that has the effect of separating it from the performance in which it has been traditionally used, so that the viability of that performance is affected, appears to come within its scope. States may need to consider administrative action in this respect.[30]

(v) Free Trade Agreements: GATT, TFEU, Florence Agreement

Here we must consider agreements aimed at freeing up world or regional trade, which include exceptions for trade in cultural objects: the General Agreement on Tariffs and Trade (1947); the Treaty on the Functioning of the European Union (2009); and the Agreement on the Importation of Educational, Scientific and Cultural Materials (1950). Can the 1970 Convention, emphasising as it does controls over trade, be regarded as compatible with any of these free trade instruments?

The General Agreement on Tariffs and Trade (GATT) provides at Article XX, inter alia, a 'cultural exception' to the general premise of free trade set out in the Agreement:

> […] nothing in this Agreement shall be construed to prevent the adoption or enforcement by any contracting party of measures: […]
>
> (f) Imposed for the protection of national treasures of artistic, historic or archaeological value […]

[26] 185 States Parties as at February 2026.
[27] Art 2(1).
[28] Art 11.
[29] Art 2(2).
[30] For more on this Convention, see J Blake, *Commentary on the UNESCO 2003 Convention on the Safeguarding of the Intangible Cultural Heritage* (Builth Wells, Institute of Art and Law, 2006).

This provision was not affected by the Uruguay Round of negotiations leading to the World Trade Agreement.[31] It appears never to have been officially interpreted, though it has been discussed by a number of authors.[32]

A similar exception to free trade exists within the European Union. It was set out at Article 36 of the Treaty on the Functioning of the European Union (TFEU), whereby the general principles of free movement of goods (established by Articles 34 and 35):

> [...] shall not preclude prohibitions or restrictions on imports, exports or goods in transit justified on grounds of ... the protection of national treasures possessing artistic, historic or archaeological value ... . Such prohibitions or restrictions shall not, however, constitute a means of arbitrary discrimination or a disguised restriction on trade between Member States.

The crucial point here is the meaning of 'national treasures', a term undefined in the relevant European treaties. Petersmann took the view that it should be construed more stringently than Article XX of GATT: that only 'necessary' and 'proportionate' measures are permitted as justification.[33] Merryman argued that 'national treasures' must be narrowly interpreted.[34] Prott examines the phrase used in other languages, all of which generally seem broader than the English.[35] The Italian, Spanish, Portuguese and Dutch texts refer instead to 'patrimony' which does indeed seem to encompass more.[36] Frigo seems to say that this should be left to the legislation of each State, until the European Court of Justice decides to intervene on the question.[37] With this in mind, and taking account of other European Union instruments[38], it would seem that the EU Treaty would not conflict with the requirement at Article 6 of the 1970 Convention that States Parties adopt export control measures for cultural property.

Going back in time, briefly, to look at an earlier free trade agreement, we come to the Agreement on the Importation of Educational, Scientific and Cultural

[31] At one stage it was said that the United States was exerting pressure at the World Trade Organization to abolish the cultural exception: N Brodie, J Doole and P Watson, *Stealing History: The Illicit Trade in Cultural Material* (Cambridge, McDonald Institute for Archaeological Research, 2000) 31.

[32] For example, T Voon, *Cultural Products and the World Trade Organization* (Cambridge, Cambridge University Press, 2007) 143; F Fiorentini, 'The Trade of Cultural Property: Legal Pluralism in an Age of Global Institutions' in JA Sánchez Cordero (ed), *The 1970 UNESCO Convention: New Challenges* (Mexico City, Instituto de Investigaciones Jurídica, 2014) 111.

[33] E-U Petersmann, *International and European Trade and Environmental Law after the Uruguay Round* (London, Kluwer, 1996) 57.

[34] JH Merryman, 'Cultural Property Internationalism' (2005) 12 *International Journal of Cultural Property* 11, 31.

[35] LV Prott, 'The International Movement of Cultural Objects' (2005) 12 *International Journal of Cultural Property* 225, 243–44.

[36] House of Commons, Culture Media and Sport Committee, *Cultural Property: Return and Illicit Trade. Volume I: Report and Proceedings of the Committee* (London, Stationery Office Ltd, 2000) xix.

[37] M Frigo, 'Italy' in JAR Nafziger and RK Paterson (eds), *Handbook on the Law of Cultural Heritage and International Trade* (Cheltenham, Edward Elgar, 2014) 234, 239.

[38] See Directive 2014/60/EU of the European Parliament and of the Council of 15 May 2014 on the Return of Cultural Objects Unlawfully removed from the Territory of a Member State, discussed below.

Materials, adopted in 1950 by the fifth General Conference of UNESCO in Florence. It requires States to facilitate the importation of cultural materials, to simplify the administrative procedure governing their importation and to assist with their expeditious and safe Customs clearance. It exhorts States to facilitate the free flow of books, publications and educational, scientific and cultural materials (Preamble) and to promote by every means the free circulation of educational, scientific or cultural materials (Article 4(a)).

Of course there is an inherent tension between the purposes of maximum exchange and the curb in illicit traffic, and there was some early suggestion that the 1970 Convention might not comply with the principles of the Florence Agreement.[39] It can be said quite firmly now that the two instruments are broadly compatible: recall here that the 1970 Convention can be implemented without resorting to import restrictions or delayed customs clearance.[40] Additionally, the 1970 Convention pays tribute to some of the benefits of free trade, an indication that the principles were intended to remain commensurate: 'the interchange of cultural property among nations for scientific, cultural and educational purposes increases the knowledge of the civilization of Man, enriches the cultural life of all peoples and inspires mutual respect and appreciation among nations' (Preamble, 1970 Convention).[41]

(vi) European Union Directives and Regulations

With the abolition of internal frontiers in the European Union (EU) in 1993 and the introduction of free movement of goods, it became necessary to prevent the illicit trade of national treasures as between EU Member States. The result was a Directive passed on 15 March 1993, and since amended and recast on 15 May 2014, as the Directive on the Return of Cultural Objects Unlawfully Removed from the Territory of a Member State.[42] A Directive is a legal act that establishes objectives that all Member States must achieve through legislative (or other) means within their domestic legal systems, leading to the eventual harmonisation of law within the EU in that particular field.

The Directive aimed to facilitate the return of cultural objects from one Member State to another. 'Cultural objects' here are defined as objects classified or defined as 'national treasures possessing artistic, historic or archaeological value' under national legislation or administrative procedures (Article 2), a definition that is

[39] The Swedish Customs authorities suggested this during the drafting process for the 1970 Convention in the late 1960s. See also the US delegation's support for free exchange of cultural goods during the drafting process: Unesdoc. SHC/MD/5 Annex I, 21.

[40] See, eg, the implementation by Canada and Australia, as discussed above.

[41] See also the Recommendation concerning the International Exchange of Cultural Property 1976, para 15.

[42] Council Directive 93/7/EEC of 15 March 1993; Directive 2014/60/EU of the European Parliament and of the Council of 15 May 2014.

meant to comply with the exception to free movement of goods set out in the TFEU (see above). Where a cultural object of this nature was 'unlawfully removed' from a Member State after 1 January 1993, that Member State will have a right to recover the object in the domestic courts of the Member State of destination (Article 6). The period to bring such claims begins after the Member State becomes aware of the location of the object and the identity of the possessor, increased from one year in the 1993 version to three years in the 2014 version (Article 8).

While the principle of return evokes the 1970 Convention, the structure of the Directive more closely follows the 1995 UNIDROIT Convention. In fact, the European Commission had urged EU Member States to adopt both Conventions in 2011, as set out at Preamble (16) to the recast Directive of 2014. Like the UNIDROIT Convention (and unlike the 1970 Convention), the Directive is not limited to the recovery of items stolen from museums, monuments or institutions[43] and creates a right of recovery through the courts (rather than diplomatic offices). Member States, having implemented the Directive, therefore have systems for return in place in their domestic legislation. Nevertheless, it is generally found that the rules created by the Directive have not led to many returns.[44]

Under the Directive, if the possessor has exercised 'due care and attention' in acquiring the object fair compensation is owed 'according to the circumstances of the case'.[45] This equates to the due diligence requirement under the 1995 UNIDROIT Convention. 'Due diligence' is perhaps a more familiar term to Americans but 'due care and attention' is likely to be clearer to Europeans, particularly non-lawyers such as art market operators and collectors.

In order to impose controls on cultural treasures at the EU's *external* borders, the EU has a harmonised export regulation: Council Regulation No 116/2009 on the Export of Cultural Goods, which replaced a similar Regulation from 1992. The Regulation ensures controls based on the age and value thresholds for specific goods set out in the Annex to the Regulation. While the list in the Annex covers similar ground to Article 1 of the 1970 Convention, it is ultimately quite different, especially due to some of the value thresholds included. Export of objects that fall within the criteria in the Annex is subject to a licence. In this regard, it could be said that the licensing requirement, in its broadest sense, is commensurate with the Article 6 requirement of the 1970 Convention. Nothing in the Regulation prevents Member States imposing stricter controls on objects leaving their territory, should they so wish.

The EU has also introduced import rules for cultural goods: Regulation 2019/880 on the Introduction and the Import of Cultural Goods. While not an

[43] Compare Art 7(b) of the 1970 Convention and Arts 3 and 5 of the Unidroit Convention. Paragraph 9 of the Preamble to the Directive provides that national treasures are covered 'whether or not they form part of other collections or are single items, and whether they originate from regular or clandestine excavations, provided they are classified or defined as national treasures.'

[44] This was recognised at para 8 of the Preamble to the recast 2014 Directive and, since that second version of the Directive was implemented, the use of it by Member States appears minimal or non-existent.

[45] Art 10.

attempt to bring into force the 1970 Convention across the EU, its impact has been in line with some of the aims of the Convention – and has gone somewhat further than the Convention in achieving those aims. To begin, the Regulation defines 'cultural goods' by reference to its Annex which effectively replicates the Article 1 categories from the Convention, though without the requirement for State designation ('Part A' cultural goods under the Regulation), and specifically limited to cultural goods derived from outside the EU.[46] It then creates a prohibition on the introduction into the EU of any such goods unlawfully removed from their place of origin (Article 3(1)). The scope of the prohibition is far wider than the import restriction at Article 7(b)(i) of the 1970 Convention, which is limited to cultural property stolen from a museum, monument or institution. As such, the EU Regulation prohibits the entry of any cultural goods that were excavated, exported or otherwise misappropriated in breach of the applicable laws or regulations in their place of origin, whenever this may have occurred (no date cut-off is set out in Article 3(1) of the Regulation).

Beyond the prohibition, the Regulation also provides a series of import controls for cultural goods originating outside the EU. Depending on the type of goods imported, their age and value, importers may need to obtain either an import licence (Article 4) or make an importer statement (Article 5), in both cases indicating through documentation that the relevant goods left their country of origin lawfully.[47] In both cases, there are exceptions if the goods left their country of origin before 24 April 1972 (the date of entry into force of the 1970 Convention) or where the country of origin cannot be reliably determined, in either case requiring proof of lawful export from the last country where the goods were located for more than five years (Article 4(4) for import licences and Article 5(2) for importer statements).

In many ways, Regulation 2019/880 is another instrument supporting and reaffirming the 1970 Convention. This is true in relation to the scope and definition of the items covered (Preamble (paragraph 7)) and the April 1972 threshold for provenance documentation, as well as an emphasis in the Regulation on Article 5 of the Convention regarding the need for national services to monitor and police the trade in cultural goods (Preamble (paragraph 9)).

(vii) Human Rights Instruments

The relationship between cultural objects and human rights has become an important area of academic research and jurisprudential development.[48] It is

[46] Art 2(1) of the Regulation, limited to cultural goods not 'either created or discovered in the customs territory of the Union' (Art 1(2)).

[47] See also the Commission's Implementing Regulations 2021/1079, at Art 8 for import licences and Art 12 for importer statements.

[48] European Court of Human Rights – Research Division, *Cultural Rights in the Case-law of the European Court of Human Rights* (Strasbourg, 2011 (updated 2017)).

therefore interesting to consider the relationship between the 1970 Convention and rights-protecting instruments such as the Universal Declaration of Human Rights (1948) or, more concretely, the European Convention for the Protection of Human Rights and Fundamental Freedoms (1950) (European Convention). Certain rights, such as the right to religion, could be said to support an international agreement restricting trade in cultural property by ensuring that ceremonial and sacred objects essential to religious practice are preserved in situ, thus benefiting the community (and its rights-bearing members) by ensuring access.[49] There is also an argument that, in certain instruments, a 'right to culture' might exist,[50] although as a single, standalone human right, it is sadly undeveloped in the jurisprudence.[51]

Another important human right, that to private property, can in fact conflict with controls imposed on the trade in such property – including cultural property. The right is enshrined in, for example, the European Convention's First Protocol, at Article 1, whereby 'Every natural or legal person is entitled to the peaceful enjoyment of his possessions'. According to the provision, no one shall be deprived of their possessions, 'except in the public interest and subject to the conditions provided for by law and by the general principles of international law'. It is therefore conceivable that a State's obligation under the 1970 Convention – to place export controls under Article 6 or to 'recover and return' under Article 7(b)(ii) – may interfere with the right to the possessor's property. The question would then be whether the deprivation of property was 'in the public interest' and 'provided for by law' and by 'the general principles of international law'. The deprivation may indeed be justified as a means of fighting illicit trade and complying with an important cultural property treaty (such as the 1970 Convention), but this may not be guaranteed in every instance. The compensation provision at Article 7(b)(ii) of the 1970 Convention would ensure that the possessor was duly compensated, thus minimising the risk of breaching a property right.

Two important cases before the European Court of Human Rights interpreting the right to peaceful enjoyment of possessions in the First Protocol offer a sense

[49] See the right to freedom of religion at Art 18 of the Universal Declaration of Human Rights (Paris, 10 December 1948) and at Art 9 of the European Convention on Human Rights (Rome, 4 November 1950).

[50] Article 27 of the Universal Declaration of Human Rights, ibid, enshrines a 'right to freely participate in the cultural life of the community', while a similar right can be found at Art 15 of the International Covenant on Economic, Social and Cultural Rights (New York, 16 Dec 1966). See R O'Keefe, 'The 'Right to Take Part in Cultural Life' Under Article 15 of the ICESCR' (1998) 47 *International and Comparative Law Quarterly* 904, 909.

[51] See, eg, *Cultural Rights in the Case-law of the European Court of Human Rights* (n 48), finding that cultural rights may be protected under core civil rights (private/family life, expression, education), but not as a standalone right. In the case of *Armenia v Azerbaijan*, the International Court of Justice linked access to cultural sites with the right against discrimination (though this related to the alleged destruction of said sites rather than looting or illicit excavation): *Application of the International Convention on the Elimination of all forms of Racial discrimination (Armenia v Azerbaijan)*, International Court of Justice, Provision Measures Order (7 Dec 2021); see A Herman, case note (April 2022) XXVII *Art Antiquity and Law* 70.

of how such a balancing can occur. In the first of these, *Beyeler v Italy*, the Court did find that Italy had a legitimate interest in policing the movement of important cultural objects on its territory.[52] Referencing the 1970 Convention (Article 4), the Court found that it was legitimate for the State to facilitate public access to works of art lawfully on its territory, even if those works were by foreign artists: at issue was a work by Van Gogh pre-empted by the State of Italy.[53] However, in this particular case, it was found that Italy's actions towards the Swiss owner of the property were disproportionate to the legitimate State interest and therefore breached the owner's right to peacefully enjoy his possession.[54] Although this was not a case of illicit traffic, it indicates that States will need to be careful when imposing restrictions on the free movement of private property. Here it related to pre-emption, but it could have easily been an export control (such as that required by Article 6 of the 1970 Convention). Even if the State has an interest in controlling trade, it must act promptly and in accordance with the law.[55]

The other important cultural property case under the European Convention involves the Victorious Youth statue, or 'Getty Bronze', claimed by Italy against the Getty Museum in California for many years: *The J. Paul Getty Trust v Italy*.[56] The case has a long, convoluted and disputed history involving a statue brought up from the seabed by Italian fishermen in 1964 and thereafter removed from Italy without an export licence. Four individuals were charged, but ultimately acquitted by the Italian courts in 1970. The piece was then sold to the Getty Trust in 1977 and has remained thereafter on display at the Getty Villa in California. In 2007 – 40 years after its removal and 30 years after the Getty's acquisition – Italian prosecutors sought a confiscation order for the sculpture from the Italian courts, which was eventually approved by the Italian Court of Cassation in 2019. Although the Italian court action is not binding on the Getty in California, the Trust nevertheless thought it wise to challenge Italy before the European Court of Human Rights (as Beyeler had done before): the Trust argued that it could not peacefully enjoy its possessions, according to the First Protocol to the European Convention.

In a startling decision dated 2 May 2024, the European Court found in favour of Italy. While the actions of the Italian authorities had indeed engaged the Trust's property right under the Protocol (thus allowing the claim to be brought), it was held that Italy had complied with the safeguards of Article 1, in that the actions

[52] [2000] ECHR 462. For a discussion of the case, see M-A. Renold, 'A Landmark Decision in Art Law by the European Court of Human Rights: Beyeler v. Italy' (2000) V *Art Antiquity and Law* 73.

[53] *Beyeler v Italy*, ibid, para 113.

[54] Specifically because Italy had attempted to use its right of pre-emption to acquire the property compulsorily from Beyeler in an unreasonable way: by waiting several years before indicating its exercise of the pre-emption right and also by seeking to acquire the work from him at an unreasonably low price. See ibid, paras 120–122.

[55] On the general issue of human rights and whether these are affected by the refusal of an export permit, the Australian case *David Waterhouse v Minister for the Arts and Territories* (1993) 119 ALR 89 is instructive: ultimately the Federal Court held that export restrictions do not breach the right to compensation for confiscated property.

[56] Application no 35271/19 (2 May 2024).

of the authorities were lawful, in the public interest and proportional. The 1970 Convention was not directly at issue: when the Trust purchased the statue in 1977, neither Italy nor the US was party to the Convention – and besides, the Convention does not impose return obligations on destination States in relation to newly discovered antiquities imported into the jurisdiction.[57] Nevertheless, the 1970 Convention was referred to approvingly by the Court: it was referenced to demonstrate the important State interest in preserving cultural property within the territory and in fighting the illicit trade in such material.[58] Any interference with property rights was in the public interest because it was done to preserve Italy's cultural heritage.[59] The Court also noted the 1970 Convention's recognition of the 'indefeasible right' of States to 'classify and declare certain cultural property as inalienable which should therefore *ipso facto* not be exported' (Article 13(1)(d)), thus rejecting the Trust's argument that Italy's latter-day attempt at confiscation was arbitrary and manifestly unreasonable.[60]

As a result of these decisions under the Protocol to the European Convention, we have two quite different conclusions on the State's role in protecting cultural heritage. Although neither case dealt directly with the 1970 Convention, each decision found support for its conclusions in the provisions of that Convention, whether relating to Article 4 or Article 13. In both cases, the moral legitimacy of the 1970 Convention – and its ability to underpin State practice – was upheld.

(viii) Nicosia Convention

The Council of Europe had initially attempted to introduce the Convention on Offences Relating to Cultural Property in 1985 (the 'Delphi Convention'), but it never received sufficient ratifications to enter into force. Much later, the idea was revived – in large part responding to the attacks on cultural heritage by ISIS in Iraq and Syria – and led to a new text proposed at the Council of Europe in Nicosia on 3 November 2017. As with the first, this new version sought to harmonise criminal offences relating to cultural property, such as theft, fraud, damage, illegal excavation, import and export. It was aimed at widening the scope of criminal offences and extending the powers of the State in providing for the enforcement of those offences (including cross-border offences), set against the backdrop of increased looting in war zones and the rise of the internet as a platform for selling looted

[57] See the limits at Art 7(b) on the import restrictions and the obligation to recover and return cultural property (only applying to such material stolen from a museum, monument or similar institution and documented on its inventory).

[58] Paras 278–79, referencing Art 13(1)(d) of the 1970 Convention and Art 5 of the UNIDROIT Convention.

[59] Paras 341 and 359–60. The Trust had argued that the 1970 Convention had no retrospective effect (para 327).

[60] Paras 354–56.

material. The Convention came into force on 1 April 2022 following the fifth ratification from a Council of Europe member (Italy). It now has seven States Parties – a very small number, rendering its impact negligible.

There are, however, some interesting parallels to the 1970 Convention in the text. A number of existing cultural conventions, including the 1970 Convention, are listed in the Preamble. Its preferred term is 'cultural property', the definition of which (at Article 2) is modelled on that found at Article 1 of the 1970 Convention. As with the 1970 Convention, Nicosia condemns the export of cultural property without appropriate authorisation, making this act a criminal offence (Article 6). Nicosia also goes further by mandating import-related offences, including for the import of illegally excavated/exported cultural property coming from a State Party either to the Nicosia or the 1970 Convention (Article 5), as well as offences for acquisition (Article 7) and placing on the market (Article 8). Seizure and confiscation by the State can lead to the repatriation of cultural property (Article 14).

The Nicosian remit is impressive, but its ambitions may have scared off more risk-averse States, which might explain the Convention's low uptake. That said, the seven ratifying States include Italy, which, in a 2022 law, amended its Criminal Code in order to incorporate all of the offences listed in the Nicosia Convention into its domestic law.[61] This provides officers with powerful tools to investigate, confiscate and forfeit foreign cultural property, as well as the ability to bring criminal proceedings against those involved in importing, exporting or dealing in such material.

(ix) Palermo Convention

The United Nations Convention Against Transnational Organized Crime (2000), known as the Palermo Convention, has a role to play in relation to crimes involving cultural artefacts.[62] The organisation responsible for administering the Convention (the United Nations Office on Drugs and Crime - UNODC) seeks to advance it, including in relation to cultural heritage. Borgstede quotes the Palermo Convention as providing the necessary legal framework for international cooperation in combating, inter alia, offences against cultural heritage, even if the same goal is pursued by other instruments, such as the 1970 Convention and the UNIDROIT Convention.[63] As it happens, the 1970 Convention refers to crimes only at Article 8, requiring 'penalties and administrative sanctions' for breaches of the export or import rules set out in the preceding articles, therefore assistance from other instruments and administrative agencies can indeed be of use in stemming illicit trade.

[61] Italian Law No 22 of 9 March 2022, 'Provisions on Crimes Against Cultural Heritage', amending the Italian Criminal Code with the insertion of new offences at Art 518bis and following.

[62] G Borgstede, 'Cultural Property, the Palermo Convention, and Transnational Organized Crime' (2014) 21 *International Journal of Cultural Property* 281.

[63] ibid 284.

An expert group on protection against trafficking in cultural property within UNODC has been operating now for many years with notable success. The group initially prepared a set of international guidelines that were adopted by the UN General Assembly on 18 December 2014.[64] The 'International Guidelines for Crime Prevention and Criminal Justice Responses with Respect to Trafficking in Cultural Property and Other Related Offences' remain useful to States, providing a consolidation of tools that can be used to improve administrative procedures, domestic criminal law and cooperation.

The Guidelines are divided into four chapters. The first sets out crime prevention strategies (eg, information/data collection, the role of cultural institutions and the private sector, monitoring, education and public awareness). The second encourages States to adhere to the relevant conventions and to criminalise specific offences (such as trafficking), or else establish administrative offences. This chapter also asks States to consider defining the term 'cultural property' for the purposes of criminal law (echoing the terminology of the 1970 Convention).[65] The third chapter encourages international cooperation (including regarding extradition, seizure and confiscation, cooperation among authorities, as well as the return, restitution or repatriation of cultural property). And the fourth sets out the general principle that States should consider applying the guidelines to situations involving trafficking in cultural property, within the framework of the relevant conventions, including the 1970 Convention. Many points around criminal legislation from the Guidelines were seemingly picked up in the Nicosia Convention of 2017 discussed above.

At the time of the publication of the Guidelines, Borgstede had warned of the danger of 'mission creep' by UNODC and the potential duplication of work in a field already short on resources.[66] However, time has shown an impressive level of commitment by UNODC in fighting illicit trade in cultural property and supporting the International Guidelines. It provided useful research in 2022 with the publication of 'False Trades: Uncovering the Scale and Scope of Trafficking in Cultural Property', which, amongst other things, emphasised the normative force of the 1970 Convention.[67] Following on from this, UNODC partnered with UNESCO and Interpol in 2023 to create the Co-Action Against Trafficking in Cultural Heritage (CATCH) initiative, a three-year programme focused on the Mediterranean region. This has provided the basis for a co-ordinated attempt by the institutions to crack down on cultural property crime, with a hope that it can

[64] Resolution 69/196.

[65] Guideline 15.

[66] Borgstede (n 62). O'Keefe has echoed this concern, pointing to the recognition by the UN General Assembly that UNESCO and INTERPOL already operate in this field: Resolution 68/186, paras 7-8. He questioned whether UNODC would have sufficient resources to devote to a matter already dealt with by others: *Protecting Cultural Objects: Before and After 1970* (Builth Wells, Institute of Art and Law, 2017) 71–72.

[67] Research and Trend Analysis Branch, UNODC (2022) 6.

continue beyond the original pilot period.[68] In parallel, UNODC has partnered with Egypt for regional programmes. It is sponsored by Cyprus, France, Greece, Italy and the UK, as well as the EU and the Antiquities Coalition from the US.[69] Its main goals are training (including specialised training of judges and prosecutors), capacity building and increased cooperation amongst criminal enforcement authorities.[70]

Chapter 2
United Nations Resolutions and Declarations

This chapter will examine resolutions that have come out of the United Nations, either from the Security Council or from the General Assembly, and which have a direct or indirect bearing on the 1970 Convention. The first category of Security Council Resolutions includes only two: those applying to illegally removed cultural property from Iraq and Syria respectively, part of the international response to the wars and looting that took place in those countries. Such Resolutions are binding on all UN Member States. The second category includes resolutions from the UN's General Assembly, along with one quite important declaration (the Declaration on the Rights of Indigenous Peoples). These are not binding upon States, but nevertheless can come to have a soft law or persuasive impact, which go towards supporting the aims of the 1970 Convention.

(i) UN Security Council Resolutions on Iraqi and Syrian Cultural Property

Following the 2003 US-UK invasion of Iraq, the National Museum in Baghdad was badly looted in April of that year, prompting action from the international community. On 22 May 2003, the United Nations Security Council adopted Resolution 1483 on Iraq, binding on all UN Member States.[71] It was long and complex, dealing with many fundamental issues concerning the war, and included the following direction to Member States:

> […] take appropriate steps to facilitate the safe return to Iraqi institutions of Iraqi cultural property and other items of archaeological, historical, cultural, rare scientific, and religious importance illegally removed from the Iraq National Museum, the

[68] UNODC Director-General's address, CCPCJ 34, 22 May 2025, which also expressed support for CATCH and the work of UNODC in cultural heritage more generally.

[69] ibid.

[70] Co-Action Against Trafficking in Cultural Heritage (CATCH) Factsheet.

[71] FL Kirgis, 'Security Council Resolution 1483 on the Rebuilding of Iraq', *American Society of International Law Insights* (May 2003).

> National Library, and other locations in Iraq since the adoption of resolution 661 (1990) of 6 August 1990, including by establishing a prohibition on trade in or transfer of such items and items with respect to which reasonable suspicion exists that they have been illegally removed, and calls upon [UNESCO], Interpol, and other international organizations, as appropriate, to assist in the implementation of this paragraph.

This provision in some ways complemented the aims of the 1970 Convention in targeting illicit cultural property, even if it applied only to cultural property illegally removed from Iraq since the beginning of the first Gulf War (6 August 1990). Unlike the 1970 Convention (and other UNESCO Conventions), UN Member States here had no choice but to adopt the rule.[72] Certain States thereafter passed new legislation to bring the Resolution into effect, including Australia, Switzerland and the United Kingdom.[73] The US President issued an executive order[74] until a more sustainable system of controls could be put in place under the Convention on Cultural Property Implementation Act of 1983, the implementing law for the 1970 Convention.

The Resolution required States to take an active role and do whatever was necessary to ensure return. Trade in and transfer of the items were prohibited. Problems could arise for items unlawfully removed from Iraq after 6 August 1990, but lawfully traded before 22 May 2003, which could fall into limbo – unable to be traded, sold, bartered or inherited. Persons may have bought objects in good faith, limitation periods may have expired, records detailing how an object was acquired may have been lost or destroyed. In such situations, the Resolution nevertheless urged States to take 'appropriate steps' to return these to Iraq.

Illegality is to be judged by Iraqi law applying at the time of removal.[75] In August 1990, the relevant law was Antiquities Law No 59 of 1936 which prohibited the export of antiquities unless accompanied by a written permit.[76] The 1936 Law was then replaced by the Antiquities and Heritage Law No 55 of 2002 which, like its predecessor, prohibited export unless in accordance with the conditions specified in the law.[77] There is thus little likelihood that any antiquity that left Iraq after August 1990 did so legally. The practical problem is, of course, proving that the object left during this time.

In early 2011, an armed conflict began in Syria between government forces and those pushing for political change, leading to the substantial destruction of monuments and sites, as well as looting by groups such as ISIS. Attempts were made at the international level to bring about an instrument to give Syrian cultural

[72] See Charter of the United Nations, Ch VII.

[73] For example, the UK's Iraq (United Nations Sanctions) Order 2003, since replaced by the Iraq (Sanctions) (EU Exit) Regulations 2020, created offences for dealing in cultural property unlawfully removed from Iraq after 6 August 1990, as well as a duty to transfer such material to a constable (s 27 of the Regulations). The offences create a presumption in favour of the prosecution, but this can be rebutted if the defence adduces evidence sufficient to raise 'an issue' (s 29(2)).

[74] Executive Order 13350 (29 July 2004).

[75] Other systems of law such as the law of the State applying the Resolution or international law are not relevant to establish illegality: I Upjohn, 'The Protection of Iraqi Cultural Heritage in Australian Domestic Law' (2006) XI *Art Antiquity and Law* 93, 97.

[76] Art 26.

[77] Art 22(3).

property the same treatment as that afforded to Iraqi cultural property. On 12 February 2015 – nearly four years after the conflict began – the Security Council adopted Resolution 2199, paragraph 17 of which required Member States to:

> [...] take appropriate steps to prevent the trade in Iraqi and Syrian cultural property and other items of archaeological, historical, cultural, rare scientific, and religious importance illegally removed from Iraq since 6 August 1990 and from Syria since 15 March 2011, including by prohibiting cross-border trade in such items, thereby allowing for their eventual safe return to the Iraqi and Syrian people and calls upon [UNESCO], Interpol, and other international organizations, as appropriate, to assist in the implementation of this paragraph.[78]

This appears to be stricter than Resolution 1483. Here, States are to 'prevent' the trade in Iraqi and Syrian cultural property. States must actively adopt administrative procedures designed to prevent 'cross border trade' including policing at the border of Member States, as well as controls on art dealers, auctioneers, museums and other collectors through prohibiting handling of cultural property covered by the Resolution. Police must be proactive in seeking out where prohibited objects are kept. Those found in the possession of persons contrary to the prohibitions must be surrendered to appropriate authorities 'for eventual safe return to the Iraqi and Syrian people'. This was implicit in Resolution 1483 but is here an explicit obligation. States will have to provide safe conditions until the objects can be returned without danger of deterioration or destruction.

Well before Resolution 2199, the European Union had taken action at a regional level: on 13 December 2013, it inserted a provision into Regulation (EU) No 36/2012 concerning restrictive measures in view of the situation in Syria.[79] These included a prohibition on the provision of 'brokering services', services that could facilitate the illicit traffic in Syrian cultural property. These can take a variety of forms but basically consist of arranging transactions between a buyer and seller for a commission. The broker might also provide information on market conditions or assist with transportation of goods. The UK, for instance, adopted import rules on Syrian cultural property through the EU Regulation, but, after Brexit, has enacted its own specific regulations that reflect in large part Resolution 2199.[80]

(ii) UN General Assembly Resolutions

The UN General Assembly has also adopted numerous statements demonstrating keen support for the 1970 Convention, even if such Resolutions are not binding

[78] Resolution 2199, unanimously adopted by Security Council.

[79] EU Council Regulation N 1332/2013, Art 11c (1).

[80] Syria (United Nations Sanctions) (Cultural Property) (EU Exit) Regulations 2020: these broadly repeat the offences created under the similar Iraq Regulations of 2020 (n 73), including the duty to transfer illegally removed Syrian cultural property to a constable (s 12), and with a general reverse onus that is rebuttable if the defence adduces evidence that raises 'an issue' (s 14(2)).

on UN Member States the way Security Council Resolutions are. As such, these Resolutions have only symbolic or persuasive force within the international community, not unlike a Declaration (as to which, see below). Every two to three years since the 1970s, Resolutions on the Return or Restitution of Cultural Property to Countries of Origin have been adopted by the General Assembly. They show support for the 1970 Convention and 'reaffirm its importance' (along with other cultural conventions, such as the UNIDROIT Convention, the World Heritage Convention and the Intangible Cultural Heritage Convention).[81] These Resolutions call on UN bodies and intergovernmental organisations to continue to 'address the issue of return or restitution of cultural property to countries of origin' and encourage all remaining UN Member States to ratify the 1970 Convention and the other cultural conventions.[82] This encouragement seems to have borne fruit: a steady average of two new States ratify the 1970 Convention every year.

In December 2024, UN General Assembly Resolution on the Return or Restitution of Cultural Property to the Countries of Origin (79/133) recognised the meetings of States Parties to the Convention, and the Subsidiary Committee, while demonstrating support for a wide variety of UNESCO-developed tools (eg Operational Guidelines to the Convention, the Code of Ethics for Dealers and the Model Export Certificates). More surprising perhaps was the expression by the General Assembly of a 'grave concern' regarding collections of cultural objects 'illegally removed before the entry into force of the 1970 Convention', calling on Member States to take 'appropriate steps' – a familiar international legal euphemism – for their 'return or restitution' to countries of origin. This is the first time the General Assembly has expressed support for the restitution of *historically* removed objects – and it is unclear at present what practical impact this statement might have.[83] What is certain is that it represents a desire amongst UN Member States to push all States to go beyond the scope of the 1970 Convention.

(iii) UN Declaration on the Rights of Indigenous Peoples

The United Nations Declaration on the Rights of Indigenous Peoples was approved by the UN General Assembly on 13 September 2007, with 143 States voting in favour, four against and eleven abstentions.[84] As a declaration, it does not create binding obligations in international law, but nevertheless has had a tremendous political and practical influence. This is due to the refinement of positions that took place over its long gestation period, as well as the large number of States that have accepted it. The Declaration exhorts States to, inter alia, 'provide effective mechanisms, which

[81] For example, UN General Assembly Resolution 79/133 (6 Dec 2024) para 8.
[82] For instance, ibid paras 7–8.
[83] Para 6.
[84] The four States voting against were Australia, Canada, New Zealand and the United States. Since 2007, each of these States has endorsed the Declaration.

may include restitution, developed in conjunction with indigenous peoples, with respect to their cultural, intellectual, religious and spiritual property taken without their free, prior and informed consent or in violation of their laws, traditions and customs' (Article 11).[85] In relation to ceremonial objects and human remains, States are asked to 'enable access and/or repatriation' (Article 12). Although it was one of the original States voting against the Declaration in 2007, Canada has now passed a statute that seeks to implement the principles of the Declaration into domestic law: the United Nations Declaration on the Rights of Indigenous Peoples Act of 2021.[86]

The principles behind Articles 11 and 12 of the Declaration, including the reference to effective mechanisms, restitution, access and repatriation, seek something much broader for Indigenous material than anything provided in the 1970 Convention. There have been attempts at aligning the two. For instance, the 2015 Operational Guidelines to the 1970 Convention highlight the importance of including indigenous cultural property within the definition of 'cultural property' at Article 1 of the Convention, referencing the Declaration ('to conform with the wishes of those communities in accordance with the principles of the [Declaration]').[87] A subsequent publication of UNESCO, Model Provisions on the Prevention and Fight Against the Illicit Trafficking of Cultural Property, intended for States seeking to implement the 1970 Convention, included a number of references to 'the cultural heritage of Indigenous Peoples', even if such a category of material was never explicitly intended by the 1970 Convention.[88]

Chapter 3
UNESCO Recommendations, Resolutions and Other Documents

(i) UNESCO Recommendations

Several relevant UNESCO Recommendations were made between the 1950s and 1970s. They were often the result of intense debate among States at the time of their drafting and, although some are now dated, contain much useful material for combatting theft and illegal traffic. They also have legal implications in that

[85] For an illuminating history of how this provision was changed and eventually adopted see S Esterling, 'One Step Forward, Two Steps Back: The Restitution of Cultural Property in the United Nations Declaration on the Rights of Indigenous Peoples' (December 2013) XVIII *Art Antiquity and Law* 323

[86] SC 2021, c 14. For commentary see O Shaw, 'Implementing UNDRIP into Canadian Law', Institute of Art and Law blog (7 August 2023).

[87] *Operational Guidelines for the Implementation of the Convention on the Means of Prohibiting and Preventing the Illicit Import, Export and Transfer of Ownership of Cultural Property*, adopted at the Third Meeting of States Parties (Paris, UNESCO, 2015) para 12. O'Keefe applauded this inclusion: *Protecting Cultural Objects* (Builth Wells, Institute of Art and Law, 2017) 117.

[88] UNESCO, *Model Provisions on the Prevention and Fight against the Illicit Trafficking of Cultural Property* (Paris, UNESCO, May 2025) 2, 4, 8. See below at p *.

Member States are required 'to apply the principles and norms … within their respective territories'. In cultural heritage law, UNESCO Recommendations are often used to establish an international standard which States can adjust to fit their diverse legal systems and harmonise the rules.

Stretching back before the 1970 Convention, UNESCO Recommendations have dealt with problems caused by theft and illicit trafficking. The first in point of time was the Recommendation on International Principles Applicable to Archaeological Excavations of 1956, which asked Member States to consider adopting rules 'to govern the trade in antiquities so as to ensure that this trade does not encourage smuggling of archaeological material or affect adversely the protection of sites and the collecting of material for public exhibit'.[89] One Recommendation from 1964 relates to the illicit trade in the run-up to the 1970 Convention. It went somewhat further than the 1970 Convention by asking States not to permit the import of cultural property until it has been cleared by the exporting State.[90] Those who see the Convention as not playing a significant role could do well to consider this earlier Recommendation and how it could be used to persuade States to become proactive in enforcing controls on theft and illicit traffic.[91]

These Recommendations often seem like UNESCO's orphan children. States and commentators seldom refer to them. Indeed, in 2006, the Executive Board of UNESCO, following a study by the Secretariat, decided to continue to follow-up on only one of the Recommendations pertaining to the Culture Sector. The other Recommendations were said to have been overtaken by the later adoption of other instruments or technological developments, otherwise the relevant principles had been accepted or applied elsewhere.[92]

(ii) UNESCO General Conference Resolutions

It should of course be noted that, from time to time, the 1970 Convention is mentioned and supported by statements from UNESCO General Conference meetings. While there are too many to note here, for present purposes it can be said that Resolution 42 of the Fortieth General Conference (November 2019) engaged quite directly with various aspects of the 1970 Convention, largely due to the fact that the Convention's fiftieth anniversary was on the horizon

[89] Para 17.

[90] Recommendation on the Means of Prohibiting and Preventing the Illicit Export, Import and Transfer of Ownership of Cultural Property (1964) para 4 (cf Art 7(b) of the 1970 Convention).

[91] There were also relevant UNESCO Recommendations from 1976 and 1978. See also Recommendation concerning the Protection and Promotion of Museums and Collections, their Diversity and their Role in Society, approved at an Intergovernmental Meeting of Experts in May 2015 (para 24 enjoins museums to adhere to the principles of international instruments for the protection and promotion of cultural heritage 'and the fight against illicit traffic of cultural property').

[92] Unesdoc 175/EX/27. See discussion of individual Recommendations in PJ O'Keefe and LV Prott, *Cultural Heritage Conventions and Other Instruments: A Compendium with Commentaries* (Builth Wells, Institute of Art and Law, 2011).

(November 2020): it included statements of support for the Convention and the various means introduced to supplement it, while also establishing the 'International Day Against Illicit Trafficking of Cultural Property', to be held on the 14 November of any given year, commemorating the date of adoption of the Convention by the General Conference in 1970.[93]

(iii) Model Provisions

Model Provisions on State Ownership of Undiscovered Cultural Objects

Jointly produced by UNESCO and UNIDROIT in 2011, the Model Provisions on State Ownership of Undiscovered Cultural Objects offered a guide for States looking to incorporate State ownership into their local law. It was intended to ensure the recognition of State ownership in such property when considered by courts in foreign jurisdictions. This invariably goes beyond the framework of the 1970 Convention, as the Model Provisions aim to ensure recognition for civil claims brought according to the private law rules of the country of destination, or else for the purposes of criminal prosecution.

Long before the publication of the Model Provisions, these issues had been considered in several important cases relating to the possession of foreign cultural material. This occurred in the lengthy litigation launched by New Zealand (through its Attorney General) to recover five Māori panels offered for sale at Sotheby's in London in 1979: *Attorney General for New Zealand v Ortiz*.[94] In that case, New Zealand was found by the English courts not to have a law that properly vested ownership of newly discovered cultural objects in the State; an export restriction alone was not enough. By contrast, the prosecution of antiquities dealer Frederick Schultz in US Federal Court was successful since the objects removed from Egypt had been vested in Egypt prior to their departure; the import into the US therefore violated the National Stolen Property Act: *US v Schultz*.[95] Similarly, the English court in *Iran v Barakat* found that Iran's law of 1979 was sufficient to vest ownership of newly discovered antiquities in the State, allowing the State to thereafter bring a claim to recover the pieces from a dealer in England.[96]

With such cases in mind, the Model Provisions provide, at Provision 3, that: 'Undiscovered cultural objects are owned by the State, provided there is no prior

[93] Records of the General Conference, Fortieth Session (Paris, UNESCO, 12–27 November 2019) Resolution 42.

[94] [1982] 3 All ER 432, [1982] QB 349, rev'd [1982] 3 All ER 432, [1984] AC 1, aff'd [1983] 2 All ER 93, [1984] AC 1. This decision is discussed in RK Paterson, 'The Legal Dynamics of Cultural Property Export Controls: *Ortiz* Revisited' (1995 Special Issue) *UBC Law Review* 241.

[95] 178 F Supp 2d 445 (SDNY 2002), aff'd, 333 F.3d.393 (2d Cir 2003).

[96] For more on these cases, see P Gerstenblith, 'Schultz and Barakat: Universal Recognition of National Ownership of Antiquities' (2009) XIV *Art Antiquity and Law* 21.

existing ownership.' Similarly, Provision 4 makes clear that: 'Cultural objects excavated contrary to the law or licitly excavated but illicitly retained are deemed to be stolen objects.'[97] Transfers of ownership of such objects are 'null and void', unless the transferor had prior title (Provision 5). The illicit nature is also to be recognised internationally, not just for domestic law (Provision 6). The model provisions are a guide and a guide only: they have no effect unless a State incorporates them into its domestic law. If it does, courts may be more likely to give effect to State ownership when it can be pointed out that the provisions have been drafted by international experts and endorsed by two international organisations.[98] In practice, a majority of 1970 Convention States Parties reporting on their implementation of the Convention indicated the existence of state ownership laws in their respective domestic legal systems – although it is not clear if this came as a result of the Model Provisions.[99]

Model Provisions on the Prevention and Fight Against the Illicit Trafficking of Cultural Property (2025)

More directly related to the 1970 Convention are the Model Provisions on the Prevention and Fight Against the Illicit Trafficking of Cultural Property. These were first commissioned by the States Parties to the Convention at their Fifth Meeting in May 2019, and are based on the 1970 Convention and its Operational Guidelines.[100] The Provisions are intended to serve as guidelines for States looking to implement the Convention into domestic legal systems. After different drafts were examined and commented upon, a finalised version was approved at the Eighth Meeting of States Parties in May 2025. The Model Provisions do reflect the general principles of the 1970 Convention, but in many respects go somewhat further. At certain points, the Provisions state clearly that they relate to 'principles deriving from other international legal instruments, adopted since 1970, and which are likely to reinforce the implementation of the 1970 UNESCO Convention': for instance, those provisions relating to the cultural property of Indigenous Peoples, a matter not contemplated in 1970.[101] Each model provision is accompanied by helpful commentary to explain its meaning and sources.

[97] Compare UNIDROIT Convention, Art 3(2). There is no equivalent in the 1970 Convention.

[98] In *Protecting Cultural Objects* (Builth Wells, Institute of Art and Law, 2017) 78, O'Keefe highlighted that the term used is not 'property' but 'ownership', which he explained has a more universally recognisable application. The term 'cultural object', found in the UNIDROIT Convention, is also used here in preference to the term 'cultural property' from the 1970 Convention. He did express reservations about the usefulness of Provisions 5 and 6: 79.

[99] For the 2019–2022 reporting cycle, UNESCO has noted that, of the 91 States reporting on implementation of the 1970 Convention, over 75% indicated the existence of State ownership of undiscovered cultural heritage: Subsidiary Committee of the Meeting of States Parties, 11th Session, C70/23/11.SC/7 (Paris, UNESCO, 1–2 June 2023) p 11.

[100] Fifth Meeting of States Parties to the 1970 Convention (Paris, UNESCO, 20-21 May 2019), Resolution 5.MSP 10(5).

[101] Provisions 2, 4 and 8.

Provision 1 sets out the general principles underlying the Convention, namely the protection of cultural property 'with a view to preserving cultural property for present and future generations'. In Provision 2, the term 'cultural property' is interpreted similarly to its definition in Article 1 of the Convention, though less categorically (it removes State designation and the list of categories from Article 1). Provisions 3 and 4 relate to public collections and Indigenous cultural heritage respectively, two topics absent from the 1970 Convention, as noted in the comments. Provision 5 sets out the relevant 'competent authorities' within the State, while Provision 6 relates to education and raising public awareness. Provision 7 requires the establishment of a national inventory of cultural heritage (as required by Article 5(b) of the Convention).

With regard to exports, Provision 8 sets out the general principle that the export of cultural property will require a certificate (reflecting Article 6 of the Convention), while Provision 9 details what information such a certificate shall include. For importation, perhaps the most vital – and contentious – aspect of the Convention and the broader attempt to curb illicit trade, Provision 10 baldly states that 'imports of cultural property removed in violation of the legislation of the State of Origin regulating the export of cultural property are illicit.' Of course this does not mirror Article 7 of the 1970 Convention, which requires only that States impose import restrictions on cultural property stolen from a museum, monument or similar institution (and documented on the inventory) after entry into force in the relevant States. Thankfully the cautionary wording accompanying Provision 10 makes clear that its intention is to go beyond the Convention itself, as the text 'refers to principles deriving from other international legal instruments, adopted since 1970, and which are likely to reinforce the implementation of the 1970 Convention'. There are additional provisions that seem to derive more from ethics than strict legal requirements (eg Provision 11 on museum acquisition and Provision 13 on restitution and repatriation).

Six years in the making, it is unclear at present how many States will adopt these Model Provisions. Presumably States can opt for selected provisions, rather than the full suite. With an already significant number of States Parties, would any look to these model provisions if they have already implemented the Convention into domestic law? And for those not yet party – States that are arguably less courageous in fighting illicit trade – it is difficult to imagine them signing up to provisions which are, in essence, far more ambitious than the rather more conservative text of the Convention.

(iv) UNESCO Code of Ethics for Dealers

The possibility of an international code of ethics was foreseen by the drafters of the 1970 Convention. Under Article 5 of the Convention, one of the functions of the heritage staff each Member State is required to establish is that of preparing rules 'in conformity with the ethical principles set forth in this Convention' for 'curators, collectors, antique dealers, etc'. Although a Code was finalised in 1994, it could not be used by UNESCO until endorsed by the General Conference, which occurred in 1999. In the rollout, there was sadly no detailed and sustained programme to engage with dealers and their organisations, limiting the effectiveness of the Code in the art business. Despite the urging of the UN General Assembly on multiple occasions for art market actors to adopt this early Code of Ethics,[102] its actual impact on the trade was negligible.[103]

Through the ICPRCP, UNESCO then introduced the text of a new iteration called the International Code of Ethics for Dealers in Cultural Property in 2026.[104] As with its predecessor, the Code is not of course directed at States but at market actors. The new Code explains in its preamble that it contains principles that are in conformity with the 1970 Convention, a simple statement that never appeared in the previous iteration. Principle 1 then requires traders not to 'import, export or transfer the ownership' of cultural property when they 'have reasonable cause to believe it has been stolen, illegally alienated, clandestinely excavated or illegally exported.' This is similar to the statement made in the British Code of Practice for the Control of International Trading in Works of Art[105] and reminiscent of Article 3 of the 1970 Convention. The term 'trader' is intended to ensure that both dealers and auctioneers are covered by the Code although auctioneers do not normally own the objects they are auctioning. The qualifier 'reasonable cause' is used to prevent any notion of an absolute duty on the part of the trader.

Principle 2 is a clear reflection of Article 10(a) of the Convention, asking traders to record provenance and details of suppliers and items traded, and to inform purchasers of relevant export prohibitions. Principle 3 then requires traders to conduct due diligence, a term that did not appear in the earlier version. The purpose of Principle 4 is to exclude clandestine material from the trade, while Principle 5 does this for illegal exports and Principle 6 for stolen or 'illegally alienated' cultural property. If traders refuse to handle such objects, their economic value will be greatly cut as they will not be attractive to collectors; it will be harder for collectors to be introduced to them and the persons involved in the excavations and trades will find their markets restricted, thus reducing the incentive to engage in these activities. Under Principle 7, traders must report to national authorities any such material they become aware of. By Principle 8, the trader shall not assist the illicit transfer or export of an object by offering specialist services such as attribution or appraisal. In its preamble and footnotes, the Code encourages

[102] United Nations General Assembly Resolutions: 70/76 (2015), 73/130 (2018), 76/16 (2021) and 79/133 (2024).

[103] SRM Mackenzie, *Going, Going, Gone: Regulating the Market in Illicit Antiquities* (Institute of Art and Law, Leicester, 2005) 106. N Brodie, 'An Archaeologist's View of the Trade in Unprovenanced Antiquities' in BT Hoffman, *Art and Cultural Heritage: Law, Policy, and Practice* (2006) 52 at p 61.

[104] This version was endorsed following its presentation to the ICPRCP in May 2026. However, it was understood to be a 'living document' that can continually be amended, to be reported on to the ICPRCP every two years: ISPRCP/26/25.COM 13.

[105] See below, ch 4.

professional associations to submit a declaration to UNESCO if they support the Code and also to receive complaints from countries of origin concerning alleged failures by their members. These create a rather gentle form of policing violations of the Code.[106]

Chapter 4
Other Voluntary Codes of Ethics and Practice

There are a number of codes promoted by private bodies to regulate their own conduct and that of their members (eg archaeologists, conservators, art historians, museum personnel, dealers and auctioneers). Usually they are organised in national groups although there are some, such as the International Council of Museums, that have a worldwide membership. Institutions can also set standards for their own conduct, such as museum policies for acquisition or loans.

Ethics provide guidance where the lawmaker has yet to venture. They may represent the unexpressed will of a group. They may be useful in attempts to sway public opinion or show the holder of a contested object in an unfavourable light. There may be some attempt to impose penalties on wayward members of the organisation – although this is never very successful if the member can simply resign. Codes are not intended to be treated as legal documents where every nuance is considered and every comma checked for its effect on meaning. Rather, they are guides prepared, in most cases, by persons concerned to express their understanding of what members of their particular profession need in order to function effectively. Thus, the language may be imprecise, but they should be interpreted in the spirit in which they were committed to writing.

An early example of a Code of this nature was produced for international art traders by the UK Government in 1984, called the Code of Practice for the Control of International Trading in Works of Art. This was supported by the big auction houses (Sotheby's and Christie's) and the major trade associations (Society of London Art Dealers, British Antiques Dealers Association), amongst others. It included a central provision to ensure members of the UK fine art and antiques trade undertook, 'to the best of their ability', not to import, export or transfer the ownership where they had cause to believe (a) the seller lacked good title, (b) the acquisition/export violated the laws of the country of origin or (c) the object came from an illegal excavation (clause 2). Where a member is in possession of an illegally exported object, that member will 'take responsible steps to co-operate in the return' to the country of export, subject to compensation if acting unintentionally (clause 4).

Despite these praise-worthy undertakings, the early life of the Code showed its inadequacy. In one example from the 1980s, Sotheby's, despite supposed

[106] For a more detailed analysis of the Code see O'Keefe, *Protecting Cultural Objects* (n 66) 79–90.

compliance with the Code, nonetheless sold unprovenanced antique Apulian vases.[107] Meanwhile, Christie's chose to proceed with the sale of a Goya, despite the Spanish Government claiming it had been exported with forged papers.[108] These two episodes reveal the problems when observance of a code is put under commercially-driven pressure, ie when an entity that has agreed to comply with its terms fails to do so because doing so would prevent it doing what it wants!

This Code was then followed by the British Art Market Federation Code of 2000, which included very similar provisions, along with the Code of the *Confédération Internationale des Négociants en Oeuvres d'Art* (CINOA), which is binding on members of the international organisation's constituent bodies.

For museums, the leading code was developed by the International Council of Museums (ICOM), first in 1986 and then amended in 2001, revised in 2004 and rebranded in 2017 (a new iteration of the Code is expected for 2026). Paragraph 2.3 of the current Code deals with provenance and due diligence in the context of acquisition:

> 2.3 Every effort must be made before acquisition to ensure that any object or specimen offered for purchase, gift, loan, bequest, or exchange has not been illegally obtained in, or exported from its country of origin or any intermediate country in which it might have been owned legally (including the museum's own country). Due diligence in this regard should establish the full history of the item since discovery or production.

While there is no mention of the 1970 date as a provenance threshold in this provision or elsewhere in the ICOM Code, the 1970 Convention is referenced elsewhere in a list of international instruments that museums are required to 'acknowledge' as a method of interpreting the Code (paragraph 7.2). Whether this could be used by museums to limit the applicability of paragraph 2.3 only to those removals dating from after the entry into force of the Convention is unclear. Probably not, as 2.3 is not restricted in such a way.

This quite strong ethical steer on museums can have an upstream impact on an object's market value, known at times as its 'merchantability': ie if a museum is incapable of acquiring an object, then the ability of dealers to sell the object becomes more limited. This can therefore have an impact on the illicit traffic in cultural property by limiting the number of parties who would want to purchase a piece with questionable provenance.

[107] For the case of the Apulian vases, see P Watson, *Sotheby's: Inside Story* (London, Bloomsbury, 1997) 116–17 and 125, and D Gill, 'Sotheby's, Sleaze and Subterfuge: Inside the Antiquities Trade' (1997) *Antiquity* 471. According to Sotheby's, the Code would only have been breached had there been actual evidence of unlawful excavation. Circumstantial evidence, no matter how strong, was not considered enough.

[108] *La Marquesa de Santa Cruz*: this led to the case of *Kingdom of Spain v Christie, Manson & Woods Ltd* [1986] 1 WLR 1120, where the Court examined the Code. Christie's claimed that Paragraph 2(b) of the Code did not apply if the seller was innocent and para 4 applied only if Spain offered reasonable compensation (per Browne-Wilkinson VC at p 1125). Ultimately the Code alone could not allow the Court to stop the sale. For commentary on this case see A Griffiths, 'Codes of Conduct' (1997) II *Art Antiquity and Law* 173, 174.

The impact of the 1970 Convention in the context of acquisition policies ultimately depends on the regard to those policies within the museum. Much more is involved than merely preparing such a document. As with dealers, the policy must be explained regularly. In reflections reproduced in his 2017 text on the Convention, O'Keefe recalled the experience of searching for an acquisitions policy drawn up by a major museum only to find it stored in the archives, forgotten by almost everyone.[109] Today, all reputable museums should be transparent to a fault when it comes to sharing and displaying such policies.

Not only are the professional rules quite strict, so too are the implications of avoiding them. Renfrew notes the case of Dietrich von Bothmer who, after six decades as curator at the Metropolitan Museum of Art, had his nomination as an Honorary Fellow of the prestigious Society of Antiquaries of London withdrawn following concerns expressed about his acquisition policies while at the Museum.[110]

[109] O'Keefe, *Protecting Cultural Objects* (n 66) 95.

[110] C Renfrew, *Loot, Legitimacy and Ownership: The Ethical Crisis in Archaeology* (London, Duckworth, 2000) 76.

V

State Implementation

Chapter 1
Introduction

It may be a truism, but when a State becomes party to an international convention it will undertake to fulfil the obligations set out in that convention. How it does this is a matter for the State concerned and depends on its political, legal and administrative structure. For certain States, an obligation may be fulfilled by administrative arrangements; for others, it may be essential for obligations to be embodied in national law; still for some, once the convention is ratified, it can become automatically part of the law of the land. Implementation can thus be achieved through a single piece of legislation, multiple pieces of legislation or sometimes no legislation at all. Federal States face a particular challenge as they will often have a complicated distribution of powers between central and regional governments, which can affect implementation and often impedes speedy ratification.

Most States implementing the 1970 Convention will have done so using specific legislation, occasionally also in combination with civil and/or criminal law.[1] Examples of States that have interpreted the 1970 Convention broadly and passed legislation giving effect to it include Canada, Australia, Germany, the Netherlands and Norway.[2] The United States implemented the Convention by passing specific legislation based on a narrow interpretation of the Convention, as explained by its Reservation and Understandings at the time of ratification.[3] However, other US instruments, as well as actions taken by law enforcement within the jurisdiction, might support a broader interpretation of that implementation, even if this was

[1] For the 2019–2022 reporting cycle, UNESCO has noted that, of the 91 States reporting on implementation of the Convention, over 70% did so by a special law either alone or in combination with civil and/or criminal law, while 66% reported a change in legal framework as a result of ratification: Subsidiary Committee of the Meeting of States Parties, 11th Session, C70/23/11.SC/7 (Paris, UNESCO, 1-2 June 2023) 6-7.

[2] For Canada, see the Cultural Property Export and Import Act (RSC, 1985, ch C-51); for Australia, see below, ch 2; for Germany see Cultural Property Protection Act (2016) and R Peters, 'Preventing Trafficking in Cultural Property: Import and Export Provisions as Two Sides of the Same Coin' (2019) 2 *Santander Art and Culture Law Review* 95; for the Netherlands see the Illicit Import, Export and Transfer of Ownership of Cultural Property (Implementation) Act 2009; for Norway, see Act Concerning Cultural Heritage (1978, amended in 2001) s 23a-b.

[3] See above, III, ch 3(ii), and below, ch 6.

not the initial intention.[4] Japan is party to the Convention and has passed specific legislation, but its implementation is extremely minimal. Switzerland also seemed to take a more restricted view of Convention obligations at the point of ratification in 2005, but this view changed significantly in the two decades that followed. Both the United Kingdom and Sweden took the view that ratification could be done relying on existing laws and administrative procedures.[5] In the United Kingdom, additional legislation was passed to criminalise certain actions, but it was done after acceptance and its long-term effectiveness can be questioned.[6] The commentary below will examine the way Australia, Japan, Switzerland, the United Kingdom and the United States have implemented the Convention.

It is also important to understand how traditional 'source States' have implemented the Convention, especially in relation to their controls over exports. Egypt passed an important antiquities laws in 1983, which effectively forbade the export of antiquities over 100 years of age, though it did not make specific reference to the 1970 Convention.[7] In fact, Fraoua's 2012 analysis of Arab States found a lack of legislative execution of the Convention in such States, with the exception of Lebanon.[8] Shyllon's detailed analysis of legislation in African States from the same time, sadly, came to the same conclusion.[9] Asian States have legislation implementing the Convention, but Lee noted at the time that 'ambiguities lurking in the Convention' led to very different conceptions of duties, with most States concerning themselves with the export, rather than the import, of cultural goods.[10] Despite these considered opinions, however, it does appear as though States themselves take the view that their implementation is

[4] Below, ch 3.

[5] For the UK, see the Ministerial Advisory Panel on Illicit Trade, *Report* (London, Department for Culture, Media and Sport, 8 Dec 2000) para 61; for Sweden, see S Lundén, 'The Scholar and the Market: Swedish Scholarly Contributions to the Destruction of the World's Archaeological Heritage' in H Karlsson (ed), *Swedish Archaeologists on Ethics* (Lindome, Bricoleur Press, 2004) 197, 217, and T Adlercreutz, 'Sweden' in JAR Nafziger and RK Paterson (eds), *Handbook on the Law of Cultural Heritage and International Trade* (Cheltenham, Edward Elgar, 2014) 381, 402.

[6] In the 20 years following the adoption of the Dealing in Cultural Objects (Offences) Act 2003, there has only been one successful prosecution, in 2016, and this related to dealing in UK cultural objects: *R v Cooper* (Hereford Crown Court, 2016, unreported). See A Herman, 'Conviction at Last Under 2003 Act' (*Institute of Art and Law blog*, 11 May 2016).

[7] Egyptian Law No 117 of 1983 Concerning the Issuance of the Antiquities Protection Law (as amended in 2010).

[8] R Fraoua, 'Legislative and Institutional Measures to Combat Trafficking in Cultural Property in Arab States' paper presented to the Second Meeting of States Parties to the 1970 Convention, UNESCO Headquarters, Paris (20–21 June 2012) 4.

[9] F Shyllon, 'Legislative and Administrative Implementation of 1970 UNESCO Convention by African States: The Failure to Grasp the Nettle' (2014) 21 *International Journal of Cultural Property* 23, 38. He did note that some countries 'have enacted laws that have inadvertently in a way implemented the Convention'; F Shyllon, 'Implementation of the 1970 Convention by African States: The Failure to Grasp the Nettle' paper presented to the Second Meeting of States Parties to the 1970 Convention, UNESCO Headquarters, Paris (20–21 June 2012) 11.

[10] K-G Lee, 'An Overview of the Implementation of the 1970 Convention in Asia' paper presented to the Second Meeting of States Parties to the 1970 Convention, UNESCO Headquarters, Paris (20–21 June 2012) 16.

on the whole appropriate – and indeed positive – as indicated in their reporting to UNESCO.[11]

For market States, it is wholly unreasonable for them to do the least possible to assist in return and recovery of stolen or illicitly exported cultural property and yet still hope to be regarded as party to the Convention. These States seldom realise that they too can be victims. This was precisely what transpired after it was revealed, in 2023, that a senior member of staff at the British Museum had been stealing collection objects and selling them online to buyers around the world.[12] Might the United Kingdom, as a result, need to rely on the 1970 Convention to recover parts of this pilfered collection, a cornerstone of its own cultural heritage? Frigo points out that the failure to legislate the rules of the 1970 Convention into national law, and the reluctance of many States to become party to the 1995 UNIDROIT Convention, are the main legal obstacles to the use of mechanisms developed to ensure restitution and return of cultural heritage items.[13]

On the other hand, many source States had originally been prepared to become party to the Convention but left effective enforcement to the market States. There were many factors at play: lack of funds for protection and conservation; a population that considered archaeological remains their inheritance to exploit by excavation and sale; large areas to supervise; a poorly paid and undermanned police force; corruption of the educated class; a long and isolated frontier… the list goes on. Whatever the excuse, a State cannot become party to the 1970 Convention and ignore its obligations. While assistance may be sought from other States and international bodies, both governmental and non-governmental, the State must ultimately do all that it can with the means available. In any event, hopefully such complacency is becoming a thing of the past, as indicated by the State reporting and the many co-operative law enforcement activities that have taken place across jurisdictions since the last edition of this commentary was published.[14]

[11] For the 2019–2022 reporting cycle, UNESCO has noted that, of the 91 States reporting on implementation of the Convention, 66% reported a change in legal framework as a result of ratification and a generally positive view of various aspects of the Convention implemented: Subsidiary Committee of the Meeting of States Parties, 11th Session, C70/23/11.SC/7 (Paris, UNESCO, 1–2 June 2023) 7.

[12] K Razzall, 'Thief at the British Museum' (BBC, 27 December 2024).

[13] M Frigo, *Circulation des Biens Culturels, Détermination de la Loi applicable et Méthodes de Règlement des Litiges* (Leiden/Boston, Nijhoff, 2015) 254.

[14] See 1970 Subsidiary Committee, 11th session (2023) (n 11) and the work of the UN Office on Drugs and Crime (UNODC), above, IV, ch 1(ix), as well as 'Operation Pandora' run as a partnership between Interpol, Europol and the World Customs Organization: latest numbers in Interpol press release, '80 arrests and more than 37,700 cultural goods seized in major art trafficking bust' (22 May 2025).

Chapter 2
Australia

Australia is not a major art market country, though it does have a lively art market and a range of collectors. It is often a transit country for objects coming from the cultural heritage of neighbouring States. Australia also has sensitive Indigenous material which it – along with many Aboriginal groups – wishes to retain in the country. The cultural heritage legislation is featured in this book because it represents arguably the most extensive implementation of the 1970 Convention in relation to import restrictions.

Australia deposited its instrument of accession to the 1970 Convention on 30 October 1989 after passing the Protection of Movable Cultural Heritage Act in 1986. Prior to that, there was some control of export of cultural heritage from Australia through Regulations made under Customs legislation. However, this was piecemeal and largely in response to publicity generated when significant items departed the country. There were no specific controls on the import of heritage objects unlawfully exported from other States, with the exception of Papua New Guinea, since the date of the latter's independence from Australia in 1975.[1]

The Commonwealth of Australia is a federal State which normally leaves matters of heritage to its component states. However, the Federal Government can pass legislation under the 'external affairs' constitutional power when implementing an international convention,[2] which was used for the passage of the Protection of Movable Cultural Heritage Act 1986. However, the Federal Parliament did not act in isolation as there was extensive consultation with the states of the Commonwealth, as well as with Aboriginal groups and the various professional bodies concerned with heritage.

At the time of becoming party to the Convention, Australia entered a reservation to the effect that it could not comply with the obligations of Article 10 that required dealers to maintain a register of transactions. Regulation of private actors is a matter for the individual states of Australia. Although existing state law relating to second-hand dealers would seem to have been adequate to support implementation of Article 10, two of the states had set up commissions to examine general provisions on trade, both considering that it might be advantageous to lessen the number of records required for commercial transactions. Rather than await the outcome of those examinations when every other step prior to ratification had already been completed, it was decided by the Commonwealth to go ahead with the ratification and to re-examine the issue at a later date. In fact,

[1] See Australia's Customs (Prohibited Imports) Regulations, Reg 4(2), Third Schedule Item No 9A, as cited in LV Prott and PJ O'Keefe, *Handbook of National Regulations Concerning the Export of Cultural Property* (Paris, UNESCO, 1988) 10.

[2] Australian Constitution, Art 51(xxix).

the legislation on second-hand dealers, which applies to the art and antiquities trade,[3] now satisfies the requirement of Article 10(a) and the reservation could be withdrawn.

Exports

The 1986 Act operates in respect of exports on the basis of the National Cultural Heritage Control List.[4] This consists of categories of objects drawn from those which are 'of importance to Australia, or to a particular part of Australia, for ethnological, archaeological, historical, literary, artistic, scientific or technological reasons'.[5] The specific classes of object to be found in each category are set out in Regulations and are defined using different thresholds of age or monetary value. They are called 'Australian protected objects'.[6] A key criterion used in establishing the content of the List is the 'significance to Australia' which means that an object must be of Australian origin, have substantial Australian content, or have been used in Australia together with additional significant associations.[7] For example, a postage stamp is subject to export control if it is of significance to Australia, no more than two examples are known to exist in Australia and it is not represented in at least two public collections in Australia by an object of equivalent quality.[8] The criterion of significance may prove hard to apply in practice in that exporters could argue that they were unaware of the significance of a particular item. Much will depend on the placement of the burden of proof.

Objects must have been in Australia for 30 years before they can qualify for the Control List.[9] Included are works by living artists once they have been sold by the artist and meet the other criteria applicable to such works. The Control List thus describes the objects 'specifically designated' as of importance to the national cultural heritage of Australia in accordance with Article 1 of the 1970 Convention.

The Control List is divided into two classes – A and B. Objects that fall in Class A cannot be exported from Australia unless they have been imported temporarily (for example, for an exhibition or to be offered for sale) and a certificate of exemption for their re-export has been granted. As currently defined, Class A objects are Indigenous sacred and secret ritual objects, carved trees, bark or log coffins used as

[3] Several Australian states have such legislation, eg Second-Hand Dealers and Pawnbrokers Act 1989 (Victoria).

[4] The 'Control List' system was inspired by that of Canada, with its Cultural Property Export and Import Act first passed in 1977. The Australian Control List was first set out in the Protection of Movable Cultural Heritage Regulations 1987, though these have been replaced by Regulations from 2018, which have since been amended in 2021 and 2025.

[5] Section 7.

[6] Section 3 (definitions).

[7] Protection of Movable Cultural Heritage Regulations 1987, s 2(1).

[8] Schedule 1, Part 8.

[9] See Protection of Movable Cultural Heritage Regulations 2018. Note that archaeological objects must be at least 50 years old: Part 2, s 2.2.

burial objects, rock art or human remains; Victoria Crosses awarded to Australians and 'every piece of the suit of metal armour worn by Ned Kelly at the event known as the siege of Glenrowan in Victoria in 1880'.[10] All other controlled objects fall within Class B and can be exported only with a permit or certificate. This accords with Article 6 of the 1970 Convention.

As noted above, a person wishing to import an Australian protected object temporarily may apply for a certificate authorising its export before bringing the object into Australia.[11] The relationship of this provision to other legislation was tested during an exhibition at Museum Victoria of Aboriginal of bark etchings lent by the British Museum and the Royal Botanic Gardens, Kew in 2004. A certificate under section 12 had been issued providing for export of the etchings at the conclusion of the exhibition. However, an inspector under the Aboriginal and Torres Strait Islander Heritage Protection Act 1984 issued a series of emergency declarations to the effect that the etchings were under threat of injury or desecration, thus preventing their return after the exhibition. The Federal Court decided that the Act allowed only one such declaration to be made.[12] The protective declarations were removed and the etchings returned to the UK. There was great concern that, unless the matter was clarified, other loans to local museums would be imperilled. As a result, in 2013 the Commonwealth passed the Protection of Cultural Objects on Loan Act 2013 which provides for clear immunity from seizure for objects loaned to approved Australian institutions for periods of up to two years.[13] Contentious Aboriginal material was loaned by the British Museum to the National Museum of Australia for the *Encounters* exhibition in 2015–16, and was protected from seizure under this Act.[14]

Any Australian protected object exported without the appropriate certificate or permit is forfeited and an offence is committed by the person responsible.[15] On forfeiture, ownership of the object vests in the Commonwealth and it is dealt with in accordance with the directions of the responsible Minister. The Act defines when the export takes place: if the object has been placed on or in a means of transport out of Australia or delivered into the control of the Australian postal system, export occurs when the transport or movement of the postal article commences.[16] This definition attempts to overcome the situation prompted by the UK courts in *Attorney-General of New Zealand v Ortiz*,[17] whereby the New Zealand export legislation was found not to have vested title in the State while the relevant heritage objects were on its territory, thus preventing the New Zealand Attorney General from recovering them once they had ended up in England.

[10] Ned Kelly was a bushranger (outlaw) and is an Australian folk hero.

[11] Section 12.

[12] *Museums Board of Victoria v Carter* [2005] FCA 645.

[13] Protection of Cultural Objects on Loan Act 2013, s 13.

[14] P Daley, 'Encounters exhibition: A Stunning but Troubling Collection of Colonial Plunder', *Guardian* (27 November 2015).

[15] Section 9.

[16] Section 9(4).

[17] [1982] 1 QB 349; [1982] 3 WLR 571; [1983] 2 WLR 809. See also above IV, ch 3(iii).

It is worth considering how Australian export controls have been interpreted by the courts. In *Waterhouse v Minister for the Arts*,[18] a painting entitled 'The Bath of Diana, Van Dieman's Land' (1837) by John Glover[19] was bought by Waterhouse in Australia in 1985 for A$575,000, prior to the Protection of Movable Cultural Heritage Act 1986 coming into force. In 1989, Waterhouse sold the painting at a Sotheby's auction to an art dealer in Los Angeles for A$1.76 million. In 1992 an application for a permit to export was refused, the Minister saying that the painting was of such importance to Australia that its loss by export would significantly diminish the cultural heritage of the country. The Australian Constitution provides, at Article 51, that any public acquisition of property must be on 'just terms'. However, the Court took the view that, although the refusal of an export permit adversely affected Waterhouse commercially, the Commonwealth did not acquire any property in the painting. Therefore, there was no need for payment of compensation by the Commonwealth for the refusal of the export permit.[20]

In *Drew v Minister for Communications and the Arts*,[21] the owner of a Herbert Badham painting called 'Snack Bar' (1944) sought to export it, but had the permit denied. He then challenged the decision to the Australian Administrative Tribunal, claiming that Badham's works rarely held interest for museums and were thus of little import to the national heritage. The Appeals Tribunal considered whether the painting was of such importance 'that its export would significantly diminish Australia's cultural heritage', accepting that this involved a 'fair degree of value-judgement'.[22] It was determined in the end that 'Snack Bar' was sufficiently important: it was painted by an important Australian artist with a small output, depicted the 'mood of relaxed tension' in wartime Sydney and included a unique interaction (for the time) between a local woman and an African-American serviceman.[23] It does seem, in these cases, that the courts defer to the experts and that the State always seems to have the upper hand against would-be exporters.[24]

Imports

Where a protected object of a foreign country is imported into Australia and its export from that country was prohibited, it is liable to forfeiture under section 14 of the Act. Such a protected object is defined as 'an object forming part of the

[18] *David Waterhouse v Minister for the Arts and Territories* (1993) 119 A.L.R. 89.

[19] Glover was an important 19th-century artist in Australia. The painting showed Aboriginal women in a pool of water.

[20] Black CJ and Gummow J (n 18) 98.

[21] [2016] AATA 601.

[22] ibid paras 67–70.

[23] ibid paras 73–75.

[24] See A Herman, 'In Matters of Export and Art, the State Always Seems to Have Its Way', Institute of Art and Law blog (7 April 2020), referring to *Drew* in the context of the UK case of *R (Simonis) v Arts Council England* [2020] EWCA Civ 374.

movable cultural heritage of a foreign country'.[25] This applies irrespective of when the object was illegally exported, provided it was imported into Australia after the operative date of the Act: 1 July 1987. Forfeiture occurs irrespective of whether or not due diligence has been exercised by the purchaser. Here the legislation goes beyond what is required, for example, by Articles 7 or 9 of the 1970 Convention, and seems to align more squarely with Article 3. Section 14 does not apply to objects imported under a loan agreement to a designated Australian institution for the purpose of public exhibition for a period not exceeding two years.[26]

Proceedings for the return of an object under section 14 are not to be instituted unless the Commonwealth has received a request from the Government of the country concerned.[27] Forfeiture is not automatic: it requires a decision by the Australian Government to forfeit the object and this is a step which it would take only after being satisfied that there is sound evidence that, on the balance of probabilities, the object in question was in fact illegally exported from the country of origin.[28] Three conditions must be satisfied before the Australian authorities will take action on a request from a foreign government: first, that the foreign government must state that the object was illegally exported; second, that it was exported in contravention of a law that protects cultural heritage (it is not necessary that the State be party to the 1970 Convention); third, that the foreign government makes explicit that it wants the object back.[29]

If the Commonwealth decides to proceed, the object may be seized and, after 30 days, is forfeited to the Commonwealth unless the person who had possession of it takes proceedings to recover it under sections 36 and 37. It is ultimately up to the court to determine, on the balance of probabilities, whether the object is one which is liable to forfeiture. If the court finds this to be the case, it must order the object to be forfeited.[30] Where the object is forfeited, its ownership is vested in the Commonwealth and it is to be dealt with and disposed of in accordance with the directions of the relevant Minister.

The application of the Act came into full view in 2014 after controversy arose regarding a high-profile object in the collection of the National Gallery of Australia: a Chola-period bronze sculpture of Shiva Nataraja, purchased from the Art of the Past gallery in New York in 2008 for $5 million. A journalistic investigation[31] had revealed the dubious nature of the provenance provided to the NGA by the commercial gallery and its owner, Subhash Kapoor. The provenance he had provided included a purchase of the statue in Delhi in 1970 (and a

[25] Section 3.

[26] Section 14(3) and also under Australian immunity from seizure legislation: Protection of Cultural Objects on Loan Act 2013.

[27] Section 41.

[28] JF Ley, *Australia's Protection of Movable Cultural Heritage: Report on the Ministerial Review of the* Protection of Movable Cultural Heritage Act *1986 and Regulations* (Canberra, Australian Government Publishing Service, 1991) 125.

[29] As per the requirements of s 14(1).

[30] Section 37.

[31] See the ABC *Four Corners* documentary, 'Dancing Shiva: Brandis Slams National Gallery of Australia over $5m purchase of Indian artefact' (*ABC News*, 24 March 2014).

purchase receipt), but it was later revealed that records of the French Institute at Pondicherry contained a photograph of the same sculpture in situ at an Indian temple in 1994 – it must therefore have been more recently looted. After initially stonewalling, the NGA was faced with seizure by the Commonwealth, followed by section 14 forfeiture. When it transpired that another problematic Indian artefact from the same New York gallery was at the Art Gallery of New South Wales, the Ardhanarishvara, the Sydney institution relented and agreed to hand it over, and it too was forfeited to the Commonwealth. Both sculptures were handed over to India by the Australian Prime Minister on an official visit in 2014.[32] The episode demonstrates the impressive tools at the Commonwealth's disposal under the Act, even if the restitution in each case was ultimately consented to by each institution.

Important judicial considerations of section 14 were later made in *Palmanova v Commonwealth of Australia*.[33] The case involved an Australian dealership that had imported an artefact into Australia in 2020, bought from a US seller for approximately US$17,000. The Commonwealth moved to seize and forfeit it, on the basis of a request from Bolivia, since the object appeared to have been unlawfully exported from that State. At trial, the Commonwealth was able to demonstrate, on a balance of probabilities, that the item had left Bolivia in the 1950s or later, thus after Bolivia's cultural heritage export law of 1906.[34] The trial judge took the view that, to fall under the forfeiture provision at section 14, the export needed to be close in time to the import into Australia.[35] The appellate court disagreed, explaining that section 14(1) makes clear that the unlawful export could have occurred *at any time* for the forfeiture to apply. In 2025, the High Court agreed. As a result, the highest court in the land affirmed the expansive scope of section 14 – and the Act as a whole – probably the most ambitious import legislation relating to the 1970 Convention in the world.

In such cases, it is assumed that the Minister would direct that an unlawfully exported protected object of a foreign country be returned to that country. This certainly occurred with the Shiva Nataraja and the Ardhanarishvara; and presumably with the Bolivian artefact in *Palmanova*. However, there remains the possibility that, in circumstances that trigger Article 7(b)(ii) of the 1970 Convention, there may be a request for compensation by the possessor. For instance, could it have been argued that the National Gallery and Art Gallery of New South Wales were owed compensation for the return of the two statues to India? The question was not publicly tested.[36]

[32] See N Palmer, *Art, Adventure and Advocacy* (Builth Wells, Institute of Art and Law, 2015) 32–36; SM Crennan, 'Review – Asian Art Provenance Project, National Gallery of Australia, Canberra' (2016).

[33] [2025] HCA 35.

[34] ibid 37–38.

[35] ibid 39–41.

[36] For more on importing and exporting cultural property into/from Australia, see S Simpson and I McDonald, *Collections Law & Ethics: Galleries, Libraries, Archives & Museums* (Sydney, Federation Press, 2025) ch 13.

Beyond the forfeiture, the person who knowingly imports such an object commits an offence punishable by fine or imprisonment.[37] The requirement of knowledge is critical to the offence, but what exactly this means has not been tested in Australia. However, some idea of the issues involved can be seen by reference to the case of *United States v Schultz* where a United States Court of Appeals had to determine whether the antiquities dealer Schultz knew of export prohibitions under Egyptian law.[38] In the Canadian case of *R v Yorke*, a somewhat lower threshold was required to convict Yorke of importing protected Bolivian artefacts into Canada.[39]

Costs are often a significant burden for a State seeking recovery of illicitly exported cultural property. However, under section 38 of the Act, the cost of transporting or disposing of a forfeited object is a debt due to the Commonwealth 'by the person who was the owner of the object immediately before it was forfeited'. The value of this provision depends on whether such person can be found and is capable of satisfying the debt.

Administration

The 1970 Convention requires that States Parties establish national services for the purposes set out in Article 5. In Australia these are handled by various departments of the Commonwealth and state governments. In relation to export and import of cultural heritage as defined in the 1986 Act, a National Cultural Heritage Committee was established to advise the Minister on the operation of the Act and to establish a register of expert examiners who assess whether an object which is the subject of an application to export is in fact covered by the Control List and, if it is, whether an export permit should be granted.[40] The expert examiner reports to the National Cultural Heritage Committee.[41] The final decision is made by the Minister after considering the Committee's recommendation and the expert report. Provision is made for the appointment of inspectors – members of the Australian Federal Police or of a state or territory police force – to enforce the Act and for delineation of their powers.[42]

Effective administration has sometimes been compromised by difficulties in obtaining information essential to process a claim. In one case, Australian Customs received anonymous information concerning the importation of 47 shipping containers of ceramics obtained from the wreck of the *Tek Sing*, a Chinese vessel sunk in 1822 in Indonesian territorial waters. It was found that the importers

[37] Section 14(2).
[38] Below ch 6.
[39] *R v Yorke* [1998] NSCA 58.
[40] Protection of Movable Cultural Heritage Act 1986, Part III.
[41] Section 10.
[42] Section 28.

did not have the documentation necessary for export from Indonesia.[43] However, before Australian authorities could obtain from Indonesia the information necessary to proceed under the 1986 Act, all but seven of the containers were exported to Europe.[44] In another case, coins from the wreck of the *Douro*, allegedly illegally exported from Spain, could not be seized due to a failure by the Spanish authorities to provide the requisite information.[45] They were also spirited out of Australia to the United Kingdom at the owner's request.

A National Cultural Heritage Account was established under Part IV of the Act to assist in the transfer of objects which have been refused an export permit from private ownership to public institutions where they may be displayed for the enjoyment of members of the public. It is funded to the amount of $500,000 per year.

Reviews of the Act were conducted in 1991, 2009 and 2015.[46]

Objects from Iraq and Syria

Security Council Resolution 1483 was first implemented into Australian law by the Iraq (Reconstruction and Repeal of Sanctions) Regulations 2003, replaced by the Australian Charter of the United Nations (Sanctions – Iraq) Regulations 2008.[47] They cover 'Iraqi cultural property and other items of archaeological, historical, cultural, rare scientific and religious importance that has been illegally removed from the Iraq National Museum, the Iraq National Library and other locations in Iraq since 6 August 1990'.[48] Regulations were made in respect of Syria in 2015. These deal with the return of 'illegally removed cultural property' which means an item of Syrian cultural property or 'archaeological, historical, cultural, rare scientific, or religious, importance' illegally removed on or after 15 March 2011.[49] In both cases, persons who suspect that they are in possession of such material must inform the Department of Foreign Affairs and Trade or the police. The objects can then be seized and repatriated. There does not appear to have been any prosecutions under either the Iraq or Syria Regulations.

[43] C Forrest, 'Australia's Protection of Foreign States' Cultural Heritage' (2004) 27 *University of New South Wales Law Journal* 605, 625 and 627.

[44] ibid.

[45] Department of Communications, Information Technology and the Arts, *Annual Report on the Operation of the Protection of Movable Cultural Heritage Act 1986 and the Administration of the National Cultural Heritage Account 1999–2000*, p 9.

[46] JF Ley, *Australia's Protection of Movable Cultural Heritage* (Australian Government Publishing Service, Canberra, 1991). D Kinsey, '"Undertake Further Consultation": A Summary of the Review of the Protection of Movable Cultural Heritage Act 1986 and Protection of Movable Cultural Heritage Regulations 1987: Report of Public Consultation 2009' (2011) XVI *Art Antiquity and Law* 25.

[47] The previous Regulations were discussed in PJ O'Keefe, *Commentary on the 1970 UNESCO Convention*, 2nd edn (Builth Wells, Institute of Art and Law, 2007) 105.

[48] Section 4.

[49] Section 4.

Chapter 3
Japan

In 2002, the Japanese Parliament passed the Law Concerning Controls on the Illicit Export and Import of Cultural Property.[1] The Law came into force on the day that Japan became Party to the Convention, 9 December 2002. Supplementary provisions state in effect that the Law is not retroactive.[2]

The Law followed a campaign by leading academics against unlawful trade in cultural property and in the context of a public perception that such trade was damaging the Japanese image.[3] Increased wealth in Japan had seen vast sums spent on the acquisition of art and antiquities some of which were under suspicion as having been stolen or unlawfully exported. Japan's restrictive laws governing attempted recovery were the subject of adverse comment overseas.[4]

Exports

Export of cultural property from Japan more generally was already governed by the Law for the Protection of Cultural Properties of 1950.[5] The 2002 Law defines 'domestic cultural property' in terms of categories covered by that earlier Law, ie important cultural properties; important tangible folk-cultural properties; historic sites, places of scenic beauty, or natural monuments. When such property is lost or stolen the Commissioner of the Agency for Cultural Affairs is to be notified and is required to announce the theft in the Official Gazette. If the property has been stolen from an institution among those referred to in Article 7(b)(i) of the 1970 Convention, the Minister of Foreign Affairs is also to be notified.[6] That Minister is obligated to notify foreign governments of the theft.[7]

These provisions allow Japanese claims for return only in extremely limited circumstances. It is perhaps unfortunate that Japan did not to put in place a more effective regime for the recovery of its own cultural heritage, either stolen or unlawfully exported. For instance, in 2012, two Buddhist sculptures were stolen from a shrine on Tsushima Island, Nagasaki and ended up in South Korea. Owing to complications relating to the history of one of the sculptures (it had allegedly

[1] An English translation is available in (2003) VIII *Art Antiquity and Law* 129.

[2] See the Act's Transitory Measures, 2–3.

[3] Prof H Fujii has recorded that: 'By the time cultural objects were disappearing from Iraqi museums, the chauvinism surrounding Japan's policy of cultural property protection was clear. Without losing time, I began to lobby important personnel of the relevant authorities …' in 'Particulars of Japan's Accession to the 1970 UNESCO Convention and an Outstanding Problem' (2004) 14 *Culture Without Context* 20, 22.

[4] C Renfrew, *Loot, Legitimacy and Ownership: The Ethical Crisis in Archaeology* (London, Duckworth, 2000) 73.

[5] Law No 214 of 1950.

[6] Article 5(1).

[7] Article 5(2).

been looted from a Korean temple by Japanese pirates in the fourteenth century) recovering them proved long and complicated; they were returned to Japan only 13 years later, following a prolonged legal dispute.[8] South Korea and Japan were both Parties to the 1970 Convention at the time of the theft. Japan had initially intended to claim return under the Convention, but a Korean court ordered an injunction stopping this due to the ownership claim to the sculpture by the Korean Temple for which it had been made in 1330 and from which it was likely looted by the pirates several decades later.[9] At first, the District Court ruled in favour of the Korean temple, acknowledging historical evidence of the illicit transfer of the sculpture to Japan, but the High Court and Supreme Court later overturned the earlier judgment and ruled in favour of the Japanese Temple, recognising its claim of adverse possession under Japanese law.[10] This process of return took many years; a far cry from the 'earliest possible restitution' predicated by the Convention.[11] Given that the Convention remains silent on ownership issues, procedures can at times be frustrated by the domestic courts of one of the States Parties.[12]

Imports

Controls placed on imported cultural property from other States by the 2002 Law are very limited. For the purposes of the legislation, 'cultural property' means property 'designated' by a State Party to the 1970 Convention in accordance with Article 1 of the Convention. That Article actually uses the phrase 'specifically designated', possible interpretations of which are discussed at length above.[13] These can range from precise itemisation in a national inventory to general categories of material. Faced with this range of possibilities, Japan undertook a survey of practice in more than 70 States Parties to establish what States have done:

> Based on the fact that a large number of States Parties have their own designating system, which became apparent from the results obtained through the survey, it was stipulated in Article 2 of the enforcement law that the scope of application of the law is focused on cultural property that other States Parties have designated.[14]

[8] H Yun-hee and K Seo-young, 'Stolen Goryeo Buddha statue to be returned to Japan after 13 years', *Chosun Daily* (24 January 2025).

[9] M Shimada, 'The Challenges of Settling International Cultural Heritage Disputes', presentation to the Union International des Avocats Art Law Commission, 31 October 2025.

[10] J Hwan-bong and R Hyung-suk, 'Korea's Supreme Court recognizes Japanese temple as owner of stolen Goryeo-era Buddha statue', *Hankyoreh Daily* (27 October 2023).

[11] Article 13(b).

[12] K Jihon, 'When Law Isn't Enough: Cultural Property, Historical Justice, and the Power of Civil Society – Case of Korea and Japan', presentation to the Hermeneutics of Restitution, Reparation, and Redress: The Case of Cultural Property, University of Bonn, Germany, 9 April 2026. The author would like to thank both Professor Makoto Shimada and Jihon Kim for their additional explanations about this complex case.

[13] Above, II, Article 1.

[14] T Kono and E Kani, 'Japan's Measures for the Implementation of the 1970 UNESCO Convention' (2003) VIII *Art Antiquity and Law* 107, 114.

It is thus apparent that Japan accepts what each State Party has chosen as its method of designation and the material covered by this. In adopting such respectful recognition, Japan has accepted a broad interpretation of the 1970 Convention.

This is then negated by the specific procedure used to implement the Convention. The import restriction applies only to cultural property designated by a State Party 'stolen from an institution stipulated in Article 7(b)(i) of the 1970 Convention' after 9 December 2002, the date of entry into force for the Law.[15] This therefore covers a 'museum or a religious or secular public monument or similar institution'.[16]

It is unclear whether the further qualifying words of Article 7(b)(i) – whereby the object must be 'documented as appertaining to the inventory of that institution' – are part of the Japanese definition in Article 3(1) of the 2002 Law. Even major museums do not have accurate inventories and the object stolen may never have been catalogued. Many religious monuments do not have an inventory of their holdings or, if they do, it may be inaccurate. The problems with this are well illustrated with the first case faced by Japanese authorities under the new legislation:

> Between December 9, 2002 and January 4, 2003, 236 objects were stolen in total from a Turkish museum. Although Japan was notified of the theft, it was difficult to identify the stolen objects. Eventually, two items were identified and designated "specific foreign cultural property" by government order in October 2003.[17]

The time taken to assess the objects and the meagre results do not redound favourably to the Japanese regime of import controls.

Kono and Kani have stated that:

> … the government of Japan has provided all other States Parties with the information as to the mechanism of Japan's import regulation. It requested other States Parties to provide sufficient information on stolen cultural property that falls in the category given in Article 7(b)(i) of the Convention whenever each State Party's designated cultural property is stolen from a museum and similar institutions (the decision as to whether or not to inform is up to each State), as such information is prerequisite for the smooth running of the enforcement law.[18]

The provision of a list does not accord with Article 7(b)(i). Cultural property must be on an inventory of the holdings of the institution concerned. This does not mean that it must also be on a list held by the State of importation. Also under Japanese law, notification of the theft must be made by the foreign government where the museum or similar institution is located. This will be difficult:

[15] Article 3 and Supplementary Provision 2.

[16] Above, II, Article 7(b).

[17] T Kono, 'UNESCO Convention on the Means of Prohibiting and Preventing the Illicit Import, Export and Transfer of Ownership of Cultural Property and Its Implementation in Japan' in N Urtnasan and N Hellmann (eds), *UNESCO Regional Workshop on the Illicit Traffic of Cultural Property, October 29 - November 2, 2003, Ulaanbaatar* (Bejing, UNESCO Office, Mongolian National Commission for UNESCO) 62, 66.

[18] Kono and Kani (n 14) 116.

governments are not normally the recipients of information on stolen cultural property, unlike police forces and the affected museums themselves.

According to the 2002 Law, the foreign government must notify the Japanese Minister of Foreign Affairs who in turn must notify the Minister of Education, Culture, Sports, Science and Technology.[19] That Minister is required to designate the object concerned as 'specified foreign cultural property'.[20] After many years, there are only five entries on this list: those from Turkey mentioned above, a crown from Madagascar and some church objects from Bolivia.[21] To gain any benefit under the 2002 Law, the designation must occur before the object in question is imported into Japan.[22]

The 2002 Law requires any person intending to import specified foreign cultural property to 'comply with the requirement to obtain import approval' in accordance with relevant Japanese Laws.[23] There are only monetary penalties for failure to comply:

> Where a person imports specified foreign cultural property without the approval of the import of specified foreign cultural property, he/she will be fined a sum not exceeding 1 million yen or imprisoned for a term not exceeding three years.[24]

Kozai and Kono point out that there is no specific prohibition on the *importation* of cultural property stolen from a museum or similar institution in another State Party to the Convention. They admit the 'possibility that even the 'Specified Foreign Cultural Property', if approved in this procedure [under the 2002 Act], could *legally* be imported'.[25] The Article is thus mainly of relevance to persons who purchase an object outside Japan and do not know if it is on the list. There is no specific provision for seizure of the object. It appears that the penalties mentioned above apply after the entry of the object into Japan if it is not stopped at Customs and this is seen as sufficient to deter transactions in such property:

> Once it turns out that the cultural property in question is specified foreign cultural property, it is envisaged that the importer of such a good will abandon it at customs.[26]

A specified foreign cultural property which is abandoned voluntarily in this way passes as an ownerless good to the Japanese State. Under the Convention it would then be required to be returned to the State whose law had been breached.[27]

There is a further provision in Article 6 of the Japanese legislation which increases the time during which claims may be made from two years to ten years

[19] Article 3(1).

[20] Article 3(2).

[21] Ministry Ordinance to Designate a Specific Foreign Cultural Property (13 April 2008), as amended (translation of the list by Google): laws.e-gov.go.jp/law/415M60000080043.

[22] Article 6(1).

[23] Article 4.

[24] Kono and Kani (n 14) 117.

[25] S Kozai and T Kono, 'Japan' in JAR Nafziger and RK Paterson (eds), *Handbook on the Law of Cultural Heritage and International* Trade (Cheltenham, Edward Elgar, 2014) 257, 264.

[26] Kono and Kani (n 14) 118.

[27] Article 7(b)(ii).

from the time of theft for specified foreign cultural property, provided that the object was added to the list before its importation into Japan. The 1970 Convention does not contain any provision on time limitations for claims. However, Japan was criticised internationally for the very short period – two years – it allowed for victims of theft to make their claims in civil law. Article 6 is the response to that criticism. Nevertheless, the system is still highly restrictive and only marginally improves the position of victims. It is a far cry from the limitation period set by the UNIDROIT Convention, for instance.[28]

When the possessor of the object in Japan is a *bona fide* purchaser, the victim is required to reimburse the price paid before the object will be returned.[29]

Article 7(a) of the 1970 Convention allows Member States to regulate museum acquisitions 'consistent with national legislation'. According to Kono and Kani, approximately 1,500 institutions in Japan were notified that they are to exercise due diligence in acquiring cultural property including compliance with the ICOM Code of Ethics.[30] In 2012, the Japanese Association of Museums adopted a Code of Ethics, requiring museums to respect the ICOM Code of Ethics and, in 2017, the Japanese Council of Art Museums adopted a similar Code.[31]

Overall, the implementation seemed designed to accommodate existing Japanese arrangements, particularly those of its Customs administration, rather than addressing the more fulsome requirements of the 1970 Convention. Little attention seems to have been paid to the need for flexibility and the necessity to look to broader ways of administering import controls.

Objects from Occupied Territories, Iraq and Syria

Japan ratified the 1954 Hague Convention, as well as its two Protocols, on 10 September 2007, prompting it to pass a new statute, the Law for the Protection of Cultural Property in the Event of Armed Conflict (2007). This law prohibits the import and dealing in cultural property removed from occupied territories, as set out in the 1954 and 1999 Protocols. By imposing an absolute prohibition on such imports, this Act goes further than the 2002 Act, though only in relation to a specified subset of material. While Japan has introduced no specific legislative rules for illegally removed Iraqi and Syrian cultural property, it abides by UN Security Council Resolutions 1483 and 2199, binding on all UN Member States, and so the import of such material is prohibited as a matter of import policy.[32]

[28] UNIDROIT Convention on Stolen or Illegally Exported Cultural Objects, Art 3: generally three years from when the claimant knows the location of the object and the identity of the possessor, and no more than 50 years from the theft (with certain exceptions).

[29] Article 6(2).

[30] Kono and Kani (n 14) 120.

[31] Thank you to M Shimada for answering the author's questions on this point by email, 14 February 2026.

[32] Thank you to M Shimada for answering the author's questions on this point by email, 14 February 2026.

Chapter 4
Switzerland

Switzerland became party to the 1970 Convention on 3 October 2003, the culmination of a long examination of options in the face of a widespread perception that the country had become a major transit point for the illicit traffic in cultural artefacts. The process had begun in earnest in 1992 when the Swiss Federal Council put ratification of the Convention on the agenda. Broad consultations were held resulting in support from major political and religious groups, with the art trade, certain collectors and some museums opposing. In 1998, an Interdepartmental Working Group on the International Transfer of Cultural Objects recommended ratification of both the 1970 Convention and the UNIDROIT Convention.[1] However, the Federal Council decided that Switzerland would become party only to the former; ratification of the UNIDROIT Convention was considered 'premature'.[2]

The Federal Act on the International Transfer of Cultural Property (referred to in English as the Cultural Property Transfer Act (CPTA)) and the Ordinance on the International Transfer of Cultural Property came into force on 1 June 2005. This was after the art trade and certain collectors had fought to limit their scope, resulting in a delay for the enactment of the Ordinance of two months and the incorporation of certain changes to reflect these interests. In terms of the nomenclature used in the title and throughout the text, the key term in the French language versions is 'bien culturel' and in German 'Kulturgut'; the Swiss government's unofficial translation into English uses 'cultural property' throughout.

Switzerland's implementation of the 1970 Convention is quite different from that of other States. In some respects, it is narrower, namely in its reliance (like the US) on bilateral agreements with source States for the imposition of import restrictions. In other respects, it goes somewhat further in supporting the objectives of the Convention, which can be seen in the requirements for Customs Declarations for the import, export and transfer of cultural property, a requirement codified in the CPTA in 2021. It can also be seen in the impositions placed in the CPTA on national museums, the art trade and auction houses – as well as the coverage of Swiss freeports, which for many years had been notorious storage hubs for looted antiquities.[3]

When Switzerland ratified the 2001 UNESCO Convention on the Protection of the Underwater Cultural Heritage in 2019, amendments were made to the CPTA to include within the definition of 'cultural property' items listed at Article

[1] Working Group, International Transfer of Cultural Objects: UNESCO Convention of 1970 and UNIDROIT Convention of 1995 (Berne, Federal Office of Culture, 1999) 31.

[2] Federal Council, Message relative *à* la Convention de l'UNESCO de 1970 et *à* la loi fédérale sur le transfert international des biens culturels (LTBC) (21 November 2001) 521.

[3] See below (n 39).

1(1) of the 2001 Convention (eg archaeological artefacts from under water that are over 100 years of age). That should be borne in mind whilst reading what follows.

Exports

Export restrictions for cultural property from Switzerland are limited under the CPTA, based on the creation of inventories at both Federal and cantonal levels. Objects placed on the Federal inventory must be the property of the Confederation and be of 'significant importance' to the Swiss cultural heritage.[4] Ownership of such objects cannot be acquired according to the good faith doctrine nor by adverse possession; claims for their return are not subject to time limitations; permanent removal of such objects from Switzerland is prohibited.[5] Subject to authorisation, they may be exported temporarily for research, conservation, exhibition or similar purposes.[6] The cantons are also entitled to create their own individual inventories.[7]

The CPTA provides in Article 6 that, if an object on the Federal inventory is exported unlawfully, the Federal Council is authorised to seek its return from another State Party to the 1970 Convention. While it is unlikely that such objects will be exported unlawfully, Switzerland, in light of its own limited provisions on return in the absence of a bilateral treaty, may well have difficulty recovering these objects based on the principle of reciprocity. For example, while an illegal export from Switzerland could be forfeited if brought into Australia, the ultimate decision to return would be at the Australian Minister's discretion,[8] which could be affected by the lack of reciprocity.

Von Segesser and Jolles stated early on that the CPTA 'grants no authority to public authorities to impose any restrictions whatsoever on the export and free disposal of privately-owned cultural property without the private owner's consent'.[9] However, the CPTA was amended in 2021 to make clear that anyone seeking to export cultural property must make a Customs Declaration (required also for imports and transit).[10] The Ordinance states that this Declaration must include precise details about the object, including where it was found if it was the result of archaeological or palaeontological discoveries or excavations.[11] Such

[4] CPTA, Art 3(1).
[5] CPTA, Art 3(2).
[6] CPTA, Art 5.
[7] CPTA, Art 4.
[8] Protection of Movable Cultural Heritage Act 1986, s 38.
[9] G von Segesser and A Jolles, 'Switzerland's New Federal Act on the International Transfer of Cultural Property: An Update and a Perspective from the Art Trade' (2005) X *Art Antiquity and Law* 175, 180.
[10] Inserted at Art 4a of the CPTA.
[11] Ordinance, Art 25. The Ordinance itself first included details about a Customs Declaration in 2007.

information can be shared to allow exported objects to be tracked in other States.[12] Any import, export or transit of stolen or looted cultural property is a specific crime under the Act, as is the appropriation of excavation finds and a failure to make a declaration.[13]

The export provisions of the Swiss legislation do implement Article 6 of the 1970 Convention, though for a relatively limited set of publicly-owned and inventoried items. However, the requirement of a Customs Declaration with details about the place of origin of the object, as well as the criminal offences created, go a long way in pursuing the goals of the Convention, namely those set out in Articles 2, 3 and 8.

Imports

To control imports of cultural property unlawfully exported from other States Parties to the 1970 Convention, Switzerland adopted a system similar to that of the United States: namely, one based on the negotiation of bilateral agreements with particular States.[14] Although there is no specific basis for such a scheme under the 1970 Convention, it is a part of the CPTA at Article 7. This provision authorises the Federal Council to enter into bilateral agreements with the aim of protecting the cultural and foreign policy interests of Switzerland and to ensure the protection of cultural heritage in general. The Working Group foresaw requests for these agreements coming from other States Parties to the 1970 Convention – not Switzerland itself.[15]

Bilateral Agreements

Three conditions govern the Swiss negotiation of a bilateral agreement. First, it must deal with cultural property of significant importance to the heritage of the State requesting the agreement. Second, the cultural property must be subject to export controls which the State concerned has designed to protect its cultural heritage. And third, the State concerned must agree to provide 'reciprocity'. Would being Party to the 1970 Convention satisfy this last requirement? If something more specific is envisaged, presumably it would have to be set out in the text of the agreement.

Bilateral agreements have been concluded with the following ten States (dates indicate entry into force): Italy (27 April 2008), Egypt (20 February 2011), Greece

[12] CPTA, Arts 18(d) and 22.

[13] CPTA, Art 24. Note that the relevant acts that constitute criminal offences were expanded in 2021.

[14] There are important differences with the US approach: in Switzerland bilateral agreements are not limited to archaeological and ethnological material and are not predicated on foreign cultural heritage being 'in jeopardy' (cf US Convention on Cultural Property Implementation Act, s 303(a)(1)).

[15] Working Group (1999) (n 1) 15.

(13 April 2011), Colombia (4 August 2011), China (8 January 2014), Cyprus (15 February 2014), Peru (19 October 2016), Mexico (25 July 2018), Turkey (4 May 2023) and Bolivia (1 January 2026). Swiss negotiators of these treaties are controlled in what they can agree to by the provisions of the CPTA.

Cultural property imported contrary to a bilateral agreement is considered an unlawful import[16] and the importer is liable to a fine or imprisonment.[17] Any person importing into Switzerland cultural property covered by a bilateral agreement, or causing such property to transit Switzerland, has to prove to Swiss Customs that all export requirements of the State concerned have been complied with. If that State requires the issue of a permit or licence for export of cultural property, it must be presented to Swiss Customs.[18]

The bilateral agreements may serve as a basis for taking action concerning seizure. Moreover, the other State may proceed in the Swiss courts with a claim for recovery under Article 9 of the CPTA, demonstrating the unlawful import and the object's 'significant importance'.[19] The limitation period is one year from when the State knows where the object is and who holds it, up to a maximum of 30 years from the theft (an unhelpfully short period).[20] Costs associated with the claim have to be paid by the claimant State,[21] which will clearly be a deterrent to States taking action. Moreover, if the object concerned has been acquired in good faith by its possessor, the claimant State has to pay compensation, calculated from the price paid for the purchase of the object plus necessary expenses.[22] The possessor has the right to retain the object until compensation is paid.[23] In exceptional circumstances, financial aid up to a maximum of 50,000 francs[24] or 50 per cent of the estimated costs[25] may be given to facilitate return to a claimant State.[26]

The court can delay return if it considers that the object could be endangered.[27] There is no provision for such a restriction in the 1970 Convention.[28] Accordingly, this provision goes somewhat against the spirit and history of the Convention. The Confederation is authorised to allocate financial assistance

[16] CPTA, Art 2(5).

[17] CPTA, Art 24.

[18] Ordinance, Art 24.

[19] CPTA, Art 9(1).

[20] CPTA, Art 9(4). These time limits were meant to follow those set out in the EU Directive on the Return of Cultural Goods, though the time limits in the latter were subsequently increased to three years from discovery: 2014/60/EU. The Swiss period inevitably makes it very onerous for a State to marshal a claim for recovery.

[21] CPTA, Art 9(2).

[22] CPTA, Art 9(5).

[23] CPTA, Art 9(6).

[24] Ordinance, Art 13(2).

[25] Ordinance, Art 10(1).

[26] CPTA, Art 14(1)(c).

[27] CPTA, Art 9(2).

[28] Nor is there in the UNIDROIT Convention: LV Prott, *Commentary on the UNIDROIT Convention* (Leicester, Institute of Art and Law, 1997) 61.

to museums or similar institutions which provide a depository and conserve cultural property of other States.[29]

Temporary Measures

Imports can also be controlled through temporary measures imposed by the Federal Council.[30] It is able to restrict or prohibit import, transit or export of cultural property, subject to possible conditions, in order to prevent risk of damage from 'exceptional events'. This is obviously based on Article 9 of the 1970 Convention, but bears no relationship to the language or concepts of that provision. The phrase 'exceptional event' appears to encompass a particular episode whereas words such as 'in jeopardy' and 'pillage' used in Article 9 relate more to a continuing situation.[31]

A Swiss Federal Ordinance adopted as a result of Russia's invasion of Ukraine in February 2022 was amended on 16 October 2024 to include specific provisions for the protection of cultural property derived from Ukraine. As a result, it is forbidden to trade in, import, export or transit cultural goods (or provide related services) if there is reason to believe they have been stolen in Ukraine, that they have been lost against the owner's will, or that they have been illicitly removed from Ukraine.[32]

Control of Transactions

Of significance in reducing the unlawful trade are provisions in the CPTA controlling transactions in cultural property within Switzerland. National bodies listed as 'Institutions of the Confederation' are prohibited from acquiring or exhibiting cultural property which has been stolen, taken against the owner's will, derived from clandestine excavations, removed as part of the cultural heritage of another State or unlawfully exported from another State.[33] This is a rather emphatic implementation of Article 7(a) of the 1970 Convention. It requires careful checks of provenance for all objects a Federal institution wishes to acquire, as well as those it wishes to bring in on loan for an exhibition, although Raschèr et al state that the latter applies only 'within reason'.[34]

[29] CPTA, Art 14.

[30] CPTA, Art 8.

[31] Ordinance, Art 1 seeks to define the phrase and includes armed conflicts, natural disasters, and 'other exceptional events that endanger the cultural heritage of a country'.

[32] Ordinance on Measures Regarding the Situation in Ukraine (SR 946.231.176.72), Art 14e (in German).

[33] CPTA, Art 15. This is seen as implementing Article 7(a) of the 1970 Convention and Article 10 of the *European Convention on the Protection of the Archaeological Heritage (Revised)* 2002.

[34] AFG Raschèr, M Bauen, Y Fischer, M-N Zen-Ruffinen, *Cultural Property Transfer* (Brussels, Zurich, Bruyland, Schulthess, 2005) 46.

Also covered by this aspect of the legislation are art dealers and auctioneers 'to the extent they transfer cultural property within Switzerland'.[35] Purely private collectors are outside this scope.[36] Article 16 of the CPTA sets out the duty of diligence for professionals: cultural property cannot be transferred in the art trade or auction business unless the person making the transfer is able to assume, in the circumstances, that the property has not been stolen, nor been taken against the will of the owner, nor derived from a clandestine excavation, nor been imported contrary to a bilateral agreement or temporary measure imposed by the Federal Council. Art dealers and auctioneers must establish the identity of the supplier or seller and obtain a written declaration that he or she has the right to dispose of the object, must inform their customers about the import and export regulations of States Parties to the 1970 Convention, must maintain records for 30 years and must provide to the authorities all information necessary to fulfil this duty of diligence. Criminal penalties are also established at Article 24.

The above requirements do not apply for cultural property worth less than CHF 5,000, with exceptions for archaeological, paleontological and ethnological material, as well as fragments and excavated material.[37] Material such as coins may cause problems as it will not necessarily be clear whether they fit within the exceptions.

Customs Declaration

According to Article 4a of the CPTA (introduced in 2021), all cultural property being imported, exported or in transit must be declared to customs. The content of the Customs Declaration is set out in the Ordinance: the type of object and, as precisely as possible, the place where the object was made or the place where it was found if it is the result of excavations or archaeological or palaeontological discoveries (regardless of the State of export); persons must indicate that it is an item of cultural property and whether it requires a licence.[38]

The consequences of such declarations are very interesting. Although the import, export or transit of certain cultural property may not be illegal as such, a declaration will nevertheless have to be made, one which may indicate information relating to unlawful export from a State of origin. This could arise, for instance, if the material comes from a State that does not have a bilateral agreement with Switzerland. Von Seggesser and Jolles, writing in 2005, had found that the declaration would not have any legal bearing, thus Customs officers would eventually have to allow such material to continue on its way.[39] Earlier editions of the present commentary took issue with this view, arguing that there may

[35] Ordinance, Art 16. And see Ordinance, Art 1(e) as to who precisely is covered.
[36] Raschèr et al (n 34) 48.
[37] Ordinance, Art 16.
[38] Ordinance, Art 25.
[39] Seggesser and Jolles (2005) (n 9) 189.

nevertheless be ways in which Swiss authorities could proceed to a seizure, either under the criminal sanctions of the CPTA or else more general penal powers.[40] But now, the point has been settled: as a result of the 2021 addition of Article 4a in the CPTA, the declaration does have significant legal consequences.

Of great importance in a place such as Switzerland is the fact that depositing cultural property in a freeport is equivalent to importation, requiring the same licences, declarations and inventories set out above.[41] Swiss freeports had for a long time been notorious for facilitating the unlawful traffic in cultural heritage.[42] The situation seems to have ameliorated as a result of the changes in law and practice following the enactment of the CPTA.

Objects from Occupied Territories, Iraq and Syria

Switzerland has implemented the 1954 Hague Convention and its two Protocols.[43] Following UN Security Council Resolutions 1483 and 2199, respectively, Switzerland passed ordinances to ban importation, exportation and transit, as well as selling, marketing, dealing in, acquiring or otherwise transferring cultural property unlawfully removed from Iraq after 2 August 1990 and from Syria after 15 March 2011, with a presumption of unlawfulness.[44] In an important case from 2023, an ancient artefact was found to have been unlawfully excavated from Syria in 1999, despite the removal having predated the 2011 date inscribed in the ordinance. The reasoning of the Court was based on the fact that the artefact belonged to the Syrian State under a vesting law of 1963 and thus possession of the artefact in Switzerland, with suspicion, violated Swiss penal law.[45] The case demonstrates that confiscation and restitution remain possible beyond the specific ordinances for Iraq or Syria – and indeed beyond the wider framework provided by the CPTA and the 1970 Convention itself.

[40] PJ O'Keefe, *Protecting Cultural Objects: Before and After 1970* (Builth Wells, Institute of Art and Law, 2014) 214.

[41] CPTA, Art 19(3). Ordinance, Art 26. See here M-A Renold and B Schönenberger, 'Switzerland' in JAR Nafziger and RK Paterson (eds), *Handbook on the Law of Cultural Heritage and International Trade* (Cheltenham, Edward Elgar, 2014) 408, 411.

[42] For example, the mosaics in *Autocephalous Greek-Orthodox Church of Cyprus v Goldberg* 917 F.2d 278 (1990) 282, or the 10,000 Italian artefacts found in the Medici freeport bust: P Watson, *Sotheby's: Inside Story* (Bloomsbury, London, 1997) 276; R Atwood, *Stealing History: Tomb Raiders, Smugglers, and the Looting of the Ancient World* (New York, St Martin's Press, 2004) 97.

[43] Federal Law on the Protection of Cultural Property in the Event of Armed Conflict, Catastrophe or Emergency (20 June 2014).

[44] Iraq Ordinance (SR 946.206); Ordinance Instituting Measures Against Syria (SR 946.231.172.7).

[45] *A c l'ordonnance de classement et de restitution rendue le 11 janvier 2023 par le Ministère public et La République Arabe Syrienne* (22 March 2023) Chambre pénale de recours, Geneva, P/18953/2017, ACPR/215/2023. The stele had been seized by UK authorities in 2014, but transferred to the Swiss authorities in 2019 because one of the dealers offering it for sale was based in Switzerland. The other dealer, based in Lebanon, was the plaintiff challenging the Swiss authorities' seizure.

Chapter 5
United Kingdom

The United Kingdom became party to the 1970 Convention on 1 November 2002. It did this in spite of having resisted both internal and external calls for such action ever since the Convention was adopted. Public perception of the trade in art and antiquities had more recently become influenced by episodes involving dealers and auction houses, particularly during the 1990s. One of the most serious involved Sotheby's, implicated in the illicit trade by an undercover operation involving the smuggling of a painting from Italy for sale in London, with several suitcases of incriminating documents revealed.[1]

In October 1999, the Culture, Media and Sport Committee of the House of Commons announced that it would conduct an inquiry into matters relating to cultural property, including measures to control illicit trade. A report flowing from the inquiry was issued in July 2000,[2] recommending that the United Kingdom not become party to the 1970 Convention, but accede to the UNIDROIT Convention instead.

The UK Government had already, by May 2000, appointed a Ministerial Advisory Panel on the Illicit Trade in Cultural Objects. The Panel reported in December 2000 to the effect that the United Kingdom should accede to the 1970 Convention, but not the UNIDROIT Convention 'under the present circumstances'.[3] This was the first time that the 1970 Convention had been examined in detail in relation to possible United Kingdom implementation. To the surprise of many, it was found that existing laws and administrative procedures would enable acceptance of the Convention without statutory change. As Norman Palmer, Chair of the Advisory Panel explained:

> It might fairly be said that a degree of myth had permeated the UK law on this point. The view that UNESCO requires extensive statutory change seems to have been shared by many shades of opinion and held in good faith.[4]

Exports

The United Kingdom has operated an integrated system of export controls with the intention of saving national treasures since 1952. This is today based on the Export of Objects of Cultural Interest (Control) Order 2003 made under the more

[1] SPM Harrington, 'Sotheby's Chastened' (1997) 50(6) *Archaeology* 30.

[2] Culture, Media and Sport Committee, *Seventh Report: Cultural Property: Return and Illicit Trade* (HC 371-1) (London, The Stationery Office Ltd, 2000).

[3] Ministerial Advisory Panel on Illicit Trade, *Report* (London, Department for Culture, Media and Sport, 8 December 2000).

[4] NE Palmer, 'The Illicit Trade Panel and the Culture Media and Sport Committee: Criminal Law Recommendations' paper.

general Export Control Act 2002. The 2003 Order applies, with a small range of exceptions, to objects of cultural interest manufactured or produced more than 50 years before the date of export. These require a licence for export, thus complying with Article 6 of the 1970 Convention. Certain objects that fall below certain age and value thresholds are allowed to leave under open licences; others require individual licences from Arts Council England.[5] Applications may be referred to expert advisers who can recommend that a licence be refused on the basis of the three 'Waverley criteria'. The criteria are as follows, asked in each case to determine if the object's departure would be 'a misfortune':

(i) Is the object closely connected with our history and national life?
(ii) Is it of outstanding aesthetic importance?
(iii) Is it of outstanding significance for the study of some particular branch of art, learning or history?[6]

A decision against export by the expert adviser means the matter is referred to the Reviewing Committee on the Export of Works of Art. If the Committee decides that one or more of the criteria is satisfied it recommends to the Minister that an export licence be deferred for a reasonable period of time, usually two to four months, to provide an opportunity for a matching offer to purchase by a UK entity. This can be extended into a second deferral period should there be a serious expression of interest to purchase.[7] If such an offer is not made, the export licence is normally granted; if an offer is made then the exporter is bound to accept it.[8]

The British system of export control has generally been praised for not overly intruding on the rights of owners, though some bemoan the insufficient funds to support fair matching offers in order to save objects for the nation.[9] But does the system comply with the 1970 Convention? While the sophisticated licensing mechanism certainly meets the export requirements of Article 6, it does not do so on the basis of a 'national inventory' list such as that set out in Article 5(b). The Advisory Panel, considering the matter in 2000, was convinced that, as with the Canadian and Australian schemes, the system of qualifying categories would meet this requirement[10] – though those countries have regulatory 'Control Lists', while the United

[5] Department for Culture, Media and Sport, *Statutory Guidance on the Criteria to be Taken into Consideration When Making a Decision About Whether or not to Grant an Export Licence* (Dec 2020), paras 2–6.

[6] ibid para 12.

[7] ibid para 18.

[8] Since 2021, the exporter must sign a binding contract to ensure that a matching offer will be accepted: ibid paras 18, 23–32, Annex I.

[9] A Hochhauser (Chair of Reviewing Committee), 'The Waverley Committee and the Creation of RCEWA', presentation at 75th anniversary event hosted by Institute of Art and Law with Historic Houses at Sotheby's, London (22 May 2025), *The World Reborn* conference papers published on Historic Houses website: www.historichouses.org/cultural-heritage-policy-gowers-report-waverley-report/. A Herman, 'UK Casts National Treasures Net Wide, But Catches Few Fish', *Art Newspaper* (November 2025) 4; S Mackenzie, *Going, Going, Gone: Regulating the Market in Illicit Antiquities* (institute of Art and Law, Leicester, 2005) 73.

[10] Advisory Panel, *Report* (n 3) para 56.

Kingdom does not. That said, any irregularities of the UK export system vis-à-vis the Convention have never been publicly raised and, following more than 20 years of ratification, it does not appear to be an issue that needs urgent addressing.

Imports

The UK employs no integrated system of import controls for cultural property. The Advisory Panel stated in its 2000 report:

> … because of administrative complications and other factors we do not at present recommend the imposition by the UK of import controls over cultural objects, beyond those general provisions which are currently in force and which are necessarily implicit in our present procedures and proposals.[11]

Chamberlain[12] notes that a request for return by a foreign State in accordance with Article 7(b)(ii) would go to the Foreign and Commonwealth Office which would pass it to the Department for Culture, Media and Sport. In the case of a criminal offence, the matter would be handed to the police who could use their powers under the Police and Criminal Evidence Act 1984 to seize and detain any object that is evidence of a crime and thereafter could seek an order to return the object to its rightful owner.[13]

The offence of handling stolen goods under the Theft Act 1968 (section 22) may be committed by a person who imports a stolen object into the UK, provided the requisite degree of knowledge/belief and dishonesty can be proven by the prosecution. Any item vested in a foreign State under a national cultural heritage law, and taken without permit, could be considered 'stolen'. As Government guidance states, dealers 'should be aware that dishonestly dealing in property of this kind could constitute the criminal offence of handling stolen goods'.[14] Likewise, a Customs offence, such as a false declaration or misdeclaration, could trigger criminal liability, leading to the object being seized and returned.[15] In addition, money laundering offences under the Proceeds of Crime Act 2002 might be relied upon to seize criminal property.

Following the UK's acceptance of the 1970 Convention, Parliament followed the Advisory Panel's additional recommendation to introduce a new criminal

[11] ibid para 83.

[12] K Chamberlain, 'UK Accession to the 1970 UNESCO Convention' (2002) VII *Art Antiquity and Law* 231.

[13] Chamberlain, ibid, suggested that return could be effectuated using the Powers of Criminal Courts (Sentencing) Act 2000, s 148 (since repealed and replaced by the Sentencing Act 2020, s 148), or the Police (Property) Act 1897.

[14] Department for Culture, Media and Sport, *The 1970 UNESCO Convention – Guidance for Dealers and Auctioneers in Cultural Property* (London, Department for Culture, Media and Sport, December 2003) 2.

[15] For an example, see *HMRC v Riad Qassas* (1 Sept 2015), Westminster Magistrates Court, Judge Zani, noted by J Ulph in 'UK Customs Seizure of Looted Libyan Statue' (*Institute of Art and Law blog*, 22 October 2015).

offence for dealing in cultural objects.[16] The Dealing in Cultural Objects (Offences) Act 2003 creates the offence of dishonestly dealing in 'tainted' cultural objects, meaning cultural objects that have been unlawfully excavated or removed from a building or similar structure of historical, architectural or archaeological interest (and had formed part thereof) whether in the UK or abroad. This offence effectively overcomes the difficulties prosecutors traditionally face in trying to prove 'theft' of an excavated foreign object under the general handling offence (Theft Act 1968, section 22). However, the 2003 Act has its limits. It does not apply retroactively, so the tainting of the object (its removal, etc) must have occurred after the Act's entry into force, that is after 30 December 2003. The Act also requires proving the 'dishonesty' and the knowledge/belief of the accused, which can be an evidential challenge.[17] The Act does not criminalise the import of, or dealing in, an object whose export had breached a foreign export law alone.[18]

At the time of its enactment, the 2003 Act was criticised for these shortcomings.[19] It was reported that the UK Government expected the level of prosecutions to be 'not more than one every two to three years'.[20] In reality, after 20 years of the Act, there has been just one prosecution, and this did not relate to overseas material, but to objects taken in the UK.[21]

With the criminal avenue proving increasingly less viable to secure the seizure of looted objects and their return, the only alternative would be for a State of origin, or indeed the entity from which cultural property had been stolen, to bring a civil suit in the UK courts.[22] For instance, in a case falling outside the Convention, the Republic of Iran had success in 2007 before the English Court of Appeal in its civil claim against a London gallery for the recovery of 18 Bronze Age artefacts unlawfully excavated from Iranian soil several years earlier.[23] But any lawsuit will invariably be time-consuming and expensive – especially in a jurisdiction that requires instructing both solicitors and barristers to issue proceedings – a far cry from the apparently straightforward 'recover and return' mechanism provided in Article 7(b)(ii) of the Convention.

[16] Advisory Panel, *Report* (n 3) paras 66–73.

[17] SRM Mackenzie, *Going, Going, Gone: Regulating the Market in Illicit Antiquities* (Leicester, Institute of Art and Law, 2005) 82.

[18] For further details on the Act see R Harwood, 'Dealing in Cultural Objects (Offences) Act 2003' (2003) VIII *Art Antiquity and Law* 347.

[19] SRM Mackenzie and P Green, 'Criminalising the Market in Illicit Antiquities: An Evaluation of the Dealing in Cultural Objects (Offences) Act 2003 in England and Wales' in SRM Mackenzie and P Green (eds), *Criminology and Archaeology: Studies in Looted Antiquities* (Oxford, Hart Publishing, 2009)145, 150.

[20] M Bailey, 'UK law to ban trade in illicit antiquities', *Art Newspaper*, No. 138, July–August 2003, p 8.

[21] See A Herman, 'Conviction at Last Under 2003 Act', Institute of Art and Law blog, 11 May 2016; *R v Cooper* (Hereford Crown Court, 2016, unreported).

[22] Chamberlain, 'UK Accession' (n 12) 247.

[23] *Iran v Barakat* [2007] EWCA Civ 1374. The case fell outside the Convention because the artefacts had been unearthed in an unlawful excavation, not stolen from an institution as per Art 7(b). Nor did they fall under the Dealing in Cultural Objects (Offences) Act 2003, since the excavation preceded the Act's entry into force (30 Dec 2003).

Indeed, the case that began this edition of the book reveals just how limited options for recovery are. Nigeria's attempts to reclaim the stolen Ife Head from the UK have been frustrated at every turn. Of course, the Head falls outside Article 7(b)(ii) because the date of the museum theft (1987) pre-dated the UK's acceptance of the Convention (2002). Had it come within that provision, one wonders what additional actions the UK authorities would have taken, if any. Leaving a Convention-mandated recovery to the requesting State's ability to bring a lawsuit within a complex court system is not, it is submitted, in line with the spirit of the Convention; nor with its letter either. In any event, it remains difficult to square the UK's inaction in this matter with certain general Convention commitments, such as those stemming from Articles 2(2), 3 and 13(b).

Roughly a quarter of a century after accession, the overall compliance of the UK with the 1970 Convention is arguably in need of review. There had initially been an intention for a subsequent review enunciated by a House of Commons committee following passage of the 2003 Act,[24] then by the Government itself.[25] Little happened for the following two decades. An opportunity presented itself to review the compatibility of the export system with the Convention on the occasion of the seventieth anniversary of the 1952 Waverley Report, but after an informal discussion with interested parties, the Minister concluded there was broad support for the system as it stood.[26] One particular criticism from the early days of adoption still rings out. In the words of Mackenzie, writing in 2005, the UK's accession may have been 'an attempt by Government to signify concern and "action" which is manifested in a flurry of symbolic legislative activity followed by a sharp decrease in the prominence of the issue on the policy radar'.[27]

Impact on Museums and the Trade

Despite the tepid legal response to the Convention, the ethical practice within the UK museum sector has undergone a sea change since 2000. In the spirit of the Convention, the Government did produce an impressive guidance document which provided a ringing endorsement of Convention principles, establishing the 1970 date as a clear ethical cut-off for provenance investigations before acquisitions. That document, *Combating Illicit Trade*, states clearly that 'Museums should acquire or borrow items only if they are certain they have not been illegally

[24] Committee, *Seventh Report* (n 2) 8.

[25] Department for Culture, Media and Sport & Home Office 'Government Response to 'Cultural Objects: Developments Since 2000' (HC 59) *Report of the Culture, Media and Sport Select Committee: Session 2003-2004* (Cm 6149) 5.

[26] Speech of Lord Parkinson, Worshipful Company of Arts Scholars (29 January 2024).

[27] S Mackenzie, *Going, Going, Gone: Regulating the Market in Illicit Antiquities* (institute of Art and Law, Leicester, 2005) 103. He called the 2003 Act 'a deliberately flawed Act': SRM Mackenzie, 'Dig a Bit Deeper: Law, Regulation and the Illicit Antiquities Market' (2005) 45 *British Journal of Criminology* 249, 265.

excavated or illegally exported since 1970'.[28] Compliance with this standard is also a requirement of museum accreditation for Arts Council England (accreditation is needed for much of the public funding in the UK).[29] This ethical push certainly aligns with Article 7(a) of the Convention, which speaks of preventing museums and other institutions (within existing legislation) from acquiring illegally exported cultural property. As the Guidance states, there is 'general agreement within museums, libraries and archives that the illicit trade in cultural material must be resisted, that they should set high ethical standards for acquisitions and that they should avoid giving tacit support to the market in unprovenanced material through their acquisition activities'.[30]

As for the trade, the DCMS did publish guidance in 2003 entitled *The 1970 Convention: Guidance for Dealers and Auctioneers in Cultural Property*,[31] though this document appears to have had less of an impact than the museum-targeted publication mentioned above. In terms of Article 10 requirements (for dealers to maintain registers and to inform purchasers of relevant export prohibitions), the UK has not followed the Swiss model of creating legislative obligations on the art trade and auction business[32] and largely allows the market to determine the ethical position in relation to returns. The *Guidance for Dealers and Auctioneers* concluded that self-regulation for the trade provided adequate ethical standards and that existing rules around tax registers and implied warranties complied with Article 10.[33] It is true that British trade associations have codes of ethics which preclude the acquisition of stolen or unlawfully exported material,[34] but – it might reasonably be asked – when was a member ever investigated for breaching the code, let alone evicted from one of these august bodies?[35]

[28] Department for Culture, Media and Sport, *Combating Illicit Trade: Due Diligence Guidelines for Museums, Libraries and Archives on Collecting and Borrowing Cultural Material* (London, DCMS, October 2005) 5.

[29] The accreditation scheme requires museums to act in accordance with the provisions of the Convention and 'reject any items that have been illicitly traded', with reference to the DCMS Guidelines of 2005, ibid: Arts Council England, *Museum Accreditation: Collections Development Policy Template* (2014) 9.3.

[30] DCMS, *Combating Illicit Trade* (2005) (n 28) 2.

[31] DCMS, *Guidance for Dealers and Auctioneers* (n 14).

[32] See above, ch 3.

[33] DCMS, *Guidance for Dealers and Auctioneers* (n 14) 5–6. Of note, the DCMS stated in this document, at p 6, that it would be 'monitoring the effectiveness' of these codes and making 'recommendations for improvement where appropriate', though there does not seem to be evidence of this continuing.

[34] For example, the British Art Market Federation, *Principles of Conduct of the UK Art Market Adopted by Members of the British Art Market Federation* (2000) 1; *Code of Practice for the Control of International Trading in Works of Art* (1985) 2.

[35] The answer appears to be 'never'. This question has been put, rhetorically, in conversation with the author by two experts on separate occasions, James Ratcfliffe (General Counsel and Head of Recoveries, Art Loss Register) and Anastasia Tennant (adviser, Tennant McQuillan).

Objects from Occupied Territories, Iraq and Syria

The UK implemented the 1954 Hague Convention for the Protection of Cultural Property in the Event of Armed Conflict on 12 September 2017, as well as the two Protocols, following the passage of the Cultural Property (Armed Conflicts) Act 2017. Section 17 of this law creates an offence of dealing in cultural property unlawfully exported from certain occupied territories. On the basis of the offence, law enforcement can seize and return relevant material that may have come from such an occupied territory.[36] Official estimates from the time of passage were that it would be used once every 30 years.[37] There has been no prosecution thus far under the Act.

As a result of UN Security Council Resolutions 1483 of 2003 and 2199 of 2015, the UK has also implemented restrictions on dealing in cultural property unlawfully removed from Iraq (after 6 Aug 1990) and Syria (after 15 March 2011). Following Brexit, the restrictions are now contained, respectively, in the Iraq (Sanctions) (EU Exit) Regulations 2020 and the Syria (United Nations Sanctions) (Cultural Property) (EU Exit) Regulations 2020. After the predecessor to the former Regulation was introduced in 2003, Brodie had commented, in relation to Iraqi material, how the 'quantities of unprovenanced seals offered for auction dropped off to nothing immediately after implementation' of the Iraq Order.[38] So it did seem to have an impact on the trade.

Under both Regulations, persons holding or controlling such unlawfully removed material must transfer it to a constable; failure to do so is an offence.[39] The onus is on the accused to prove that they 'did not know and had no reasonable cause to suspect that the goods… were illegally removed' from Iraq or Syria (as the case may be), a reversal of the usual burden of proof in criminal law. However, the 2020 Regulations make clear that if the accused can raise 'an issue with respect to the defence' then it is up to the prosecution to prove knowledge or suspicion beyond reasonable doubt[40] – effectively making the above-mentioned reversal somewhat illusory. After more than 20 years of the prohibition relating to Iraqi material, and after 10 years for Syrian material, there has yet to be a prosecution under either instrument.

[36] Cultural Property (Armed Conflicts) Act 2017, ss 18–27.

[37] E Gould, 'UK Ratification of the Hague Convention' (Oct 2017) XXII *Art Antiquity and Law* 244, 256.

[38] NJ Brodie, 'The Plunder of Iraq's Archaeological Heritage 1991–2004 and the London Antiquities Trade' in NJ Brodie, M Kersel, C Luke and KW Tubb (eds), *Archaeology, Cultural Heritage, and the Trade in Antiquities* (Gainesville, University Press of Florida, 2006) 409.

[39] Iraq Regulations, s 27(2); Syria Regulations, s 12(1).

[40] Iraq Regulations, s 29(2); Syria Regulations, s 14(2).

Chapter 6
United States of America

The United States was significantly involved in the negotiation process leading to the adoption of the 1970 Convention, though with a somewhat different attitude than most other States present.[1] In 1972, the US Senate gave its advice and consent to accept the Convention by a vote of 79-0, but thereafter developed a major struggle over implementing legislation. The House of Representatives passed a Bill in 1977, but negotiations still continued for a number of years. The United States finally became party to the 1970 Convention on 2 September 1983, the first major art market country to do so, with the passage of the Convention on Cultural Property Implementation Act (CCPIA).[2] As we shall see, it included substantial limitations which undercut several of the Convention's express obligations.

The US deposited its acceptance at UNESCO along with one Reservation and six 'Understandings'. The reservation was to retain the right to determine whether to impose export controls over cultural property leaving the US. The first understanding was that the Convention was 'neither self-executing nor retroactive', which was and remains a broadly accepted position amongst States Parties. The other understandings involved particular interpretations of provisions in the Convention. Article 3 was understood not to 'modify property interests in cultural property', Article 7(a) was found only to apply to institutions under national control (in the US, this is limited to the museums of the Smithsonian Institution in Washington DC) and Article 7(b) was said to be 'without prejudice' to other recovery remedies that may not require payment of compensation to a possessor. Article 10(a) was understood to allow each State Party to decide whether to regulate its antique dealers at all, which in the US context would involve determinations at the state and municipal level, while Article 13(d) was found to apply only prospectively and to be subject to the law of the requested State.[3]

There were some conflicts of interpretation with UNESCO's Secretariat after the instrument was deposited, but it seems the US approach was in the end tolerated.[4] Mexico had expressed some disagreement with the manner in which its northern neighbour had adopted the Convention, but this was never escalated.[5]

The CCPIA implemented the Convention into US domestic law. Considering the reservation and understandings set out above, the only two provisions of the

[1] See above, I, ch 2(ii). See also the commentary in PM Bator, 'An Essay on the International Trade in Art' (1982) 34 *Stanford Law Review* 275.

[2] 19 USC, ss 2601–13.

[3] Unesdoc LA/Depository/1984/3 Annex III. For more analysis of whether such 'understandings' should be acceptable insofar as accepting US adoption of the Convention, see PJ O'Keefe, *Protecting Cultural Objects* (Builth Wells, Institute of Art and Law, 2017) 223.

[4] See above, III, ch 3(ii); O'Keefe, ibid 222–23. See also Unesdoc LA/Depository/1984/3 Annex I, V and VI.

[5] See above, III, ch 3(ii).

Convention that the US considered necessary for direct domestic implementation were Articles 7(b)(ii) and 9. The manner in which this was done will be explored below.

Exports

Due to the US reservation at the moment of adopting the Convention, it was understood that the US would not impose export licensing for US cultural property leaving the jurisdiction. It appears to be the only State to take such an approach, a reflection of US support for the free market. The assumption is that US institutions and collectors have sufficient funds to acquire nationally important cultural objects and thus to keep them in the country, and require no State mechanisms to assist them. This is an obvious – and intended – disregard for Article 6 of the Convention, arguably for Article 3 as well.[6]

That said, it would be wrong to assume that, without export licensing, there are no export restrictions in the United States to speak of. The Archaeological Resources Protection Act of 1979, for instance, makes it an offence to traffic in archaeological resources unlawfully excavated, removed, or sold in violation of state or local law, subjecting such material to forfeiture.[7] Congress passed the Safeguard Tribal Objects of Patrimony Act (or STOP Act) in 2022, which will introduce export restrictions on cultural objects originating from Native American communities.[8] There do not appear to be examples of objects under either Act being claimed back by the US after unlawful export, nor has either prompted an official reassessment of the Article 6 reservation to the 1970 Convention. The effectiveness of these Acts might need to be reassessed. Gerstenblith has proposed a formal recognition of Article 6 compliance, for reasons she explains would benefit the United States.[9]

Imports

Import restrictions are taken much more seriously in the US, with detailed provisions in the CCPIA implementing Articles 7(b)(ii) and 9 of the Convention. The first of these is dealt with at section 308, 19 USC 2607, placing an import bar on articles of cultural property entering the US that were stolen from a museum, monument or similar institution in another State Party to the Convention ('documented as appertaining to the inventory' of the institution) after the Convention's entry into force in both States. While US law already had a federal stolen property

[6] See O'Keefe, *Protecting Cultural Objects* (2017) (n 3) 223.
[7] 16 USC 470ee(c).
[8] Safeguard Tribal Objects of Patrimony (STOP) Act, 2021 Pub L No 117–196.
[9] P Gerstenblith, 'Evolving Implementation of the 1970 UNESCO Convention' in *Essays on Cultural Heritage in Honour of Francesco Francioni*, forthcoming 2026.

statute that could be (and has been) used to seize and return foreign cultural objects (the National Stolen Property Act), the CCPIA did not have the earlier statute's $5,000 minimum value requirement and also made the placement and level of the burden of proof more favourable to the federal government in a civil forfeiture.

The second, and more complex, series of import controls is found at sections 303-04, 19 USC 2602-03, and reflects Article 9 of the Convention (in a partly tangential way). First, the President is authorised, on certain conditions, to make bilateral agreements to restrict imports of archaeological and ethnological material.[10] These are defined in the Act in a particular way, requiring that they be of 'cultural significance' and over 250 years in age. As Feldman explained in relation to an early version of the Bill:

> The enabling legislation … establishes an agreement to agree, and a process permitting us to negotiate, bilaterally or multilaterally, with individual states on particular items to be covered by the import/export control …. The result will be a program which can be implemented over time with a gradual increase of controls.[11]

While the Act speaks of the 'President', this authority has been delegated to the Secretary of State and to lower officials, typically the Assistant Secretary of State for Educational and Cultural Affairs. The bilaterial agreements are managed by the 'Cultural Heritage Center' within the Bureau of Educational and Cultural Affairs of the State Department. Central to the administration is the Cultural Property Advisory Committee (CPAC), which considers requests for bilateral agreements and makes recommendations to the Assistant Secretary as to whether the four statutory criteria for an agreement are satisfied. The CPAC is composed of 11 members: two members representing museums, three experts in archaeology, anthropology, ethnology, or related fields, three experts in the international sale of cultural property and three members representing the interests of the general public.[12]

The authority to make an agreement with a State Party is set out in section 303(a)(1), 19 USC 2602. A request must come under Article 9 of the Convention and demonstrate how the requesting State has satisfied the four required determinations: (A) the requesting State's cultural patrimony is 'in jeopardy from the pillage of archaeological or ethnological materials', (B) the requesting State has taken measures to protect its cultural patrimony,[13] (C) US import restrictions would be of substantial benefit in deterring the pillage and there are no less drastic alternatives, and (D) import restrictions are in the general interest of the international community in the interchange of cultural materials.

Alternatively, if the situation is dire, the President may implement import restrictions pursuant to an emergency action, without the need for a bilateral

[10] Section 2602(a)(2).

[11] MB Feldman, 'Proceedings of the Panel on the U.S. Enabling Legislation of Import, Export and Transfer of Ownership of Cultural Property' (1976) 4 *Syracuse Journal of International Law and Commerce* 97, 114–15.

[12] CCPIA, s 306, 19 USC 2605. It might be argued that this infrastructure contributes to some of the functions set out at Article 5 of the Convention.

[13] The elements for evaluating this criterion are derived from Articles 5 and 6 of the Convention.

agreement with the State of origin. However, the other State Party must first submit a request for a bilateral agreement and demonstrate how it satisfies the criteria for both an agreement and an emergency action.[14] An emergency action can relate to a newly discovered type of material, material coming from a site of high cultural significance or material from a particular culture or civilisation, the record of which is threatened to be wiped out – 'of crisis proportions', in the language of the legislation.[15]

Both agreements and emergency actions are accompanied by a Designated List. The import restrictions go into effect only after publication of the Designated List. The Designated List is a list of categories of types of archaeological and ethnological materials, rather than a list of specific objects. If an importer attempts to introduce an object that falls into one of the categories on the Designated List, the importer must either present an export certificate from the State of origin or evidence that the object was exported before the import restrictions went into effect. Agreements last a maximum of five years and may be renewed an unlimited number of times. Emergency actions can last a maximum of five years and may be renewed only one time for an additional three years.

The first actions under the CCPIA were made under this latter power for emergency actions: these related first to pre-Hispanic objects from El Salvador (1987), then antique ceremonial textiles from Bolivia (1989), then pre-Columbian archaeological materials from Sipan, Peru (1990) and from Petén, Guatemala (1991), followed by archaeological material from the Niger River Valley and Bandiagara Escarpment, Mali, (1993). These emergency measures were then replaced by bilateral agreements with the respective States once time and resources allowed: El Salvador in 1995, Peru, Guatemala and Mali in 1997, and – in a more comprehensive manner – Bolivia in 2001. After that slow start, the process of entering bilateral agreements gained steam in the mid-2000s and has really taken off over the last few years: 31 bilateral agreements are in place as of early 2026, half of which were first entered into since 2018.[16] The Cultural Heritage Center of the State Department claims on its website that, since 2021, nearly 2,500 trafficked objects were prevented from entering the US market from countries with cultural property agreements.[17]

The format of these bilateral agreements is largely standardised. They commence with an undertaking by the US Government to restrict the importation into the United States of certain categories of archaeological and ethnological material unless the other State certifies that their export had been lawful.[18] The US

[14] CCPIA, s 304, 19 USC 2603 (c)(1).

[15] CCPIA, s 304, 19 USC 2603 (a).

[16] Note that a number of these are referred to as 'Memoranda of Understanding', although their status under the CCPIA are as bilateral agreements.

[17] Cultural Heritage Center, Department of State website: www.state.gov/cultural-heritage-center: 'Between 2021 and the present, nearly two-thousand five hundred trafficked objects were prevented from entering the U.S. market from countries with cultural property agreements.'

[18] CCPIA, s 307, 19 USC 2606.

will offer any forfeited material for return to the other State Party.[19] Then there are undertakings by the other State Party. These vary depending on local conditions but in many cases the undertaking is qualified by such phrases as 'shall use its best efforts', 'will seek' and 'will continue to endeavour'. The general thrust is to improve security, training and education. Sometimes there will be more specific demands placed on the other State.[20]

The proliferation of import restrictions is not without its critics. Senator Patrick Moynihan introduced a Bill in Congress as far back as 1999 to try to limit the powers of entering into bilateral agreements, but this failed.[21] Some in, or associated with, the dealer community have, at times, reacted vociferously to the CPAC's activities.[22] In 2009, an association of coin collectors brought a test case against the inclusion of import restrictions on certain coins from Cyprus and China, but this was ultimately rejected by the Fourth Circuit Court of Appeals.[23]

Beyond the CCPIA: Legislation, Case Law, Forfeiture and Repatriation

The ability to control imports of looted cultural objects coming into the United States – and to provide for their forfeiture and potential repatriation – is not limited to the CCPIA. There is a long history of legislation being used to control the entry of suspect material into the country. It is possible that, by assisting in achieving some of the aims of the 1970 Convention (namely Articles 2, 3 and 13), even if only by implication, these have served to strengthen the US's place as a committed party to the Convention.

In 1972, before the CCPIA was passed, the US had enacted a bespoke law to address the problem of the importation of looted material from its southern neighbours. The Importation of Pre-Columbian Monumental or Architectural Sculpture or Murals Act[24] dealt specifically with large-scale material coming from

[19] CCPIA, s 310, 19 USC 2609.

[20] For instance, in the case of Italy, for Italy to share information on looting with the USA, to pursue the goals of the 1970 Convention, to engage with other countries in the fight against looting: see Memorandum of Understanding Between the USA and Italy (Washington DC, 29 October 2020).

[21] Introduced in the Senate, S 1696, on 6 October 1999.

[22] WG Pearlstein, 'Implications of the Schultz Case', letter to *Art Newspaper*, No 133, February 2003, p 4; PK Tompa, '2025 Year in Review – Repatriation on Demand Continues as Law of the Land', *Cultural Property News* website, 9 January 2026.

[23] *Ancient Coin Collectors Guild v US Customs and Border Protection, et al*, 698 F 3d 171 (4th Cir 2012), on remand, *United States v 3 Knife-Shaped Coins*, 246 F Supp 3d 1102, aff'd sub nom, *United States v Ancient Coin Collectors Guild*, 899 F.3d 295 (4th Cir 2018), one of only two reported cases concerning the bilateral agreements under the CCPIA: P Gerstenblith and Y Wang, 'Article 9 of the 1970 UNESCO Convention: International Cooperation and Bilateral Agreements' in AF Vrdoljak, A Jakubowski and A Chechi, *The 1970 UNESCO and 1995 Unidroit Conventions on Stolen or Illegally Transferred Cultural Property* (Oxford, Oxford University Press, 2024) 280, 287.

[24] 19 USC ss 2091–2095 (1972).

Central and South America. If the objects fall into a category of stone carvings or wall art listed under the regulation, then entry is prohibited unless the importer can produce an export licence or proof that the material left the country of origin before the date of listing of this category. A violation can lead to seizure and forfeiture under Customs laws.[25] While the law was undoubtedly important, and established a blueprint for the CCPIA, it remained limited in terms of the objects covered (stone carvings, wall art) and the region affected (the Americas).

More general powers under Customs legislation can be used to cover such violations as smuggling, entry of goods using false statements, fraud, civil penalties for failure to declare, loading or unloading of merchandise or baggage without permit and false descriptions in ocean bills of lading.[26] The operation of this type of legislation was evident in the case of *United States v An Antique Platter of Gold* (the '*Phiale* case') from the late 1990s.[27] In that case, a fourth-century BCE golden phiale had been smuggled out of Sicily and eventually sold through intermediaries to the well-known antiquities collector Michael Steinhardt, who displayed it in his home from 1992 to 1995. The customs broker had listed the country of origin in the Customs entry form as Switzerland ('CH'), which was patently untrue. It also misstated the value of the phiale by close to a million dollars. The Italian Government found out and issued Letters Rogatory to the US authorities for the phiale to be seized, which occurred pursuant to a warrant in November 1995. The forfeiture was ultimately affirmed by the Second Circuit Court of Appeals on the basis that the import had violated Customs law (18 USC, section 545), which prohibits the smuggling of goods into the US by means of a false statement in the entry form. The Court concluded that the misstatement was material because it could significantly affect the 'integrity or operation of the importation process'.[28]

The Archaeological Resources Protection Act (ARPA), referred to above in relation to US archaeological sites, has been used by prosecutors to obtain the seizure and forfeiture of foreign cultural objects. In 1996, the US Attorney's Office filed a forfeiture complaint for violation of section 470ee(c) of the Act, as well as New York Penal Law, in relation to an archaic Etruscan ceremonial vase believed to have been looted in Italy.[29] In the end, there was no trial, as the dealer in possession waived his claims and the piece was forfeited, then returned to Italy. It is unclear whether this was a proper use of ARPA. The activity was not without its critics:

[25] 19 USC s 2093.

[26] PJ O'Keefe and LV Prott, *Law and the Cultural Heritage: Volume III: Movement* (London, Butterworths, 1989) 600–601. This document, required for the transportation of goods to foreign countries, specifies the details of the goods being transported, such as quantity, type and destination.

[27] 991 F Supp 222 (1997); 184 F 3d 131 (1999). The case is discussed in CJ Shapreau, 'Second Circuit Holds That False Statements Contained in Customs Forms Warrant Forfeiture of Ancient Gold Phiale – Hotly Contested Foreign Patrimony Issue Not Reached by the Court: *United States v. An Antique Platter of Gold*' (2000) 9 *International Journal of Cultural Property* 49.

[28] *United States v An Antique Platter of Gold*, ibid 136.

[29] *US v Archaic Etruscan Pottery Ceremonial Vase*, No 96-Civ 9437 (SDNY, filed 16 Dec 1996, unreported).

Urice listed it as 'an extralegal cultural property practice'.[30] ARPA was subsequently used to recover from several museums and dealers in southern California artefacts looted from Thailand and elsewhere in 2008.[31]

Another legislative basis on which smuggled material can be seized and forfeited is through the National Stolen Property Act (NSPA), a federal law that prohibits the cross-border transit, whether international or interstate, of stolen goods worth more than $5,000.[32] This law was used rather early on – well before the US accepted the 1970 Convention – in the case of *United States v McClain*, to prosecute defendants who had brought into the US recently-excavated pre-Columbian artefacts from Mexico.[33] The question the prosecution had to answer was whether these particular artefacts had indeed been 'stolen'. The Fifth Circuit Court of Appeals concluded that, where a State had declared itself the owner of undiscovered antiquities which were found and unlawfully exported in violation of a national ownership law, they were 'stolen' for the purposes of the NSPA. The first conviction of the *McClain* defendants was reversed as the Court considered the Mexican law prior to 1972 too vague to form the basis of criminal liability in the United States.[34] However, the defendants' subsequent conviction for conspiring to import stolen artefacts in violation of the 1972 law was upheld on appeal.[35] The case established the '*McClain* doctrine' whereby smuggled archaeological material could, in principle, be considered stolen, provided the State of origin has a clear law that vested title in the State and the artefacts were removed after enactment of the vesting law.[36]

In the *Phiale* case, the Second Circuit had found that the *McClain* doctrine had given the Customs official a reasonable basis for seizing the phiale for having been exported in violation of Italian ownership laws, rendering the phiale stolen property,[37] even if it did not reach a conclusion on the doctrine itself.[38] As mentioned above, the case was decided on the basis of a false Customs statement, and the Second Circuit did not need to decide it under the NSPA.

[30] SK Urice and AL Adler, 'Unveiling the Executive Branch's Extralegal Cultural Property Policy' (13 August 2010) *Miami Law Research Paper Series*, SSRN.

[31] It had earlier been used to recover manuscripts stolen from the Vatican and other repositories in Europe: *United States v Melnikas*, 929 F Supp 276 (SD Ohio 1996).

[32] 18 USC ss 2314–15. In the absence of a conviction, such objects can be forfeited civilly under 19 USC s 1595a(c)(1)(A), which allows for seizure of merchandise that is introduced into the United States 'contrary to law' if the merchandise is 'stolen, smuggled, or clandestinely imported or introduced.' The law in the 'contrary to law' provision can be the National Stolen Property Act or other relevant laws, such as those requiring truthful declarations upon import.

[33] 545 F 2d 988 (5th Cir 1977); 593 F 2d 658 (5th Cir 1979). See also JF Fitzpatrick, 'A Wayward Course: The Lawless Customs Policy Toward Cultural Properties' (1983) 15 *New York University Journal of International Law and Politics* 857, 862.

[34] *McClain*, 545 F2d at 1000–04.

[35] *McClain*, 593 F2d at 660, 670–72.

[36] See P Gerstenblith, 'Schultz and Barakat: Universal Recognition of National Ownership of Antiquities' (April 2009) XIV *Art Antiquity and Law* 21, 25–27.

[37] *Antique Platter of Gold* (Phiale case) (1999) (n 27) 137.

[38] The lower court, the US District Court for Southern New York, had decided the NSPA point in favour of the prosecution.

The opportunity eventually came in the case of *United States v Schultz*.[39] That involved the prosecution of a well-known American antiquities dealer, Frederick Schultz, in 2001. He was charged under the NSPA with conspiring to receive stolen Egyptian antiquities that were being transported in foreign commerce. The question was whether the antiquities were 'stolen' and whether Schultz had the requisite knowledge of this fact. The Court considered the Egyptian antiquities legislation, Law No 117 of 1983, which declared that all antiquities were the property of the Egyptian Government and prohibited all trade in antiquities.[40] The Court found that Schultz's actions 'violated the NSPA if the antiquities he conspired to receive in the United States belonged to someone who did not give consent for Schultz (or his agent) to take them. That "someone" is the nation of Egypt'.[41] Under the *McClain* doctrine, it had to be shown that the Egyptian law actually vested ownership, and was not merely an export restriction, and that the law was in fact used within Egypt. The Court concluded that the law complied with both requirements, therefore the artefacts were considered stolen for the purposes of the NSPA.[42] Schultz was also found to have had the requisite knowledge based on a jury instruction using 'conscious avoidance'. Schultz was convicted and sentenced to a 33-month prison sentence.

The *Schultz* case has been called by Gerstenblith 'probably the most significant US decision concerning the international art market for this generation.'[43] It ushered in a new era in the fight against trafficking in cultural property, one that went well beyond the strictures of the CCPIA. In fact, the Second Circuit Court of Appeals had specifically rejected Schultz's argument that the CCPIA was intended to exclude application of any other law in the area of cultural property.[44] It is noteworthy that this case was decided long before the United States had a cultural property agreement in place with Egypt: such an agreement only came to be in 2016.[45]

The approach has been taken even further by the office of the District Attorney of the County of New York (Manhattan), which has an Antiquities Trafficking Unit that has been highly active in this field. Between 2017 and 2025, the DA seized over 6,000 antiquities in New York and repatriated the vast majority of them to over 30 countries of origin, including Iran, India, Pakistan, Greece, Italy, Egypt, Lebanon, China, Turkey, Cambodia, Thailand and Iraq.[46] These cases are not based

[39] 178 F Supp 2d 45 (2002); 333 F 3d 393 (2003).

[40] Article 6.

[41] ibid (2003), 399.

[42] ibid (2003), 400–402.

[43] P Gerstenblith, 'Schultz and Barakat: Universal Recognition of National Ownership of Antiquities' (April 2009) XIV *Art Antiquity and Law* 21, 27.

[44] *US v Schultz* (n 39) 408–409

[45] The only remedy allowed under the CCPIA is civil forfeiture. Unlike the NSPA, which is a criminal statute, the CCPIA does not provide for criminal penalties.

[46] See Office of Manhattan District Attorney, 'DA Bragg Announces Return of 43 Antiquities to the People of Türkiye', press release (10 December 2025).

on the NSPA – nor indeed on the CCPIA – but on the state-level Penal Law,[47] upon the allegation that such antiquities had been stolen from their country of origin. The approach undoubtedly owes a debt to *Schultz*, in that the characterisation of these antiquities as 'stolen' relies on that case's analysis. Most of the possessors, whether collectors, dealers or museums, in the end agree to voluntarily hand over the property for its eventual repatriation, though admittedly this comes as a result of pressure from the DA.[48] At the end of 2025, the Unit stated that it had convicted 18 individuals for their roles in criminal activity.[49]

Taken together, the activities of US law enforcement agencies have been relentless, leading as they have to countless outcomes of forfeiture and repatriation. While the scope of the CCPIA was admittedly narrow to begin with, the substantial number of bilateral agreements has now made the return of antiquities to many parts of the world that much easier. And law enforcement, using tools well outside the CCPIA, has progressed the matter even further. By implication, it could be said that the United States has clearly imbibed the spirit of the 1970 Convention – even if this had never been its intention at the start.[50]

Objects from Iraq, Syria and other Conflict Areas

The United States had continuing economic sanctions against Iraq following the 1990 invasion of Kuwait, which effectively banned the import of most goods, including cultural property. Following the 2003 conflict, the broad economic sanctions were dropped. In light of the looting of the Iraq Museum followed by adoption of UN Security Resolution 1483, these sanctions were replaced by an Executive Order, which prohibited 'transactions with respect to Iraqi cultural property or other items of archaeological, historical, cultural, rare scientific, and religious importance illegally removed from the Iraq National Museum, the National Library, and other locations in Iraq since August 6, 1990'.[51] The Emergency Protection for Iraqi Cultural Antiquities Act of 2004 enabled the President to impose import restrictions pursuant to emergency action under section 304, 19 USC 2603 of the CCPIA. These import restrictions on categories of archaeological and ethnological material went into effect in 2008. However, the restrictions 'relate back' to

[47] New York Penal Law, s 165.54, with a reverse onus at s 165.55(2).

[48] A Herman, *Restitution: The Return of Cultural Artefacts* (Lund Humphries, 2021) 76–79.

[49] See 'DA Bragg Announces Return' (n 46).

[50] Though note that, while this may be the case, Gerstenblith and Wang, 'Article 9' (n 23) 296–7, still refer to the approach as a 'patchwork' leading to 'chaos'.

[51] Executive Order 13350, 31 CFR s 575.533(b)(5).

the 1990 date of the original sanctions.[52] Gerstenblith and Wang explain that the legislation was required in order to comply with the broader category of cultural property required by the Security Council Resolution 1483 (in comparison with the CCPIA), to waive the necessity for a request for a bilateral agreement from Iraq and to ensure the restrictions did not expire after five years (standard under the CCPIA).[53]

For Syria, a similar legislative regime was created with the Protect and Preserve International Cultural Property Act in 2016,[54] which also triggered an emergency action under the CCPIA.[55] However, the Syria import restrictions may sunset if certain conditions are met. At that point, the usual CCPIA process would have to be used to achieve a proper bilateral agreement.

In respect of cultural property coming from certain other conflict areas – Afghanistan, Ukraine and Lebanon – import restrictions were imposed on an emergency basis under the CCPIA following requests for bilateral agreements: this was done for Afghanistan in 2022,[56] for Ukraine in 2024[57] and for Lebanon in 2025. [58]

There are many ways to recover illicitly exported cultural property located in the United States. The legal structure is admittedly complex, but it does mean that the United States has been able to effectively implement the 1970 Convention, in spite of its earlier apparent reluctance.

[52] This was demonstrated in the forfeiture of the 'Gilgamesh Dream Tablet', which had been removed from Iraq before the imposition of the import restrictions in 2008: United States v One Cuneiform Tablet Known as the 'Gilgamesh Dream Tablet', Amended Verified Complaint in Rem, 20-CV-2222 (filed 16 July 2021). See P Gerstenblith, 'Hobby Lobby, the Museum of the Bible and the Law: A Case Study of the Looting of Archaeological Artifacts from Iraq' in L Hashemi and L Shelley (eds), *Antiquities Smuggling: In the Real and Virtual World* 59 (Routledge, 2022).

[53] Gerstenblith and Wang, 'Article 9' (n 23) 286.

[54] 19 USC 2601.

[55] Under CCPIA, s 304, 19 USC 2603, see above.

[56] Emergency Import Restrictions Imposed on Archaeological and Ethnological Material of Afghanistan, 2022-03663 (87 FR 9439).

[57] Emergency Import Restrictions Imposed on Categories of Archaeological and Ethnological Material of Ukraine, 2024-20385 (89 FR 73280).

[58] Emergency Import Restrictions on Categories of Archaeological and Ethnological Material of Lebanon, 2025-08615 (90 FR 20384).

Appendix I

Chronological List of State Party Ratification to the 1970 UNESCO Convention

This Convention entered into force on 24 April 1972. It subsequently entered into force for each State three months after the date of deposit of that State's instrument, except in cases of notifications of succession, where the entry into force occurred on the date on which the State assumed responsibility for conducting its international relations.

	Country	Date of deposit	Type of ratification
1	Ecuador	24 March 1971	Acceptance
2	Bulgaria	15 September 1971	Ratification
3	Nigeria	24 January 1972	Ratification
4	Central African Republic	01 February 1972	Ratification
5	Cameroon	24 May 1972	Ratification
6	Kuwait	22 June 1972	Acceptance
7	Cambodia	26 September 1972	Ratification
8	Mexico	04 October 1972	Acceptance
9	Niger	16 October 1972	Ratification
10	Libya	09 January 1973	Ratification
11	Argentina	11 January 1973	Ratification
12	Iraq	12 February 1973	Acceptance
13	Brazil	16 February 1973	Ratification
14	Dominican Republic	07 March 1973	Ratification
15	Egypt	05 April 1973	Acceptance
16	Panama	13 August 1973	Acceptance
17	Poland	31 January 1974	Ratification
18	Jordan	15 March 1974	Ratification
19	Algeria	24 June 1974	Ratification
20	Democratic Republic of the Congo	23 September 1974	Ratification
21	Iran (Islamic Republic of)	27 January 1975	Acceptance
22	Syrian Arab Republic	21 February 1975	Acceptance
23	Tunisia	10 March 1975	Acceptance
24	Nepal	23 June 1976	Ratification
25	Saudi Arabia	08 September 1976	Acceptance
26	Bolivia (Plurinational State of)	04 October 1976	Ratification
27	India	24 January 1977	Ratification
28	Nicaragua	19 April 1977	Ratification
29	Qatar	20 April 1977	Acceptance
30	Mauritania	27 April 1977	Ratification
31	United Republic of Tanzania	02 August 1977	Ratification
32	Uruguay	09 August 1977	Ratification
33	El Salvador	20 February 1978	Ratification
34	Mauritius	27 February 1978	Acceptance
35	Canada	28 March 1978	Acceptance
36	Oman	02 June 1978	Acceptance
37	Italy	02 October 1978	Ratification
38	Hungary	23 October 1978	Ratification
39	Guinea	18 March 1979	Ratification
40	Honduras	19 March 1979	Ratification
41	Cyprus	19 October 1979	Ratification

42	Peru	24 October 1979	Acceptance
43	Cuba	30 January 1980	Ratification
44	Sri Lanka	07 April 1981	Acceptance
45	Türkiye	21 April 1981	Ratification
46	Pakistan	30 April 1981	Ratification
47	Greece	05 June 1981	Ratification
48	Republic of Korea	14 February 1983	Acceptance
49	Democratic People's Republic of Korea	13 May 1983	Ratification
50	United States of America	02 September 1983	Acceptance
51	Senegal	09 December 1984	Ratification
52	Guatemala	14 January 1985	Ratification
53	Zambia	21 June 1985	Ratification
54	Portugal	09 December 1985	Ratification
55	Spain	10 January 1986	Ratification
56	Mali	06 April 1987	Ratification
57	Burkina Faso	07 April 1987	Ratification
58	Bangladesh	09 December 1987	Ratification
59	Belarus	28 April 1988	Ratification
60	Russian Federation	28 April 1988	Ratification
61	Ukraine	28 April 1988	Ratification
62	Colombia	24 May 1988	Acceptance
63	Madagascar	21 June 1989	Ratification
64	Australia	30 October 1989	Acceptance
65	China	28 November 1989	Acceptance
66	Belize	26 January 1990	Ratification
67	Côte d'Ivoire	30 October 1990	Ratification
68	Mongolia	23 May 1991	Acceptance
69	Angola	07 November 1991	Ratification
70	Croatia	06 July 1992	Notification of succession
71	Lebanon	25 August 1992	Ratification
72	Tajikistan	28 August 1992	Ratification
73	Grenada	10 September 1992	Acceptance
74	Georgia	04 November 1992	Notification of succession
75	Slovenia	05 November 1992	Notification of succession
76	Czechia	26 March 1993	Notification of succession
77	Slovakia	31 March 1993	Notification of succession
78	Bosnia and Herzegovina	12 July 1993	Notification of succession
79	Armenia	05 September 1993	Notification of succession
80	Romania	06 December 1993	Acceptance
81	Kyrgyzstan	03 July 1995	Acceptance
82	Estonia	27 October 1995	Ratification
83	Costa Rica	06 March 1996	Ratification
84	Uzbekistan	15 March 1996	Ratification
85	France	07 January 1997	Ratification
86	North Macedonia	30 April 1997	Notification of succession
87	Bahamas	09 October 1997	Ratification
88	Lithuania	27 July 1998	Ratification
89	Finland	14 June 1999	Ratification
90	Azerbaijan	25 August 1999	Ratification
91	Serbia	11 September 2001	Notification of succession
92	Rwanda	25 September 2001	Ratification
93	Barbados	10 April 2002	Acceptance
94	Albania	13 June 2002	Acceptance
95	United Kingdom of Great Britain and Northern Ireland	01 August 2002	Acceptance
96	Japan	09 September 2002	Acceptance
97	Bhutan	26 September 2002	Ratification
98	Sweden	13 January 2003	Ratification
99	Morocco	03 February 2003	Ratification
100	Denmark	26 March 2003	Ratification
101	Gabon	29 August 2003	Acceptance
102	Switzerland	03 October 2003	Acceptance
103	South Africa	18 December 2003	Acceptance
104	Seychelles	28 May 2004	Ratification
105	Iceland	09 November 2004	Ratification
106	Paraguay	09 November 2004	Ratification
107	Venezuela (Bolivarian Republic of)	21 March 2005	Acceptance

108	Afghanistan	08 September 2005	Acceptance
109	Viet Nam	20 September 2005	Ratification
110	Zimbabwe	30 May 2006	Acceptance
111	New Zealand	01 February 2007	Acceptance
112	Norway	16 February 2007	Ratification
113	Montenegro	26 April 2007	Notification of succession
114	Republic of Moldova	14 September 2007	Ratification
115	Germany	30 November 2007	Ratification
116	Chad	17 June 2008	Ratification
117	Belgium	31 March 2009	Ratification
118	Netherlands (Kingdom of the)	17 July 2009	Acceptance
119	Haiti	08 February 2010	Ratification
120	Equatorial Guinea	17 June 2010	Ratification
121	Kazakhstan	09 February 2012	Ratification
122	State of Palestine	22 March 2012	Ratification
123	Eswatini	30 October 2012	Acceptance
124	Lesotho	17 July 2013	Ratification
125	Myanmar	05 September 2013	Ratification
126	Bahrain	07 March 2014	Ratification
127	Chile	18 April 2014	Ratification
128	Luxembourg	03 February 2015	Ratification
129	Austria	15 July 2015	Ratification
130	Lao People's Democratic Republic	22 December 2015	Acceptance
131	Ghana	20 January 2016	Ratification
132	Benin	01 March 2017	Ratification
133	Botswana	23 August 2017	Acceptance
134	Monaco	25 August 2017	Ratification
135	United Arab Emirates	09 October 2017	Ratification
136	Ethiopia	22 November 2017	Ratification
137	Djibouti	09 April 2018	Ratification
138	Togo	19 November 2018	Ratification
139	Latvia	21 January 2019	Ratification
140	Yemen	03 June 2019	Ratification
141	Comoros	17 March 2021	Ratification
142	Turkmenistan	01 June 2022	Ratification
143	Malawi	07 July 2022	Acceptance
144	Gambia	10 November 2023	Ratification
145	Kenya	15 February 2024	Ratification
146	Malta	15 July 2024	Ratification
147	Sao Tome and Principe	03 October 2024	Ratification
148	Sierra Leone	19 June 2025	Ratification
149	San Marino	07 October 2025	Ratification

Appendix II

Alphabetical List of State Party Ratification to the 1970 UNESCO Convention

1	Afghanistan	8 September 2005
2	Albania	13 June 2002
3	Algeria	24 June 1974
4	Angola	7 November 1991
5	Argentina	11 January 1973
6	Armenia	5 September 1993
7	Australia	30 October 1989
8	Austria	15 July 2015
9	Azerbaijan	25 August 1999
10	Bahamas	9 October 1997
11	Bahrain	7 March 2014
12	Bangladesh	9 December 1987
13	Barbados	10 April 2002
14	Belarus	28 April 1988
15	Belgium	31 March 2009
16	Belize	26 January 1990
17	Benin	1 March 2017
18	Bhutan	26 September 2002
19	Bolivia (Plurinational State of)	4 October 1976
20	Bosnia and Herzegovina	12 July 1993
21	Botswana	23 August 2017
22	Brazil	16 February 1973
23	Bulgaria	15 September 1971
24	Burkina Faso	7 April 1987
25	Cambodia	26 September 1972
26	Cameroon	24 May 1972
27	Canada	28 March 1978
28	Central African Republic	1 February 1972

29	Chad	17 June 2008
30	Chile	18 April 2014
31	China	28 November 1989
32	Colombia	24 May 1988
33	Comoros	17 March 2021
34	Costa Rica	6 March 1996
35	Côte d'Ivoire	30 October 1990
36	Croatia	6 July 1992
37	Cuba	30 January 1980
38	Cyprus	19 October 1979
39	Czechia	26 March 1993
40	Democratic People's Republic of Korea	13 May 1983
41	Democratic Republic of the Congo	23 September 1974
42	Denmark	26 March 2003
43	Djibouti	9 April 2018
44	Dominican Republic	7 March 1973
45	Ecuador	24 March 1971
46	Egypt	5 April 1973
47	El Salvador	20 February 1978
48	Equatorial Guinea	17 June 2010
49	Estonia	27 October 1995
50	Eswatini	30 October 2012
51	Ethiopia	22 November 2017
52	Finland	14 June 1999
53	France	7 January 1997
54	Gabon	29 August 2003
55	Gambia	10 November 2023
56	Georgia	4 November 1992

57	Germany	30 November 2007
58	Ghana	20 January 2016
59	Greece	5 June 1981
60	Grenada	10 September 1992
61	Guatemala	14 January 1985
62	Guinea	18 March 1979
63	Haiti	8 February 2010
64	Honduras	19 March 1979
65	Hungary	23 October 1978
66	Iceland	9 November 2004
67	India	24 January 1977
68	Iran (Islamic Republic of)	27 January 1975
69	Iraq	12 February 1973
70	Italy	2 October 1978
71	Japan	9 September 2002
72	Jordan	15 March 1974
73	Kazakhstan	9 February 2012
74	Kenya	15 February 2024
75	Kuwait	22 June 1972
76	Kyrgyzstan	3 July 1995
77	Lao People's Democratic Republic	22 December 2015
78	Latvia	21 January 2019
79	Lebanon	25 August 1992
80	Lesotho	17 July 2013
81	Libya	9 January 1973
82	Lithuania	27 July 1998
83	Luxembourg	3 February 2015
84	Madagascar	21 June 1989
85	Malawi	7 July 2022
86	Mali	6 April 1987
87	Malta	15 July 2024
88	Mauritania	27 April 1977
89	Mauritius	27 February 1978
90	Mexico	4 October 1972
91	Monaco	25 August 2017
92	Mongolia	23 May 1991
93	Montenegro	26 April 2007

94	Morocco	3 February 2003
95	Myanmar	5 September 2013
96	Nepal	23 June 1976
97	Netherlands (Kingdom of the)	17 July 2009
98	New Zealand	1 February 2007
99	Nicaragua	19 April 1977
100	Niger	16 October 1972
101	Nigeria	24 January 1972
102	North Macedonia	30 April 1997
103	Norway	16 February 2007
104	Oman	2 June 1978
105	Pakistan	30 April 1981
106	Panama	13 August 1973
107	Paraguay	9 November 2004
108	Peru	24 October 1979
109	Poland	31 January 1974
110	Portugal	9 December 1985
111	Qatar	20 April 1977
112	Republic of Korea	14 February 1983
113	Republic of Moldova	14 September 2007
114	Romania	6 December 1993
115	Russian Federation	28 April 1988
116	Rwanda	25 September 2001
117	San Marino	7 October 2025
118	Sao Tome and Principe	3 October 2024
119	Saudi Arabia	8 September 1976
120	Senegal	9 December 1984
121	Serbia	11 September 2001
122	Seychelles	28 May 2004
123	Sierra Leone	19 June 2025
124	Slovakia	31 March 1993
125	Slovenia	5 November 1992
126	South Africa	18 December 2003
127	Spain	10 January 1986
128	Sri Lanka	7 April 1981
129	State of Palestine	22 March 2012
130	Sweden	13 January 2003
131	Switzerland	3 October 2003

132	Syrian Arab Republic	21 February 1975
133	Tajikistan	28 August 1992
134	Togo	19 November 2018
135	Tunisia	10 March 1975
136	Türkiye	21 April 1981
137	Turkmenistan	1 June 2022
138	Ukraine	28 April 1988
139	United Arab Emirates	9 October 2017
140	United Kingdom of Great Britain and Northern Ireland	1 August 2002
141	United Republic of Tanzania	2 August 1977
142	United States of America	2 September 1983
143	Uruguay	9 August 1977
144	Uzbekistan	15 March 1996
145	Venezuela (Bolivarian Republic of)	21 March 2005
146	Viet Nam	20 September 2005
147	Yemen	3 June 2019
148	Zambia	21 June 1985
149	Zimbabwe	30 May 2006

Bibliography

Abramson, RD and Huttler, SB. 'The Legal response to the Illicit Movement of Cultural Property' *Law and Policy in International Business* [1973, 5, 932].

Abranches, H *Report on the Situation in Africa* Unesdoc CLT-83 CONF/216.3, 1983.

Adlercreutz, T. 'Sweden' in Nafziger, JAR and Paterson, RK [editors]. *Handbook on the Law of Cultural Heritage and International Trade* Edward Elgar, Cheltenham, 2014.

Almeida Luis, LM and Ramos Díaz, M. 'Control in Cuban Customs' in Hooff H [editor], *Culture & Development: Stop the Illicit Traffic of Cultural Property* Havana, UNESCO Regional Office, 2013.

Alva Guerrero, B. 'Peru in Egypt: Archaeological Recovery' in van Hooff H [editor], *Culture & Development: Stop the Illicit Traffic of Cultural Property* UNESCO Regional Office, Havana, 2013.

American Association of Art Museum Directors. *The Acquisition of Archaeological Material and Ancient Art* 2013.

American Museum of Natural History. 'Willamette Meteorite Agreement' 22 June 2000.

Apor, P. 'The National Museums of Hungary' in Aronsson, P and Elgenius, G [editors]. EuNaMus Report No 1, *Building National Museums in Europe 1750–2010* conference proceedings from EuNaMus, *European National Museums: Identity Politics, the Uses of the Past and the European Citizen* [Bologna 28–30 April 2011], Linköping University Electronic Press.

Askerud, P and Clément, E. *Preventing the Illicit Traffic in Cultural Property* Paris, UNESCO, 1997.

Arts Council England. *Restitution and Repatriation: A Practical Guide for Museums in England* 2022.

The Art Newspaper, No 69, April 1997.

The Art Newspaper, No. 127, July–August 2002.

Asaf, S. 'Crown of thorns returns to Notre-Dame Cathedral after fire' *BBC News*, 13 December 2024.

Association of Art Museum Directors. *The Acquisition of Archaeological Material and Ancient Art* [updated 2013].

Atwood, R. *Stealing History: Tomb Raiders, Smugglers, and the Looting of the Ancient World* New York, St Martin's Press, 2004.

Aust, A. *Modern Treaty Law and Practice* [first edition] Cambridge, Cambridge University Press, 2000.

Aust, A. *Modern Treaty Law and Practice* [3rd edition] Cambridge, Cambridge University Press, 2013.

Australian Department of the Environment and Heritage Annual Report. 2004–2005.

Bailey, M. 'British Museum to digitise collection as one million objects are found to be undocumented' *The Art Newspaper* 19 October 2023.

Bailey, M. 'UK law to ban trade in illicit antiquities' *Art Newspaper*, No. 138, July–August 2003.

Bákula, C. 'Combating Trafficking in Cultural Property: The 1970 Convention: Evaluation and Prospects' Second Meeting of States Parties to the 1970 Convention, Paris, UNESCO, 20–21 June 2012.

Barton, A. 'Smuggled fossils found in Yorkshire return to Brazil' *BBC News*, 4 June 2024.

Bassiouni, MC. *A Draft International Criminal Code and Draft Statute for an International Criminal Tribunal* Dordrecht, Nijhoff, 1987.

Bator, PM. 'An Essay on the International Trade in Art' *Stanford Law Review* [1982, 34, 275].

Becerril, E. 'The Necessary Evolution of the Mexican Law Under the New Paradigm of the 1972 UNESCO Convention in Order to Strengthen the Fight Against the Illicit Trafficking of Cultural Property' in Sánchez Cordero JA [editor], *The 1970 UNESCO Convention: New Challenges* Mexico City, Instituto de Investigaciones Jurídica, 2014.

Bernard, J. 'Church and State Disagree over Management of Religious Heritage' *The Art Newspaper* July–August 1996.

Berrios, F. 'Lessons Learned in the Andean Region and Central America' in van Hooff, H [editor]. *Culture & Development: Stop the Illicit Traffic of Cultural Property* Havana, UNESCO Regional Office, 2013.
Blake, J. *Commentary on the UNESCO 2003 Convention on the Safeguarding of the Intangible Cultural Heritage* Builth Wells, Institute of Art and Law, 2006.
Blake, J. 'Turkey' in Nafziger JAR and Paterson RK [editors], *Handbook on the Law of Cultural Heritage and International Trade* Cheltenham, Edward Elgar, 2014.
Bolla, G. 'Keynote Address: the UNESCO Convention on Illicit Traffic of Art' *New York University Journal of International Law and Politics* [1983, 15, 765].
Borgstede, G. 'Cultural Property, the Palermo Convention, and Transnational Organized Crime' *International Journal of Cultural Property* [2014, 21, 281].
Bos, C. '"How Our Heritage is Looted": Legal Meaning-Making, Cultural Property, and Customs Enforcement in Nigeria, 1938–79' *Journal of African History* [2024, 1, 9].
British Museum. 'An update on the progress of the recovery programme' London, British Museum, 26 September 2023.
British Museum. 'Acquisition Policy' House of Commons Select Committee for Culture, Media and Sport, Annex II, 2000.
Brodie, N. 'An Archaeologist's View of the Trade in Unprovenanced Antiquities' in Hoffman BT, *Art and Cultural Heritage: Law, Policy, and Practice* Cambridge, Cambridge University Press, 2006.
Brodie, N Doole, J and Watson, P. *Stealing History: The Illicit Trade in Cultural Material* Cambridge, McDonald Institute for Archaeological Research, 2000.
Brodie, N. 'The Plunder of Iraq's Archaeological Heritage 1991–2004 and the London Antiquities Trade' in Brodie, NJ Kersel, M, Luke C and Tubb, KW [editors]. *Archaeology, Cultural Heritage, and the Trade in Antiquities* Gainesville, University Press of Florida, 2006.
Browning, J. 'A Layman's Attempts to Precipitate Change in Domestic and International 'Heritage'Llaws' in Tubb, KW [editor]. *Antiquities Trade or Betrayed: Legal, Ethical and Conservation Issues* Archetype, 1995.
Byrnes, AC. 'The Implementation of Treaties in Australia After the Tasmanian Dams Case: The External Affairs Power and the Influence of Federalism' *Boston College International and Comparative Law Review* [1985, 8, 275].
Byrne-Sutton, Q and Renold, MA. 'Rôle et contenu d'une nouvelle réglementation Suisse en matière de circulation des biens culturels' in Byrne-Sutton Q; Marièthoz, F and Renold, MA [editors]. *La réglementation Suisse de l'importation et de l'exportation des biens culturels* Schulthess Polygraphischer Verlag, 1994.
Cameron, DF. *An Introduction to the Cultural Property Export and Import Act* [2nd edition], Ottawa, Department of the Secretary of State, 1980.
Campbell, PB. 'The Illicit Antiquities Trade as a Transnational Criminal Network: Characterizing and Anticipating Trafficking of Cultural Heritage' International Journal of Cultural Property [2013, 20, 113].
Carducci, G. *La restitution internationale des biens culturels et des objets d'art* Paris, LGDJ, 1997.
Cassese, A [editor]. *The New Humanitarian Law of Armed Conflict – Proceedings* Naples, Editoriale Scientifica, 1980.
RR, Cater. 'The Taranaki Panels – a case-study in the recovery of cultural heritage' *Museum* [1982, 34, 256].
Chamberlain, K. 'UK Accession to the 1970 UNESCO Convention' *Art Antiquity and Law* [September 2002, VII, 231].
Chamberlain, K. *War and Cultural Heritage: A Commentary on the Hague Convention and its two Protocols* [2nd edition], Builth Wells, Institute of Art and Law, 2013.
Chatelain, J. 'Means of Combating the Theft of and Illegal Traffic in Works of Art in the Nine Countries of the EEC' Commission of the European Communities, Doc.XII/920/79-E, 1976.
Cicero. *Against Verres*, Book IV.

Clark, IC. 'The Cultural Property Export and Import Act of Canada: An Appraisal Nine Years After Implementation' in Prott LV and Specht J [editors], *Protection or Plunder? Safeguarding the Future of Our Cultural Heritage* Canberra, AGPS, 1989.

Committee of Experts on the Establishment of an Intergovernmental Committee concerning the Restitution or Return of Cultural Property, Unesdoc CC-78/Conf.609/6, Dakar, 1978.

Cornu, M. 'Implementation of the 1970 Convention in Europe' UNESCO, Paris, 2012.

Cornu, M and Renold, MA. 'New Developments in the Restitution of Cultural Property: Alternative Means of Dispute Resolution' *International Journal of Cultural Property* [2010, 17, 1].

Crennan, SM. 'Review – Asian Art Provenance Project, National Gallery of Australia, Canberra' 2016.

Crystal, E. 'Rape of the Ancestors: Discovery, Display, and Destruction of the Ancestral Statuary of Tana Toraja' in Taylor PM [editor], *Fragile Traditions: Indonesian Art in Jeopardy* Honolulu, University of Hawaii Press, 1994.

Culture, Media and Sport Committee. *Seventh Report: Cultural Property: Return and Illicit Trade* (HC 371-1) London, The Stationery Office Ltd, 2000.

'Dancing Shiva: National Gallery of Australia to Return Allegedly Stolen Statue to India' *ABCNews*, 26 March 2014.

Davis, T and Mackenzie, SRM. 'Crime and Conflict: Temple Looting in Cambodia' in Kila, JD and Balcells, M [editors]. *Cultural Property Crime: An Overview and Analysis of Contemporary Perspectives and Trends* Leiden, Brill, 2015.

Department for Culture, Media and Sport. *The 1970 UNESCO Convention – Guidance for Dealers and Auctioneers in Cultural Property* London, 2004.

Department for Culture, Media and Sport. *Combating Illicit Trade: Due Diligence Guidelines for Museums, Libraries, Archives on Collecting and Borrowing Cultural Material* 2005.

Department for Culture, Media and Sport. *Export of Objects of Cultural Interest 2023–24* 2024.

Department for Culture, Media and Sport & Home Office. 'Government Response to 'Cultural Objects: Developments Since 2000' (HC 59) *Report of the Culture, Media and Sport Select Committee: Session 2003–2004* (Cm 61490.

Department for Culture, Media and Sport. *Statutory Guidance on the Criteria to be Taken into Consideration When Making a Decision About Whether or not to Grant an Export Licence* December 2020.

Department for Culture, Media and Sport Statutory Guidance. *Export Controls on Objects of Cultural Interest* 2020.

Department of Communications (Canada). *Annual Report 1979–1980.*

Department of Communications, Information Technology and the Arts. *Annual Report on the Operation of the Protection of Movable Cultural Heritage Act 1986 and the Administration of the National Cultural Heritage Account 1999–2000.*

Digital State UA (Ministry of Digital Transformation of Ukraine). 'How Ukraine's Digital Museum Fund Protects Cultural Heritage in Wartime' 5 August 2025.

Ding, J. 'China' in Nafziger, JAR and Paterson, RK [editors]. *Handbook on the Law of Cultural Heritage and International* Trade Edward Elgar, Cheltenham, 2014.

Dural, S. *Protecting Çatalhöyük: Memoir of an Archaeological Site Guard* Walnut Creek, Left Coast Press, 2007.

Egloff, B and Kelly, K. *Sacred Caves of Tam Ting (Pak Ou). Luang Prabang, Laos: Mystery, Splendor, and Desecration* Bangkok, White Lotus, 2015.

Einhorn, T. 'Israel' in Nafziger JAR and Paterson RK [editors], *Handbook on the Law of Cultural Heritage and International Trade* Cheltenham, Edward Elgar, 2014.

Eldem, E. 'From Blissful Indifference to Anguished Concern: Ottoman Perceptions of Antiquities, 1799–1869' in Bahrani, Z Çelik, Z and Eldem, E [editors]. *Scramble for the Past: A Story of Archaeology in the Ottoman Empire, 1753–1914* Istanbul, SALT, 2011.

Ellis, R. 'The Fred Schultz Case – An Example of International Cooperation Between Police, Archaeologists and Legal Experts' in Korean National Commission for UNESCO. *Return of Cultural Property and the Fight Against Its Illicit Trafficking: 30 September–3 October 2002, Seoul, Korea.*

Elsen, A. 'An Outrageous Anomaly' originally published in *ARTNews*, reprinted in *International Journal of Cultural Property* [1992, 1, 129].
Esterling, S. 'One Step Forward, Two Steps Back: The Restitution of Cultural Property in the United Nations Declaration on the Rights of Indigenous Peoples' *Art Antiquity and Law* [2013, XVIII, 323].
European Court of Human Rights Research Division. *Cultural Rights in the Case-law of the European Court of Human Rights* Strasbourg, 2011, updated 2017.
Explanatory Memorandum' Council of Europe. *The Art Trade* 1988.
Explanatory Memorandum to the 1970 Convention on the Illicit Import, Export and Transfer of Ownership of Cultural Property (Implementation) Act 2009.
Eyster, J. 'United States v. Pre-Columbian Artifacts and the Republic of Guatemala: Expansion of National Stolen Property Act in Its Application to Illegally Exported Cultural Property' *International Journal of Cultural Property* [1966, 5, 185].
Federal Government of Germany. *Framework Principles for Dealing with Collections from Colonial Contexts* 2019.
Federal Government of Germany. 'Report of the Federal Government on the Protection of Cultural Property in Germany' 2013).
Federal Register. Vol 79, No 8, 13 January 2014.
Feldman, MB. 'Proceedings of the Panel on the U.S. Enabling Legislation of the UNESCO Convention on the Means of Prohibiting and Preventing the Illicit Import, Export and Transfer of Ownership of Cultural Property' *Syracuse Journal of International Law and Commerce* [1976, 4, 97].
Fiorentini, F. 'The Trade of Cultural Property: Legal Pluralism in an Age of Global Institutions' in Sánchez Cordero JA [editor], *The 1970 UNESCO Convention: New Challenges* Mexico City, Instituto de Investigaciones Jurídica, 2014.
Fitzpatrick, JF. 'A Wayward Course: The Lawless Customs Policy Toward Cultural Properties' *New York University Journal of International Law and Politics* [1983, 15, 857].
Fitzpatrick, JF. 'Cultural Property and Art Theft: The Misguided Quest: The Clear Case Against UNIDROIT' *Journal of Financial Crime* [1996, 4, 54].
Forrest, C. 'Australia's Protection of Foreign States' Cultural Heritage' *University of New South Wales Law Journal* [2004, 27, 605].
Fossey, JM. 'Illicit Traffic in Antiquities: Some Canadian Experiences' in Kila, JD and Balcells, M [editors]. *Cultural Property Crime: An Overview and Analysis of Contemporary Perspectives and Trends* Leiden, Brill, 2015.
Freidel, D. *The Mayan Temple Facade* in Prott, LV. *Witnesses to History* Paris, UNESCO, 2009.
Franca, M 'Article 3 of the 1970 UNESCO Convention: Definition of "Illicit"' in AF Vrdoljak, A Jakubowski and A Chechi, *The 1970 UNESCO and 1995 Unidroit Conventions on Stolen or Illegally Transferred Cultural Property* (Oxford, Oxford University Press, 2024) 82.
Fraoua, R. *Convention concernant les mesures à prendre pour interdire et empêcher l'importation, l'exportation et le transfert de propriété illicites des biens culturels* (Unesdoc CC-86/WS/40) 1986.
Fraoua, R. 'Legislative and Institutional Measures to Combat Trafficking in Cultural Property in Arab States' UNESCO, Paris, June 2012.
Frigo, M. *Circulation des Biens Culturels, Détermination de la Loi applicable et Méthodes de Règlement des Litiges* Nijhoff, Leiden/Boston, 2015.
Frigo, M. *La protezione dei beni culturali nel diritto internazionale* Milan, Giuffrè Editore, 1986.
Fujii, H. 'Particulars of Japan's Accession to the 1970 UNESCO Convention and an Outstanding Problem' *Culture Without Context* [2004, 14, 20].
Gascoigne, B. *How to Identify Prints* New York, Thames and Hudson, 1988.
Gerstenblith, P. 'Schultz and Barakat: Universal Recognition of National Ownership of Antiquities' *Art Antiquity and Law* [2009, XIV, 14].
Gerstenblith, P. 'The Meaning of 1970 for the Acquisition of Archaeological Objects' (2013) 38 *Journal of Field Archaeology* 364; K Hausler and E Selter, *Beyond Restitution: Exploring the Stories of Cultural Objects after their Return* (Oxford, Hart, 2025).

Gerstenblith, P and Yunxia, W. 'Article 9 of the 1970 UNESCO Convention: International Cooperation and Bilateral Agreements' in AF Vrdoljak, A Jakubowski and A Chechi, *The 1970 UNESCO and 1995 Unidroit Conventions on Stolen or Illegally Transferred Cultural Property* (Oxford, Oxford University Press, 2024) 280

Gerstenblith, P. 'Evolving Implementation of the 1970 UNESCO Convention', *Tribute to Francesco Francioni*, forthcoming 2026.

Gerstenblith, P. 'The 1970 UNESCO Convention: Past Present and Future' in S Vigneron and J Ulph, *Research Handbook on Art, Culture and Heritage Law* (London, Edward Elgar, 2026) 232–40.

'Giant gold nugget discovered in Australia' *The Perth Mint*, 17 January 2013.

Gibney, E. 'Brazil Clamps Down on Illegal Fossil Trade' *Nature*, 4 March 2014.

Gill, D. 'Sotheby's, Sleaze and Subterfuge: Inside the Antiquities Trade' *Antiquity* [1997, 471].

Giorgallis, A. 'On the Definition of Heritage' *Art Antiquity and Law* [2025, 30, 309].

Glatthard, N. 'China, Switzerland and the Transfer of Cultural Goods: On the Agreement Regarding the Illicit Import, Export and Restitution of Cultural Goods'.

Gordon, JB. 'The UNESCO Convention on the Illicit Movement of Art Treasures' *Harvard International Law Journal* [1971, 12, 537].

Goy, R. 'Le Régime international de l'Importation, de l'Exportation et du Transfert de Propriété des Biens culturels' *Annuaire français de droit international* [1970, 16, 605].

Gould, E. 'UK Ratification of the Hague Convention' *Art Antiquity and Law* [2017, XXII, 244].

Griffiths, A. 'Codes of Conduct' *Art Antiquity and Law* [1997, II, 173].

Grotius, H. *The Law of War and Peace* [published in 1868].

Haertel, LM. 'The Past, Present: The Parthenon Sculptures dispute as an Example of the ICPRCP's Role on Claims Barred by the Non-Retroactivity of the 1970 UNESCO Convention' (2021) 28 *International Journal of Cultural Property* 479–504.

Hall, AR. 'The Recovery of Cultural Objects Dispersed during World War II' *Department of State Bulletin* [1951, United States, 337].

Hallett, F. 'Does the Art Trade Turn a Blind Eye to Church Thefts?' *ArtWatch UK*, 2015.

Hardy, S. 'Threats to Cultural Heritage in the Cyprus Conflict' in Grove L and and Thomas S [editors], *Heritage Crime: Progress, Prospects and Prevention* New York, Palgrave Macmillan, 2014.

Harrington, SPM. 'Sotheby's Chastened' *Archaeology* [(1997, 50 (6), 30.]

Harvey, H. 'Motunui panels returned to Taranaki' *Taranaki Daily News*, 20 March 2015.

Hausler, L and Selter, E. *Beyond Restitution* Oxford, Hart Publishing, 2025.

Harwood, R. 'Dealing in Cultural Objects (Offences) Act 2003' *Art Antiquity and Law* [2003, VIII, 347].

van Heese, M. 'The Fight Against Illicit Traffic in Cultural Goods – The Dutch Approach' *Art Antiquity and Law* [2006, XI, 85].

Herman, A. *Armenia v Azerbaijan Art Antiquity and Law* [2022, XXVII, 70].

Herman, A. 'Conviction at Last Under 2003 Act' *Institute of Art and Law Blog*, 11 May 2016.

Herman, A. 'In Matters of Export and Art, the State Always Seems to Have Its Way' *Institute of Art and Law Blog*, 7 April 2020.

Herman, A. *The Parthenon Marbles Dispute: Heritage, Law, Politics* Oxford, Hart Publishing, 2023.

Herman, A. *Restitution: The Return of Cultural Artefacts* London, Lund Humphries, 2021.

Herman, A. 'UK Casts National Treasures Net Wide, But Catches Few Fish' *Art Newspaper*, November 2025.

Hicks, D. *The Brutish Museums* London, Pluto Press, 2020.

Historic England. *The Nighthawking Survey* 2009.

Hochhauser, A. 'The Waverley Committee and the Creation of RCEWA', presentation at 75th anniversary event hosted by Institute of Art and Law with Historic Houses at Sotheby's, London, 22 May 2025.

House of Commons, Culture Media and Sport Committee. *Cultural Property: Return and Illicit Trade. Volume I: Report and Proceedings of the Committee* London, Stationery Office Ltd, 2000.

ICPRCP, Report on the use of the ICPRCP Fund, 24th Session, Paris, May 2024, Annex I: Financial Report of the Fund as of 31 December 2023.

Institute of International Law. 'The Laws of War on Land' [Oxford Manual] Oxford , 9 September 1880.

Internal Oversight Service, Evaluation of UNESCO's Standard-setting Work of the Culture Sector Unesdoc IOS/EVS/PI/133 REV, 2014.

Interpol. '80 arrests and more than 37,700 cultural goods seized in major art trafficking bust' 22 May 2025.

Jakubowski, A. *State Succession in Cultural Property* New York, Oxford University Press, 2015.

Johnson, D. 'Simone de Sartre' *London Review of Books* [7 June 1985, No 10, 11].

Kaplan, W. 'Assistance Under the 1970 Unesco Cultural Property Convention: Canada's Request to the United States' *Stanford Journal of International Law* [1986, 22, 123].

Kenney, N. 'UNESCO under fire for using Met objects in anti-trafficking campaign' *The Art Newspaper*, 13 November 2020.

Kinsey, D. '"Undertake Further Consultation": A Summary of the Review of the Protection of Movable Cultural Heritage Act 1986 and Protection of Movable Cultural Heritage Regulations 1987: Report of Public Consultation 2009' *Art Antiquity and Law* [2011, XVI, 25].

Kirgis, FL. 'Security Council Resolution 1483 on the Rebuilding of Iraq', *American Society of International Law Insights* [May 2003].

Kishkovsky, S. 'These are Terrible Crimes: A Ukrainian Museum Director's Fight to Recover Art' *The Art Newspaper*, 16 July 2024.

Kono, T. 'UNESCO Convention on the Means of Prohibiting and Preventing the Illicit Import, Export and Transfer of Ownership of Cultural Property and Its Implementation in Japan' in Urtnasan, N and Hellmann, N [editors]. *UNESCO Regional Workshop on the Illicit Traffic of Cultural Property, October 29–November 2, 2003, Ulaanbaatar* Bejing, UNESCO Office, Mongolian National Commission for UNESCO.

Kono, T and Kani, E. 'Japan's Measures for the Implementation of the 1970 UNESCO Convention' *Art Antiquity and Law* [2003, VIII, 107.

Kozai, S and Kono, T. 'Japan' in Nafziger, JAR and Paterson, RK [editors]. *Handbook on the Law of Cultural Heritage and International* Trade (Cheltenham, Edward Elgar, 2014) 257, 266.

Kreder, JA and Beteta, X. 'Understanding Guatemala's Cultural Heritage: Extending Protection to Colonial Art in the MoU between the US and Guatemala' *Art Antiquity and Law* [2010, XV 161].

Lalbekova, G. 'Imperial Legacies and Displaced Heritage: The case for repatriation of Pamiri Ismaili manuscripts from Russian State Archives' LLM dissertation, Queen Mary University of London, unpublished, 2025.

Latournerie, M-A. 'L'inaliénabilité: histoire d'un concept' in Cornu M et al [editors], *L'Inalienabilité des collections, performances et limites?* Paris, L'Harmattan, 2012.

Lawson-Tancred, J. 'British Museum Seeks Treasure Hunter to Recover Stolen Antiquities' *ArtNet News* 5 January 2026.

Lee, K-G. 'An Overview of the Implementation of the 1970 Convention in Asia' UNESCO, Paris, 2012.

Leniaud, JM. 'Les fondements de la règle d'aliénabilité dans le droit du patrimoine culturel' in Cornu M et al [editors], *L'Inalienabilité des collections, performances et limites?* Paris, L'Harmattan, 2012.

Ley, JF. *Australia's Protection of Movable Cultural Heritage: Report on the Ministerial Review of the Protection of Movable Cultural Heritage Act 1986 and Regulations* Canberra, Australian Government Publishing Service, 1991.

Llywelyn Evans, T. 'Collecting Copper Alloy Portrait Heads: A History of the Acquisition and Export of the Wúnmọníjẹ̀ Heads in Late Colonial Nigeria' *Journal of the History of Collections* [2024, 36, 101].

Lobay, G. 'Border Controls in Market Countries as Disincentives to Antiquities Looting at Source? The US-Italy Bilateral Agreement 2001' in Mackenzie, S and Green, P [editors]. *Criminology and Archaeology: Studies in Looted Antiquities* Oxford, Hart Publishing, 2009.

Logan, MJ. 'Limiting Access to Art in Hopes of Decreased Cultural Property Destruction: An Assessment of the United States and China's Memorandum of Understanding for 2014' *Art Antiquity and Law* [2014, XIX, 1].

Lord Parkinson. Worshipful Company of Arts Scholars, 29 January 2024.
Lufkin, MGB. 'Criminal Liability for Receiving State-Claimed Antiquities in the United States: The 'Schultz' Case' *Art Antiquity and Law* [2003, VIII, 321].
Lufkin, MGB. 'End of the Era of Denial for Buyers of State-Owned Antiquities: United States v. Schultz' *International Journal of Cultural Property* [2002, 11, 305].
Lundén, S. 'The Scholar and the Market: Swedish Scholarly Contributions to the Destruction of the World's Archaeological Heritage' in Karlsson, H [editor]. *Swedish Archaeologists on Ethics* Bricoleur Press, Lindome, 2004.
Mackenzie, SRM. 'Dig a Bit Deeper: Law, Regulation and the Illicit Antiquities Market' *British Journal of Criminology* [2005, 45, 249].
Mackenzie, SRM. *Going, Going, Gone: Regulating the Market in Illicit Antiquities* Leicester, Institute of Art and Law, 2005.
Mackenzie, SRM. 'Illicit Antiquities' *Trafficking Culture.*
Mackenzie, SRM and Green, P. 'Criminalising the Market in Illicit Antiquities: An Evaluation of the Dealing in Cultural Objects (Offences) Act 2003 in England and Wales' in Mackenzie, SRM and Green, P [editors]. *Criminology and Archaeology: Studies in Looted Antiquities* Oxford, Hart Publishing, 2009.
Macleod, I. 'Shipwreck Graves and Their Conservation Management' *AICCM Bulletin* [2008, 31 (1)].
Martorell-Carreño, A. 'Cultural Patrimony and Property Rights in Peru' in Hoffman, B. (ed). *Art and Cultural Heritage: Law, Policy and Practice* New York, Cambridge University Press, 2006.
Mattern, E. 'The Role of Photography in the Protection, Identification, and Recovery of Cultural Heritage' *International Journal of Cultural Property* [2012, 19, 133].
Matyk, S. 'The Restitution of Cultural Objects and the Question of Giving Direct Effect to the Protocol to the Hague Convention for the Protection of Cultural Property in the Event of Armed Conflict 1954' *International Journal of Cultural Property* [2000, 9, 341].
M'Bow, AM. 'Address by Director-General of UNESCO at the Ceremony of Tribute to the Memory of René Maheu' 1984, Unesdoc DG/76/10.
McCarthy, C. 'The Practice of Repatriation: A Case Study from New Zealand' in L Tythacott and K Arvanitis [editors], *Museums and Restitution: New Practices, New Approaches* Farnham, Ashgate, 2014.
Melikian, S. 'A Splendid Art Collection Goes on Display in Japan' *International Herald Tribune*, 6 November 1997.
Merryman, JH. 'Cultural Property Internationalism' *International Journal of Cultural Property* [2005, 12, 11].
Merryman, JH & Elsen, AE. *Law, Ethics and the Visual Arts* [3rd edition] London, Kluwer Law, 1998.
'Model Provisions on the Prevention and Fight Against the Illicit Trafficking of Cultural Property' Eighth Meeting of States Parties to the 1970 Convention Paris, UNESCO, 19-20 May 2025.
'Model Provisions on the Prevention and Fight against Illicit Trafficking in Cultural Property' UNESCO 11 July 2022.
'Model Provisions on State Ownership of Undiscovered Cultural Objects' UNESCO, 2011.
Moustaira, EN. 'Greece' in Nafziger JAR and Paterson RK [editors], *Handbook on the Law of Cultural Heritage and International Trade* Cheltenham, Edward Elgar, 2014.
Müller-Katzenburg A, *Internationale Standards im Kulturgüterverkehr und ihr Bedeutung für das Sach- und Kollisionsrecht* Berlin, Duncker & Humblot, 1996.
Museums Association (UK), *Supporting Decolonisation in Museums* 2021.
Musteaţă, S. 'Archaeological Heritage Crimes in Romania and Moldova: A Comparative View' in Grove, L and Thomas, S [editors]. *Heritage Crime: Progress, Prospects and Prevention* New York, Palgrave Macmillan, 2014.
'Mystery Over Vatican Pages' *Times Higher Education Supplement*, 9 June 1995.
National Film and Sound Archive. 'The Story of the Kelly Gang' *Australian Screen.*
Nafziger, JAR. 'The 1970 UNESCO Convention: Insights, Circumspections, and Outlooks' in Sánchez Cordero, JA [editor]. *The 1970 UNESCO Convention: New Challenges* Mexico, Instituto de Investigaciones Jurídica, 2014.

Nafziger JAR, 'Article 7(a) of the UNESCO Convention' in DuBoff LD, *Art Law: Domestic and International* South Hackensack, Fred B. Rothman & Co., 1975.
Nagashima, M. *The Lost Heritage: The Reality of Artifact Smuggling in Southeast Asia* Bangkok, Post Books, 2002.
Nahlik SE, 'International Co-operation to Prevent Illicit Traffic of Cultural Property' *Annuaire de l'Association des Anciens Auditeurs de l'Académie de La Haye* [1981–88,) 51–53].
Nahlik, SE. 'La Protection des Biens culturels en Cas de Conflit armé' *Recueil des Cours de l'Académie de droit international de La Haye* [1967, I, 113].
Nahlik SE, *Polish Yearbook of International Law* 1981.
New York County District Attorney's Office. 'DA Bragg Announces Return of 43 Antiquities to the People of Türkiye' [10 December 2025].
Niec, H. *Ojczyzna Dzieta Sztuki* Warsaw-Krakow, Panstwowe Wydawnictwo Naukowe, 1980.
Niec, H. 'Sovereign Rights to Cultural Property' *Polish Yearbook of International Law* [1971, 4,239].
Nudds, JR. 'Ethics, science and the trade: let's get together' *The Geological Curator* [2001, 7 (6), 191].
O'Keefe PJ, *Commentary on the 1970 Convention* [1st edition] Leicester, Institute of Art and Law, 2000.
O'Keefe, PJ. '"Commercial Exploitation": Its Prohibition in the Unesco Convention on Protection of the Underwater Cultural Heritage 2001 and Other Instruments' (2013) XVIII *Art Antiquity and Law* [2013, XVIII, 129].
O'Keefe, PJ. 'The First Protocol to the Hague Convention Fifty Years On' *Art Antiquity and Law* [2004, IX, 99].
O'Keefe, PJ. 'Foreign Investment and the World Heritage Convention' *International Journal of Cultural Property* [1994, 3, 259].
O'Keefe, PJ. *Protecting Cultural Objects: Before and After 1970* Builth Wells, Institute of Art and Law, 2017.
O'Keefe, PJ. *Shipwrecked Heritage: A Commentary on the UNESCO Convention on Underwater Cultural Heritage* [2nd edition] Builth Wells, Institute of Art and Law, 2014.
O'Keefe, PJ. *Trade in Antiquities: Reducing Destruction and Theft* Paris, London, UNESCO Publishing, Archetype, 1997.
O'Keefe, R. *The Protection of Cultural Property in Armed Conflict* Cambridge, Cambridge University Press, 2006.
O'Keefe, R. 'The 'Right to Take Part in Cultural Life' Under Article 15 of the ICESCR' *International and Comparative Law Quarterly* [1998, 47, 904].
O'Keefe, PJ and Prott, LV [editors]. *Cultural Heritage Conventions and Other Instruments* Builth Wells, Institute of Art and Law, 2011.
O'Keefe, PJ and Prott, LV. 'Cultural Heritage or Cultural Property?' *International Journal of Cultural Property* [1992, 1, 307].
O'Keefe, PJ and Prott, LV. *Handbook of National Regulations Concerning the Export of Cultural Property* Paris, UNESCO, 1988.
O'Keefe, PJ and Prott, LV. 'Implementation of the 1970 UNESCO Convention on the Means of Prohibiting and Preventing the Illicit Import, Export and Transfer of Ownership of Cultural Property' Unesdoc CLT-83/WS/16, 1983.
O'Keefe, PJ and Prott, LV. *Law and the Cultural Heritage* London, Butterworths, 1984–1989.
O'Keefe, PJ and Prott, LV. *National Legal Control of Illicit Traffic in Cultural Property* UNESCO, Paris, 1983.
'Operational Guidelines for the Implementation of the Convention on the Means of Prohibiting and Preventing the Illicit Import, Export and Transfer of Ownership of Cultural Property' Third Meeting of States Parties to the Convention, Paris, UNESCO, 2015.
Oxford Uehiro Institute, *Decision Aid for the Restitution of Cultural Artefacts* (Oxford, 2026), developed with the Institute of Art and Law.
Palmer, NE. *Art, Adventure and Advocacy* Builth Wells, Institute of Art and Law, 2015.
Palmer, NE. 'The Illicit Trade Panel and the Culture Media and Sport Committee: Criminal Law Recommendations' paper.
Palmer, NE. *Museums and the Holocaust* [2nd edition], Redmond-Cooper R [editor], **2020.

Papageorge Kouroupas, M. 'Illicit Trade in Cultural Objects' *Conservation, The GCI Newsletter* [1998, 13, 5].
Passmore, D. 'Australia Loses Out as George Stubbs Painting of Kangaroo Stays in UK' News.Com. AU, 7 November 2013.
Paterson, RK. 'The Legal Dynamics of Cultural Property Export Controls: *Ortiz* Revisited' *UBC Law Review* [1995, Special Issue, 241].
Pavoni, R. 'Sovereign Immunity and the Enforcement of International Cultural Property Law' in Francioni, F and Gordley, J [editors]. *Enforcing International Cultural Heritage Law* Oxford, Oxford University Press, 2013.
Pearlstein, WG. 'Implications of the Schultz Case' *The Art Newspaper*, No. 133, February 2003.
Pérez Ortega, R. 'Rare dinosaur heads home as Germany agrees to return Brazilian fossil' *Science*, 19 July 2022.
Perrottet, T. 'The Marquis de Sade Crimes of Passion' *Smithsonian* [2015, 45–10, 72]. Petersmann EU, *International and European Trade and Environmental Law after the Uruguay Round* London, Kluwer, 1996.
Peters, R. 'Preventing Trafficking in Cultural Property: Import and Export Provisions as Two Sides of the Same Coin' (2019) 2 *Santander Art and Culture Law Review* 95.
Phillips, B. 'Nigerian Ife Head: Why UK Police are Holding a Priceless Sculpture' *BBC News*, 26 June 2022.
'Pioneering Programme Using Archaeology to Empower Young People' *Historic England*, 28 May 2023.
Pitt Rivers Museum. 'Shrunken heads' 2020.
The Plundered Past, Athenaeum, New York, 1974.
Polybius. *Histories*, Book 39.
'Principles for Partnership in Cross-Cultural Human Sciences Research with a Particular View to Archaeology' Swiss Academy of Humanities and Social Sciences and the Swiss Liechtenstein Foundation for Archaeological Research Abroad, 1994.
Prott, LV. *Commentary on the UNIDROIT Convention* [1st edition] Leicester, Institute of Art and Law, 1997.
Prott, LV. *Commentary on the 1995 UNIDROIT Convention*, [2nd edition] Builth Wells, Institute of Art and Law, 2021.
Prott, LV. 'Inalienability and Other Modes of Protection in Current Legal Systems' in Cornu, M et al [editors]. *L'Inalienabilité des collections, performances et limites?* Paris, L'Harmattan, 2012.
Prott, LV. 'The International Movement of Cultural Objects' *International Journal of Cultural Property* [2005, 12, 225].
Prott, LV. 'Movables and Immovables as Viewed by the Law' *International Journal of Cultural Property* [1992, 1, 389].
Prott, LV. 'Repatriation of Cultural Property' *University of British Columbia Law Review* [1995, Special Issue, 229].
Prott, LV. 'The Sphinx Within the Wall: A Tale of Two Germanies and Three Sphinxes' *Art Antiquity and Law* [2010, XV, 147].
Prott, LV. 'UNESCO and UNIDROIT: A Partnership Against Trafficking in Cultural Objects' *Uniform Law Review* [1996, 59].
Prott, LV [editor]. *Witnesses to History: Documents and Writings on the Return of Cultural Objects* Paris, UNESCO Publishing, 2009.
'Provenance project: works from Art of the Past Gallery' Art Gallery of New South Wales. 2022.
Prott, LV Redmond-Cooper, R and Urice, S [editors]. *Realising Cultural Heritage Law: Festschrift for Patrick O'Keefe* Builth Wells, Institute of Art and Law, 2013.
Purkait, H, Douet, S and Tabacchi, N. Audit of the Working Methods of Cultural Conventions Unesdoc IOS/AUD/2013/06.
Quynn, DM. 'The Art Confiscations of the Napoleonic Wars' *The American Historical Review* [1945, L, 437].
Raschèr, AFG Bauen, M Fischer, Y and Zen-Ruffinen, MN. *Cultural Property Transfer* Brussels, Zurich, Bruyland & Schulthess, 2005.

Razzall, K. 'Thief at the British Museum' *BBC* 2024.

Recommendation on International Principles Applicable to Archaeological Excavations New Delhi, UNESCO, 1956.

Redmond-Cooper, R. 'Good Faith Acquisition of Stolen Art' *Art Antiquity and Law* [1997, II, 55].

Renfrew, C. *Loot, Legitimacy and Ownership: The Ethical Crisis in Archaeology* London, Duckworth, 2000.

Renold, MA. 'A Landmark Decision in Art Law by the European Court of Human Rights: Beyeler v. Italy' *Art Antiquity and Law* [2000, V, 73].

Renold, MA. 'The International Protection of Archaeological Heritage: Questions of Private International Law and of Legal Harmonization' in Sánchez Cordero JA [editor], *The 1970 UNESCO Convention: New Challenges* Mexico City, Instituto de Investigaciones Jurídica, 2014.

Renold, MA and Schönenberger, B. 'Switzerland' in Nafziger, JAR and Paterson, RK [editors]. *Handbook on the Law of Cultural Heritage and International* Trade Cheltenham, Edward Elgar, 2014.

Report of the Ministerial Advisory Panel on Illicit Trade, 2000.

Report of the United States Delegation to the Special Committee of Governmental Experts to Examine the Draft Convention on the Means of Prohibiting and Preventing the Illicit Import, Export and Transfer of Ownership of Cultural Property Paris, UNESCO, 13–14 April 1970.

'Report of the Working Party on International Regulations Designed to Prohibit and Prevent the Illicit Export, Import and Sale of Cultural Property' *Records of the General Conference Twelfth Session*, Unesdoc 283, Paris, 1962.

Research Report: Export Licensing and Provenance (London, Department for Culture, Media and Sport, 3 June 2025).

Rodotà, S. 'The Civil Law Aspects of the International Protection of Cultural Property' in *International Legal Protection of Cultural Property* 1984.

'Rules of Procedure concerning recommendations to Member States and international conventions covered by the terms of Art IV, para 4, of the Constitution 111', Basic texts, Paris, UNESCO, 2014.

Russell, JM. *The Final Sack of Nineveh: The Discovery, Documentation, and Destruction of King Sennacherib's Throne Room at Nineveh, Iraq* New Haven, Yale University Press, 1998.

Sandrock O, 'Foreign Laws Regulating the Export of Cultural Property: the Respect Due to them by the Judge of the Lex Fori' in Lalive P [editor], *International Sales of Works of Art* Paris, Institute of International Business Law and Practice and Faculté de Droit de Genève, 1988.

Sarr, F and Savoy, B. *Rapport sur la restitution du patrimoine culturel africain, vers une nouvelle éthique relationnelle* (*The Repatriation of African Cultural Heritage: A New Relational Ethics*), Report to the French President, 2018.

Savoy, B. '1815. Année zéro. L'Europe à l'heure des restitutions d'oeuvres d'art', Lecture series, Paris, Collège de France, 19 April 2019.

Scanlon, J. 'CITES Shares Experience with UNESCO' 15 March 2011.

Schechter, R. 'Preventing Pillage and Promoting Politics: The Dual Goals of the 2009 US-China Bilateral Agreement to Restrict Imports of Chinese Cultural Property' *Art Antiquity and Law* [2009, XIV 317].

Schrader, A. 'UNESCO has teamed up with Interpol to Build a Virtual Museum of Stolen Cultural Artifacts' *Artnet*, 13 October 2023.

von Schorlemer, S. *Internationaler Kulturgüterschutz: Ansätze zur Prävention im Frieden sowie im bewaffneten Konflikt* Berlin, Duncker & Humblot, 1992.

Scovazzi, T. 'Evolutionary Trends as regards the Return of Removed Cultural Property' in L Durbán and A Lazari [editors], *El tráfico de bienes culturales* Valencia, Tirant lo Blanch, 2015.

Scovazzi, T. 'Un'Importante missione diplomatica di Antonio Canova' in *Scritti in onore di Ugo Draetta* Naples, Editoriale Scientifica, 2011.

Scovazzi, T and Ferri, PG. 'Recent Developments in the Fight Against the Illicit Export of Archaeological Objects: The Operational Guidelines to the 1970 Convention' *Art Antiquity and Law* [(2015, XX, 195].

Slayman, A. 'Recent Cases of Repatriation of Antiquities to Italy from the United States' *International Journal of Cultural Property* [1998, 7, 456.

Senate Committee on Foreign Relations [United States]. *Convention on Ownership of Cultural Property* S.Exec. Rep. No. 29, 92nd Congress, 2nd session, 1972.
von Segesser, G and Jolles, A. 'Switzerland's New Federal Act on the International Transfer of Cultural Property: An Update and a Perspective from the Art Trade' *Art Antiquity and Law* [2005, X, 175].
Shapreau, CJ. 'The Purloined Stradivari' *IFAR Journal* [(2015, 16 (no. 3), 19].
Shapreau, CJ. 'Second Circuit Holds That False Statements Contained in Customs Forms Warrant Forfeiture of Ancient Gold Phiale – Hotly Contested Foreign Patrimony Issue Not Reached by the Court: *United States v. An Antique Platter of Gold' International Journal of Cultural Property* [2000, 9 49].
Shaw, O. 'Implementing UNDRIP into Canadian Law' *Institute of Art and Law Blog*, 7 August 2023.
Shimada, M. Presentation at Union Int des Avocats, 2025.
Schwimler, D. 'Stolen fossils back in Argentina' *BBC News*, 4 July 2008.
Shyllon, F. 'Legislative and Administrative Implementation of 1970 UNESCO Convention by African States: The Failure to Grasp the Nettle' *International Journal of Cultural Property* [2014, 21, 23].
Shyllon, F. 'Return of the Makonde Mask from Switzerland to Tanzania – A Righteous Conclusion?' *Art Antiquity and Law* [2011, XVI, 79].
Siehr, KG. 'Globalization and National Culture: Recent Trends Toward a Liberal Exchange of Cultural Objects' *Vanderbilt Journal of Transnational Law* [2005, 38 1067, 1076].
State Council of the People's Republic of China. 'China Appreciates Italy's Cultural Heritage Protection, Lost Relics Return Work: Spokesperson' 11 November 2024.
PP Stewens, 'Ubirajara and Irritator Belong to Brazil: Achieving Fossil Returns Under German Private Law', *International Journal of Cultural Property*, 20 March 2024.
'Stubbs's Kangaroo and Dingo Paintings Saved for the Nation' *Heritage Fund*, 6 November 2013.
Subsidiary Committee of the Meeting of States Parties, 11th Session, C70/23/11.SC/7 (Paris, UNESCO, 1–2 June 2023)
Toman, J. *The Protection of Cultural Property in the Event of Armed Conflict* Dartmouth, Aldershot, 1966.
Thornes, R Dorrell, P and Lie, H. 'Introduction to Object ID: Guidelines for Making Records that Describe Art, Antiques and Antiquities' Getty Information Institute, Los Angeles, J Paul Getty Trust, 1999.
Tietze, H. 'L'Accord Austro-Hongrois sur la répartition des collections de la Maison des Habsbourgs' *Mouseion* [1933, 23–24, 22].
Treaty of Osnabrück between Sweden and the Austrian Empire, 1648.
Truslow, FJ. 'The IFAR Inventory of Cuzco Churches and Its Lessons' *IFAR Journal* [2013, 14, 28].
Ulph, J. 'Acquiring fossils: a complex picture', *The Geological Curator* [2018, 10 (10), 657].
Ulph, J. 'UK Customs Seizure of Looted Libyan Statue' *Institute of Art and Law Blog* 22 October 2015.
UNESCO. 'A Plea for the Return of an Irreplaceable Cultural Heritage to Those Who Created It' 1978.
UNESCO. Decision of the ICPRC, 24th Session, ICPRCP24/24.COM 3(14), Paris, May 2024.
UNESCO. 'French customs return 998 stolen fossils to UNESCO Global Geopark in Brazil' 3 June 2022).
UNESCO. 'Implementation of the Convention on the Means of Prohibiting and Preventing the Illicit Import, Export and Transfer of Ownership of Cultural Property (1970): Reports by Member States and Other States Parties on the Action They Have Taken to Implement the Convention' Unesdoc 32 C/24, 31 July 2003.
UNESCO. 'The Real Price of Art, International UNESCO campaign reveals the hidden fact of art trafficking' 20 October 2020.
UNESCO. *Policy on Engaging with Indigenous Peoples* Paris, 2018.
UNESCO. *Workshop on the Fight Against the Illicit Trafficking of Cultural Property in Melanesia* Port Vila, Vanuatu, 5–7 August 2015.
UNESCO. 'Virtual Museum of Stolen Cultural Objects' October 2025.
Upjohn, I. 'The Protection of Iraqi Cultural Heritage in Australian Domestic Law' *Art Antiquity and Law* [2006, XI, 93].
Urice, SK. 'Unveiling the Executive Branch's Extralegal Cultural Property Policy' *Miami Law Research Paper Series* [2010].
Urice, SK and Levy, GA. 'Article 7(b)(ii) of the 1970 UNESCO Convention: Cooperation for the Return of Cultural Property' in Vrdoljak, AF, Jakubowski, A and Chechi, A [editors]. *The 1970*

UNESCO and 1995 UNIDROIT Conventions on Stolen or Illegally Transferred Cultural Property: A Commentary Oxford, Oxford University Press, 2024.
US Customs and Border Protection. *Works of Art, Collector's Pieces, Antiques, and Other Cultural Property.*
US Immigration and Customs Enforcement. 'ICE returns huge cache of rare fossils smuggled into US from Argentina' 10 May 2008.
de Vattel, E. *The Law of Nations* 1758.
Velarde, J. 'The Protection of Cultural Patrimony in Peru' in Hoffman, B [editor. *Art and Cultural Heritage: Law, Policy and Practice* New York, Cambridge University Press, 2006.
Veres, Z. 'The Fight Against Illicit Trafficking of Cultural Property: The 1970 UNESCO Convention and the 1995 UNIDROIT Convention' *Santa Clara Journal of International Law* [2014, 12(2), 4].
Vincent, S. 'Fred Schultz Found Guilty' *Art & Auction* [2002, 24, 20].
Vincent, S. 'The Secret War of Maria Kouroupas') *Art & Auction* [2002, March, 62].
Viscount Castlereagh. *Note XV delivered to the Allied Ministers respecting the Restitution of the Works of Art* Paris, 11 September 1815.
de Visscher, C. **'La protection internationale des objets d'art et des monuments historiques' *Revue de droit internationale de législation comparée* [1935, 32].
de Visscher, C. 'La protection des patrimoines artistiques et historiques nationaux; nécessité d'une réglementation' *Mouseion* [1938, 43–44, 19].
de Vitoria, F. *De Indis et de jure belli relectiones* 1532 (*Dissertations on the Indians and the Law of War*) James Brown Scott [editor], Washington, Carnegie Institution of Washington, 1917.
Voon, T. *Cultural Products and the World Trade Organization* Cambridge, Cambridge University Press, 2007.
Vrdoljak, AF. *International Law, Museums and the Return of Cultural Objects* Cambridge, Cambridge University Press, Cambridge, 2008.
Wang Yunxia. 'Enforcing Import Restrictions of China's Cultural Objects: The Sino-US Memorandum of Understanding' in Francioni, F and Gordley, J [editors], *Enforcing International Cultural Heritage Law* (Oxford, Oxford University Press, 2013.
Warner, K. 'Theft of Cultural Heritage: *R v Hakimzadeh*' *Art Antiquity and Law* [2010, XV, 95].
Watson P and Todeschini C, *The Medici Conspiracy: The Illicit Journey of Looted Antiquities* New York, Public Affairs, 2007.
Watson, P. 'The Investigation of Frederick Schultz" *Culture Without Context: The Newsletter of the Illicit Antiquities Research Centre* [2002, 10, 21].
Watson, P. *Sotheby's: Inside Story* London, Bloomsbury, 1997.
William Shakespeare. *Henry V*, Act III, Scene 6.
Williams, SA. *The International and National Protection of Movable Cultural Property* Dobbs Ferry, Oceana, 1978.
Working Group. *International Transfer of Cultural Objects: UNESCO Convention of 1970 and UNIDROIT Convention of 1995* Berne, Federal Office of Culture, 1999.
Woodhead, C. 'Article 7(b)(i) of the 1970 Convention: Prohibition of Import of Inventoried Cultural Property' in AF Vrdoljak, A Jakubowski and A Chechi (eds), *The 1970 UNESCO and 1995 UNIDROIT Conventions on Stolen or Illegally Transferred Cultural Property: A Commentary* (Oxford, Oxford University Press, 2024) 226
The World Reborn conference papers, Historic Houses.
Yun-hee, H and Seo-young, K. 'Stolen Goryeo Buddha statue to be returned to Japan after 13 years', *Chosun Daily*, 24 January 2025.

INDEX

Note: **Convention** refers to the **Convention on the Means of Prohibiting and Preventing the Illicit Import, Export and Transfer of Ownership of Cultural Property (1970)**. All entries refer to the 1970 Convention unless otherwise stated.

www.ingramcontent.com/pod-product-compliance
Ingram Content Group UK Ltd.
Pitfield, Milton Keynes, MK11 3LW, UK
UKHW022205220926
475873UK00003B/55

9 781509 986927